Dumbarton Oaks Studies
XXXVI

SIEGECRAFT

SIEGECRAFT

Two Tenth-Century Instructional Manuals
by "Heron of Byzantium"

Denis F. Sullivan

Dumbarton Oaks Research Library and Collection
Washington, D.C.

Library of Congress Cataloging-in-Publication Data

Siegecraft : two tenth-century instructional manuals / by "Heron of Byzantium"; [edited by] Denis F. Sullivan.
     p. cm. — (Dumbarton Oaks studies ; 36)
    Includes bibliographical references and index.
    ISBN 0-88402-270-6
    1. Siege warfare—Byzantine Empire—Early works to 1800. I. Sullivan, Denis F. II. Heron, of Byzantium. III. Series.

    UG443 .S54 2000
    355.4′4—dc21   99-052629

Contents

Foreword

The texts commonly called the *Parangelmata Poliorcetica* and the *Geodesia* are products of tenth-century Byzantium; internal references indicate that they were created to assist in the construction and measurement of devices for the Byzantine offensive against Arab cities. The author of these works is anonymous, although he is often referred to as "Heron of Byzantium." His texts are in large part compilations and interpretations of earlier works on siegecraft, particularly those by Apollodorus of Damascus (1st–2nd century A.D.) and Heron of Alexandria (1st century A.D.). However, the generally static nature of methods of fortification and references by tenth-century historians and in military manuals suggest that some of the machines described in the earlier works still had practical application centuries later. Nevertheless, a few of the devices are apparently included for their historical interest (e.g., Hegetor's ram, the largest known from antiquity) and perhaps for their novelty (e.g., an inflatable leather ladder).

The manuals are in the tradition of didactic handbooks stretching back to the fourth-century B.C. work by Aeneas Tacticus, *On Defense of Fortified Positions,* and including a number of other tenth-century Byzantine texts that have been the subject of recent scholarly attention. The texts presented here in critical editions based on the archetype manuscript, Vaticanus graecus 1605, are notable for the author's particular interest in effective methods of conveying technical information. He specifically formulates and subsequently employs a method of exposition in which concern with levels of vocabulary, order of presentation, depth of explication, use of "situated" examples for geometrical problems (he explains, "they learn pottery on the pot"), and realistic illustration set him apart from his predecessors. He also shows a degree of concern for the safety and motivation of troops not found in his sources. While by no means an error-free technical writer, the so called Heron of Byzantium offers a distinctly new approach to technical pedagogy in the tradition of didactic military handbooks.

Foreword

It is a pleasure to extend my thanks to the many colleagues who have shared their expertise and to two institutions that furnished assistance during the preparation of these texts. Eric McGeer first suggested the project to me and was helpful at many points. George T. Dennis, Nicolas Oikonomides, and Alice-Mary Talbot offered early and continuing support. A sabbatical granted by the University of Maryland and a fellowship awarded by Dumbarton Oaks (1991–92) provided σχολή, excellent library facilities and a warmly collegial atmosphere for which I am most grateful. At various points I have consulted, with great benefit, Alexander Alexakis, Robert Farber, Stamatina McGrath, John Nesbitt, and Gabriele and Helmut Sieg. I am particularly grateful to Lee Sherry for reading through the penultimate version of the Greek text with me and to Jonathan Bardill for help with the realia of the Hippodrome. The anonymous readers provided a number of perceptive suggestions; I am most indebted to reader "B" for detailed comments. I am deeply grateful to the Biblioteca Apostolica Vaticana for permission to reproduce the forty-two illustrations from Vaticanus graecus 1605; I am also grateful to the Bibliothèque nationale de France and the Österreichische National Bibliothek for permission to reproduce illustrations from Parisinus supplementus graecus 607 and Vindobonensis phil. gr. 120, respectively. I have also benefited from the assistance of the staff of the publications office at Dumbarton Oaks, and particularly from the expertise of Frances Kianka, Karen Rasmussen, and Glenn Ruby.

The book is dedicated to the memory of my parents, Denis F. and Helen R. (Girard) Sullivan.

Dumbarton Oaks and
the University of Maryland,
March 1999

List of Abbreviations and Bibliography

Texts and Translations of "Heron of Byzantium"

Barocius

> *Heronis Mechanici liber de machinis bellicis necnon liber de geodaesia a Francisco Barocio* ... (Venice, 1572) (a Latin translation of the *Parangelmata* and the *Geodesia* with annotations and illustrations, based on ms. Bononiensis Universitatis 1497)

Martin

> T. H. Martin, *Recherches sur la vie et les ouvrages d'Héron d'Alexandrie, disciple de Ctésibius, et sur tous les ouvrages mathématiques grecs, conservés ou perdus, publiés ou inédits, qui ont été attribués à un auteur nommé Héron* ... (Paris, 1854) (includes a study of the works of the so-called Heron of Byzantium, pp. 243–323, with partial edition and French translation of and commentary on the *Parangelmata*, pp. 446–73, based on ms. Paris. suppl. gr. 817, a 19th-century copy made from the Oxford ms. Baroc. 169)

Rochas D'Aiglun

> A. de Rochas D'Aiglun, *Traité de fortification d'attaque et de défense des places par Philon de Byzance* (Paris, 1872) (pp. 169–200 contains a partial French translation, following Martin, of the *Parangelmata* with annotations, based on Wescher's edition)

Schneider

> R. Schneider, *Griechische Poliorketiker, mit den handschriftlichen Bildern, herausgegeben und übersetzt, II: Anweisungen zur Belagerungskunst* (Berlin, 1908) (= Abhandlungen der Königlichen Gesellschaft der Wissenschaften zu Göttingen, Philologisch-historische Klasse, Neue Folge, XI:1) (an edition with German translation and annotations of the *Parangelmata* based on ms. Bononiensis Universitatis 1497)

Vincent

> A. J. H. Vincent, *Extraits des manuscrits relatifs à la géométrie pratique des grecs* ... (Paris, 1858) (pp. 348–407 contains an edition with French translation of the *Geodesia* based on ms. Paris. suppl. gr. 817)

Wescher

> C. Wescher, *Poliorcétique des grecs* (Paris, 1867) (pp. 195–279 contains an edition of the *Parangelmata* based on ms. Bononiensis Universitatis 1497)

Primary Sources

Aeneas Tacticus
> *Énée le Tacticien: Poliorcétique,* ed. A. Dain, trans. A.-M. Bon (Paris, 1967)

Afric., *Cest.*
> Sextus Julius Africanus, Cesti, ed. J.-R. Vieillefond, *Jules Africain, Fragments des Cestes* (Paris, 1932)

Apollod.
> Apollodorus of Damascus, Πολιορκητικά, ed. C. Wescher, *Poliorcétique des grecs* (Paris, 1867), 137–93

Archim. *Circ.*
> Archimedes, *Dimensio circuli,* ed. J. L. Heiberg, corrigenda adiecit E. Stamatis, *Archimedis opera omnia,* 4 vols. (Stuttgart, 1972–75), I:232–43

Archim. *Method.*
> Archimedes, *Ad Eratosthenem methodus,* ed. J. L. Heiberg, corrigenda adiecit E. Stamatis, *Archimedis opera omnia,* 4 vols. (Stuttgart, 1972–75), III:426–507

Archim. *Sph. Cyl.*
> Archimedes, *De sphaera et cylindro* ed. J. L. Heiberg, corrigenda adiecit E. Stamatis, *Archimedis opera omnia,* 4 vols. (Stuttgart, 1972–75), I:2–229

Arist. *Top.*
> Aristotle, *Topica,* ed. W. D. Ross, *Aristotelis topica et sophistici elenchi* (Oxford, 1958; repr. 1970), 1–189

Ath. Mech.
> Athenaeus Mechanicus, Περὶ μηχανημάτων, ed. C. Wescher, *Poliorcétique des grecs* (Paris, 1867), 3–40

Biton
> Biton, Κατασκευαὶ πολεμικῶν ὀργάνων καὶ καταπαλτικῶν, ed. E. W. Marsden, *Greek and Roman Artillery: Technical Treatises* (Oxford, 1971), 66–103

De admin.
> Constantine Porphyrogenitus, *De administrando imperio,* ed. G. Moravcsik, trans. R. Jenkins, rev. ed., CFHB 1 (Washington, D.C., 1967)

De cer.
> *De cerimoniis aulae byzantinae,* ed. J. J. Reiske, 2 vols. (Bonn, 1829–30)

De obsid.
>*Anonymous de obsidione toleranda*, ed. H. van den Berg (Leiden, 1947)

Elias Phil., *In Cat.*
>Elias (olim David) Philosophus, *In Aristotelis Categorias commentarium*, ed. A. Busse, *Commentaria in Aristotelem graeca* XVIII:1 (Berlin, 1900), 107–225

Euc.
>*Euclidis elementa*, ed. E. S. Stamatis (after J. L. Heiberg), 4 vols. (Leipzig, 1969–73)

Geoponika
>*Geoponica*, ed. H. Beckh (Leipzig, 1895)

Hero(n), *Bel.*
>Heron of Alexandria, Βελοποιϊκά, ed. E. W. Marsden, *Greek and Roman Artillery: Technical Treatises* (Oxford, 1971), 18–60

Hero(n), *Dioptr.*
>Heron of Alexandria, Dioptra, ed. H. Schöne, *Heronis Alexandrini opera quae supersunt omnia III* (Leipzig, 1903), 141–315

Leo diac.
>Leo the Deacon. *Leonis diaconi Caloensis historiae libri decem*, ed. C. B. Hase (Bonn, 1828)

Leo, *Taktika*
>*Taktika* of Leo VI, PG 107: 671–1094

Maurice, *Strategikon*
>G. T. Dennis and E. Gamillscheg, *Das Strategikon des Maurikios*, CFHB 17 (Vienna, 1981)

Nicom., *Ar.*
>Nicomachus of Gerasa, *Introductio arithmetica*, ed. R. Hoche (Leipzig, 1866)

Nik. Chon., *Hist.*
>Niketas Choniates, *Historia*, ed. J. L. Van Dieten (Berlin–New York, 1975)

Nikephoros Ouranos
>*Taktika*, chaps. 56–65, ed. E. McGeer, *Sowing the Dragon's Teeth: Byzantine Warfare in the Tenth Century* (Washington, D.C., 1995), 79–167

Nikephoros Phokas
>*Praecepta militaria*, ed. E. McGeer, *Sowing the Dragon's Teeth: Byzantine Warfare in the Tenth Century* (Washington, D.C., 1995), 3–78

Olymp. Phil., *Proll.*
Olympiodorus Philosophus, *Prolegomena*, ed. A. Busse, *Commentaria in Aristotelem graeca XII:1* (Berlin, 1902), 1–25

Onasander
Aeneas Tacticus, Asclepiodotus, Onasander, with an English translation by members of the Illinois Greek Club (New York, 1923), 342–526

⟨Περὶ Στρατηγίας⟩
ed. G. T. Dennis, *Three Byzantine Military Treatises,* CFHB 25 (Washington, D.C., 1985), 1-135

Philo Mech.
Μηχανικὴ σύνταξις, book V, ed. Y. Garlan, *Recherches de poliorcétique grecque* (Paris, 1974), 291–404

Pl. *Charm.*
Plato, *Charmides*, ed. J. Burnet, *Platonis opera* (Oxford, 1900–1907; repr. 1967–68), III:153–176d

Pl. *Grg.*
Plato, *Gorgias*, ed. J. Burnet, *Platonis opera* (Oxford, 1900–1907; repr. 1967–68), III:447–527e

Pl. *Soph.*
Plato, *Sophista*, ed. J. Burnet, *Platonis opera* (Oxford, 1900–1907; repr. 1967–68), I:216–268c

Porph. *Plot.*
Porphyrius, *Vita Plotini*, ed. P. Henry and H.-R. Schwyzer, *Plotini opera* (Leiden, 1951), I:1–41

Proc. *Theol. Plat*
Proclus, *Theologia Platonica*, ed. D. Saffrey and L. G. Westerink, *Proclus. Théologie platonicienne*, 3 vols. (Paris, 1968–78)

Souda
Suidae Lexicon, ed. A. Adler, 5 vols. (Leipzig, 1928–38)

Theo. Sim.
Theophylaktos Simokattes, *Historiae*, ed. C. de Boor, rev. P. Wirth (Stuttgart, 1972)

Theoph.
Theophanis Chronographia, ed. C. de Boor, 2 vols. (Leipzig, 1883–85; repr. Hildesheim, 1963)

Secondary Sources

André, "Résine"
J. André, "La résine et la poix dans l'antiquité, technique et terminologie," *L'Antiquité classique* 33 (1964), 86–97

Atsalos, *Terminologie*

B. Atsalos, *La terminologie du livre-manuscrit à l'époque byzantine* (Thessalonike, 1971)

Blyth, "Apollodorus"
P. H. Blyth, "Apollodorus of Damascus and the Poliorcetica," *Greek, Roman and Byzantine Studies* 33 (1992), 127–58

BMGS
Byzantine and Modern Greek Studies

Bryer, "Implements"
A. Bryer, "Byzantine Agricultural Implements: The Evidence of Medieval Illustrations of Hesiod's Works and Days," *Annual of the British School at Athens* 81 (1986), 45–80

Callebat and Fleury, *Vitruve*
L. Callebat and P. Fleury, *Vitruve: De l'architecture, livre X* (Paris, 1986)

Cameron, *Porphyrius*
A. Cameron, *Porphyrius the Charioteer* (Oxford, 1973)

CFHB
Corpus Fontium Historiae Byzantinae

Dagron, *Constantinople*
G. Dagron, *Constantinople imaginaire: Études sur le recueil des Patria* (Paris, 1984)

Dagron, *Naissance*
G. Dagron, *Naissance d'une capitale: Constantinople et ses institutions de 330 à 451* (Paris, 1974)

Dagron, *Traité*
La traité sur la guérilla (De velitatione) de l'empereur Nicéphore Phocas (963–969), ed. G. Dagron and H. Mihăescu, trans. (into French) G. Dagron (Paris, 1986)

Dain, "Stratégistes"
A. Dain, "Les stratégistes byzantins," *Travaux et mémoires* 2 (1967), 317–90

Dain, *Tradition*
>A. Dain, *La tradition du texte d'Héron de Byzance* (Paris, 1933)

Dar.-Sag., *Dictionnaire*
>C. Daremberg and E. Saglio, *Dictionnaire des antiquités grecques et romaines d'après les textes et les monuments* (Paris, 1877–1919)

Demetrakos, *Lexikon*
>Δημητράκου Μέγα λεξικὸν τῆς Ἑλληνικῆς γλώσσης, 9 vols. (Athens, 1949–50)

Dennis, *Treatises*
>G. T. Dennis, *Three Byzantine Military Treatises*, CFHB 25 (Washington, D.C., 1985)

DOP
>*Dumbarton Oaks Papers*

D'Ooge, *Nicomachus*
>M. L. D'Ooge, *Nicomachus of Gerasa, Introduction to Arithmetic* (London, 1926)

Downey, "Architects"
>G. Downey, "Byzantine Architects," *Byzantion* 18 (1948), 99–118

Downey, "Mesarites"
>G. Downey, "Nikolaos Mesarites: Description of the Church of the Holy Apostles at Constantinople," *Transactions of the American Philosophical Society* 47.6 (1957), 855–924

Drachmann, *Technology*
>A. G. Drachmann, *The Mechanical Technology of Greek and Roman Antiquity* (Copenhagen, 1963)

Du Cange, *Glossarium*
>C. D. F. Du Cange, *Glossarium ad scriptores mediae et infimae graecitatis* ... (Lyons, 1688; repr. Graz, 1958)

Dunn, "Exploitation"
>A. Dunn, "The Exploitation and Control of Woodland and Scrubland in the Byzantine World," *BMGS* 16 (1992), 235–98

Fleury, *Mécanique*
>P. Fleury, *La mécanique de Vitruve* (Caen, 1993)

Garlan, *Recherches*
>Y. Garlan, *Recherches de poliorcétique grecque* (Paris, 1974)

Guilland, "Hippodrome"
R. Guilland, "Études sur l'Hippodrome de Byzance. XI. Les dimensions de l' Hippodrome," *Byzantinoslavica* 31 (1970), 1–11

Guilland, *Topographie*
R. Guilland, *Études de topographie de Constantinople byzantine*, 2 vols. in 1 pt. (Amsterdam, 1969)

Heath, *Elements*
T. L. Heath, *The Thirteen Books of Euclid's Elements*, 3 vols. (Cambridge, 1912; repr. New York, 1956)

Heath, *History*
T. L. Heath, *A History of Greek Mathematics*, 2 vols. (Oxford, 1927)

Humphrey, *Circuses*
J. Humphrey, *Roman Circuses* (London, 1986)

Janin, *Constantinople*
R. Janin, *Constantinople byzantine: Développement urbain et répertoire topographique*, 2nd ed. (Paris, 1964)

Kolias, *Waffen*
T. Kolias, *Byzantinische Waffen* (Vienna, 1988)

Koukoules, *Bios*
Ph. Koukoules, Βυζαντινῶν βίος καὶ πολιτισμός, 6 vols. in 7 pts. (Athens, 1948–57)

Koumanoudes, *Synagoge*
S. A. Koumanoudes, Συναγωγὴ λέξεων ἀθησαυρίστων ἐν τοῖς ἑλληνικοῖς λεξικοῖς (Athens, 1883)

Kustas, *Rhetoric*
G. L. Kustas, *Studies in Byzantine Rhetoric* (Thessalonike, 1973)

Lacoste, "Poliorcétiques"
E. Lacoste, "Les Poliorcétiques d'Apollodore de Damas," *Revue des études grecques* 3 (1890), 230–81

Lammert, "Apollodoros"
F. Lammert, "Zu den Poliorketikern Apollodoros und Athenaios und zur Poliorketik des Vitruvius," *Rheinisches Museum für Philologie* 87 (1938), 304–32

Landels, *Engineering*
J. G. Landels, *Engineering in the Ancient World* (Berkeley, Calif., 1981)

List of Abbreviations and Bibliography

Lawrence, *Fortification*
A. W. Lawrence, *Greek Aims in Fortification* (Oxford, 1979)

Lefort, *Géométries*
J. Lefort et al., *Géométries du fisc byzantin* (Paris, 1991)

Lendle, *Schildkröten*
O. Lendle, *Schildkröten: Antike Kriegsmaschinen in poliorketischen Texten* (Wiesbaden, 1975)

Lendle, *Texte*
O. Lendle, *Texte und Untersuchungen zum technischen Bereich der antiken Poliorketik* (Wiesbaden, 1983)

LSJ
H. G. Liddell, R. Scott, and H. S. Jones, *A Greek-English Lexicon* (Oxford, 1968)

LSJRS
LSJ Revised Supplement, ed. P. G. W. Glare (Oxford, 1996)

Mamboury, "Fouilles"
E. Mamboury, "Les fouilles byzantines à Istanbul et dans banlieue immédiate aux XIXe et XXe siècles," *Byzantion* 11 (1936), 229–83

Mamboury, *Kaiserpaläste*
E. Mamboury and T. Wiegand, *Die Kaiserpaläste von Konstantinopel zwischen Hippodrom und Marmara-meer* (Berlin, 1934)

Mango, "L'euripe"
C. Mango, "L'euripe de l'Hippodrome de Constantinople," *REB* 7 (1950), 180–193

Mango, "Palace"
C. Mango, "The Palace of the Boukoleon," *Cahiers archéologiques*, 45 (1997), 41–50

Marsden, *Development*
E. W. Marsden, *Greek and Roman Artillery: Historical Development* (Oxford, 1969)

Marsden, *Treatises*
E. W. Marsden, *Greek and Roman Artillery: Technical Treatises* (Oxford, 1971)

McGeer, "Tradition"
E. McGeer, "Tradition and Reality in the *Taktika* of Nikephoros Ouranos," *DOP* 45 (1991), 129–40

McGeer, *Warfare*
> E. McGeer, *Sowing the Dragon's Teeth: Byzantine Warfare in the Tenth Century* (Washington, D.C., 1995)

Meiggs, *Trees*
> R. Meiggs, *Trees and Timber in the Ancient World* (Oxford, 1982)

Miracula Demetrii
> P. Lemerle, *Les plus anciens recueils des Miracles de s. Démétrius*, 2 vols. (Paris 1979–81)

Mugler, *Dictionnaire*
> C. Mugler, *Dictionnaire historique de la terminologie géométrique des grecs* (Paris, 1958)

Müller, "Handschriftliches"
> K. K. Müller, "Handschriftliches zu den Poliorketika und der Geodäsie des sogenannten Hero," *Rheinisches Museum fur Philologie* 38 (1883), 454–63

Müller-Wiener, *Bildlexikon*
> W. Müller-Wiener, *Bildlexikon zur Topographie Istanbuls* (Tübingen, 1977)

ODB
> *The Oxford Dictionary of Byzantium*, 3 vols., ed. A. Kazhdan et al. (New York, 1991)

Partington, *History*
> J. R. Partington, *A History of Greek Fire and Gunpowder* (Cambridge, 1960)

PG
> *Patrologiae cursus completus, Series graeca*, ed. J.-P. Migne, 161 vols. in 166 pts. (Paris, 1857–66)

RE
> *Paulys Real-Encyclopädie der classischen Altertumswissenschaft* (Stuttgart, 1893–)

REB
> *Revue des études byzantines*

Rochas D'Aiglun, "Athénée"
> A. de Rochas D'Aiglun, "Traduction du traité des machines d'Athénée," in *Mélanges Ch. Graux* (Paris, 1884), 781–801

Sackur, *Vitruv*
> W. Sackur, *Vitruv und die Poliorketiker* (Berlin, 1925)

Schilbach, *Metrologie*
> E. Schilbach, *Byzantinische Metrologie* (Munich, 1970)

Schneider, *Apollodoros*

R. Schneider, *Griechische Poliorketiker, mit den handschriftlichen Bildern, herausgegeben und übersetzt, I: Apollodorus* (Berlin, 1908) (= Abhandlungen der Königlichen Gesellschaft der Wissenschaften zu Göttingen, Philologisch-historische Klasse, Neue Folge, X:1)

Schneider, *Athenaios*

R. Schneider, *Griechische Poliorketiker, mit den handschriftlichen Bildern, herausgegeben und übersetzt, III: Athenaios über Maschinen* (Berlin, 1912) (= Abhandlungen der Königlichen Gesellschaft der Wissenschaften zu Göttingen, Philologisch-historische Klasse, Neue Folge XII:1)

Schöne, "Dioptra"

H. A. Schöne, "Die Dioptra des Heron," *Jahrbuch des Kaiserlich Deutschen Archäologischen Instituts* 14 (1899), 91–103

Singer, *Technology*

A History of Technology, ed. by C. Singer et al., 3 vols. (Oxford, 1954–58)

Sophocles, *Lexicon*

E. A. Sophocles, *Greek Lexicon of the Roman and Byzantine Periods* (New York, 1900; repr. New York, 1957)

TLG

Thesaurus Linguae Graecae, CD-ROM (Version D) produced by the Department of Classics, University of California at Irvine

Toomer, *Almagest*

G. J. Toomer, *Ptolemy's Almagest* (London, 1984)

Trapp, *Lexikon*

E. Trapp, *Lexikon zur byzantinischen Gräzität* (Vienna, 1994–)

Vogt, *Livre*

A. Vogt, *Constantin VII Porphyrogénète, Le livre des cérémonies*, 4 vols. (Paris, 1935–40)

Whitehead, *Aineias*

D. Whitehead, *Aineias the Tactician: How to Survive under Siege* (Oxford, 1990)

Winter, *Fortifications*

F. E. Winter, *Greek Fortifications* (Toronto, 1971)

List of Illustrations

List of Illustrations

Introduction

Vaticanus graecus 1605, a richly illustrated manuscript dated on palaeographical grounds to the eleventh century, contains just two treatises — instructional manuals on the fabrication of siege machines and on the use of a dioptra (a kind of surveyor's theodolite) with applied geometry, ostensibly to estimate the required sizes of the machines — generally referred to as the *Parangelmata Poliorcetica* and the *Geodesia*. K. K. Müller first showed that the unedited Vaticanus was the archetype of the tradition of these texts,[1] which had been edited previously from the sixteenth-century Bononiensis Universitatis 1497 or its descendants.[2] In his monograph *La tradition du texte d'Héron de Byzance,* Alphonse Dain elaborated on Müller's demonstration and provided an exhaustive study of the tradition.[3] The two treatises represent the work of an anonymous tenth-century Byzantine compiler and commentator, who updated and supplemented for his contemporaries the works of classical poliorcetic authors,[4] particularly Apollodorus of Damascus (1st–2nd cen-

---

[1] Müller's argument rests on the observations that all manuscripts of the tradition exhibit significant lacunae, noticed by earlier editors, which correspond to the loss of folios in the Vaticanus, and incorrect sequences of text that can be shown to result from a faulty rebinding of the Vaticanus. Müller concludes ("Handschriftliches," 456): "Klar ist nun, dass alle Hss., welche die eben verzeichneten Lücken und die oben dargestellte Unordnung im Texte zeigen, ohne Ausnahme direkt oder indirekt auf den Vat. 1605 zurückgehen." Müller also provides a list of the readings in the Vaticanus that differ from the editions of Wescher and Vincent, based in part on his own observations and in greater part those of A. Mau.

[2] See the editions and translations by Barocius, Martin, Schneider, and Wescher of the *Parangelmata,* and Vincent of the *Geodesia* listed in the bibliography; for the stemma see Dain, *Tradition,* 155.

[3] Dain concludes (*Tradition,* 42) on the archetype value of the Vaticanus: "On sait aussi que le *Vaticanus* 1605 présentait dans la *Poliorcétique,* comme dans la *Géodésie,* des lacunes dues à la chute de folios; ces mêmes lacunes se retrouvent dans tous nos manuscrits, et comme elles correspondent à des fins ou à des débuts de folios du *Vaticanus* 1605, il en résulte que la parenté avec ce manuscrit est amplement démontrée."

[4] For the classical and Byzantine poliorcetic works and manuscripts, see Dain "Stratégistes," passim, and H. Hunger, "Kriegswissenschaft" in *Die hochsprachliche profane Literatur der Byzantiner* (Munich, 1978), II:321–40.

tury A.D.),[5] but also Athenaeus Mechanicus (1st century B.C.), Biton, and Philo Mechanicus (perhaps 3rd century B.C.), as well as Heron of Alexandria's (1st century A.D.) *Dioptra*. He also presents the material with a new pedagogical approach to both text and illustration which he indicates is more appropriate for his "nonengineering" audience. As noted below, he does so with a mix of both insightful and at times inaccurate interpretations.

The Author, The So-called Heron of Byzantium

The rubrication of the Vaticanus was never carried out, leaving the headpiece of the manuscript blank as well as initial letters of paragraphs and the space left between the two treatises. Thus the name of the author and the titles of the works were never recorded. A later hand (Dain, *Tradition,* 13, suggests 14th–15th century) added the words Ἥρων(ος) (sic) – προοίμ(ιον) to the headpiece,[6] perhaps deriving the name Heron from the Byzantine author's use of Heron of Alexandria and the fact that the Alexandrian was the best known of the classical writers on technology. The Byzantine commentator nowhere mentions his own name and makes no claim to be Heron of Alexandria; there is no indication that the author of the addition to the headpiece had any external evidence for the name. The numerous Byzantine references in the texts, however, show that the author was not Heron of Alexandria. Various epithets have also been added to distinguish the Byzantine from his predecessor(s), thus Hero tertius, Heron the Younger and Heron of Byzantium.[7] The last is now the more common designation and, while again nowhere mentioned in the text, is at least appropriately descriptive. In the *Geodesia* the commentator employs a number of examples set in the Hippodrome of Constantinople[8] and says (*Geodesia* **11:36–38**) that he engraved longitude and latitude lines "in the ... admirable imperial terrace balcony (?) ... near Boukoleon's" (ἐν τῷ ἀξιαγάστῳ βασιλικῷ ... παρακυπτηρίῳ ⟨ἐν⟩ τοῖς Βουκολέοντος), that is in an area

---

[5] For the view that the *Poliorcetica* attributed to Apollodorus was not actually authored by him and includes significant later additions, see Blyth, "Apollodorus," passim.

[6] See fig. A.

[7] For discussion of the epithets see Dain, *Tradition,* 15.

[8] This was noted by Martin, 285–304; see also Vincent, 352–53.

overlooking the shore of the Sea of Marmara. Whether he was born in Constantinople we have no indication, but that he worked there and chose examples for an audience familiar with the city is clear. Most modern scholars refer to the author as the Anonymus Byzantinus, which is the factually correct position. In the interest of clarity of identification and given numerous other "anonymi byzantini," I have chosen to retain "Heron of Byzantium"[9] on the title page, but generally refer to him as the Anon. Byz.

Date of Composition

A date for the composition of the two texts was proposed with detailed argumentation and a critique of earlier proposals, by T. H. Martin (267–75) who noted that the Anon. Byz. in the *Geodesia* (**11**:73–76, 86–87) says: "For Regulus, with the onward movement of the time since Ptolemy, is found to have now 10 1/2 degrees in Leo; and the Bright Star of the Hyades 20 2/3 degrees in Taurus" (Ὁ γὰρ Βασιλίσκος, σὺν τῷ ἐπικινήματι τῶν ἀπὸ τοῦ Πτολεμαίου χρόνων, ι´ ϛ´ μοίρας ἐπὶ τοῦ Λέοντος νῦν εὑρίσκεται ἐπέχων· καὶ ὁ Λαμπρὸς τῶν Ὑάδων ἐπὶ τοῦ Ταύρου κ´ β´´), and "For Arcturus now is at the fifth degree in Libra, with the onward movement" (Ὁ γὰρ Ἀρκτοῦρος νῦν ε´ μοῖραν τοῦ Ζυγοῦ, σὺν τῷ ἐπικινήματι, ἐπέχει). Martin proposed that the Anon. Byz. had not observed the stars himself but had taken the values for the same stars given in the *Star Catalog* in Ptolemy's *Almagest* and simply added Ptolemy's precession rate of 1 degree per century to get the values he gives. The exactly 8 degree difference in all three cases between the Anon. Byz. and Ptolemy would thus place the composition of the texts eight centuries after the date of Ptolemy's work or, as Martin (275) concluded, "Héron le Jeune écrivait donc cet ouvrage en l'an 938 ou à

---

[9] See Dain, *Tradition,* passim; Wescher, 197: Ἀνωνύμου ἤτοι Ἥρωνος Βυζαντίου. Cf. K. Tittel, *RE* 8 (1913), cols. 1074–80: "Heron von Byzanz (auch H. der Jüngere genannt)." Heath, *History,* II:318–19 tentatively suggested that the author might be Nikephoros Patrikios, the teacher of geometry appointed by Constantine VII, based on his possible connection with editions of Heron of Alexandria's *Geometria* and *Stereometrica* and the fact that he was a contemporary of "Heron of Byzantium." There appears to be no further basis for the suggestion, and the Anon. Byz.'s mathematical errors would seem to militate against it. For Nikephoros Patrikios see P. Lemerle, *Byzantine Humanism* (Canberra, 1986), 307.

peu près." Martin also argued (275–77) that the Anon. Byz.'s reference to the use of his work against the "cities of Agar" (*Parangelmata* **58**) best fits the period of Romanos I Lekapenos and Constantine Porphyrogennetos.[10]

Alphonse Dain accepted Martin's basic conclusion, while reasonably cautioning about acceptance of the precise year, and added that the Byzantine was using a corpus of classical poliorcetic authors that did not exist in collected form until the beginning of the tenth century.[11] Dain also noted the Anon. Byz.'s references in the *Parangelmata* to siege devices that reflect tenth-century practice, particularly the handheld tube for projecting Greek fire (**49**:20: μετὰ στρεπτῶν ἐγχειριδίων πυροβόλων, depicted on folio 36r).[12] One might add the Anon. Byz.'s comparison of a base of a scout-ladder to an "uncial" *eta* (**27**:15, **28**:4: ἦτα λιτόν), a use of λιτός not found before the late 9th century;[13] also his characterization of the enemy with the rare adjective θεόλεστος (**58**:9) which accords well with a mid-tenth-century date, as discussed below.

Method of Presentation

The Anon. Byz. indicates in his opening paragraph his concerns with the presentation method (which he calls the καθολικὴ τεχνολογία) of his classical sources, naming specifically (in an apparently corrupt passage that, given the authors he actually uses, may have originally contained additional names) Apollodorus of Damascus, Athenaeus Mechanicus, and Biton. He thus had access to a manuscript of the poliorcetic corpus that, as Dain has shown, was from the branch of the tradition now most closely preserved in a fragmentary state in the six-

---

[10] Schneider (85) suggested a possible connection with the encyclopedic work commissioned by Constantine Porphyrogennetos and concludes that this would insure the anonymity of the author. There is no evidence for such a connection and for doubts see Dain, *Tradition*, 16–17.

[11] Dain, *Tradition*, 16 and n. 3

[12] Ibid., 16 and n. 2. It is worth adding that Leo VI (*Taktika* XIX:57) also mentions the devices, which he describes as "recently fabricated" (παρὰ τῆς ἡμῶν βασιλείας ἄρτι κατεσκευασμένα).

[13] For this usage and date see Atsalos, *Terminologie*, 106ff. I am grateful to Alice–Mary Talbot for bringing this reference to my attention.

teenth-century Vindobonensis phil. gr. 120, and paralleled by another branch found with more complete text in Paris. suppl. gr. 607 dated to the second quarter of the tenth century.[14] The Byzantine commentator indicates that to understand his sources one would need one of the "engineers" (μηχανικοί) who composed them. He states that his objective is to make it possible for siege machines to be constructed "by anyone" (παρὰ τῶν τυχόντων), phrasing derived from Apollodorus; he subsequently describes his potential users as military leaders seeking to besiege Arab cities (*Parangelmata* **58**). He also indicates (*Geodesia* **6**) that he has added examples, particularly mathematical examples, for "beginners" (οἱ εἰσαγόμενοι), referring "the more accomplished" (οἱ ἐντελέστεροι) to the works of Archimedes and Heron. He thus writes for a mixed audience, but with the express intent of making his sources' engineering descriptions accessible to nonengineers. He also provides generic statements of his own methodological approach to achieve this objective, an approach that incorporates a new view of how to present technical material in a format that will lead to practical results. The anonymous author illustrates his general statements with numerous specific examples in both treatises.

Textual Changes

The Anon. Byz. describes the core of his method of textual presentation at two points in the *Parangelmata:* "Having clarified only the works of Apollodorus as it were in toto, with additional elaborations and secondary arguments, we have drawn our conclusions, finding and adding ourselves numerous concordant <items>. Everything we have collected here and there from the remaining <writers> is easy to know and apprehend truthfully, "axioms of common intuition" as Anthemios says, and capable of being comprehended from the problem alone and the illustration; they require no instruction or interpretation" (**1:**25–33); "all writing on siege warfare requires . . . sometimes also repetitions and reiterations and secondary arguments (ταυτολογιῶν καὶ ἐπαναλήψεων καὶ ἐπενθυμημάτων) for comprehension of the concepts and operations" (**3:**4–8). He also indicates (**1:**33–

---

[14] Dain, *Tradition,* 19–20, following Wescher, xxxviii.

34) that he will use common diction (ἰδιωτείᾳ λέξεων) and simple style (ἁπλότητι λόγου), although this is clearly a topos.[15]

The rhetorical terminology (ἐπεργασίαι, ἐπενθυμήματα, ταυτολογίαι, and ἐπαναλήψεις) employed here may reflect an acquaintance, direct or more likely through handbooks, with the Hermogenic corpus.[16] The precision with which the Anon. Byz. uses the technical terms, however, is uncertain; he is not writing a rhetorical piece but an instructional manual. Yet he is clearly attempting to give his method a consciously articulated framework unlike anything found in his sources. His reworkings and clarifications of these sources are varied in nature and at times helpful, in other cases obvious and pedantic. He sometimes changes aspects of the sequence of presentation in his sources: for example, at *Parangelmata* **13**:13–14 the Anon. Byz. mentions early in his description that excavating tortoises are wheeled, a fact mentioned by his source Apollodorus only at the end. He also inserts lengthy mathematical examples: for example, at *Parangelmata* chap. **38** he compares in detail the dimensions of two mobile siege towers with special emphasis on their proportional relationships and in chap. **51** adds dimensions for a mobile landing tube, again with emphasis on proportion. He frequently inserts similes in the *Parangelmata,* comparing the blade of a borer to a garden spade (**17**:12–13), the base of a scout-ladder to an uncial letter H (**27**:15), clamping caps to pivot sockets (**22**:35–37), metal washers to clay pipes (**44**:24), and so on. Finally, he adds his own interpretations of technical issues, for example on the nature of a torsion system attached to a battering ram (**44**:18–20) and on a system for maintaining equilibrium between two yoked ships (**53**:33–34).

Two other methods of clarification deserve examination in greater detail. First, the Anon. Byz. frequently adds directional information: for example, at **5**:2–3 Apollodorus' "rolling objects" (τὰ ἐπικυλιόμενα) become "objects being rolled down from above by the enemy" (τὰ ἄνωθεν ἀπὸ τῶν ἐναντίων ἐπικυλιόμενα); at **7**:2–3 to Apollodorus' instruction

---

[15] For the *topos* in the 10th century see R. Browning, "The Language of Byzantine Literature," in S. Vryonis, ed., *The Past in Medieval and Modern Greek Culture* (Malibu, Calif., 1978), 103–33 (repr. in R. Browning, *History, Language and Literacy in the Byzantine World* [Northampton, 1989], XV), esp. 103–4 with citations of similar sentiments in Leo VI, *Taktika* and *De admin.*

[16] On the rhetorical terminology see the related notes in the commentary.

for besiegers to dig a defensive ditch the Anon. Byz. adds at the outset, "Beginning from below from the foot of the slope" (ἐκ γὰρ τῆς ὑπωρείας κάτωθεν ἀρχομένους); and at **16**:10–11 the addition "from the outer facade" (ἀπὸ δὲ τῆς ἔξωθεν ὄψεως) indicates more precisely where a hole is to be drilled in a metal laminated jar. Second, the author provides logical explanations of statements made by his sources. For example, at **11**:14–15, drawing on Philo Mechanicus' defensive tactic of burying empty jars over which troops can walk, but which siege machines cause to collapse, halting the machines, he adds the (obvious) explanation that it is the weight of the machines that causes the collapse (λίαν βαρυτάτοις οὖσι) and a specific mention that the jars break under the weight (ἐπὶ τῇ θραύσει καὶ ἐπιδόσει τῶν ὑποκειμένων κεραμίων). At **12**:16–18 he adds to Philo's description of inflatable leather ladders the explanation: "For when they are inflated and full of air <and> kept from deflating, they necessarily become upright, held firm for climbing by the air" (ἐμφυσωμένων γὰρ καὶ πνεύματος πληρουμένων τοῦ διαπνεῖν κωλυομένων, ἐξορθοῦσθαι αὐτὰς ἀνάγκη, ὑπὸ τοῦ πνεύματος ἀντεχομένων πρὸς τὴν ἀνάβασιν). At **13**:10–11 to Apollodorus' recom-mendation for the use of three, four, or five beams in constructing an excavating tortoise the Anon. Byz. adds, to explain the five-beam ap-proach, "for thicker and more solid results" (διὰ τὸ πυκνότερον καὶ στερεώτερον τοῦ ἔργου). Again, at **39**:6–7 he adds "so that the tower may be maintained steadfast in position when turbulent battle is joined" (ὅπως ἐπὶ τῇ συμβολῇ καὶ τῷ κλόνῳ τῆς μάχης ἀκλινὴς πρὸς τὴν στάσιν ὁ πύργος συντηρῆται) to explain the purpose of the underplate of the portable siege tower of Apollodorus. It is presumably such directional and explanatory insertions that the author characterizes as "additional elaborations and secondary arguments" (ἐπεργασίαι and ἐπενθυμήματα), which he believes will aid the reader's comprehension.

The Anon. Byz.'s third named category, tautology, can be seen, for ex-ample, at **15**:5, "greasy and viscous" (λιπαρὸν καὶ κολλώδη); **39**:2, "even and level" (ὁμαλὸς καὶ ἰσοπέδιος); **53**:5, "well known and obvious" (εὐγνώστους ... καὶ φανεράς). In each case he has added the second adjective to the text of his source. Tautology is combined with vocabulary change at **22**:2, "to shatter and break" (ῥηγνύειν καὶ διασπᾶν) for "shake" (σεῖσαι) in Apollodorus, and at **44**:10–11, "being pulled up and falling (ἐκσπῶνται ... ἐκπίπτωσι) for Apollodorus' "be dislodged" (ἐξάλλωνται).

Introduction

The Anon. Byz. also mentions in his methodological discussion (**1**:21–22) a concern that "the scientific terms are not familiar to the common speech" (καὶ ἀσυνήθη κοινοῖς τυγχάνει λόγοις τὰ τῶν ἐπιστημῶν ὀνόματα). While the phrase is taken directly from his source Apollodorus, the Anon. Byz. clearly shares his concern and makes numerous changes in the interest of clarity. In many cases these appear to involve substitutions of general terms or periphrases for technical or rarer ones, distinctions sometimes difficult to capture in translation: for example, "poles" for "vine-poles" (ξύλα for κάμακες) at **10**:4; "points" for "spikes" (ξίφη for στύρακες) at **10**:14; "openings" for "niches" (διάχωρα for ζωθήκαι) at **14**:2; "bindings" for "ties" (δεσμά for ἄμματα) at **56**:12; "blade ... narrowed ... in front" for "apex" (πέταλον ... ἐπὶ τὸ ἔμπροσθεν ... ἐστενωμένον for ὁ οὐραχός) at **17**:10–12; "these beams that come down" for "swipes" (ταῦτα ... κατερχόμενα for τὰ κηλώνια) at **27**:30–31. Others may reflect contemporary usage: for example, σαθρότερα for ἀσθενεστάτους (**4**:10); λαός for ὄχλος (**10**:1); λακκίσματα for τέλματα (**11**:7); ὑποδήμασι for ἐνδρομίδες (**11**:20); αὐλίσκον for σύριγξ (**16**:13); πέταλον for λεπίς (**17**:10); ἐπανάπτεσθαι for ἐρεθίζεσθαι (**19**:24).

Thus the Anon. Byz. explicitly states his own methodological approach to updating and clarifying the textual aspects of his classical sources and can be shown to apply the method extensively, adding explanations and simplifying vocabulary for nonengineering readers. These changes are noted in more detail in the commentary.

Changes in Illustrations

Even more interesting in terms of methodology is the Anon. Byz.'s description of his new approach to illustration of the devices described and their actual illustration in the archetype.[17] In his introductory sentence to the *Parangelmata* the Anon. Byz. comments that poliorcetic

[17] For an earlier version of this argument see the abstract of my paper "Technical Illustration and Neoplatonic Levels of Reality in Vaticanus Graecus 1605," *Abstracts of the 19th Annual Byzantine Studies Conference, 4–7 November 1993* (Princeton, N.J.), 96–97, and my "Tenth Century Byzantine Offensive Siege Warfare: Instructional Prescriptions and Historical Practice," *Byzantium at War (9th–12th c.)* (Athens, 1997), 179–200, esp. 198–99.

concepts (νοήματα) are hard to grasp, that they are perhaps comprehensible by "'ignorance' alone" (τῇ ἀγνωσίᾳ μόνῃ), as they do not obtain clarity "from looking at the drawings" (ἀπ' αὐτῆς τῆς τῶν σχημάτων θέας). Examples of the drawings in his sources which evoked this response are presumably contained in Vindonbonensis phil. gr. 120 and closely paralleled in Paris. suppl. gr. 607. The drawings in those manuscripts may be characterized as peculiar in their combination of ground plan and elevation in a single composition and in the addition of some depth to the elevations. Also various parts of the devices are sometimes presented and labeled individually to clarify their function, but with resulting loss of an indication of their relationship to the whole. In some illustrations reference letters are employed and cited in the text.[18] In origin technical plans, by the tenth century they have become a strange hybrid.[19] A number of these characteristics are visible in the drawings of the ram-tortoise of Hegetor reproduced in fig. B. The Anon. Byz. indicates (**1**:37–39) that to facilitate understanding he will not employ the method of drawing that he finds in his sources, but combine his improved verbal descriptions "with the drawings, giving these precise definition" (σὺν τοῖς σχήμασιν ἀκριβῶς διορισάμενοι), thus producing "an illustration . . . well defined" (σχηματισμὸς καλῶς διορισθείς).

The reading "ignorance" (ἀγνωσίᾳ), emended by previous editors[20] working from apographs, is also in the archetype and, I suggest, correct, employed here as used frequently in the sense "unknowing" employed by Pseudo-Dionysius. For example, *De mystica theologia* I:3: "into the darkness of unknowing in which one rejects all the perceptions of knowing" (εἰς τὸν γνόφον τῆς ἀγνωσίας . . . καθ᾽ ὃν ἀπομυεῖ πάσας τὰς γνωστικὰς ἀντιλήψεις), and II:1: "through unseeing and unknowing to see and know what is beyond seeing and knowing" (δι᾽ ἀβλεψίας καὶ ἀγνωσίας ἰδεῖν καὶ γνῶναι τὸ ὑπὲρ θέαν καὶ γνῶσιν). This "negative cognition," a condition accomplished by the rejection of apprehension

---

[18] See Wescher, xxiv.

[19] The relationship, if any, between the drawings in the Paris manuscript and the original drawings of the classical poliorcetic authors is, of course, a very remote one; see Sackur, *Vitruv,*19–21; Lendle, *Texte,* xx and n. 8; idem, *Schildkröten,* 122; and Marsden, *Treatises,* 62.

[20] ἐννοίᾳ (in the margin of London add. 15276, 16th century); εὐγνωσίᾳ (Martin); διαγνωσίᾳ (Wescher); εὐγνωμοσύνη (for ἀγνωσίᾳ μόνῃ) (Schneider).

through the senses, results from ἀφαίρεσις, variously translated "removal," "abstraction," or "denial," which involves ascent to universals by removal of particulars (ibid., II:1: ἀπὸ τῶν ἐσχάτων ἐπὶ τὰ ἀρχικώτατα τὰς ἐπαναβάσεις ποιούμενοι, τὰ πάντα ἀφαιροῦμεν, ἵνα ἀπερικαλύπτως γνῶμεν ἐκείνην τὴν ἀγνωσίαν).[21] On this reading the source drawings the Anon. Byz. criticizes are conceptualized by him as at a level of reality beyond normal sense perception and thus beyond the capability of anyone but trained engineers to comprehend. A comparison of the illustrations of the ram-tortoise of Hegetor found in Vindobonensis phil. gr. 120 and Paris. suppl. gr. 607 with the same tortoise as illustrated in the Vaticanus conveys this difference clearly (fig. B). The choice of the term may represent an example of a major principle of Byzantine rhetoric, that "obscurity" is a virtue of style, a principle connected with "the sense of the mystical, the understanding of the relation between the universal and the particular."[22]

The Anon. Byz.'s contrast of "drawing" vs. "illustration" (σχῆμα/σχηματισμός) (the latter term occurs twice in the introductory paragraph, once in the conclusion to the *Parangelmata,* and again in a scholion in the *Geodesia*) is also paralleled in Neoplatonism. Simplicius' use of the contrast has been characterized by C. Luna as representing "le rapport de participation entre la figure transcendante et l'objet sensible."[23] At *In Aristotelis Categorias commentarium* 8:271:26, for example, Simplicius, following Archytas, comments that Aristotle's fourth category, "quality" (ποιότης), resides not ἐν σχήματι . . . ἀλλ᾽ ἐν σχηματισμῷ; earlier (8:21:14–19), commenting on the distinction between Socrates and a picture (εἰκών) of Socrates, he defines the latter as an "illustration of colors" (χρωμάτων οὖσα σχηματισμός), which he later (8:21:18–19) calls

---

[21] For discussion of the concept see S. Lees, *The Negative Language of the Dionysian School of Mystical Theology* (Salzburg, 1983), esp. I:140–41: "Ps. Dionysius effectively proposes a new method of apprehension which is appropriate to the incomprehensibility of its object — a method whose alienation from natural processes of sensual and intellectual perception is imaged in, rather than properly described by, the paradoxical construction of the individual words." For the *via negativa* in mathematics, see J. Whittaker, "Neopythagoreanism and Negative Theology," *Symbolae Osloenses* 44 (1969), 109–125.

[22] See Kustas, *Rhetoric,* 12.

[23] I. Hadot et al., *Simplicius: Commentaire sur les Catégories,* fasc. III (Leiden, 1990), 148.

a "surface σχῆμα" (σχήματος ἐπιπολαίου); he also says (8:261:24–26) regarding "quality" that "it must be comprehended according to the σχηματισμός of the surface" (ληπτέον … κατὰ τὸν τῆς ἐπιφανείας ποιὸν σχηματισμόν). "Quality" here is used in the sense of Aristotle, *Categoriae* 10a11: "the external form of each thing" (ἡ περὶ ἕκαστον ὑπάρχουσα μορφή). These and other passages in Simplicius, then, specifically use the σχῆμα/σχηματισμός contrast to distinguish between the generalized concept and the individual reality the senses perceive. This is particularly clear in the definition in the passage cited above of the σχηματισμός as a "surface σχῆμα" (ἐπιπόλαιον σχῆμα).[24]

Finally, the term "give definition to" (διορίζεσθαι), used to describe how a σχῆμα will become a σχηματισμός, is paralleled by references in Neoplatonic authors. At *In Aristotelis Categorias commentarium* 8:217:27–29, for example, Simplicius has τὰ ἀσώματα εἴδη, διὰ τούτων ἐμφαίνεται, ἀλλ' ἄτακτα καὶ ἀδιόριστα πάντα τὰ τοιαῦτα φέρεται παρ' αὐτοῖς, and at 8:261:21–23 where the category of ποιότης is described: διότι ἐπιπολῆς καὶ οἷον ἔξωθεν ἐπ' ἐσχάτῳ τοῦ σώματος συνίσταται. πολυμερὲς δέ ἐστιν καὶ πολυειδὲς τὸ γένος τοῦτο. καὶ ἔστιν ἐν αὐτῷ σχῆμα μὲν τὸ ὑπό τινος ἢ τινῶν ὅρων περιεχόμενον.[25] Thus "to give definition or definiteness" (ὅρος) to a σχῆμα is used in some Neoplatonists of giving it the externalities or particulars of quality.[26] Here then the Anon. Byz. seems to complete,

---

[24] Similar uses of σχηματισμός alone as a representation of superficial appearance can also be found in Pseudo–Dionysius (e.g., *Epistula* 9.2: προσέτι δὲ καὶ τῶν νοητῶν ἅμα καὶ νοερῶν ἀγγέλων οἱ θεοειδεῖς διάκοσμοι ποικίλαις μορφαῖς διαγράφονται καὶ πολυειδέσι, καὶ ἐμπυρίοις σχηματισμοῖς) and in Macarii Aegyptii *Epistolae* (PG 34:413C): ἕκαστος ἡμῶν νοητὴ συκῆ, παρ' ἧς ὁ κύριος τὸν ἔνδον καρπὸν ἐπιζητεῖ, καὶ οὐ τὸν ἐκ φύλλων ἐπικείμενον σχηματισμόν, among others. The distinction can also be seen at different levels of reality in Plotinus, *Ennead* VI:7:14: ἐν ἑνὶ σχήματι νοῦ οἷον περιγραφῇ ἔχων περιγραφὰς ἐντὸς καὶ σχηματισμοὺς αὖ ἐντός….

[25] See also Simplicius, *In Aristotelis Physica commentaria* 9:537:15–16: τὸ δέ ἐστι πέρας καὶ ὅρος τοῦ ἀορίστου διαστήματος ὁριστικόν τε καὶ περιεκτικόν, καὶ τοῦτο μέν ἐστι τὸ εἶδος ("there is boundary and a defining limit which makes the indefinite extension definite and embraces it, and this is form"); trans. R. Sorabji, "Simplicius: Prime Matter as Extension," in I. Hadot, *Simplicius: Sa vie, son oeuvre, sa survie* (Berlin, 1987), 148–65, specifically 163. Cf. Simplicius, *In Aristotelis Categorias commentarium* 8:28:4–6: τὸ δὲ κοινὸν καὶ ἀόριστον … ὅπερ μετὰ τοῦ διορισμοῦ ληφθὲν τὸ κοινὸν ἰδιωθὲν καὶ ἀπομερισθὲν παρίστησιν.

[26] For discussion see Sorabji (as in previous note) and cf. Aristotle, *Analytica Posteriora* 81b7–8: τῶν γὰρ καθ' ἕκαστον ἡ αἴσθησις ("sense perception apprehends particulars").

by choice of terminology, his conceptualization of his new approach to technical illustration as at the level of what the senses see, the surface appearance, while suggesting that the approach found in his sources is at a higher level of abstraction.

The validity of this interpretation is strengthened not only by the nature of the illustrations in Vat. gr. 1605, but also by overt references in the texts. The Anon. Byz. (3:9–14) cites Porphyry (ὁ πολὺς ἐν σοφίᾳ), on Plotinus (ὁ μέγας), that Plotinus was "concerned only with the concept and the things. For he knew that reality is tripartite: words, concepts, and things" (μόνου τοῦ νοῦ καὶ τῶν πραγμάτων ἐχόμενος. Τριττὰ γὰρ τὰ ὄντα ἠπίστατο, ἔν τε φωναῖς νοήμασί τε καὶ πράγμασι). The phrase "and the things" (καὶ τῶν πραγμάτων) is not in any manuscript of the cited passage of Porphyry's *Vita Plotini* and has apparently been added here by the Anon. Byz. to the citation. The view of reality as tripartite is found in the sixth-century Neoplatonists Olympiodorus and Elias.[27] The sentence also seemingly reflects what S. Gersch[28] has described in another context as the extensive Neoplatonic controversy about the subject of Aristotle's *Categories*,[29] whether it classifies "words" (φωναί), "things" (πράγματα), or "concepts" (νοήματα), and which as Gersch notes was commented on by Porphyry and is, among extant works, best documented in Simplicius. The Anon. Byz. next argues (3:18–22) that one who errs about "things," his worst-case scenario, falls into Plato's "double ignorance," ἄγνοια ("knowing that one knows and not understanding that one is ignorant"). Thus the Anon. Byz. cites Plato and Neoplatonists by name, deliberately supplements the text of the *Vita Plotini* to mark a contrast between "concepts" and "things" (νοήματα and πράγματα), shows a specific, if unsophisticated,[30] knowledge of Neoplatonic epistemology,

[27] See Olymp. Phil., *Proll.* 18:25–27, and Elias Phil., *In Cat.*129:9–11.

[28] *From Iamblichus to Eriugena* (Leiden, 1978), 96 n. 76.

[29] On the centrality of Aristotles' *Categories* and Porphyry's commentary thereon in Byzantine philosophical education, as well as the growing interest in Neoplatonism in the late 9th and 10th centuries before the "renaissance" associated with M. Psellos, see R. Browning, *The Byzantine Empire,* rev. ed. (Washington, D.C., 1992), 138, and Lemerle, *Byzantine Humanism,* 251–55.

[30] The Anon. Byz. appears to use two levels of reality, that of sense perception and a level above, which he uses of both νοήματα and mathematical objects ἐν φαντασίᾳ, levels that are often distinguished by some Neoplatonists (see, e.g., the distinction between φαντασία and διάνοια in Syrianus below, note 31). Gersch, however, observes

and evinces a clear preference for the sensible realities (πράγματα).

In the *Geodesia* (**6**:29, 37) the Anon. Byz. describes geometrical figures as existing "in concept and reality ... in reality and imagination" (νοήσει τε καὶ αἰσθήσει ... αἰσθήσει τε καὶ φαντασίᾳ), reflecting again dual levels of reality, here most similar to those found especially in Proclus.[31] A number of the geometrical figures in Vat. gr. 1605 are notable in their realistic qualities, for example, a circle depicted with rocks and bushes on its perimeter (chap. **7**), a human figure with a rope measuring a circle (chap. **7**), and a cistern depicted with individual bricks visible and filled with water to illustrate calculation of the volume of a rectangular solid (chap. **9**).[32] Finally, the Anon. Byz.'s stated purpose for his modified verbal descriptions in the introductory passage of the *Geodesia* (**1**:28–30)exemplifies as well his approach to illustration: "to bring down to a low and more sensible level the height of their theory concerning these concepts" (καὶ τὸ ὑψηλὸν τῆς περὶ τὰ νοήματα θεωρίας ἐπὶ τὸ ταπεινὸν καὶ αἰσθητικώτερον κατενεγκεῖν).[33]

(94 n. 61, as above in note 29) that for convenience of argument the Neoplatonists "sometimes speak simply of two levels: sensible (immanent) Forms and psychic Forms (concepts)."

[31] See esp. Proclus, *In primum Euclidis librum commentarius* 51:14–21 and G. Morrow, *Proclus, A Commentary on the First Book of Euclid's Elements* (Princeton, N. J., 1970) 41 n. 5 on the idea of φαντασία as a form of νόησις. See also the interesting passage in Syrianus (*In Metaphysica commentaria* 6:98:26ff (on 1078a14) on the place of φαντασία in practical construction: ὁμοίως καὶ ὁ μηχανικὸς τὴν ὕλην σχηματίζων ἐπανάγει πᾶσαν ἑαυτοῦ τὴν ποίησιν ἐπὶ τὰ ἄυλα σχήματα καὶ ἐν φαντασίᾳ μὲν διαστατῶς, ἐν διανοίᾳ δὲ ἀμερῶς τὴν ὑπόστασιν ἔχοντα. G. Watson, *Phantasia in Classical Thought* (Galway, 1988), 119 comments on this passage: "When someone is making something, for instance, he shapes his matter in accordance with an immaterial blueprint (schemata), which exists unextended in the mind and in extended fashion in phantasia." The Anon. Byz., I suggest, is arguing for the educational value of descending still one level of reality further down.

[32] One other passage provides evidence of the author's interest in the effect of realistic representation. In a recommendation in the *Parangelmata* (**52**:5–10) not found in his classical sources he suggests for the doors of a *sambuca* (a tubelike troop carrier): Αἱ δὲ τοῦ αὐτοῦ στομίου θύραι ἔξωθεν καταπληκτικαὶ διὰ γλυφῆς ἐκφανοῦς καὶ πολυχρώμου γραφῆς σὺν τῷ ἐμπροσθίῳ μέρει τοῦ αὐλοῦ γινέσθωσαν, δράκοντος ἢ λέοντος πυροφόρον ἐπιφερόμεναι προτομὴν εἰς κατάπληξιν καὶ φόβον τῶν ἐναντίων προσερχομένην.

[33] It is worth noting that even the traditional geometrical drawings found in the *Geodesia* (used to show measurement of the height of a wall, distances between points in the horizontal plain, and so on) are given a concrete quality by examples in the text

I suggest, then, that the approach to poliorcetic, and to a lesser extent geometric, illustration in Vat. gr. 1605 is consciously articulated in his text by the Anon. Byz.[34] Reversing the Neoplatonic[35] idea of ascent from what the senses perceive to the νοήματα, he replaces "schematic" drawings, conceived of as objects "in thought" and "in imagination," with "sensibles" to achieve a practical educational purpose, and specifically describes the process, "give definition to, particularize" (ἀκριβῶς διορίζεσθαι) the σχήματα. Such use of depictions of finished devices was perhaps initially more acceptable in an "original" Byzantine compilation, one not bound by the dictates of the classical tradition. Therefore, the so-called Heron of Byzantium would appear to be the first adapter of realistic representation to the poliorcetic genre, with a new pedagogical vision, both textual and especially pictorial, of how his contemporaries could best learn to create physical objects. He brings to the genre a method that is quite new, even though one flawed by misinterpretations and errors.

The Errors

Otto Lendle comments that the Anon. Byz. interpreted the work of Apollodorus "nach seinem (manchmal überzeugenden, gelegentlich in

---

set in the Hippodrome of Constantinople, e.g. (*Geodesia* **2**:15–16), ὡς [τοῦ] ἀπὸ τοῦ ⟨ἐπὶ⟩ ἐδάφους τῶν θυρῶν ὑποτεθέντος B πρὸς τὸ ἐπὶ μέρους τινὸς τοῦ τεθρίππου σημειωθὲν A ("from <point> B assumed at the bottom of the doors to point A noted on some part of the quadriga").

[34] The illustrations in Vat. gr. 1605 are, of course, at least once removed from those that accompanied the Anon. Byz.'s original work. Given the specific verbal description he provides of his approach to illustration and the conservatism of illustrators, it seems reasonable to assume that many of the main characteristics of the illustrations in the Vaticanus follow those in the autograph. Whether the illustrator of the Vaticanus introduced additional innovations is uncertain.

[35] Other indications of Neoplatonic influence in the Anon. Byz. include his characterization in the *Geodesia* (**7**:47–48) of the radius of a circle as ἐν ἀρχῇ … ἀπ᾽ ἀρχῆς … ἐπ᾽ ἀρχήν, an image widely found in Neoplatonic authors, especially Plotinus (e.g, *Ennead* V.1:10), Pseudo-Dionysius (e.g., *De divinis nominibus* 5) and Proclus (e.g., *In primum Euclidis librum commentarius* 155:6–8: Ἀλλ᾽ ὡς μὲν τῆς διαστάσεως ἀρχὴ τῶν γραμμῶν τῷ "ἀφ᾽ οὗ" σημαίνεται, ὡς δὲ μέσον τῆς περιφερείας τῷ "πρὸς ὅ"), and his reference to Pythagorean views of the cube as representing "harmony" (*Geodesia* **8**:13–15).

die Irre gehenden) Verständnis."[36] In addition to occasional and serious misinterpretations of the sources, the Byzantine author also makes some errors in mathematics and in his "astronomical" methodology. In the first category, for example, W. Sackur observed that the Anon. Byz. misinterprets the method of diminishing the size of each upward story of the portable siege tower of Diades as one based on area rather than on width (*Parangelmata* **30**), with resulting errors in his description of Apollodorus' tower.[37] In the second category the Byzantine author (*Geodesia* **8**) incorrectly computes the surface area of a cone, apparently due to his misinterpretation of Archimedes. Finally, T. H. Martin (394–95) has noted, among a number of problems, that the Byzantine "paraît avoir confondu, de même que les anciens astrologues, les *ascensions droits* avec les *ascensions obliques,* et avoir confondu aussi *déclinaisons* avec les *latitudes.*" Such errors are noted in the commentary. Sackur's general characterization (*Vitruv,* 106) seems not unfair: "Der Anonymus Byzantinus ist ein sehr gewissenhafter Arbeiter . . . aber ein eigentlich technisches Denken . . . dürfen wir bei ihm nicht erwarten."

The Tenth-Century Context

The tenth century witnessed a flowering of interest in codifying and transmitting methods of warfare. This interest occurred in large part as a response to the Arab threat and the accompanying shift from a defensive to an offensive posture on the part of the Byzantine state.[38] One primary focus of the shift was Crete, lost in about 826 and the objective of numerous expeditions, including the failed expedition in 949 (the preparations for which are described in detail in *De cerimoniis,* 669ff) and the final success of Nikephoros Phokas in 960–961. Other foci of the tenth-century offensive included Muslim territory in Cilicia and northern Syria. The taking of walled cities and fortifications was a significant part of such expeditions (e.g., Melitene, Edessa, Chandax, and Aleppo). The list of military manuals compiled during the period includes Leo VI's *Taktika* (ca. 905), *De obsidione toleranda* (after 924), the

---

[36] Lendle, *Texte,* xx.

[37] Sackur, *Vitruv,* 106.

[38] See E. McGeer, "Infantry vs. Cavalry: The Byzantine Response," *REB* 46 (1988), 135.

Sylloge tacticorum (ca. 950), the *Praecepta militaria* attributed to Nikephoros Phokas (ca. 965), the *De re militari* (ca. 975), *De velitatione* (ca. 975), and the *Taktika* of Nikephoros Ouranos (ca. 1000).[39] Most of these take a comprehensive view of warfare; some, however, present siege warfare as one facet of the whole enterprise. Thus chap. 15 of Leo's *Taktika* is entitled Περὶ πολιορκίας πόλεων, chap. 21 of the *De velitatione* Περὶ πολιορκίας κάστρου, chap. 21 of the *De re militari* Περὶ πολιορκίας, and chap. 65 of Ouranos' *Taktika* Περὶ καστροπολέμου.

The degree of realism in these texts has been the subject of recent scholarly interest.[40] Among the issues considered have been the extent to which they simply preserve classical sources and with what intent, how useful the classical techniques were in the tenth-century context, and how much specifically contemporary material they contain. Gilbert Dagron has suggested three criteria for judging relative modernity: (1) the attention paid to the evolution of military technology, although this, as Dagron notes, admittedly saw no radical transformation; (2) the description of the enemy, for example, ethnic nature, social composition, and military methods; and (3) the composition and structure of the Byzantine army, including recruitment, administrative and political status, and the appearance of a military caste.[41] Of Dagron's latter two criteria there is little evidence in the Anon. Byz. With regard to the enemy the Anon. Byz., in explaining the purpose of his work, says that if they (i.e., the Byzantines) construct siege machines by the methods he describes, military leaders "will easily capture cities, especially those of Agar and themselves suffer nothing fatal from the God-damned enemy" (εὐχερῶς τὰς τῆς Ἄγαρ μάλιστα λήψονται πόλεις, αὐτοὶ μηθὲν ἀνήκεστον ὑπὸ τῶν θεολέστων ἐχθρῶν πάσχοντες, chap. **58**). It is thus specifically against Arab cities that he sees his work as being employed. The use of the adjective θεόλεστος may also be indicative. The word occurs three times in *De cerimoniis* (514:5 and 9, 651:15) in the phrase "against God-damned Crete" (κατὰ τῆς θεολέστου Κρήτης) with regard

---

[39] For a review of the military manuals see Dain, "Stratégistes," passim. Individual articles on most of these are contained in the *ODB*.

[40] See T. G. Kolias, "The Taktika of Leo VI the Wise and the Arabs," *Graeco-Arabica* 3 (1984), 129–35; G. Dagron, *Traité,* 139–60; E. McGeer, "Infantry," 136; and McGeer "Tradition," 129–40.

[41] Dagron, *Traité,* 142.

to the expedition of 911 under Himerios, and in the Δημηγορία Κωνσταντίνου βασιλέως πρὸς τοὺς τῆς ἀνατολῆς στρατηγούς 5:13: κατὰ τῶν χωρῶν καὶ κάστρων τῆς θεολέστου Ταρσοῦ.[42] Theophanes (ὑπὸ τοῦ θεολέστου αὐτῶν ἔθνους) also uses the term in connection with Arabs.[43] The adjective, as well as the specific reference to Arab cities, thus sets the intent of the treatise in line with Byzantine objectives of the 940s and 950s.

Concerning the third criterion, the Anon. Byz. says nothing on issues of military recruitment, or the political and administrative nature of the army and makes only brief, but interesting, mention of the army's officer class. At the end of the *Parangelmata,* in the sentence whose conclusion was quoted above, he begins: "If army commanders carefully complete with logic and continuous diligence these siege machines, which have been selectively compiled for description and illustration, and always contemplate divine justice, being honored for their fairness and reverence, and strengthened and guarded by the powerful hand and cooperation and alliance of the God crowned and Christ-loving emperors of Rome" (⟨Τ⟩αῦτα τοίνυν τὰ πρὸς ἀναγραφὴν καὶ σχηματισμὸν κατ᾽ ἐκλογὴν συνταχθέντα πολιορκητήρια μηχανήματα οἱ τῶν στρατευμάτων ἐξάρχοντες μετὰ λόγου καὶ συνεχοῦς μελέτης ἐπιμελῶς κατεργαζόμενοι, τὴν θείαν διὰ παντὸς ἐνοπτριζόμενοι δίκην, ἐπὶ δικαιοσύνῃ καὶ εὐσεβείᾳ κεκοσμημένοι καὶ τῇ κραταιᾷ χειρὶ συνεργείᾳ τε καὶ συμμαχίᾳ τῶν θεοστέπτων καὶ φιλοχρίστων ἀνάκτων Ῥώμης ἐνδυναμούμενοί τε καὶ φρουρούμενοι). It is thus the military leaders whom he sees as employing his treatise and they are characterized as closely associated with the emperors. Earlier in the treatise, immediately following the introductory material, he says (chap. 4): "The most competent military commander, kept safe by Providence above because of his piety, and obedient to the command and judgment and good counsel of our most divine emperors" (⟨Τ⟩ὸν ὑπὸ τῆς ἄνω προνοίας ἐπ᾽ εὐσεβείᾳ συντηρούμενον στρατηγικώτατον ἄρχοντα, τῇ κελεύσει καὶ γνώμῃ καὶ εὐβουλίᾳ τῶν θειοτάτων αὐτοκρατόρων ὑπείκοντα), again linking military leaders with the emperors and here, perhaps rhetorically, but nev-

[42] Ed. R. Vári, "Zum historischen Exzerptenwerke des Konstantinos Porphyrogennetos," *Byzantinische Zeitschrift* 17 (1908), 75–85.

[43] *Chronographia* 499:21 (ed. C. de Boor; repr. Hildesheim, 1963).

ertheless explicitly, describing them as highly skilled. General officers are thus portrayed as close to the emperors and learned in their profession.

On Dagron's first criterion the treatise presents issues of greater complexity. The Anon. Byz. specifically indicates that he is working from classical sources, and thus his work is obviously heavily derivative; he also tells us that he will add material. The author's description of the classical material should, however, be set in the context of his modernization of the method of presentation discussed above, by which both textually and pictorially he seeks to make the classical material more accessible. Further, as Dagron notes, evolution of military technology was not radical, a point that can be substantiated by specific references in tenth-century texts. The historians provide one source of information about siege techniques. John Kaminiates, for example, describes the Arabs besieging Thessalonica in 904 as using siege towers on paired ships, a technique described by the Anon. Byz. in *Parangelmata* **53**, following Athenaeus Mechanicus. Whether Kaminiates' description is actually tenth-century, however, has been questioned.[44] Leo the Deacon (*Historiae* II:7) describes Nikephoros Phokas' siege of Chandax (961) as involving a battering ram and methods of undermining walls also described by the Anon. Byz. (*Parangelmata* chaps. **22–23** and **13–14**); but Leo's account has been shown to be heavily dependent on a siege description in Agathias (*Historiae* 1:10).[45] Anna Comnena (e.g., *Alexiad* XI:1:6–7; XIII:2:3, 3:9) describes portable siege towers, tortoises for filling and excavating, undermining walls, ram-tortoises, and even the importance of the dioptra in correctly constructing siege engines, all items discussed by the Anon. Byz. Yet even here literary influence cannot be completely ruled out.

More helpful are inventory lists and comments of practitioners. In the list of items prepared for the expedition against Crete in 949 the *De cerimoniis* lists a "wooden tower," ξυλόπυργος (670:10–11), "tortoises,"

[44] A. P. Kazhdan, "Some Questions Addressed to the Scholars Who Believe in the Authenticity of Kaminiates'"Capture of Thessalonica," *Byzantinische Zeitschrift* 71 (1978), 301–14. For an opposing view, however, see J. Frendo, "The Miracles of St. Demetrius and the Capture of Thessaloniki," *Byzantinoslavica* 58 (1997), 205–24.

[45] C. B. Hase, *Leonis Diaconi Historiae libri X* (Bonn, 1828), 419, note 25: 19.

χελῶναι (670:11), and "ram-tortoises" εἰς ... τὰς χελώνας κριοί (670:13, 671:4–5, 673:1), all classical devices covered in considerable detail by the Anon. Byz. Nikephoros Ouranos (*Taktika* 65:22) comments: "The men of old, in their pursuit of siege warfare, constructed many devices such as battering rams, wooden towers, scaling ladders with various features, tortoises, and all kinds of other things which our generation can hardly imagine. It has, however, tried all these devices and found that out of all of them, the most effective way, one which the enemy cannot match, is undermining the foundations, all the more so if one does so with careful scrutiny and method, and has the accompanying and extremely helpful protection of *laisai* (mantlets)" (Οἱ μὲν γὰρ παλαιοὶ ἔχοντες τὴν σπουδὴν εἰς καστροπόλεμον ἐποίουν καὶ μηχανήματα πολλὰ οἷον κριοὺς καὶ πύργους ξυλίνους καὶ σκάλας ἐχούσας ἄλλα καὶ ἄλλα ἰδιώματα, καὶ χελώνας καὶ ἄλλα περισσότερα ἅπερ ἡ ἡμετέρα γενεὰ οὐδὲ ἰδεῖν ἴσχυσε· πλὴν ἀπεπείρασε ταῦτα πάντα καὶ εὗρεν ἐκ πάντων τούτων ἐπιτηδειότερον καὶ ἀναπάντητον τοῖς ἐχθροῖς τὸ διὰ τῶν θεμελίων ὄρυγμα, ἂν ἄρα καὶ μετὰ διακρίσεως καὶ τάξεως ποιήσῃ τις αὐτό, ἔχων συνακολουθοῦσαν καὶ βοηθοῦσαν πολὺ καὶ τὴν σκέπην τῶν λαισῶν).[46] Ouranos thus indicates that his generation has tested various classical siege devices (rams, <mobile> wooden towers, ladders, and tortoises) and found that undermining walls using *laisai* (light weight shelters plaited from branches, a contemporary Byzantine technology) is the most effective technique. The Anon. Byz. includes all of the classical devices mentioned by Ouranos, including methods of undermining walls as well as the contemporary *laisai*. Ouranos' detailed description (65:18–21) of the undermining of walls using an "excavate, prop, and burn" method has a number of similarities with the description of the Anon. Byz. (*Parangelmata* **13–14**). Finally, in the eleventh century, Kekaumenos comments: "Since those wondrous men who have written treatises on war machines constructed rams and engines and many other tools by which they captured cities, I say also to you to construct one of these engines, but if you can to also invent something new. For this is more worthy of praise." (Ἐπεὶ δὲ οἱ θαυμαστοὶ ἄνδρες ἐκεῖνοι οἱ περὶ μηχανημάτων στρατηγικῶν συγγραψάμενοι ἐμηχανήσαντο κριοὺς καὶ μηχανικὰ καὶ ἄλλα πολλὰ ὄργανα ἐν οἷς εἶλον πόλεις, λέγω σοι κἀγὼ

---

[46] Trans. McGeer, "Tradition," 161–63.

μηχανήσασθαι μηχανήν τινα ἐξ αὐτῶν, εἰ δὲ δύνασαι, καὶ καινόν τι ἐπινοήσασθαι. Τοῦτο γὰρ μᾶλλον ἐπαίνου ἐστιν ἄξιον).[47] Thus classical devices were still considered of value, but even more praiseworthy was innovation, based in part on a knowledge of classical sources.

The Anon. Byz. also indicates (*Parangelmata* 1:27–28) that he will add related information to his paraphrase of Apollodorus, πλεῖστα καὶ αὐτοὶ σύμφωνα προσευρόντες καὶ παραθέμενοι. Much of this material is drawn from other classical sources, but some is clearly contemporary. Dain has listed among them the wheeled ladder with drop-bridge (chap. **46**), excavating tortoise with drop-bridge (chap. **47**), various remarks on ladders and bridges, including the handheld στρεπτόν for shooting Greek fire (chap. **49**), and improvements to Athenaeus Mechanicus' landing tube (chap. **52**).[48] Eric McGeer has noted references to the clearly contemporary *laisai* (chaps. **9, 17, 47**).[49] A number of other briefer references not found in the classical sources are scattered through the text, for example, the use of urine for cracking heated stones (chap. **16**), τοξοβολίστραι (chap. **15**), alternate bases for a scout-ladder (chaps. **27, 28**), and silk (νήματα σηρικά) for torsion springs (chap. **44**). The illustrations in Vat. gr. 1605 also provide evidence of contemporary practice. The *laisai* are depicted on folios 8r and 35r, the στρεπτόν on folio 36r, and the human figures are shown in contemporary military dress, felt hats, tunics, and boots (καμελαύκια, καβάδια, and ὑποδήματα).

Thus while the *Parangelmata* and the *Geodesia* are clearly heavily derived from classical sources, the potential practical value that the Anon. Byz. ascribes to them (to "capture cities, especially those of Agar") is verified by other tenth-century theory and practice for at least some of the devices and methods described. Classical devices were still tried and used in the tenth century: the *De cerimoniis* indicates the use of siege towers, tortoises, and rams; Ouranos indicates trial of numerous such devices, together with innovation, as does the advice of Kekaumenos.

[47] Ed. G.G. Litavrin, *Sovety i rasskazy Kekavmena* (Moscow, 1972), 148:23–28.

[48] Dain, *Tradition,* 16 n. 2. Dain's comment, "A dire vrai, dans le texte relatif au πυροβόλον, Héron ne dit rien qui ne se trouve dans Apollodore: ce qui est nouveau c'est la vignette," is questionable. The Anon. Byz. says μετὰ στρεπτῶν ἐγχειριδίων πυροβόλων (*Parangelmata* 49:20), a description not in his source and clearly referring to a middle Byzantine device.

[49] McGeer, "Tradition," 136.

The Anon. Byz.'s new method of presentation is intended to improve his readers' understanding of classical engineering descriptions, while his inclusion of tenth-century material indicates his awareness of innovation. The contemporary value of such a book is also attested by the remark of Constantine VII, in describing for his son the items to be included in the imperial baggage: "books on mechanics, including siege machinery and the production of missiles and other information relevant to the enterprise, that is to say wars and sieges" (βιβλία μηχανικά, ἐλεπόλεις ἔχοντα, καὶ βελοποιϊκὰ καὶ ἕτερα ἁρμόδια τῇ ὑποθέσει ἤγουν πρὸς πολέμους καὶ καστρομαχίας).[50] At the same time, however, it is clear that some items in the text would seem to have only antiquarian interest (e.g., the ram of Hegetor, the largest from antiquity) and others, although derived from the classical sources, are of questionable value (e.g., the inflatable leather ladder from Philo Mechanicus and the raft of Apollodorus). The utility of the works is also compromised by the Anon. Byz.'s errors.

Editorial Principles

K. K. Müller's and Alphonse Dain's studies of the manuscript tradition of the two texts associated with "Heron of Byzantium" convincingly established the archetype value of Vat. gr. 1605; it led Dain to recommend a new edition based on it. Dain also noted the sound state of the text in the Vaticanus and proposed that there were few intermediaries between the original and this copy. His description of Vat. gr. 1605, coupled with those of Müller and Cyrus Gianelli, leaves little to be added.[51] The manuscript is parchment, 258 mm x 210 mm, with 58

---

[50] Trans. J. Haldon, *Constantine Porphyrogenitus, Three Treatises on Imperial Military Expeditions* (Vienna, 1990), 106, lines 196–98.

[51] C. Gianelli, *Codices Vaticani Graeci: Codices, 1485–1683* (Vatican City, 1950), 260–62. Gianelli noted that the final folio contains the designation "AND," taken to be the bookmark of Charles of Anjou, suggesting that Vat. gr. 1605 may have been among the books given to the pope after the battle of Beneventum; see also P. Canart, "Le livre grec en Italie méridionale sous les règnes Normand et Souabe: aspects matériels et sociaux," *Scrittura e civiltà* 2 (1978), 103–62, esp. 149 n. 113, and N. Wilson, *Scholars of Byzantium* (Baltimore, Md., 1983), 214. However, A. G. Bagliani, "La provenienza 'angioina' dei codici greci della biblioteca de Bonifacio VIII," *Italia medioevale e umanistica* 26 (1983), 27–69, esp. 43–44, has argued persuasively that the abbreviation is not to be connected with Charles of Anjou and "sembra essere destinata a rimanere misteriosa e sibillina." I am grateful to an anonymous reader for this last reference.

extant folios, and notably contains only the two treatises of "Heron of Byzantium." Dain's suggestion of a mid-eleventh-century date (Müller and Gianelli say only 11th century without further specification) might be questioned in light of the recent tendency to place manuscripts earlier.[52] Of the origin of the manuscript and the reasons for the lack of rubrication we know nothing. Later interlinear annotations[53] on folios 4r–v, 6v, 7r, 53v, and 54r and their subsequent erasure have obscured some accents and the upper portion of some letters. The first folio is reproduced in fig. A.

The edition, then, is based on the archetype, Vat. gr. 1605, previously not used in any edition.[54] Where I have recorded the conjectures of the previous editors, I have, for the sake of clarity, generally also included the related reading of the apograph as they report it; in some instances a negative entry appeared sufficient. In those instances where I have preferred the reading of an apograph to the Vaticanus, the reading of the apograph is also derived from the printed edition. I have not noted in the apparatus editorial conjectures or errors and omissions in the apographs for which the archetype provides correct readings. I have supplied in angle brackets and generally without further notice initial paragraph letters omitted in the Vaticanus[55] due to lack of rubrication. As the text has generally been cited from Wescher's and Vincent's editions, their page numbers are noted in the margin preceded by "Wes" and "Vin"; I have not attempted to retain their line breaks. I have allowed the scribe's inconsistency in employing elision and *nu* movable

---

[52] For such earlier dating generally, see, e.g., Dagron, *Traité,* 14–15.

[53] On their likely nature see Gianelli (as above, note 51), 262.

[54] I note the following errors in Müller's recorded readings of V, using his listing by Wescher's and Vincent's page and line numbers: 217, 2 ἐπαλιφθέντα: ἐπαλιφέντα V ‖ 252, 9 ὑπεμβαίνονται: ὑπεμβαίνοντα V ‖ 264, 15 σχάριον: σχαρίον V ‖ 264, 17 διάμετρα: διάμετροι V ‖ 348, 17 ὀλίγον διὰ γραμμάτων: ὀλίγων (–ων per compendium) διάγραμμάτων V ‖ 350, 5 πρός τε γεωδεσίαν καὶ: πρός τε γεωδεσίαν τε καὶ V ‖ 350, 6 τε om.: τε V ‖ 350, 8 εὖ κρινῆσαι: εὐκρινῆσαι V ‖ 350, 10 εὐλήπτως: εὐλήπτων (–ων per compendium) V ‖ 376, 14 ἅπερ: ἅσπερ V ‖ 378, 6 οἱ δ': ὁ ιδ' V ‖ 390, 6 βολιβοῦν: μολιβοῦν V ‖. In one instance Müller has not recorded a significant difference, i.e., Vincent 396, 8 has λβ' (i.e., "32"); Müller makes no comment, while V has λβ' β'' (i.e., "32 2/3"), on which see the related note in the commentary.

[55] *Parangelmata* 1, 4, 11, 13–20, 22, 24, 25, 27–29, 39[1, 17], 42, 43, 45–50, 52, 53, 55–58 and *Geodesia* 1, 3–7, 8[1, 60, 85, 96, 105], 9[1, 46], 10[1, 19], 11.

to remain as it appears in the manuscript. Errors resulting from iota-cism, homophonic confusions, dittography (e.g., πέταλλον for πέταλον in all but one instance), and incorrect accents and breathings are not recorded unless a different meaning is possible.

Measurement Units in the Text

For specific numerical measurements of length the author uses the δάκτυλος ("finger"), πούς ("foot"), πῆχυς ("cubit"), and ὀργυά ("fathom"); the στάδιον ("stade") is employed in a scholion. He also mentions the παλαιστή ("palm") and the σπιθαμή ("span"). Proportional relationships between units of measure are explicitly stated in *Parangelmata* **18** and **38** and in the scholion at *Geodesia* **6**. The author uses 16 δάκτυλοι = 1 πούς, 11/2 πόδες = 1 πῆχυς, 4 πήχεις = 1 ὀργυά; also the παλαιστή = 4 δάκτυλοι, the σπιθαμή = 12 δάκτυλοι. The author compares (*Parangelmata* **38**) for commensurability different siege towers built using πήχεις and πόδες respectively as the units of measure. In *Geodesia* **9** in measuring the volume of the cistern of Aspar, he makes a comparison between the cubic πῆχυς and ὀργυά a major part of his presentation. An analogous situation exists for units of liquid volume, the κεράμιον and the κάδος. Given the integral nature of the specific measurement units to the text and the differences between, for example, the Byzantine *pous* and the English "foot," it has seemed best to simply transliterate the measurement terms. The units of length have the following values; for in-depth treatment see Schilbach, *Metrologie*.

1 δάκτυλος, pl. δάκτυλοι *(daktylos, daktyloi)*	1.95 cm
1 παλαιστή, pl. παλαισταί *(palaiste, palaistai)*	7.8 cm
1 σπιθαμή, pl. σπιθαμαί *(spithame, spithamai)*	23.4 cm
1 πούς, pl. πόδες *(pous, podes)*	31.23 cm
1 πῆχυς, pl. πήχεις *(pechys, pecheis)*	46.8 cm
1 ὀργυά, pl. ὀργυαί *(orgya, orgyai)*	1.87 m

Sigla: Variae lectiones et coniecturae

V	Vaticanus graecus 1605, XI
B	Bononiensis Universitatis 1497, XVI
P	Parisinus supplementus graecus 817, XIX
< >	addenda
< . . . >	lacuna
[ ]	delenda
Dain	Dain, *Tradition*
Mango	Mango, "Palace"
Mar	T. H. Martin
Marsden	Marsden, *Treatises*
Sch	R. Schneider
Vin	A. J. H. Vincent
Wes	C. Wescher

Texts and Translations

Parangelmata Poliorcetica

Geodesia

⟨ ΠΑΡΑΓΓΕΛΜΑΤΑ ΠΟΛΙΟΡΚΗΤΙΚΑ ⟩

    1. ⟨῞Ο⟩σα μὲν τῶν πολιορκητικῶν μηχανημάτων δυσχερῆ καὶ
δυσέφικτα πέφυκεν, εἴτε διὰ τὸ ποικίλον καὶ δυσδιάγνωστον
τῆς τούτων καταγραφῆς, εἴτε διὰ τὸ τῶν νοημάτων δύσληπτον
ἢ μᾶλλον εἰπεῖν ἀκατάληπτον τοῖς πολλοῖς, ἴσως δὲ τῇ ἀγνωσίᾳ
5   μόνῃ περιληπτῶν, ὡς μηδ᾽ ἀπ᾽ αὐτῆς τῆς τῶν σχημάτων θέας
τὸ σαφὲς κεκτημένων καὶ εὔληπτον, ἅτε μὴ πᾶσιν ὄντων
εὐκόλων τε καὶ γνωστῶν, μήτε μὴν πρὸς κατασκευὴν καὶ
τεκτόνευσιν εὐχερῶν, μόνων δὲ τῶν ταῦτα ἐξευρηκότων καὶ
συγγεγραφηκότων μηχανικῶν εἰς τὴν τούτων ἐξάπλωσιν καὶ
10   σαφήνειαν δεομένων· οἷον τὰ Ἀπολλοδώρου | πρὸς Ἀδριανὸν   Wes 198
αὐτοκράτορα συνταχθέντα Πολιορκητικά, τὰ Ἀθηναίου πρὸς
Μάρκελλον ἐκ τῶν Ἀγησιστράτου καὶ ἑτέρων σοφῶν πρὸς
πολιορκίαν ἐκτεθέντα ὑπομνήματα, τὰ Βίτωνος πρὸς Ἄτταλον
Περὶ Κατασκευῆς Πολεμικῶν Ὀργάνων ἐκ διαφόρων
15   συλλεγέντα προγενεστέρων μηχανικῶν ⟨ . . . ⟩ βελοποιϊκά, καὶ
τὰ πρὸς πολιορκίαν ἀντιμηχανήματα φυλακτικά τε καὶ
διαιτητικά, ἐπί τε συστάσει καὶ ἁλώσει πόλεων διάφορα
παραγγέλματα. Ταῦτα κατὰ τὴν πάλαι ‖ συνταχθεῖσαν τῶν   f. 1v
ἀνδρῶν καθολικὴν τεχνολογίαν, ὡς τοῖς πολλοῖς νῦν
20   ἀπεξενωμένα πάντῃ καὶ δυσδιάγνωστα, διά τε τὴν ἐκ τοῦ
χρόνου παραδραμοῦσαν λήθην, ἀλλ᾽ ὅτι καὶ ἀσυνήθη κοινοῖς
τυγχάνει λόγοις τὰ τῶν ἐπιστημῶν ὀνόματα, τῇ παρούσῃ βίβλῳ
μὴ ἐντάξαι πρέπον ἐκρίναμεν· ὡς ἂν μή, τῆς ἐπιπολαζούσης ἐν
αὐτοῖς ἀσαφείας τὸν νοῦν ἀντιπερισπώσης πρὸς ἑαυτήν, καὶ

1: 21–22 ἀσυνήθη – ὀνόματα: cf. Apollod. 138:14–15.

Tit. ΠΑΡΑΓΓΕΛΜΑΤΑ ΠΟΛΙΟΡΚΗΤΙΚΑ Sch: om. VB: Ἡρων(ος) προοίμ(ιον) add. m. rec. V
(s. 14–15 ? v. Dain, 13): *1605 Heronis Poliorcetica* add. m2. rec. V (? A.D. 1650 Allatii, Dain, 33):
ΠΟΛΙΟΡΚΗΤΙΚΑ Wes ‖ **1:** 4 ἀγνωσίᾳ VBP: ἐννοίᾳ marg. ms. Lond. add. 15276: εὐγνωσίᾳ
Mar: διαγνωσίᾳ Wes ‖ 4–5 ἀγνωσίᾳ μόνῃ VB: εὐγνωμοσύνη Sch ‖ 5 περίληπτον (sic) Mar
‖ 6 εὐλήπτων Mar ‖ 15 < . . . > Sch

<Instructions for Siege Warfare>

1. Everything about siege machines is difficult and hard to understand, either because of the intricacy and inscrutability of their depiction, or because of the difficulty of comprehending the concepts, or, to say it better, because of their incomprehensibility to most men; perhaps they are comprehensible only through <mystical> "unknowing." For the <machines> do not obtain clarity and comprehensibility even from looking at the drawings of them, since these are neither easy nor understandable for all, nor indeed readily useful for construction and carpentry. The engineers alone who have invented and described these <machines> are required for explanation and clear knowledge of them. For example, the *Siege Machines* compiled by Apollodorus for the emperor Hadrian; the commentaries on siege warfare by Athenaeus for Marcellus, extracted from the works of Agesistratus and other skillful men; also those by Biton for Attalus *On the Construction of War Engines,* collected from the works of different earlier engineers; < . . . > artillery construction, and defensive and provisioning countermeasures against siege warfare, different instructions for the protection and capture of cities. These we have judged appropriate not to insert in the present volume according to the general systematic method compiled by men long ago (for this is wholly foreign now to most men and difficult to understand, because of the oblivion that comes with the passage of time, but also because the scientific terms are not familiar to the common speech) lest, with the obscurity that predominates in these <works> diverting the <reader's> mind to

25 περὶ τὴν τῶν σαφῶν τις ἀτονήσῃ διάγνωσιν. Μόνα δὲ τὰ
Ἀπολλοδώρου, ἅπερ εἰς τέλος, διασαφήσαντες δι᾽ ἐπεργασιῶν
καὶ ἐπενθυμημάτων συνεπεράναμεν, πλεῖστα καὶ αὐτοὶ
σύμφωνα προσευρόντες καὶ παραθέμενοι.

Ὅσα δ᾽ ἐκ τῶν λοιπῶν σποράδην | συνελεξάμεθα εὔγνωστα   Wes 199
30 καὶ πρὸς ἀλήθειαν εὐκατάληπτα, "κοινῆς ἐννοίας ἀξιώματα"
κατὰ Ἀνθέμιον ὄντα καὶ ἀπὸ μόνου προβλήματος καὶ
σχηματισμοῦ καταλαμβάνεσθαι δυνάμενα, μηδεμιᾶς
διδασκαλίας ἢ ἑρμηνείας δεόμενα, ἰδιωτείᾳ λέξεων καὶ
ἁπλότητι λόγου ὑφ᾽ ἡμῶν καὶ αὐτὰ μεταποιηθέντα πρὸς τὸ
35 σαφέστερον, ὥστε παρὰ τῶν τυχόντων εὐκόλως καὶ
τεκτονεύεσθαι καὶ κατασκευάζεσθαι, τοῖς τοῦ Ἀπολλοδώρου
καὶ ταῦτα συμπλέξαντες, σὺν τοῖς σχήμασιν ἀκριβῶς
διορισάμενοι, κατετάξαμεν, εἰδότες ὅτι δύναται καὶ μόνος
σχηματισμὸς καλῶς διορισθεὶς τὸ περὶ τὴν κατασκευὴν ‖   f. 2
40 σκοτεινὸν καὶ δύσφραστον κατάδηλον ἀπεργάζεσθαι.

2. Χρεία δέ ἐστι τῶν εἰς πολιορκίαν μηχανημάτων· χελωνῶν
διαφόρων τε καὶ ἑτεροσχήμων, οἷον ὀρυκτρίδων, χωστρίδων,
κριοφόρων, προτρόχων, καὶ τῶν νῦν ἐκ πλοκῆς ἐφευρεθεισῶν
ἐλαφροτάτων λαισῶν, πρὸς δὲ τὰ κυλιόμενα βάρη σφηνοειδῶν
5 ἐμβόλων, γερροχελωνῶν, καὶ ξυλίνων πενταπηχῶν τριβόλων,
κριῶν συνθέτων τε καὶ μονοξύλων, ξυλοπυργίων φορητῶν
εὐπορίστων, κλιμάκων συνθέτων τε καὶ ἐλαφροτάτων εἴδη
διάφορα, προφυλακῇ δὲ πάλιν καὶ πρὸς τὰ εἰς ὕψος αἰρόμενα
βάρη καὶ πρὸς τὰ ὑπὸ | τῶν πυροβόλων ἀναπτόμενα, σκοποὶ εἰς   Wes 200
10 καταθεώρησιν τῶν ἔνδον, διορυγαὶ τειχῶν διαφόρων διάφοροι,
διαβάθραι πρὸς παντοίας τάφρους εὐμήχανοι, δίχα κλιμάκων
μηχαναὶ τοῖς τείχεσιν ἐπιβαίνουσαι, πολιορκητήρια παραλίων
πόλεων ἀπαράπτωτα, πολλῶν ὄχλων κατὰ τάξιν ἀθρόαι ἐπὶ
ποταμῶν διαβάσεις. Ταῦτα κατασκευάζειν κατὰ τοὺς πάλαι
15 ἀρχιτέκτονας εὐπόριστα τῇ ὕλῃ, ποικίλα τοῖς σχήμασιν,
ἐλάχιστα τοῖς μέτροις, ἐλαφρὰ τοῖς βάρεσιν, ὑπὸ τυχόντων

---

40 δύσφραστον κατάδηλον: cf. Ath. Mech. 39:1.   **2:** 1–19 Χρεία – εὐδιάλυτα: cf. Apollod.
138:18–139:8.

2: 1 τῶν VB: τούτων Wes (cf. Apollod. 138:18)

itself, one be too exhausted for comprehension even of what is clear. Having clarified only the works of Apollodorus as it were in toto with additional elaborations and secondary arguments, we have drawn our conclusions, finding and adding ourselves numerous concordant <items>.

Everything we have collected here and there from the remaining <writers> is easy to know and apprehend truthfully, "axioms of common intuition" as Anthemios says, and capable of being comprehended from the problem alone and the illustration; they require no instruction or interpretation. We have recast these with common diction and simplicity of style for greater clarity so that <machines> can be both carpentered and constructed easily by anyone. After weaving this <material> also into the works of Apollodorus we have arranged it with the drawings, giving these precise definition, knowing that even an illustration alone, when well defined, is able to render quite clear aspects of construction that are obscure and difficult to express.

2. There is a need of machines for conducting a siege: different types and forms of tortoises, such as excavating tortoises, filler tortoises, ram-carrying tortoises, tortoises with wheels in front, and plaited *laisai*, recently invented and very light, wedge-shaped beak <tortoises> to protect against heavy rolling objects, wicker tortoises; and wooden caltrops 5 *pecheis* in height; rams both composite and of a single piece of wood; portable wooden towers, which are easy to procure; different forms of ladders, composite and very light; also protection against heavy objects that are raised high <to drop> and against <flames> ignited by incendiaries; scout-ladders for viewing things inside <cities>; different tools for digging through different kinds of walls; drop-bridges useful for all types of ditches; machines for mounting walls without ladders; siege machines that do not fall over for use against coastal cities; bridges for en masse river crossings of large numbers of men in good order. <It is necessary> to construct these following the ancient master builders, of materials that are easy to procure, varied in form, as small as possible, light in weight, able to

τεχνιτῶν ταχέως γίνεσθαι δυνάμενα, εὐδιόρθωτα,
δυσεπιβούλευτα, εὐμετάγωγα, ἀσφαλῆ, δυσκάτακτα,
εὐσύνθετα πρὸς τὴν χρείαν ὄντα καὶ εὐδιάλυτα. Ταῦτα δὲ ‖   f. 2v
20 πάντα, στρατηγικὴν ἐπιστήμην ὡς πρὸς πολιορκίαν ῥαδίως
ἐφοδιάζειν δυνάμενα, ἐν τῇδε τῇ δέλτῳ πρός τε κατασκευὴν
καὶ χρείαν καθεξῆς προϊόντες, κατὰ τάξιν ἀναγράψαντες
ἐξεθέμεθα.

3. Καὶ μή τις λέξεων ἐξονυχιστής, συνθήκην ἀττικίζουσαν
ἐρευνῶν ἢ δεινότητα λόγου, κάλλος τε καὶ ἁρμονίαν καὶ
σχημάτων εὐρυθμίαν, περὶ τὸ ἰδιωτικὸν καὶ ὕπτιον ἡμᾶς
εὐθύνῃ, τῶν πάλαι σοφῶν ἀκούων ὅτι ὁ πρὸς πολιορκίαν
5 γινόμενος ἅπας λόγος σαφηνείας τε καὶ τῆς δεούσης ἐπιδεῖται
συντομίας, ἔστιν δὲ ὅτε καὶ ταυτολογιῶν καὶ ἐπαναλήψεων καὶ
ἐπενθυμημάτων πρὸς κατάληψιν τῶν τε διανοημάτων καὶ
πράξεων, διαλεκτικῶν δὲ παραγγελμάτων ἢ τῶν τούτοις
ἀντιστρόφων ἀνοίκειος | τυγχάνει· εἰδὼς δὲ ὅτι καὶ Πλωτῖνος ὁ   Wes 201
10 μέγας "ἔγραφεν," ὥς φησιν ὁ πολὺς ἐν σοφίᾳ Πορφύριος, "οὔτε
εἰς κάλλος ἀποτυπούμενος τὰ γράμματα, οὔτε εὐσήμως τὰς
συλλαβὰς διαιρῶν, οὔτε τῆς ὀρθογραφίας φροντίζων, ἀλλὰ
μόνου τοῦ νοῦ καὶ τῶν πραγμάτων ἐχόμενος." Τριττὰ γὰρ τὰ
ὄντα ἠπίστατο, ἔν τε φωναῖς νοήμασί τε καὶ πράγμασι· καὶ τὸν
15 μὲν περὶ τὰς φωνὰς σφαλλόμενον μηδὲν διασύρεσθαι, ὡς οὐδὲν
τὸ νόημα ἢ τὸ πρᾶγμα λυμαινόμενον· τὸν δὲ περὶ τὰ νοήματα
ἁμαρτάνοντα πικρῶς διελέγχεσθαι, ὡς ‖ ἀδιανοήτως   f. 3
φθεγγόμενον· πολλῷ δὲ ἄρα τὸν περὶ τὰ πράγματα τυφλώττοντα
καταγινώσκεσθαι, ὡς ἠλίθιον ὄντα καὶ ψευδογράφον, εἰς τὴν
20 κατὰ διάθεσιν ἐμπίπτοντα ἄγνοιαν, ἥντινα διπλῆν ὁ Πλάτων
καλεῖ, διὰ τὸ εἰδέναι μὲν ὅτι γινώσκει, μὴ ἐπίστασθαι δὲ ὅτι
ἀγνοεῖ. Ἀλλὰ καὶ ὁ ἱστοριογράφος Καλλισθένης φησίν, "δεῖν
τὸν γράφειν τι πειρώμενον μὴ ἀστοχεῖν τοῦ προσώπου, ἀλλ᾽

3: 4–9 ὁ – τυγχάνει: cf. Ath. Mech. 7:4–6.   10–13 ἔγραφεν – ἐχόμενος: cf. Porph. Plot. VIII.
13–14 Τριττὰ – ὄντα: cf. Olymp. Phil., Proll. 18:25–27, Elias Phil., In Cat. 129:9–11.   20–22
διπλῆν – ἀγνοεῖ: cf. Pl. Sph. 229b, Chrm. 166d.   22–24 ὁ – θεῖναι: cf. Ath. Mech. 7:1–4.

3: 13 Post τὰ add. ἁμαρτήματα Mar ‖ 21 Post μὲν add. οἴεσθαι Sch ‖ 22 δεῖν Wes (cf. Ath.
Mech. 7:2): δεῖ VB

be made quickly by any craftsman, easy to repair, difficult to damage, easy to transport, secure, difficult to break, easy to assemble for use and to disassemble. All these <devices>, which can easily supply knowledge for generals on conducting sieges, we have set forth in this book for both construction and use, proceeding in order and recording them in sequence.

3. And let no scrutinizer of diction, searching for Attic composition or forcefulness of style, and beauty and harmony and gracefulness of <rhetorical> figures, fault us for our commonplace and flat writing, after hearing from the wise men of the past that all writing on siege warfare requires clarity and the necessary conciseness, but sometimes also repetitions and reiterations and secondary arguments for comprehension of the concepts and operations, but that it is not suited to dialectic precepts or their <rhetorical> counterparts and knowing that even the great Plotinus "has written," as the most wise Porphyry says, "without forming his letters calligraphically, not dividing syllables clearly, nor being concerned for correct spelling, but concerned only with the concept and the things." For he knew that reality is tripartite: words, concepts, and things. And the one who errs regarding words is not disparaged, as he does not harm the concept or the thing; but the one missing the mark on concepts is severely reproached for speaking incomprehensibly; but the one who is blind to things is then especially condemned, as a fool and writer of falsehoods. For this one falls into the ignorance by disposition that Plato calls double, "knowing that one knows and not understanding that one is ignorant." But the historian Kallisthenes says: "It is necessary for one who undertakes to write something not to depart from his personality, but to suit the

οἰκείως αὐτῷ τε καὶ τοῖς πράγμασι τοὺς λόγους θεῖναι" [τῆς
25 σοφίας]. Τουτὶ γὰρ ἄν τις εἰς πραγμάτων λόγον ὠφεληθεὶς | Wes 202
ἀπέλθοι, ἢ ἐκ τῶν Φιλολάου καὶ Ἀριστοτέλους, Ἰσοκράτους
τε καὶ Ἀριστοφάνους καὶ Ἀπολλωνίου καὶ τῶν παραπλήσια
ἐκείνοις γεγραφότων· νεωτέροις μὲν γὰρ φιλομαθοῦσιν οὐκ
ἄχρηστα πρὸς ἕξιν τοῦ στοιχειωθῆναι φανήσονται, τοῖς δὲ
30 βουλομένοις ἤδη τι πράττειν πόρρω παντελῶς ἂν εἴη καὶ
ἀπῳκισμένα τῆς πραγματικῆς θεωρίας. Ὅθεν καὶ Ἥρων ὁ
μαθηματικός, συνεὶς τὸ Δελφικὸν ἐκεῖνο παράγγελμα τὸ
ὑπομιμνῆσκον ἡμᾶς χρόνου φείδεσθαι καὶ ὅτι τὰ τοῦ καιροῦ
μέτρα δεῖ εἰδέναι ὡς ὑπάρχοντος ὅρου ⟨τῆς σοφίας⟩, τὸ μέγιστον
35 καὶ ἀναγκαιότατον μέρος τῆς ἐν φιλοσοφίᾳ διατριβῆς καὶ μέχρι
τοῦ νῦν παρὰ πολλῶν ζητούμενον περὶ ἀταραξίας ὑπάρχειν
ᾤετο, καὶ μηδέποτε διὰ τῶν λόγων τέλος ἕξειν ἔλεγεν. Μηχανικὴ
δέ, τὴν ἐν λόγοις δι' ἔργων ὑπερβᾶσα διδασκαλίαν, πάντας || f. 3v
ἀνθρώπους ἐδίδαξεν ἀταράχως ζῆν ἐπίστασθαι δι' ἑνὸς αὐτῆς
40 μέρους τοῦ κατὰ τὴν βελοποιίαν καλουμένου· ὡς μήτε ἐν
εἰρηνικῇ καταστάσει ταράττεσθαί ποτε ἐχθρῶν καὶ πολεμίων | Wes 203
ἐφόδους μήτε πολέμου ἐνστάντος, εἰ ἐν παντὶ χρόνῳ καὶ
καταστήματι σὺν τοῖς σκευαζομένοις τροφίμοις ἔν τε
πολιορκίαις καὶ στρατεύμασιν ὀλιγαρκέσιν ἐπιμονιδίοις

25–31 Τουτὶ – θεωρίας: cf. Ath. Mech. 4:13–5:7.   32–33 τὸ – φείδεσθαι: cf. Ath. Mech. 3:2–
4.   33–34 τὰ – σοφίας: Ath. Mech. 4:12–13.   34–43 τὸ – καταστήματι: cf. Hero Bel. 71–72.
44–45 ἐπιμονιδίοις – φαρμάκοις : cf. Philo Mech. 88:29.

24 αὐτῷ Wes (cf. Ath. Mech. 7:3): αὐτοῦ VBP: αὐτῷ Mar || 24–25 τῆς σοφίας secl. Mar || 25
Τουτὶ VBP (cf. Ath. Mech. 4:13): τούτῳ Mar || Post λόγον add. πλέον Mar || 34 δεῖ Mar: δεῖν
VBP || ὅρου Mar (cf. Ath. Mech. 4:13): ἀόρου VBP || τῆς σοφίας add. Mar || 44 ἐπιμονιδίοις:
in marg. VB: Συντίθεται δὲ τοῦτο τὸ ἐπιμονίδιον φάρμακον ἀφεψηθείσης σκίλλης καὶ
πλυθείσης ὕδατι καὶ ξηρανθείσης κατακοπείσης τε εἰς λεπτότατα, καὶ μετὰ ταῦτα
παραμιχθέντος εἰς αὐτὴν σησάμου τοῦ ε΄ μέρους, μήκωνος ὡς ιε΄, καὶ πάντων τούτων
λεανθέντων ἐν τῷ αὐτῷ ὡς βελτίστῳ μέλιτι φυράσαντα (φυράσαντι V; cf. Philo Mech.
88:37), διελεῖν ὅσον εἰς ἐλαίας τὰς μεγίστας γινομένας. Καὶ τούτων ἓν μὲν περὶ β΄ ὥραν,
ἓν δὲ περὶ ι΄ ἀναλίσκοντες, οὐθὲν ὑπὸ λιμοῦ πάθοιεν δεινόν. Ἄλλη σύνθεσις φαρμάκου
συντιθεμένη τοῦτον τὸν τρόπον. Λαβὼν σήσαμον Ἀττικὸν ἡμίεκτον καὶ μέλιτος ἡμίχουν
καὶ ἐλαίου κοτύλην καὶ χοίνικα ἀμυγδάλων γλυκέων λελεπισμένων, φρύξαντες τὸν
σήσαμον καὶ τὰ ἀμύγδαλα, καταλέσαι καὶ σεῖσαι· εἶτα τὰς σκίλλας περιλεπίσαντα καὶ
τὰς ῥίζας καὶ τὰ πέταλα ἀποτεμόντα καὶ διελόντα μικρά, εἰς θυίαν (θύϊαν V; cf. Philo

words both to himself and to things." For in this way one might come off with benefit in the discussion of things, more than from the <works> of Philolaus and Aristotle, Isocrates and Aristophanes and Apollonius and those who have written like them. For on the one hand, for the young who are eager to learn, these will not seem useless for the acquisition of basic principles; but for those wishing to accomplish something beyond that, they would be completely distant and remote from practical science. Whence Heron the mathematician, understanding that Delphic dictum reminding us to be sparing of time and that it is necessary to know the measures of time, as there is a limit on wisdom, considered the largest and most necessary part of the study of philosophy and the one investigated even to this day by the greatest number to be that concerning tranquility; and he said that it will never achieve a conclusion by argument, but that mechanics, which surpasses teaching by argument through actions, has taught all men to know how to live without anxiety through one of its branches, that called artillery construction; and in conditions of peace and war never to be anxious about attacks of domestic or foreign enemies, provided that at all times and in all conditions, with nourishment prepared for both sieges and expeditions, minimum requirements called long-lasting[1]

---

[1] [Marginal scholion] This long-lasting ration is compounded of squill, boiled, washed with water, dried and cut very thin; then sesame is mixed into it, one fifth part, and poppy one fifteenth, and all this is crushed and the best honey kneaded into it. Divide this into pieces the size of large olives. If one uses one of these at the second hour, another at the tenth, he will not be severely affected by hunger.

Another compound ration is put together as follows. Take an Attic *hemiekton* of sesame and a *hemichoun* of honey and a *kotule* of oil and a *choinix* of peeled sweet almonds; roasting the sesame, grind and sift the almonds, peel the squill and cut away the roots and leaves, separating it into small pieces, put it in a mixing bowl, pound it very smooth. Next pound evenly an equal amount of the pounded squill with honey and olive oil and, pouring it into a pot, boil it placed on the coals.

When it begins to boil adding the sesame and almonds, stir with a stick until everything is homogenized. And when it is quite stiff, taking it out divide it into small morsels. Someone taking this, one in the morning and one in the afternoon, will have sufficient sustenance. This ration is good also for expeditions; for it is sweet and filling and causes no thirst.

45 λεγομένοις φαρμάκοις καί τισι σμικροτάτοις βρώμασιν
πλησμίοις ἀδιψίαν ἐμποιοῦσιν, καὶ τὴν τῶν βελοποιϊκῶν
ὀργάνων μάλιστα ποιούμεθα πρόνοιαν. Καὶ ἐπεὶ οἱ τὰ πρὸς
πολιορκίαν καθ᾽ ὅλου ἐπιστάμενοι ὀρθῶς καὶ τὰ ἀντικείμενα
ἴσασι, τῶν δὲ ἀντικειμένων μία ἐστὶν ἐπιστήμη, οἱ διὰ
50 μηχανικῆς ἄρα παρασκευαστικῆς τε ὀλιγαρκοῦς πανημερίου
βρώσεως καὶ κοινῆς ἁπάσης ἐπ᾽ εὐταξίᾳ διαίτης πολιορκίαν
συνιστᾶν ἢ λύειν δυνάμενοι ἀεὶ ἐν ἀταραξίᾳ διάξουσιν. Οὐκ
ἀπεικὸς οὖν πρὸς τοὺς πολυγραφοῦντας καὶ εἰς οὐκ ἀναγκαίους
λόγους τὸν χρόνον καταναλίσκοντας, ἀνθηρολεκτοῦντάς τε
55 πρὸς ⟨τὸ⟩ κενοὺς λόγους ἄψυχα ἐκφράζοντας κοσμεῖν καὶ ζῷα
αἰνοῦντας ἢ ψέγοντας οὐ κατ᾽ ἀξίαν δι᾽ ἔμφασιν τῆς ἑαυτῶν
πολυμαθείας, καὶ Κάλανον τὸν ‖ Ἰνδὸν εἰρηκέναι· "Ἑλλήνων   f.4
φιλοσόφοις οὐκ ἐξο|μοιούμεθα παρ᾽ οἷς ὑπὲρ μικρῶν καὶ   Wes 204
ἀφελῶν πραγμάτων πολλοὶ καὶ δεινοὶ ἀναλίσκονται λόγοι·
60 ἡμεῖς γὰρ ὑπὲρ τῶν μεγίστων καὶ βιωφελεστάτων ἐλάχιστα καὶ
ἁπλᾶ, ὡς πᾶσιν εὐμνημόνευτα, παραγγέλλειν εἰώθαμεν." ‖   f. 4v
   4. ⟨Τ⟩ὸν ὑπὸ τῆς ἄνω προνοίας ἐπ᾽ εὐσεβείᾳ συντηρούμενον
στρατηγικώτατον ἄρχοντα, τῇ κελεύσει καὶ γνώμῃ καὶ εὐβουλίᾳ
τῶν θειοτάτων αὐτοκρατόρων ὑπείκοντα, καὶ δυσμενεῖς καὶ
ἀποστάτας πολιορκεῖν μέλλοντα, τὰς τῶν πόλεων θέσεις
5 ἀκριβῶς διερχόμενον ἐπισκέπτεσθαι χρὴ πρότερον, καὶ τὴν τοῦ
ἰδίου λαοῦ πρὸ πάντων ἀβλαβῆ ποιούμενον φύλαξιν τῆς

---

46 πλησμίοις – ἐμποιοῦσιν: cf. Philo Mech. 89:9–10.   46–47 καὶ – πρόνοιαν: cf. Hero *Bel.*
72.   47–49 Καὶ – ἴσασι: cf. Ath. Mech. 39:1–5.   49 τῶν – ἐπιστήμη: cf. Arist. *Top.* 163a:2–
3.   52 ἀεὶ – διάξουσιν: cf. Hero Bel. 71–73.   52–54 Οὐκ – καταναλίσκοντας: cf. Ath.
Mech. 4:9–10.   56–57 ἔμφασιν – πολυμαθείας: cf. Ath. Mech. 4:10–11.   57–61 Κάλανον
– εἰώθαμεν: Ath. Mech. 5:8–11.

Mech. 88:49) ἐμβαλόντα, τρῖψαι ὡς λειότατα. Μετὰ δὲ ταῦτα τῶν τετριμμένων σκιλλῶν
(τὸν τετριμμένον σκίλον V; cf. Philo Mech. 88:50–51) ἴσον τῷ μέλιτι τρῖψαι ὁμαλῶς ἅμα
τῷ ἐλαίῳ καὶ ἐγχέοντας εἰς χύτραν ἑψεῖν ἐπιθέντας ἐπ᾽ ἀνθρακιᾶς. Ὅταν δὲ ἄρξηται
ζεῖν, παρεμβαλόντα τοῦ σησάμου καὶ τῶν ἀμυγδάλων ἅμα ξύλῳ διακινεῖν, μέχρις ἂν
ἅπαντα ἑνωθῇ. Ὅταν δὲ γένηται στερεὸν ἰσχυρῶς, ἀφελόντα διελεῖν εἰς ψωμοὺς μικρούς·
καὶ ἕνα πρωΐ, ἕνα δείλης, ἀναλίσκων τις ἱκανὴν ἔχει τροφήν. Τυγχάνει δὲ καὶ πρὸς
στρατιὰς τοῦτο τὸ φάρμακον ἀγαθόν· ἡδὺ γάρ ἐστι καὶ πλήσιμον, καὶ δίψαν οὐκ ἐμποιεῖ.
‖ 55 τὸ addidi ‖ ἄψυχα Mar: ἀψύχοις VBP ‖ 56 οὐ κατ᾽ ἀξίαν Mar: οὐκ ἀταξίαν VBP ‖ 60
βιωφελεστάτων Wes: βιωφιλεστάτων VB ‖ 61 Post εἰώθαμεν reliqua p. vac. V ‖ 4: 6 Post
φύλαξιν ras. 4–5 litt. V

rations, and with certain very small amounts of food that is filling and does not cause thirst, we also especially have provision for artillery engines. And since those who are fully knowledgeable about the details of siege warfare also know how to defend against it correctly, and there is really one subject <composed> of these two opposites, they will always live then without anxiety, being able to mount or break a siege through the mechanical preparations, minimum daily food, and a common regimen completely in good order. And in opposition to those who write at length and spend time on unnecessary words, speaking in a flowery manner to the adornment of empty phrases that describe inanimate objects and praise or censure living creatures, not appropriately, <but> to stress their own learning, the Indian Kalanos has not unfairly said: "we are not like the philosophers of the Hellenes, among whom many and awesome words are lavished on small and simple things; for we are accustomed to recommend the least and simplest about those things that are the greatest and most important to life, as this is the easiest way for all to remember them."

4. The most competent military commander, kept safe by Providence above because of his piety, and obedient to the command and judgment and good counsel of our most divine emperors, when he is about to besiege the enemy and rebels, must first, by going about <himself>, precisely observe the position of the cities; and having provided for the secure protection of his own

πολιορκίας ἀπάρχεσθαι, πρὸς ἄλλους μὲν τόπους καστρομαχεῖν
ἐνδεικνύμενον, εἰς τὸ ἐκεῖσε τοὺς ἐχθροὺς ἀπατωμένους
παρασκευάζεσθαι, καὶ πρὸς ἄλλους εἰσφέρειν τὰ μηχανήματα,
10 τὴν δὲ προσβολὴν πρὸς τὰ σαθρότερα τῶν τειχῶν ἐκ διαδοχῆς
στρατιωτικῶν ταγμάτων κατὰ συνέχειαν ποιεῖσθαι, σὺν πολλῷ
θορύβῳ τοὺς ἔνδον περισπῶντα καὶ σάλπιγγας νύκτωρ ἐπὶ τὰ
ὀχυρώτερα μέρη ἀνίεσθαι, ἵνα ὑπολαμβάνοντες οἱ πλεῖστοι
ταῦτα ἁλίσκεσθαι, ἀπὸ τῶν μεταπυργίων μετὰ τῶν ἄλλων
15 ἐκφύγωσι.

5. Καὶ εἰ μὲν ἐφ' ὑψηλῶν λόφων ἢ κρημνῶν δυσβάτων ὦσιν
αἱ πόλεις κείμεναι, δεῖ τὰ ἄνωθεν ἀπὸ τῶν ἐναντίων
ἐπικυλιόμενα | παραφυλάττεσθαι βάρη, ἅτινά εἰσι ‖ λίθοι   Wes 205
στρογγύλοι, κίονες, τροχοί, σφόνδυλοι, ἅμαξαι τετράτροχοι   f. 5
5 φορτίοις βεβαρημέναι, ἀγγεῖα ἐκ πλοκῆς διάφορα κόχλακος ἢ
γῆς πεπιλημένης γέμοντα, καὶ οἷα τὰ ἐκ σανίδων κυκλοτερῶς
συνηρμοσμένα καὶ δεσμοῖς ἔξωθεν περιειλημμένα τὰ πρὸς
ὑποδοχὴν οἴνου γινόμενα ἐλαίου τε καὶ παντὸς ὑγροῦ· ἄλλα τε
ὅσα πρὸς ἄμυναν ἐνδεχόμενόν ἐστι παρὰ τῶν ἐναντίων
10 ἐπινοεῖσθαι.

6. Καὶ χρὴ πρὸς ταῦτα ἀντιμηχανωμένους τριβόλους
κατασκευάζειν ξυλίνους πενταπήχεις, ὑπό τινων λαβδαραίας
καλουμένους, πάχους ἑκάστου σκέλους τὸν γῦρον ἔχοντος ὡσεὶ
ποδῶν δύο, ὥστε μὴ θραύεσθαι ἢ διακλᾶσθαι, ἀλλὰ ἀντέχειν
5 πρὸς τὰ καταφερόμενα βάρη· ἱκανοὺς δὲ τῷ πλήθει
κατασκευάζειν αὐτούς, ἵνα τριπλῆ ἢ καὶ τετραπλῆ ἡ τούτων
γίνηται θέσις· οὕτως γὰρ τὰ δυσανάφορα καὶ δυσχερῆ τῶν
τόπων περιορίζοντα δυνατόν ἐστιν ἐκτὸς βέλους ἀκινδύνως
ἀνέρχεσθαι· ἡ γὰρ τῶν λίθων βιαία καταφορὰ ἐπὶ τῇ τῶν
10 τριβόλων ἀναστροφῇ ἐνεχθεῖσα ἠρεμήσει.

7. Ἔστι δὲ καὶ κατ' ἄλλον τρόπον τὴν ἐκ τῶν κατερχομένων
παρα|φυλάξασθαι βλάβην· ἐκ γὰρ τῆς ὑπωρείας κάτωθεν   Wes 206

4: 7–9 πρὸς – μηχανήματα: cf. Philo Mech. 98:14–17. 10–15 τὴν – ἐκφύγωσι: cf. Philo
Mech. 98:45–52. **5:** 1–6 Καὶ – γέμοντα: cf. Apollod. 139:9–12. **6:** 1–10 τριβόλους – ἠρεμήσει:
cf. Ath. Mech. 38:2–9.

6: 8 περιορίζοντας Mar

[36]

host above all, begin the siege, first appearing to attack the fortifications in certain locations, in order that the enemy be tricked into making their preparations there, and then deploying machines against other places. He should continuously attack the weaker parts of the walls with relays of *tagmata* of soldiers, with loud noise distract those inside and sound trumpets by night at the stronger parts, in order that the majority, assuming that these parts are captured, might flee from the curtain walls with the others.

5. And if the cities are situated on high hill crests or impassable crags, it is necessary to guard against heavy objects being rolled down from above by the enemy. These are: round stones, columns, wheels, column drums, heavily loaded four-wheeled wagons, different plaited containers full of gravel or compacted earth, and the kind <made> of boards fitted together in a circle and surrounded with bands on the outside, which are for storage of wine and oil and every liquid, and other things such as can be devised for defense by the enemy.

6. And it is necessary when devising countermeasures against these to construct wooden caltrops 5 *pecheis* tall, which some call *labdaraiai,* each leg having the circumference of about 2 *podes* thick, so as not to be shattered and broken, but to withstand the heavy descending objects; and to construct these in sufficient number so that they can be placed three and four deep. For by thus surrounding the hard to reach and difficult places, it is possible to move upward without danger outside missile range. For the forceful rush of the stones will be stilled when checked by the resistance of the caltrops.

7. One can guard in yet another way against harm from objects coming down. For beginning from below from the foot of the

ἀρχομένους πλαγίας ὀρύσσειν δεῖ τάφρους, καὶ πρός ‖ τινα μέρη   f. 5v
τῶν τειχῶν ἀφορᾶν καὶ ἀνέρχεσθαι, βάθος ἐχούσας ὡσεὶ ποδῶν
5   πέντε, καὶ ἕνα τοῖχον ὀρθὸν τὸν ἐκ τοῦ αὐτοῦ ὀρύγματος ἐπ᾽
ἀριστερὰ ὄντα, πρὸς ὃν ἐπιφέρεται τὰ κυλιόμενα βάρη,
προτείχισμα καὶ ἀσπίδα τῶν ἀνερχομένων γινόμενον. Τὸν δὲ
προορυχθέντα τόπον ἀσφαλίζεσθαι τοὺς ὀρύσσοντας οὕτως·
ξύλα ὡς ἐξάπηχα ἢ νεάκια κάτωθεν ὀξύνοντας ὡς πασσάλους
10 πρὸς τὸν ῥηθέντα ἐκ τοῦ χώματος ὀρθὸν τοῖχον ἐπ᾽ ἀριστερὰ
πρὸς τὸ ἀντέχειν πηγνύειν, λελοξευμένα πρὸς τὴν κατωφερῆ
τοῦ λόφου κλίσιν· καὶ σανίδας ἐπ᾽ αὐτὰ ἔξωθεν ἐπιθέντας,
κλάδους δένδρων ἀπαγκαλίζοντας περιδεσμεῖν· καὶ τὴν
ὀρυσσομένην ἅπασαν ὕλην ἐκεῖσε ἀπορρίπτοντας ὁδοὺς
15 εὐθείας ἐξομαλίζειν πρὸς τὰς τῶν χελωνῶν ἀναβάσεις. Τὰς δὲ
προσφερομένας χελώνας ἐμβόλους κατὰ πρόσωπον γίνεσθαι,
τουτέστι σφηνοειδεῖς ἐκ τριγώνων ἢ πενταγωνοειδῶν βάσεων
συνεστώσας πρὸς ὀξεῖαν κατ᾽ ἔμπροσθεν γωνίαν, ἐκ δὲ τοῦ
κάτω πλάτους πρὸς ὕψος ἀνερχομένας καὶ μέχρι τῆς κατὰ
20 κορυφὴν ῥάχεως εἰς ὀξὺ προϊούσας, ὁμοιουμένας ἔμπροσθεν
πλοίων πρῴραις πρὸς γῆν ἐπισκηφθέντων ὡς τῶν καλουμένων ‖   f. 6
τοξικίων· μικρὰς δὲ αὐτὰς εἶναι καὶ πλείονας διὰ τὸ ταχέως
καὶ εὐκόλως κατασκευάζεσθαι καὶ ὑπὸ ὀλίγων ἀνδρῶν εὐκόπως
φέρεσθαι, λεῖα ξύλα ποδιαῖα περὶ | τὴν βάσιν ἐχούσας, καὶ ἀντὶ   Wes 207
25 τροχῶν ἥλους σιδηροῦς διὰ τὸ τιθεμένας πρὸς τῇ γῇ πήγνυσθαι
καὶ μὴ ὑπὸ τῆς ἐμβολῆς κατασύρεσθαι· ἔχειν δὲ καὶ πλάγιον
ξύλον ἑκάστην κατὰ μέτωπον, ὥσπερ ἐν τοῖς ῥυμοῖς ἔχουσιν αἱ
ἅμαξαι, ἵνα ὑποστρέφουσαν αὐτὴν πρὸς τὸ κατωφερὲς ἀντέχῃ
καὶ ἐπιστηρίζῃ, καὶ μάλιστα ὅταν οἱ προσάγοντες αὐτὴν ἐπὶ τὸ
30 ἀνωφερὲς ἀτονήσωσι καὶ πρὸς μικρὸν ἀναπαύεσθαι μέλλωσι.
Συμβήσεται οὖν, ἢ τῇ τάφρῳ πλαγίᾳ οὔσῃ ἐμπίπτοντα
παραφέρεσθαι τὰ βάρη, ἢ τοῖς λοξοῖς πασσάλοις πλαγίαν
ἔχουσι θέσιν ἐνσείοντα ἀπορραπίζεσθαι, ἢ τοῖς ἐμβόλοις
ἐγκρούοντα πρὸς θάτερον μέρος παράγεσθαι, τὸ δὲ διὰ μέσου
35 χωρίον τῆς πληγῆς ἀπαλλάττεσθαι.

7: 3–35 πλαγίας – ἀπαλλάττεσθαι: cf. Apollod. 140:3–141:3.

7: 9 ἐξάπηχα Wes: ἐξάπιχα VBP: ἐξαπηχῆ Mar ‖ 21 ἐπισκηφθέντων Sch: ἐπισκυφισθεισῶν
V: –ών B: ἐπὶ συνφισθεισῶν P: ἐπισυσφιγχθείσαις Mar

slope it is necessary to dig ditches diagonally and to aim at and advance upward toward certain parts of the wall; the <ditches> should have a depth of about 5 *podes* and a single wall <that rises> vertically from the same excavation on the left side, against which the heavy rolling objects strike, as it is a rampart and shield for those advancing upward. The diggers should fortify the area already dug thus: sharpening at the bottom pieces of wood about 6 *pecheis* in length, or trunks of young trees, like stakes, affix them to the aforementioned vertical wall <made> on the left side from the excavated soil, to offer resistance; these stakes should be set on a slant corresponding to the downslope of the hill. And having placed boards on the outside of these <stakes>, bind them together by interweaving tree branches. And having thrown up there all the excavated material, level straight paths for the ascents of the tortoises. The tortoises being deployed should be beaked in front, that is, wedge-shaped, constructed from triangular or pentagonal bases to a sharp angle in front, but rising upward from the wide <area> below and proceeding to a sharp <angle> at the ridge on top, similar in front to the prows of ships set upside down on the ground, like the so-called *toxikia*. These <tortoises> should be small and numerous, because they are <then> quickly and easily constructed and readily carried by a few men, having smooth 1-*pous* pieces of wood around the base and iron nails instead of wheels, so that when set down they are fixed in the ground and not overturned by <any> impact. And each should have a diagonal piece of wood at the front, such as wagons have in their poles, so as to stop it and prop it up if it turns back downward, and especially whenever those who are pushing it uphill grow tired and are going to rest for a short time. It will follow, therefore, that the heavy objects, falling into the ditch which is diagonal, are diverted, or, striking against the slanted stakes which are in a diagonal position, are repelled, or hitting against the beaks are deflected to either side, but the midsection is spared the blow.

8. Βέλτιον δὲ προσάγειν καὶ τὰς λεγομένας γερροχελώνας, ἐλαφροτέρας τῶν ῥηθέντων ἐμβόλων καὶ ὁμοιοσχήμους οὔσας, κατασκευαζομένας ἐκ πλοκῆς ἰτείνων βεργῶν νεοτμήτων ἢ ἐκ μυρίκης ἢ φιλύρας, ὀξείας καὶ αὐτὰς κατὰ πρόσωπον οὔσας
5 ἄχρι τῆς κατὰ κορυφὴν ῥάχεως.

9. Τὰς δὲ καλουμένας λαίσας, ἐλαφροτάτας οὔσας, ‖ ἐκ πλοκῆς   f. 6v
καὶ αὐτὰς ἀμπελίνων κλημάτων ἢ νεοτμήτων βεργῶν ἐν σχήματι
τροπικῶν διὰ τάχους γινομένας, οὐ δεῖ πρὸς κατωφερεῖς καὶ
κρημνώδεις εἰσφέρειν τόπους, μήπως ὄλεθρον τοῖς ἄγουσιν
5 ἐμποιήσωσιν, ἀδυνατοῦσαι ἀντέχεσθαι πρὸς τὰ ὑπέρογκα τῶν
βαρῶν· χρᾶσθαι δὲ αὐταῖς μᾶλλον, ὅταν ἐν ἐπιπέδοις καὶ
ὁμαλοῖς τόποις ὦσιν αἱ πόλεις κείμεναι· τότε γὰρ ἔσονται
εὔχρηστοι. | Wes 208

10. Ὁ δὲ πρὸς τὴν καστρομαχίαν ἀνερχόμενος λαὸς
ἀκολουθήσει πρὸς τὰ πλάτη τῶν ἐμβόλων φυλαττόμενος ἤτοι
τῶν χελωνῶν ὄπισθεν, καὶ ταῖς ἀμπελοχελώναις σκεπόμενος διά
τε τὰς τοξείας καὶ τὰς σφενδονήσεις. Εἰσὶ δὲ τοιαῦται· ξύλα
5 βαστάζουσιν οἱ ὁπλῖται ὀρθά, πρὸς ὕψος ἄνισα ὄντα ἐν παρ᾽
ἕν, πάχος ἔχοντα γυρόθεν ὡσεὶ δακτύλων δώδεκα, κατὰ δὲ πέντε
πόδας πρὸς ἕτερα πλάγια ἐπ᾽ εὐθείας ἐπεζευγμένα, ἵνα
φυλάττηται τὸ τῶν πέντε ποδῶν πρὸς ἄλληλα μεταξὺ διάστημα·
καὶ τὰ μὲν ὑψηλότερα αὐτῶν ὑπὲρ ἀνδρὸς ἡλικίαν καὶ ἥμισυ,
10 τὰ δὲ ταπεινότερα ὑπὲρ ἄνδρα ἔστωσαν· ἄνωθεν δὲ σκεπόμενα,
διὰ τὸ ἄνισον ἐξομοιοῦνται ἀναδενδράσιν, τὸ δὲ ἀπὸ τῆς
κορυφῆς τοῦ ἐμβόλου ἄχρι τῶν σκεπομένων ἀνίσων ξύλων ἐν
σχήματι ἅμα φανήσεται ‖ χελώνης. Τὰ δὲ ὑπὸ τῶν ὁπλιτῶν   f. 7
βασταζόμενα ξύλα κάτωθεν ὡς ξίφη ἐχέτωσαν, ὅπως τῇ γῇ
15 ἐμπησσόμενα τοὺς φέροντας ἀναπαύωσι. Δέρματα δέ, ἢ λίνα
παχέα, ἢ τρύχινα κρεμῶνται ἔξωθεν καὶ κατὰ πρόσωπον· ἐπὶ
δὲ τοῖς ἀνίσοις ξύλοις δέρματα ἐπικείσθωσαν ἄνωθεν διπλᾶ,
οὐκ ἀπεκτεταμένα πρὸς ὁμαλὴν καὶ ἴσην ἐπιφάνειαν, ἀλλ᾽

8: 1–5 γερροχελώνας – ῥάχεως: cf. Philo Mech. 99:29–37.   10: 1–23 Ὁ – ὑπόκεινται: cf. Apollod. 141:5–143:5.

9: 5 ἀδυνατοῦσαι Mar: ἀδυνατούσας VBP ‖ 10: 15 ἢ λίνα Mar: η λινα V: ἤλινα BP: ἤ λινᾶ Wes ‖ 16 τρύχινα VBP: τρίχινα Mar

8. It is better to deploy the so-called wicker tortoises, as they are lighter than the aforementioned beaks and similar in form, constructed from plaiting of freshly cut branches of willow, tamarisk, or lime; these too are sharp in front up to the ridge on top.

9. The so-called *laisai*, being the lightest, are themselves quickly made by plaiting vine stalks or freshly cut <willow> branches in the form of arches; these should not be deployed against steep and precipitous places, lest they bring destruction on those carrying them. For they are too weak to withstand the great bulk of heavy objects; but rather one should use them whenever the cities are situated on even and level terrain; then they will be useful.

10. And the host that is moving upward to an attack on fortifications will follow protected at the widths of the beaks, that is, behind the tortoises, and shielded against archery and slinging by vine tortoises. These are as follows: the hoplites hold upright poles that are alternately unequal in height, about 12 *daktyloi* in circumference, and joined on top on a straight line to other cross<-poles> at 5 *podes,* in order to retain the intervening 5-*pous* distance to one another. The taller of these <poles> are one and a half times a man's height, the shorter ones stand <just> taller than a man. When covered from the top, they resemble vine trellises because of their unequal length. The <part> from the top of the beak as far as the unequal poles, when covered, will appear at the same time in the form of a tortoise. The poles held up by the hoplites should have points at their lower ends, so that when pressed into the ground, they give the carriers a rest. And hides, or thick canvas, or patchwork <coverings> should be hung down on the outside and in front. And double hides should be placed from above on the unequal poles, not stretched taut to an even and equal surface, but drawn together slightly

ἐπισυνηγμένα κατὰ μικρὸν καὶ προσκεχαλασμένα πρὸς τοῖς
20 ἀνίσοις ξύλοις, ἵνα τῇ τούτων χαυνότητι τὰ ἐπιπίπτοντα βέλη
πρὸς τὴν πληγὴν ἀτονῇ καὶ ἐκλύηται, οἱ δὲ | ἔνδον σκεπόμενοι   Wes 209
ἀβλαβεῖς διαμένωσι. Τὰ δὲ ὑπογεγραμμένα πάντα σὺν τοῖς
σχήμασι κατὰ τάξιν ὑπόκεινται. ‖   f. 7v, 8, 8v

11. ⟨Ε⟩ἰ δὲ ἐν ἐπιπέδοις καὶ ὁμαλοῖς τόποις ὦσιν αἱ πόλεις
κείμεναι, τὰς χωστρίδας δεῖ προσάγεσθαι χελώνας, ὑποτρόχους
αὐτὰς οὔσας καὶ ἔμπροσθεν καταστεγεῖς, ἵνα οἱ τὰς τάφρους
χωννύοντες ἀπὸ τῶν ἐναντίων μὴ πλήττωνται· ἢ τὰς
5   προειρημένας λαίσας, ὡς ἐλαφροτάτας καὶ χρησίμους πρὸς τὸ
χωννύειν τάφρους, τόπους τε ἐνύδρους καὶ ὑπόμβρους
ἀναγεμίζειν καὶ παντοῖα λακκίσματα ἐξομαλίζειν τοῖς τείχεσι
πλησιάζοντα, ὅπως εὐδιάβατον καὶ ἀκίνδυνον τὴν τῶν
μηχανημάτων ἀγωγὴν ποιησώμεθα. Δεῖ δὲ ἀκριβῶς σκοποῦντας
10 ἀνερευνᾶν τὰς ἐπὶ τὰς τάφρους φαινομένας ἰσοπέδους
διαβάσεις διὰ τὰ κάτωθεν πολλάκις κρυπτόμενα ὑπὸ τῶν
ἐναντίων κεράμια, καὶ τοῖς μὲν ἀνθρώποις εὐδιάβατον καὶ
ἀκίνδυνον τὴν ὁδὸν ἀποφαίνεσθαι, τοῖς δὲ προσφερομένοις
ὀργάνοις λίαν βαρυτάτοις οὖσι καταδύνειν καὶ διασπᾶσθαι ἐπὶ
15 τῇ θραύσει καὶ ἐπιδόσει τῶν ὑποκειμένων κεραμίων. Ὅθεν χρὴ
μετὰ | ἀκοντίων εὐτόνων λόγχας ἀσφαλεῖς ἐχόντων ἢ   Wes 210
ὁλοσιδήρων ἢ τρυπάνων τινῶν ἐπιτηδείων τὴν ἀπόπειραν
ποιεῖσθαι· πρὸς δὲ | τοὺς κατεσπαρμένους ὑπὸ τῶν ἐχθρῶν   Wes 211
σιδηροῦς τριβόλους τῇ γῇ | ἀναμιγνυμένους καὶ ἀφανεῖς ὄντας   Wes 212
20 ξύλινα ὑποθέματα πρὸς τοὺς πόδας τοῖς ὑποδήμασι κά‖τωθεν   f. 9
ὑποθέντας ἀβλαβῶς διαβαίνειν ἢ τοῖς γεωργικοῖς κτεσὶν οὓς
καὶ γριφάνας τινὲς καλοῦσιν, ὀδοντωτοῖς οὖσιν, τούτους
ἀνακαθαίρειν· καὶ πρὸς τὰς ἐπὶ βοθρεύμασι τιθεμένας θύρας
πρόπειραν ποιουμένους ταῖς δικέλλαις ἀνασκάπτειν. Χρὴ δὲ
25 καὶ τὰς ὑπὸ γῆν πρὸς τῷ τείχει γινομένας ὑπορύξεις κρυφίας
βαθείας πρὸς τοῖς θεμελίοις ποιεῖσθαι, καὶ μὴ εἰς ὄψιν τῆς γῆς,

---

11: 2–4 χωστρίδας – πλήττωνται: cf. Philo Mech. 99:41–44. 9–15 Δεῖ – κεραμίων: cf. Philo
Mech. 85:23–29. 15–24 Ὅθεν – ἀνασκάπτειν: cf. Philo Mech. 100:4–11. 24–29 Χρὴ –
ἀπολέσωσι: cf. Philo Mech. 99:11–13; 18–19.

---

23 Post ὑπόκεινται vac. reliqua p. V   **11:** 4 ἀπὸ VBP: ὑπὸ Mar ‖ 15 ἐπιδόσει VBP: ὑφιζήσει
Mar ‖ 22 τούτους Mar: τούτοις VBP

and left loose against the unequal poles so that the missiles striking it may be sapped of their force due to the slackness of these
<hides> and lose their power, and those covered inside remain
unharmed. All the <devices> that have been described are below with the drawings sequentially.

<figs. 1 and 2>

11. If the cities are situated on level and even terrain, one should
deploy filler tortoises, which are wheeled and covered in front in
order that those filling the ditches not be hit by the enemy; or
the aforementioned *laisai,* as these are very light and useful for
filling ditches, for filling terrains that are swampy and subject to
rain, and for leveling all kinds of depressions near the walls, so as
to make the deploying of the machines smooth and without
danger. It is necessary to examine with precise reconnaissance
those passages over ditches that appear level, since clay pots are
often hidden underground by the enemy; and for men the route
appears passable and without danger, but under the weight of
engines being deployed, since they are quite heavy, it collapses
and is torn asunder with the breaking and collapse of the clay
pots below the surface. Hence it is necessary to probe with strong
lances with secure <iron> points, or all-iron ones, or with appropriate boring tools. And against the iron caltrops sown by the
enemy, which are mixed in the earth and invisible, one should put
wooden supports under the boots on one's feet to cross unharmed,
or clear these away with farm rakes with large tines which some also
call *griphanai.* And after first probing for <trap->doors placed over
holes, one should dig them up with two-pronged drag-hoes. And
one should also make underground tunnels to the foundations
of the walls, secret, deep and below the surface of the ground,

ἵνα μὴ διαγνόντες οἱ πολέμιοι ἔνδον ἀντορύξωσι καὶ τῷ τείχει ἀντιτρυπήσαντες καπνῷ ἢ ὕδατι τοὺς τὴν ὀρυγὴν κατεργαζομένους ἀπολέσωσι.

12. Τὸν δὲ βουλόμενον εὐκόπως πορθεῖν τὰς πόλεις, κατὰ Φίλωνα τὸν Ἀθηναῖον, δεῖ μάλιστα τρυγητοῦ ὄντος ἢ ἑορτῆς ἔξω τῆς πόλεως ἀγομένης ἀθρόαν τὴν ἐπίθεσιν ποιεῖσθαι· πλείστους γὰρ ἔξω τότε χειρούμενον εὐάλωτον ἢ ὑπόφορον καὶ
5 τὴν πόλιν ἐκ τῶν λοιπῶν οἰκητόρων διὰ τὴν πρὸς αὐτοὺς στοργὴν ἢ συγγένειαν ἀνταλλαττόμενον ἕξειν. Εἰ δὲ κατὰ κλοπὴν νυκτὸς τὴν πόλιν βουλόμεθα λαβεῖν τῶν πολιτῶν τὴν ἔλευσιν ἡμῶν ἀγνοούντων καὶ ἀνελπίστων ὄντων, χειμῶνος καταλαβόντος ὅτε τῷ κρύει τούτων οἱ πλείους ἐν ταῖς οἰκίαις
10 συστέλλονται καὶ ἀπαράσκευοι πρὸς μάχην τυγχάνουσιν, ἢ πανδήμου ἑορτῆς ἐν τῇ πόλει τελουμένης καὶ τοῦ | πλήθους ‖   Wes 213 ἐπὶ τῇ τελετῇ παιγνίοις σχολάζοντος ἢ καταφόρου ὑπὸ τῆς μέθης   f. 9v ὄντος, κλίμακας ποιήσαντες δερματίνας τῷ τείχει προσάξομεν, αἵτινες ῥάπτονται καθάπερ οἱ ἀσκοὶ καὶ τῇ ἀλοιφῇ
15 ἐμφραττόμεναι περὶ τὰς ῥαφὰς ἀναγεμίζονται ὥστε μὴ διαπνεῖν· ἐμφυσωμένων γὰρ καὶ πνεύματος πληρουμένων τοῦ διαπνεῖν κωλυομένων, ἐξορθοῦσθαι αὐτὰς ἀνάγκη, ὑπὸ τοῦ πνεύματος ἀντεχομένων πρὸς τὴν ἀνάβασιν. Εἰ δὲ ὑψηλότερον τῶν κλιμάκων τὸ τεῖχος εἴη, ἐπὶ ταῖς στυππίναις προϋποτίθενται
20 κλίμαξιν, αἳ κατασκευάζονται διὰ πλοκῆς καὶ ῥαφῆς δεσμούμεναι, δικτυωταὶ οὖσαι ὡς τὰ λεγόμενα σάρκινα· εἰς δὲ τὰ ἄκρα αὐτῶν | ἄγκιστρα προσβάλλονται, ἵνα ἀπὸ τῶν   Wes 214 προϋποτεθέντων δερματίνων ἐπιρριπτόμενα ἐπιλαμβάνηται τῶν προμαχώνων καὶ οὕτως τὴν ἐπὶ τὸ τεῖχος ἀνάβασιν τοῖς
25 βουλομένοις διευθετίζωσι. Τὰ δὲ τῶν κλιμάκων σχήματα ὑπογέγραπται. ‖   f. 10

13. ⟨Τ⟩ὰ δὲ ἀνωτέρω προρρηθέντα ἔμβολα σὺν ταῖς ἀμπελοχελώναις ὅταν ἐγγὺς τοῦ τείχους ἀνέλθωσι, χελώνας δεῖ

12: 1–6 Τὸν – ἕξειν: cf. Philo Mech. 96:27–32.   6–13 Εἰ – ὄντος: cf. Philo Mech. 96:32–34. 13–24 κλίμακας – προμαχώνων: cf. Philo Mech. 102:12–19. 13: 2–39 ὅταν – ὑπόκειται: cf. Apollod. 143:6–144:11.

27 τὸ τεῖχος Mar ‖ 12: 6 ἀνταλλαττόμενον Wes: ἀνταλαττόμενον VB ‖ 16 διαπνεῖν Sch: διαπνέειν VB

lest the enemy within spot them and dig a countertunnel and, boring through the wall, kill by smoke or water those working on the tunnel.

12. According to Philo the Athenian, one who wishes to take cities without great labor should attack suddenly, especially at vintage time or when a festival is going on outside a city. For by seizing many people who are outside at the time, he will easily capture the city as well or subject it to tribute, getting this in exchange from its remaining inhabitants out of their affection for or kinship with the <captives>. And if we wish to take the city with stealth by night, <we should act> while the citizens are unaware of our coming and not expecting it, in wintertime when, because of the cold, the majority of them are gathered in their houses and unprepared for battle, or when a public festival is being celebrated inside the city and the majority are playing festival games or are sluggish from drinking. Making ladders of hides we shall bring them to the wall; these are stitched like wineskins and, smeared around the stitches with grease, filled so as not to deflate. For when they are inflated and full of air <and> kept from deflating, they necessarily become upright, held firm for climbing by the air. But if the wall should be higher than the ladders, they are placed beneath ladders of tow which are constructed by being bound together with plaiting and stitching, net-like, similar to the so-called soldiers' packs. Hooks are attached to the ends of these <nets> so that when thrown from the leather ladders placed beneath, they catch on the merlons and thus facilitate the ascent of the wall at will. The drawings of the ladders are delineated.

<fig. 3>

13. And whenever the beaks discussed above go up close to the wall with the vine tortoises, one should then deploy different

τότε διαφόρους προσάγειν, ἄλλας μὲν πρὸς τὸ ὀρύξαι τὸ τεῖχος,
ἑτέρας δὲ πρὸς τὸ κριοκοπῆσαι· ἐπὶ μὲν οὖν τοῦ ὀρύξαι τὰς
5 λεγομένας ὀρυκτρίδας· ταύτας δὲ ἢ διρρύτους εἶναι καὶ κατὰ
πρόσωπον σκεπομένας προσάγεσθαι καὶ προσεγγίζειν τῷ τείχει,
ἢ μονοπτέρους, ὄπισθεν μὲν κατωφερεῖς, κατὰ δὲ πρόσωπον
τετραγώνους, καὶ ἐκ πλαγίων τραπεζοειδεῖς ὡς τριγώνους,
κατασκευαζομένας οὕτως· ξύλα λαβόντας τρία ἢ τέσσαρα,
10 ἔστιν δὲ ὅτε καὶ πέντε διὰ τὸ πυκνότερον καὶ στερεώτερον τοῦ
ἔργου, μῆκος ἔχοντα μὴ ἔλασσον ποδῶν δέκα, πάχος δὲ ὡσεὶ
ποδὸς ἑνός, ὁμοίως δὲ καὶ πλάτος, ταῦτα ἀποκόπτειν ἄνωθεν
λοξῶς ὡς πρὸς ὄνυχα, ἵνα προσφερόμενα δι' ὑποτρόχων
ἀξόνων, ὑπὸ ὀρθίων ξύλων ἔσωθεν βασταζόμενα, προσεγγίσωσι
15 τῷ τείχει· ἱστάσθω δὲ πρὸς τῷ τείχει στῦλος ὑπόθεμα κάτωθεν
ἔχων, ὅστις καὶ τὰ ἐπικείμενα ξύλα καὶ τὰ ὑποστηρίζοντα
βαστάσει πάρορθα, ἵνα τὰ ἄνωθεν καταφερόμενα μηδὲν
παραβλάπτοντα τὴν στέγην παρεκπίπτῃ ὄπισθεν. Τὰ δὲ πάρορθα
ξύλα καὶ πρὸς ὄνυχα ἔμπροσθεν ἐκκεκομμένα κέντρα σιδηρᾶ
20 ἐχέτωσαν ὄπισθεν, ἵνα ἐμπήσ‖σωνται τῇ γῇ καὶ μὴ | f. 10v
παρασύρωνται· εἰς δὲ τὰ πλάγια κρεμάσθωσαν δέρματα ἢ ῥάκη   Wes 215
σκέποντα, ἢ τὰ ἐκ βεργῶν ἢ φοινίκων πεπλεγμένα διὰ τὰ
ἑκατέρωθεν ἐπιφερόμενα βέλη· ὡσαύτως δὲ καὶ ἐπὶ τὰ
ἔμπροσθεν. Ὅταν δὲ προσεγγίζωσι τῷ τείχει, ἀναπεταξέσθωσαν
25 ἐπὶ τὰ ἄνω τὰ ἔμπροσθεν· ὑποκρύπτεσθαι δὲ καθ' ἑκάστην
χελώνην ἄνδρας δύο ὀρθοὺς ἱσταμένους καὶ σκάπτοντας τὸ
τεῖχος, πρὸς μὲν πάχος πλέον τοῦ ἡμίσους, κατὰ δὲ πλάτος ὅσον
καὶ τὸ τῆς χελώνης ἐστί, πρὸς δὲ τὸ ὕψος ἀπὸ τριῶν ποδῶν
ἄνωθεν τῆς γῆς ἀρχομένους ὀρύσσειν, ἵνα τὰ ἐκ τῆς ⟨ὀρυ⟩γῆς
30 κατερχόμενα πρὸς τὸν ἑαθέντα κάτωθεν πίπτωσι τόπον· ἐπὶ δὲ
τὸ ἀνώτερον μέρος τοσοῦτον σκάπτειν ὅσον οἱ ὀρύσσοντες
ἀπαρεμποδίστως δυνήσονται. Ἐγγύτερον δὲ εἴκοσι ποδῶν
διεστηκέτωσαν ἀπ' ἀλλήλων αἱ χελῶναι, | ἵνα καὶ πολλαὶ ὦσι   Wes 216
καὶ πολὺν τόπον οἱ ὀρύσσοντες ἐπὶ τὸ τεῖχος ἐργάζωνται· καὶ
35 μικραὶ οὖσαι, ἵνα ταχέως καὶ εὐκόπως παράγωνται, καὶ ἵνα μὴ
ἐπ' εὐθείας πρὸς τὸν σκοπὸν φέρηται καὶ εὐστοχῇ πρὸς τὰ
πλάγια τῶν χελωνῶν τῶν τοσαύτην διάστασιν ἀπ' ἀλλήλων

13: 29 γῆς V: ὀρυ s. s. m. rec. V: ὀρυγῆς B ‖ 32 δυνήσονται Wes: δυνήσωνται VB

tortoises, some for excavating the wall, others for ramming. For excavating, therefore, there are the so-called excavating tortoises; these are either saddle roofed and are moved forward and approach the wall covered in front, or are single winged and sloping in back, but quadrangular in front and on the sides trapezoidal, almost triangular. These are constructed thus: taking three or four beams, but sometimes five for thicker and more solid results, with a length of no less than 10 *podes,* a thickness of about 1 *pous,* and a similar width, cut these at the top on a precise diagonal, in order that, carried by wheels on axles <and> held up inside by upright beams, they may approach the wall. A pillar with a counterplate at the bottom should be set up against the wall to hold the beams lying on top with the supports in slanting position, in order that objects coming down from above may slide off behind without harming the roof. And the slanting beams that have been cut precisely in front should have iron spurs on the bottom so that they may fix themselves in the ground and not be dragged out of position. And hides should be hung at the sides, or patchwork coverings or material plaited from <willow> branches or palms, against missiles striking from either side. Let them also be the same in front. When they get close to the wall, the front <coverings> should be furled upward. Two men standing upright and digging through the wall can find shelter under each tortoise; <they should> excavate to a depth greater than one-half <the wall>, to a width as much as that of the tortoise, and in height beginning 3 *podes* above the ground in order that the material coming down from the excavating may fall to the place left below. And the excavators should dig on the upper portion as far as they can without difficulty. The tortoises should stand closer than 20 *podes* apart so that there may be many of them, and the excavators may work at a sizable portion of the wall. <The tortoises> should also be small, so as to be moved sideways quickly and without great labor and so that the missiles thrown by the enemy from the walls may not hit the mark directly and strike the sides of the tortoises, since they have

ἐχουσῶν τὰ ἀπὸ τοῦ τείχους ὑπὸ τῶν ἐναντίων βαλλόμενα. Τὰ
δὲ ὑπογεγραμμένα σχήματα ὑπόκειται. ‖ f. 11

    14. ⟨Ὅ⟩ταν δὲ τρυπηθῇ τὸ τεῖχος ἀπὸ τῆς ὄψεως ἔνδον ἐπὶ τὸ
πάχος καὶ διάχωρα κατὰ πλάτος τοσαῦτα λάβῃ ὅσαι καὶ αἱ
χελῶναί εἰσιν, καὶ οἱ ῥηθέντες δύο ἄνδρες ἀπ᾽ ἀλλήλων
ἀπεστραμμένοι ἔσωθεν ἀπαρεμποδίστως ἐπὶ τὰ διάχωρα
5 σκάπτωσιν, οὐκέτι χελώνης ἔχουσι χρείαν πρὸς τὰ πλάγια μέρη
ὀρύσσοντες καὶ ὑπὸ τοῦ πάχους τοῦ τείχους ἔνδον
φυλαττόμενοι. Ἵνα δὲ τοῖς σκάπτουσι μὴ συνεμπίπτῃ τὸ τεῖχος,
ὑποστυλούσθω ἔσωθεν καὶ βασταζέσθω στυλαρίοις λεπτοῖς
μᾶλλον καὶ πυκνοῖς, καὶ μὴ παχέσι καὶ ἀραιοῖς, ἐπάνω καὶ
10 ὑποκάτω σανίδος τιθεμένης, ἵνα μὴ πρὸς τῇ γῇ ὑποχαλῶντα τὰ
στυλάρια οὐ βαστάσῃ. ‖ Ὅταν δὲ τελειωθῇ τὸ ὄρυγμα καὶ f. 11v
ἐπιστυλωθῇ, ⟨ἀναπληρούσθω⟩ τὸ κατὰ μέσον τῶν ἐπιστύλων
ὑλῶν εὐκαύστων, οἷον φρυγάνων, ξύλων ξηρῶν ἐσχισμένων,
δᾳδῶν καὶ ὅσα τούτων ἕτερα πρὸς ἔκκαυσιν ἐπιτήδεια· καὶ
15 οὕτως ἀναφθήτω. Εἰ δέ τις ἐλλείπει τόπος, πυροβόλοις
ὑφαπτέσθω·‖ ἐχέτω δὲ καὶ ξύσματα ξύλων ξηρὰ περιεσπαρμένα Wes 217
σὺν ὑγρᾷ πίσσῃ ἢ ἐλαίῳ ἐπαλιφέντα· καὶ οὕτως ἐκκαέντων τῶν
ὑποστυλωμάτων καταπεσεῖται τὸ τεῖχος. Καὶ ἔστιν ἡ ὄψις τοῦ
σχήματος τοιαύτη. ‖ f. 12

    15. ⟨Τ⟩οῖς δὲ τῶν χελωνῶν τούτων παρορθίοις ξύλοις ἧλοι
πλατυκέφαλοι ὕψους δακτύλων ὀκτώ, ἤτοι καρφία ἐκ σιδήρου
εἰργασμένα ἄνωθεν ἐμπησσέσθωσαν ἄχρι δακτύλων τεσσάρων·
τοὺς δὲ λοιποὺς τέσσαρας ὑπερανέχοντας ἐχέτωσαν· τὸν δὲ διὰ
5 μέσου τόπον πηλὸν λιπαρὸν καὶ κολλώδη μετὰ τριχῶν χοιρείων
ἢ τραγείων μεμαλαγμένον ἐπιχρίειν καὶ ἀναγεμίζειν, ἵνα μὴ
διασπᾶται μηδὲ διασχίζηται. Κρατηθήσεται γὰρ καὶ διὰ τὴν
πυκνότητα τῶν ἥλων καὶ διὰ τὸ πλάτος τῶν κεφαλῶν αὐτῶν.
Ῥάκη δὲ ἐκ πλαγίων ἢ δέρματα ἐπικρεμάσθωσαν, ἵνα μήτε
10 ἄμμος θερμὴ μήτε ‖ πίσσα μήτε τήλη ἀφεψηθεῖσα μήτε ἔλαιον Wes 218

14: 1–7 ⟨Ὅ⟩ταν – φυλαττόμενοι: cf. Apollod. 145:1–5. 7–19 Ἵνα – τοιαύτη: cf. Apollod.
145:6–146:3.   **15:** 1–22 ⟨Τ⟩οῖς – ὑπόκειται: cf. Apollod. 146:4–147:6.

14: 4 ἀπαρεμποδίστως Wes: ἀπαραποδίστως VB ‖ 10 ὑποχαλῶντα Sch: ὑποχαλῶνται VB ‖
11 Post στυλάρια add. καὶ Wes ‖ 12 ἀναπληρούσθω add. Wes ‖ μέσον B: μέσου V

such <a small> distance between them. And the drawings described are below.

<fig. 4>

14. Whenever the wall has been perforated from the facade
inward toward its depth and receives as many openings along its
width as there are tortoises, and the aforementioned two men,
back to back inside, dig at the openings without difficulty, they
no longer have need of a tortoise, as they are digging toward the
sides and are protected inside by the depth of the wall. To keep
the wall from collapsing on the diggers, it should be propped up
inside and held up preferably by numerous and thin supports,
but not by thick and sparsely placed ones. A board should be
placed above and below the supports, lest they sink into the
ground and not hold <the wall> up. When the excavating is
completed and propped up, the area between the props <should
be filled> with flammable material such as dry sticks, split dry
timbers, pine torches, and other such combustible materials and
so be ignited. And if any place fails <to catch fire>, it should be
ignited by incendiaries, which contain dry wood shavings covered with liquid pitch or smeared with oil. And so the wall will
collapse as the props burn. The view of the drawing is as follows.

<fig. 5>

15. Flat-headed nails 8 *daktyloi* long, that is, small iron spikes,
should be driven from above into the slanting beams of these
tortoises to a depth of 4 *daktyloi;* and the remaining 4 <*daktyloi*>
should rise above the surface. The area between <the nails> should
be smeared and filled with greasy and viscous clay, softened with
swine or goat hair to keep it from being broken or split. For it
will hold fast on account of the denseness of the nails and the
width of their heads. Patchwork materials or hides should be
hung from the sides to keep hot sand or pitch or boiled fenugreek

ἐπιχεόμενον, ὡς ταχέως φύσει θερμαινόμενον καὶ ψυχόμενον
βραδέως, τοῖς ἔνδον ἐργαζομένοις ἐνστάζῃ· παρομοίως γὰρ πυρὶ
τὰς τῶν ἀνθρώπων ἀναλίσκουσι σάρκας. Οὕτως οὖν
κατεργαζόμεναι αἱ χελῶναι διαφυλαχθήσονται πρὸς τὸ μὴ
15 καίεσθαι ἐκ τῶν ἐπιβαλλομένων ἄνωθεν πυροφόρων καὶ
ἀναπτομένων φλογῶν, μηδὲ διέρχεσθαι ἔνδον τὰ ἐπιχεόμενα
τεθερμασμένα ὑγρά. Ὡσαύτως δὲ λαῖσαί τε καὶ γερροχελῶναι
ἐπὶ τὰ πλέγματα σκεπέσθωσαν δέρμασι διαβρόχοις βοῶν
νεοσφαγῶν ὡς δυναμένοις πυρὶ ἀντιμάχεσθαι. ‖ Αὗται δὲ αἱ   f. 12v
20 χελῶναι πόρρωθεν λιθοβόλων ὀργάνων καὶ τοξοβολιστρῶν
χριέσθωσαν, συμπεπηγυῖαι δὲ καὶ ὑπότροχοι συμβληθεῖσαι τοῖς
τείχεσι προσαγέσθωσαν. Καὶ τὸ σχῆμα ὑπόκειται. | Wes 219
   16. ⟨Τ⟩ινὲς δὲ ἐπὶ λιθίνων τειχῶν ξύλα ὡς ἔθος περιτιθέασι
προσεγγίζοντα κάτωθεν, ὥστε ἀνάπτεσθαι καὶ θρύπτειν τοὺς
λίθους. Δύσχρηστον δὲ τὸ ἔργον ἐνίοτε καὶ ἐπισφαλὲς γίνεται,
ὅτι καὶ ὕδωρ ἄνωθεν ἐπιχεόμενον σβεννύει τὸ πῦρ, καὶ
5 ἀσθενεστέρα πρὸς πλάγιον ἡ τοῦ πυρὸς φορὰ γίνεται, ὡς φύσει
ἀνωφερὴς καὶ πρὸς ἐνέργειαν ἰσχυροτέρα τυγχάνουσα· καὶ οὐ
δυνήσονται ἐπὶ τῇ τῆς φλογὸς ὁρμῇ οἱ ἔνδον ἐργαζόμενοι ὑπὸ
χελώνην εἶναι· συγκαήσονται γάρ. Γίνονται οὖν κύθρινοι
ὀστράκινοι διὰ ‖ πετάλων σιδηρῶν ἐπὶ τοῦ ἔξωθεν μέρους   f. 13
10 συνδεδεμένοι καὶ γεμίζονται ἀνθράκων λεπτῶν· ἀπὸ δὲ τῆς
ἔξωθεν ὄψεως τοῦ πετάλου πρὸς τὸν πυθμένα τέτρηνται
ἀνεῳγότες ἄχρι δακτυλιαίου τρυπήματος καὶ σιδηροῦν
αὐλί|σκον ἐκεῖθεν δεχόμενοι, πρὸς ὃν ἄλλος ἐμβάλλεται   Wes 220
ἄσκωμα ἔχων. Πῦρ δὲ λαβόντες οἱ ἄνθρακες καὶ ἐμφυσώμενοι
15 ὁμοίαν φλογὸς ἀπεργάζονται ἔκκαυσιν ὑπεμβαίουσαν τῷ λίθῳ
καὶ θρύπτουσαν, ἢ ὄξους ἢ οὔρου ἤ τινος ἄλλου τῶν δριμέων
ἐπιχεομένου. Καὶ ἔστιν τὸ σχῆμα οἷον ὑπογέγραπται. Κέχρηνται
δὲ αὐτῷ συνεχῶς οἱ μολιβδουργοί. ‖   f. 13v
   17. ⟨Ἐ⟩ὰν πλίνθινα τείχη καταβαλεῖν ταχέως θελήσωμεν,
πυκνοτάτας ἐπ’ αὐτὰ τρήσεις διὰ τρυπάνων ποιήσομεν, ὑπὸ

16: 1–18 ⟨Τ⟩ινὲς – μολιβδουργοί: cf. Apollod. 152:7–153:7.   **17:** 1–34 ⟨Ἐ⟩ὰν – τοιοῦτον: cf.
Apollod. 148:2–150:3.

16: 8 κύθρινοι Wes: χύθρινοι VB ‖ **17:** 2 ποιήσομεν Wes: ποιήσωμεν VB

or oil, when poured down, from dripping upon those working within. For these substances naturally heat up quickly and cool slowly <and> destroy men's flesh like fire. Tortoises so prepared will then be protected against burning by incendiaries launched from above and by ignited flames, nor can the hot liquids that are poured upon them penetrate inside. Similarly *laisai* and wicker tortoises should be covered on the plaited parts by wet hides of freshly slaughtered cattle as these are able to withstand fire. These tortoises should be coated far away from stone-throwing engines and arrow shooters, and brought forward to the walls <already> assembled and supplied with wheels. And the drawing is below.

<fig. 6>

16. In the case of stone walls, some customarily put wood beams near the bottom, so that they can be ignited and shatter the stones. This operation is at times difficult and precarious, both because water poured from above quenches the fire and because the impetus of fire is weaker to the side, as by nature it rises up and is stronger in its effect <in that direction>. Those working within will not be able to remain under the tortoise because of the force of the flame; for they will be burned. Therefore, earthenware pottery is secured on the outside with iron plates and filled with powdered charcoal. <The pots> are perforated from the outer facade of the plate toward the bottom <and> opened with a hole up to 1 *daktylos* <in diameter> and receive a small iron tube therein. Into <this tube> another <tube> is inserted which has a bellows. When the charcoal is ignited and fanned, it creates a combustion like an <open> flame that goes in under the stone and breaks it, when vinegar or urine or some other acidic <liquid> is poured upon it. And the drawing is such as has been described. Lead workers also regularly employ this <device>.

<fig. 7>

17. If we wish to bring down brick walls quickly, we shall make numerous perforations in them with borers while <we are>

χελωνῶν ἄνωθεν ἐπικεχρισμένων σκεπόμενοι, ἢ λαισῶν
ἀσφαλεστάτας στέγας ἐχουσῶν καὶ δέρμασι βοῶν νεοσφαγῶν
5 περὶ τὰ πλέγματα σκεπομένων διά τε τὰ πεμπόμενα κατ᾽ αὐτῶν
βάρη καὶ τὰ ἐγχεόμενα τεθερμασμένα ὑγρά. Τὰ δὲ τρύπανα
ἔστωσαν τεκτονικοῖς ὀργάνοις παρόμοια· μοχλὸς γὰρ γίνεται
σιδηροῦς μήκους ποδῶν μὴ ἔλασσον πέντε, δακτυλιαίαν τὴν
διάμετρον ἔχων καὶ πάχος γυρόθεν ὡσεὶ δακτύλων τεσσάρων,
10 πέταλον ὁμοίως σιδηροῦν ἐπὶ τὸ ἔμπροσθεν ἄκρον
προσηλωμένον ἔχων πλάτους δακτύλων δώδεκα καὶ ὕψους
ὀκτώ, ἐστενωμένον κατὰ μέσον ἔμπροσθεν ἐν σχήματι
κηπουρικοῦ πλατυλισγίου· πρὸς δὲ τὸ ἕτερον ἄκρον ξύλινον
ἀπὸ τόρνου μεσόστενον εἰσδέχεται κύλινδρον ὑπὸ ἀρίδος
15 στρεφόμενον, ἔχοντα κατὰ μέσον τοῦ ὀπισθίου μέρους
κεφαλοειδῆ παρεξοχὴν ὑπεμβαίνουσαν καὶ ἀναστρεφομένην
ἐπὶ τὴν ὀνομαζομένην πυελίδα ἤτοι ἐπικεφαλίδα τινὰ οὖσαν,
κανόνος τῇ γῇ ἐπικειμένου τοῦ προσ|άγοντος αὐτὴν καὶ   Wes 221
ἐπακολουθοῦντος ἀεὶ τῷ τρυπωμένῳ τόπῳ. Περιστραφήσεται ‖ f. 14
20 δὲ πρὸς τὴν αὐτὴν ἐργασίαν καὶ διὰ χειρῶν κινούμενος ὁ
κύλινδρος σὺν τῷ τρυπάνῳ, ἐὰν κανόνια πρὸς τὸ μέσον
εἰσδέξηται ὡς φρεατίας ἠλακάτης σταυροειδῶς διεκβληθέντα,
ἅ τινες ἐκ τοῦ σχήματος ἀστερίσκους καλοῦσιν. Τὰς δὲ
γινομένας ἐπὶ τῷ τείχει τρυπήσεις πλαγίας τε καὶ ἀνωφερεῖς
25 ποιεῖσθαι ὡς πρὸς τὸ ἐνδότερον μέρος ὑψηλοτέρας, ὅπως τὰ ἐκ
τῆς πλίνθου ὑπὸ τῶν τρυπάνων περιξεόμενα εὐκατάφορα
γίνηται καὶ τὸ ἐπ᾽ ἄκρον τοῦ μοχλοῦ προσηλωθὲν πέταλον
καλῶς πρὸς τὴν ἐργασίαν ἀναβαστάζηται στηριζόμενον ὑπὸ
τοῦ τῇ γῇ πλαγίου ἐπικειμένου κανόνος καὶ πρὸς αὐτῇ
30 ἀντιστηριζομένου. Ἡ δὲ ἐκ τῶν τρυπάνων γινομένη ἀνωφερὴς
σύντρησις οὐ ποιεῖ συγκάθεσιν μόνην τοῦ τεί|χους, ἀλλὰ καὶ   Wes 222
παρεγκεκλιμένην ἐπὶ τὴν ἔξω καταφοράν. Καὶ γίνεται ἀθρόως
πολὺ περὶ τὸ τεῖχος τὸ σύμπτωμα. Καὶ ἔστιν τὸ τῆς κλίσεως
σχῆμα τοιοῦτον. ‖   f. 14v
    18. ⟨Τ⟩ρυπάσθω δὲ ἐξ ἴσου τὸ τεῖχος ἐπὶ τῆς αὐτῆς εὐθείας,

---

18: 1–2 ⟨Τ⟩ρυπάσθω – τέταρτον: cf. Apollod. 150:4–5.

---

24 Post ἀνωφερεῖς add. δεῖ Wes ‖ 31 συγκάθεσιν Wes: συγκάθησιν VB

covered by tortoises coated on top or by *laisai* that have very secure roofs and are covered on the plaited parts with hides of freshly slaughtered cattle to ward off the heavy objects sent against them and the hot liquids poured on them. The borers should be similar to a carpenter's tools: for this is an iron bar no less than 5 *podes* in length with a diameter of 1 *daktylos* and a circumference of about 4 *daktyloi*. It has a blade that is also iron affixed to the front end, 12 *daktyloi* wide and 8 long, narrowed in the center in front like a garden spade. At the other end it receives a wooden cylinder <made> on a lathe, narrow in the middle <and> turned by a bow. It has at the center of the rear section a head-shaped projection that goes in under and turns in what is termed a socket, that is, a type of cap. A rod resting on the ground applies and directs it continuously at the place being bored. The cylinder with the borer will be whirled around with the same effect even when moved by hand, if it should receive small rods in its mid-section, inserted in the form of a cross like a well windlass, which some from the shape call little stars. Make the holes in the wall at an upward angle, higher toward the interior, so that the material routed from the brick by the borers may easily fall down; and so that the blade affixed to the end of the bar may be properly raised up to its task, supported by the rod that rests on the ground at an angle and supports itself thereon. The joint-channel of the bore holes made by the borers, since it slants upward, will not only cause the wall to sink, but to fall outward, with a sudden, quite massive collapse of the wall. And the drawing of the inclination is as follows.

<figs. 8 and 9>

18. The wall should be bored evenly along the same straight

ἀπεχομένων ἀπ᾽ ἀλλήλων τῶν τρυπημάτων πόδα καὶ τέταρτον,
τουτέστι δακτύλους εἴκοσι, ἤτοι σπιθαμὴν καὶ δύο παλαιστάς·
ἔστι γὰρ ἡ σπιθαμὴ δακτύλων δώδεκα, ἡ δὲ παλαιστὴ τεσσάρων.
5 Τὰς δὲ τρυπήσεις ἀπὸ τῆς γῆς ἄνωθεν ἀπαρχομένους ‖ ποιεῖσθαι   f. 15
ὡς ἀπὸ ποδῶν τριῶν, καθάπερ καὶ ἐπὶ τῶν λιθίνων προειρήκαμεν
τειχῶν, ἵνα ἡ ἐκ τῶν τρημάτων κατερχομένη ὕλη ἐπὶ τὸν ἐαθέντα
κάτωθεν πίπτῃ τόπον.

19. ⟨Ὅ⟩ταν δὲ τρυπηθῇ κατὰ τάξιν τὰ μέτωπα τοῦ τείχους,
ἀναγεμί‖ζονται τὰ τρήματα ἐκ τῆς ἔξωθεν ὄψεως ἐπὶ τὰ ἔνδον,   Wes 223
οὐ πρὸς ὅλον τὸ πάχος ἀλλ᾽ ἐπὶ πόδα μόνον, ξύλοις ξηροῖς
ἐσχισμένοις, μὴ τετραγώνοις ὥστε κατὰ πλάτος ἐφαρμόζειν
5 ἀλλήλοις, ἀλλὰ παραστρογγύλοις ὡς πασσάλοις, πάχος ἔχουσι
πρὸς τὴν βάσιν δακτύλων μὴ πλέον τριῶν, πρὸς δὲ τῇ κορυφῇ
μᾶλλον ἐστενωμένοις πρὸς τὸ βαστάζειν τὸ τεῖχος κατὰ τὸν τῆς
ἐργασίας καιρόν. Καί, εἰ ἐνδέχεται, δᾷδες οἱ πάσσαλοι
ἔστωσαν· εἰ δὲ μή, ξύλα ξηρὰ πεπισσωμένα ἢ θείῳ τετριμμένῳ
10 σὺν ὑγρᾷ πίσσῃ ἢ ἐλαίῳ ἐπαλιφέντα· στρογγύλοι δὲ γίνονται
οἱ πάσσαλοι, ἵνα μεταξὺ πρὸς ἀλλήλους διαλείμματα ἔχωσιν,
ἔνθα τὸ πῦρ ὑπεμβαῖνον καὶ ἀναστρεφόμενον ἐπανάπτηται, καὶ
μὴ τῇ πυκνότητι συμπνιγόμενον σβεννύηται. Ὅταν δὲ
γεμισθῶσι πάντα τὰ τρήματα ποδὸς ἄχρι κατὰ βάθος, ὡς
15 εἴρηται, πάλιν ἐπὶ τῆς αὐτῆς εὐθείας τρυπάσθωσαν κατὰ μέσον
τὰ καταλειφθέντα διάχωρα κατὰ τάξιν ἐξ ἴσου πρὸς τὰ πρότερα.
Τὰ δὲ ἔσχατα ‖ τρήματα πλαγιαζέσθωσαν ἐφ᾽ ἑκάτερον μέρος,   f. 15v
ἵνα ἐπὶ τὰ πρότερα ἡ τῶν ὑστέρων ἐπεισέρχηται σύντρησις, καὶ
γεμισθήτωσαν καὶ αὐτὰ ξυσμάτων ἤτοι πελεκημάτων ἢ
20 ῥυκανισμάτων ξηρῶν καὶ εὐκαύστων φρυγάνων ἢ σχιδάκων,
καθ᾽ ὧν τὸ πῦρ ἐπιδρασσόμενον ταχεῖαν τὴν ἔκκαυσιν ποιεῖται.
Ἐξεπίτηδες οὖν οἱ πάσσαλοι οὐκ ἔχουσιν ἴσην τὴν ἐπιφάνειαν
κατὰ τὸ ὅλον ὕψος, ἀλλὰ μείζονές εἰσι κάτωθεν, ὥστε κρατεῖν
δύνασθαι τὸ πῦρ καὶ ἀνέμου ἐμπνέοντος ἐπανάπτεσθαι. Εἰ δὲ
25 νηνεμία κατὰ τὸν τῆς ἐργασίας καιρὸν ἢ τόπον εἴη,

5–8 Τὰς – τόπον: cf. Apollod. 144:6–7.   **19:** 1–29 ⟨Ὅ⟩ταν – ἔχοντες: cf. Apollod. 150:6–
152:4.

18: 5 Post ἀπαρχομένους add. δεῖ Wes

line, with the borings 11/4 *podes* apart, that is, 20 *daktyloi,* that is, 1 *spithame* and 2 *palaistai;* for the *spithame* is 12 *daktyloi,* the *palaiste* 4. Make the holes starting about 3 *podes* up from the ground, as we also mentioned earlier for stone walls, so that the material coming down from the apertures may fall into the space left below.

19. When the face of the wall has been bored in sequence, the apertures are filled from the facade inward, not to their complete depth, but only to 1 *pous,* with <pieces of> split dry timbers, which are not squared so as to fit <tightly> against one another on their sides, but rounded like stakes, with a thickness at the base of no more than 3 *daktyloi,* but narrower toward the top, to hold the wall up during the course of the work. And, if possible, the stakes should be pine torches; otherwise they should be dry wood covered with pitch or smeared with pulverized sulphur <mixed> with liquid pitch or with oil. The stakes are rounded so as to have spaces between one another, where fire going in under and coming back may ignite and not be extinguished, choked off by obstruction. Whenever all the apertures have been filled up to a depth of 1 *pous,* as mentioned, the remaining areas between them should be bored in sequence evenly with the earlier ones, again on the same straight line. And these last apertures should be made diagonally in both directions, in order that the channels of these latter ones may join with the earlier ones; and these too should be filled with <combustible> particles, that is, chips or dry shavings and combustible dry sticks or split wood through which the fire catches <and> creates rapid combustion. Intentionally, therefore, the stakes do not have an equal surface over their entire length, but are thicker at the bottom, so that the fire is able to catch and ignite when the wind blows. And if there should be no wind at the time or place of the work, reeds should be joined

συμβαλλέσθω|σαν κάλαμοι τετρυπημένοι δι᾽ ὅλου ἔσωθεν, Wes 224
οἵους οἱ ἰξευταὶ ἔχουσιν, ἀσκώμασι χαλκικοῖς ἐμφυσώμενοι·
πρὸς ὃν γὰρ ἄν τις ἐθέλῃ μεταφέρονται τόπον καὶ ἀνάπτουσι τὸ
πῦρ, σιδηροῦν αὐλίσκον ἔμπροσθεν τοῦ πυρὸς ἔχοντες. Καὶ τὸ
30 σχῆμα ὑπόκειται. ‖ f. 16

   20. ⟨Τ⟩ῆς συντρήσεως ἐπὶ τῇ ὑποστυλώσει καὶ ἐκκαύσει
τελεσθείσης καὶ τοῦ τείχους ἀκλινῶς ἡδρασμένου καὶ
ἀτρεμοῦντος ἐπὶ τῷ συμπάχῳ τῆς πλινθίνης οἰκοδομῆς
τεχνουργήματι, κριομαχεῖν ἀνάγκη. Εἰ γὰρ καὶ ἔκλυτος καὶ
5 ἀνίσχυρος ἡ τοῦ κριοῦ πρὸς τὴν πλίνθον γίνεται πληγή,
λακκίζουσα μᾶλλον διὰ τὸ χαῦνον καὶ μαλακὸν ἢ σείουσα καὶ
ῥηγνύουσα διὰ τὸ σκληρὸν καὶ ἀντίτυπον ὡς ἐπὶ λίθων, ἀλλ᾽
οὖν διὰ τῆς προγεγονυίας κάτωθεν ἐργασίας ἀτονῆσαν πρὸς
τῇ βάσει τὸ τεῖχος οὐ δυνήσεται ἀντέχειν πρὸς τὰς συνεχεῖς
10 τῶν κριῶν κερατίσεις, ἀλλὰ τῇ βίᾳ πληττόμενον πρὸς τῇ
συντρήσει τὴν κλίσιν εἰσδέξεται. | Wes 225

   21. Τὰς δὲ συμβολὰς καὶ συνδέσεις τῶν κατὰ μῆκος
συμβεβλημένων κριῶν, τάς τε περὶ τὰ κῶλα αὐτῶν καὶ τὰς ἐπὶ
τῶν μονοξύλων κατὰ διάστασιν ἀνηκούσας ἀρτήσεις ἐπί τε
κριοφόρων χελωνῶν πύργων τε καὶ τῶν διπλῶν κλιμάκων, καὶ
5 ἔτι τὰς δι᾽ αὐτῶν πρὸς τὸ τεῖχος γινομένας εὐεργεῖς διαβάθρας,
πρὸς τὴν ἁρμόζουσαν ἐφεξῆς ἑκάστῳ ἐργασίαν ἐπὶ τῆς
προκειμένης πραγματείας λεπτομερῶς διασαφήσαντες
ἐξεθέμεθα. ‖ f. 16v

   22. ⟨Ἐ⟩ὰν τάχιον μετὰ κριῶν θελήσωμεν τείχη ἢ πόρτας
ῥηγνύειν καὶ διασπᾶν, κριοφόρους ποιήσομεν χελώνας
τετρατρόχους ὑψηλάς, ἄνωθεν ἀλύσεις ἢ σχοινία εὔτονα κατὰ
πάχος ἐχούσας τὰ τὸν κριὸν βαστάζοντα καὶ ἀνέχοντα· ἀφ᾽
5 ὑψηλοῦ γὰρ βασταζόμενος ὁ κριὸς πλέον ὄπισθεν διάστημα
πρὸς τὴν κίνησιν λαμβάνει, καὶ ἐκ μακροῦ ἐπιφερόμενος καὶ
ἐνσειόμενος πλέον ἐνδυναμοῦται καὶ προσκρούων τῷ τείχει
βιαίαν καὶ ἰσχυρὰν ἀποτελεῖ τὴν πληγήν. Ἔστω δὲ τῷ εἴδει
ὑψηλὴ ἡ χελώνη καὶ μὴ τοσοῦτον μεγάλη, ἵνα πρὸς τὴν κίνησιν
10 εὐπαράγωγος ᾖ, διπλάσιον τὸ ὕψος τοῦ πλάτους ἔχουσα, τὸ δὲ

22: 1–65 ⟨Ἐ⟩ὰν – ὑπόκειται: cf. Apollod. 153:8–156:2.

together, totally hollowed out inside, such as fowlers have; they are blown into by a bronzesmith's bellows. These are brought to any place one wishes and kindle the fire, having an iron pipe in front where the fire is. The drawing is below.

<fig. 10>

20. When the interconnected perforation as well as the propping and combustion have been completed, if the wall should <still> stand steadfastly and be unshakable because of the thick fabrication of the brick construction, it is necessary to attack with rams. For even if the blow of the ram against the brick is dissipated and weak, and it makes pit holes because of the porousness and softness <of the brick> — rather than shaking and shattering as occurs with stones that are hard and offer resistance — yet due to the earlier work at the bottom, the wall, weakened at its base, will be unable to withstand the continuous batterings of the rams, but struck by force it will begin to incline because of the interconnected perforation.

21. As for the couplings and bindings of the rams that are joined lengthwise, the suspension systems that are appropriate in spacing for both the sections of the <composite> rams and single-beam ones (those on ram-bearing tortoises, on <portable> towers, and on double ladders), and further the drop-bridges that are effective against the wall through them — having clarified these minutely we have set them forth in the present treatise according to the operation successively fitting for each.

22. If we wish to use rams to shatter and break through walls and gates more quickly, we shall make ram-bearing tortoises, four-wheeled tall ones, which have chains or strong, thick ropes <suspended> from above to lift and hold up the ram. For if lifted up from a height, the ram obtains more space behind for movement, and carried and launched over a long distance, it gathers more momentum and, striking the wall, renders a forceful and strong blow. The tortoise should be tall in form and not <otherwise> very large, so that it may be easily positioned for movement, having a height twice its width, the length equal to

μῆκος τοῦ ὕψους ἴσον ἢ μικρῷ ἔλασσον, ἵνα ὀξύρρυτος καὶ
ἐπιμήκης εἴη, ὡς ἂν τὰ ἐν αὐτῇ ἐπιπίπτοντα βάρη πλαγιαζόμενα
παρεκτρέχῃ κάτωθεν. Κατασκευάζεται δὲ οὕτως. Ζυγὰ δύο καὶ
δύο τίθενται μήκους ὄντα ἀνὰ ποδῶν κδ΄, διεστῶτα ἀπ᾽
15   ἀλλήλων | ποδῶν οὐκ ἔλασσον δώδεκα· καὶ πρὸς αὐτὰ   Wes 226
ἐμβάλλονται ξύλα δακτύλων κατὰ πάχος δώδεκα, πλάτους
ποδὸς οὐκ ἔλαττον, εἴκοσι τεσσάρων ποδῶν πρὸς ὕψος, ἀριθμῷ
ὄντα ὀκτώ, τέσσαρα καὶ τέσσαρα ἀφ᾽ ἑκατέρων τῶν πλαγίων
μερῶν ἐφιστάμενα· συννεύοντα δὲ ἄνωθεν κατὰ κορυφὴν
20   συμβάλλει ἀλλήλοις, περιλαμβάνοντα ‖ ξύλον, ὅ ἐστι ῥάχις   f. 17
τῆς χελώνης, μακρότερον τοῦ περὶ τὰ ζυγὰ μήκους, καὶ
παρεξέχον ἔμπροσθεν δι᾽ ἃς προϊόντες λέξομεν αἰτίας, καθ᾽ ὃ
δὲ μέρος τὴν χελώνην προσνεύειν βουλόμεθα· κατὰ μέσους τοὺς
ὀρθοστάτας τούτοις ἄλλα ζυγὰ προσηλούσθω, καὶ ἐκ τοῦ
25   ἔσωθεν μέρους ὑποβεβλήσθωσαν παραστάται ἀντέχοντες καὶ
στηρίζοντες τὰ μέσα ζυγὰ καὶ τὴν ῥάχιν· τῇ δ᾽ ἔξωθεν
ἐπιφανείᾳ σανίσι κατὰ πάχος τετραδακτύλοις οἱ ὀρθοστάται
σκεπέσθωσαν. Καὶ οὕτως συντελεῖται τὸ σχῆμα. Ἀπὸ δὲ τοῦ
ἐδάφους τῶν ἔσω ζυγῶν ὑποστυλούσθω τὰ ἔσω ξύλοις ὀρθοῖς,
30   ἀκλινέσι κατὰ κάθετον οὖσι· τὸ δὲ μεταξὺ κένωμα τὸ περὶ τὰ
κάτω ζυγά, τουτέστι τὸ διάστημα, τροχοὺς τέσσαρας ἐχέτω τοὺς
ἀνέχοντας καὶ βαστάζοντας τὸ ὅλον περὶ τὴν χελώνην
σύμπηγμα. Ἵνα δὲ μὴ ἀνοίγηται τὰ κάτω ζυγά, περιτομίδας
προσλάβοι οὐκ ἔξω τομῆς | γινομένης, ἀλλὰ χελωνίων   Wes 227
35   προσηλώσει κρατούσας, ὡσανεὶ γρονθαρίων τινῶν
περικεκομμένων καὶ ἡμισφαιρίων ἐγγεγλυμμένων, παρομοίων
τοῖς ἐπὶ τῶν στροφίγγων τῶν θυρῶν τιθεμένοις, αἳ βάσεις
ἔσονται τῆς ὀξυρρύτου χελώνης. Γίνεται δὲ ὀτὲ ἀμβλυτέρα καὶ
ταπεινοτέρα ἡ τῆς χελώνης στέγη, ὅταν ἐπὶ ⟨τῶν⟩ μεσοστατῶν
40   τῶν ἐπὶ τὰ ζυγὰ ὀρθίων ἑστώτων ἄνωθεν προστεθῶσιν οἱ
λεγόμενοι ‖ συγκύπται καὶ τὴν ἀνωτάτην τοῦ ἀετώματος   f. 17v
περιλάβωσι ῥάχιν, μακροτάτου δηλονότι τοῦ κριοῦ ὄντος καὶ

22: 22 λέξομεν B: λέξωμεν V ‖ 23 βουλόμεθα B: βουλώμεθα V ‖ 24 τούτοις Wes: τούτους
V: τούτου B ‖ 29 ἔσω² VB: ξ s.s. m. rec. VB: ἔξω Wes ‖ 33 περιστομίδας Sch ‖ 34
γινομένης Sch: γινομένας VB ‖ 38 ὀτὲ Sch: ὅτε VB ‖ 39 τῶν add. Sch ‖ 42 μακροτάτου m.
rec. V, B: μικροτάτου V

or slightly less than the height; thus it will be steep-roofed and
oblong, so that heavy objects striking it may be deflected <and>
fall sideways to the ground. It is constructed thus. Beams of about
24 *podes* in length are placed two by two, no less than 12 *podes*
apart; and upon them are placed timbers about 12 *daktyloi* thick,
not less than 1 *pous* wide, 24 *podes* high, eight in number, standing four by four on both sides. Leaning above toward one another they meet at the peak, encompassing a timber that is the
ridge-pole of the tortoise. This <ridge-pole> is longer than the
length of the <base->beams and projects forward — for reasons
we shall discuss as we proceed — at that part where we wish the
tortoise <roof> to slope forward. At the middle of the uprights
other <horizontal> beams should be nailed to these, and on the
inside supports should be placed beneath to hold and prop up
these middle beams and the ridge-pole. On the outside surface
the uprights should be covered with boards 4 *daktyloi* thick. Thus
the frame is completed. From the bottom of the interior beams
let the inner ones be supported by uprights that are perpendicular <and> straight. The empty space between the lower beams,
that is, the interval, should have four wheels that hold up and lift
the entire superstructure of the tortoise. In order that the lower
beams not come apart, they should receive angle braces with the
cut edge unexposed, but these get their strength by having shell-
caps affixed to them, like some cutout little fists and hollowed-
out hemispheres, similar to those placed on door pivots. These
will be the bases of the steep-roofed tortoise. Sometimes the
roof of the tortoise is blunter and flatter, whenever the so-called
rafters rest up top upon the midsupports that stand upright on
the beams, and encompass the uppermost ridge-pole of the gable;
<this is possible> when the ram is obviously quite long and the

τῆς χελώνης πόρρω τοῦ τείχους ἀφεστώσης. Εἰ γὰρ ἐλάσσων ὁ
κριὸς κατὰ μῆκος τύχῃ καὶ ἡ χελώνη τοῦ τείχους ἔγγιον εἴη, οὐ
45 δυνήσεται ἀντέχειν πρὸς τὰ ἐπικρημνιζόμενα καὶ πρὸς αὐτὴν
ἐπιπίπτοντα βάρη διὰ τὸ τῆς στέγης ταπείνωμα, ἀλλὰ ῥῆξιν ἢ
θραῦσιν ἐπὶ ταῖς τῶν ἁρμονιῶν λαβοῦσα συμβολαῖς ἐπισφαλὴς
ἑαυτῇ τε καὶ τοῖς κριομαχοῦσι γενήσεται. Τὴν δὲ ὑπὸ τῶν
προειρημένων παρορθίων μονοξύλων ἐπιλαμβανομένην ἄνωθεν
50 ῥάχιν χρὴ παρέξειν ἔμπροσθεν κατὰ πρόσωπον τοῦ τείχους, ἵνα
ἐπ’ αὐτὴν προστέγασμα ᾖ καὶ τὰ ἐπὶ τῷ κριῷ πεμπόμενα
προσδέχηται· εἰ γὰρ οἱ ἀπὸ τοῦ τείχους καταφερόμενοι μέγιστοι
λίθοι καὶ τὰ πλάγια ξύλα τὰ ἐξ ἴσου ἰσοβαρῶς καὶ ἰσοζύγως
κατερχόμενα ἀστέγαστον τύχωσι τὸν κριὸν τῷ τείχει
55 ἐπιφερόμενον, εἴτε αὐτὸς ὁ κριὸς περινεύσας διασπασθήσεται,
ἢ τοὺς κινοῦντας ἀπορρίψει καὶ διαφθερεῖ. Τοιαύτη μέν ἐστιν
ἡ ἔμπροσθεν χελώνη | ἡ καὶ τὰς βασταγὰς τοῦ κριοῦ κατὰ   Wes 228
διάστασιν ἔχουσα. Ἡ δὲ δευτέρα ταπεινοτέρα πρὸς ὕψος καὶ
ἐλάσσων· καὶ ἄλλαι δύο κατόπισθεν ἔτι ἐλάσσονες· πρὸς
60 ἀσφάλειαν γὰρ παρόδου ἀναγκαῖαι τυγχάνουσι. Πλείονας δὲ
αὐτὰς εἶναι καὶ μικράς, ὡς προείπομεν, διὰ τὸ εὐκόπως
προσάγεσθαι καὶ ἐκ μικρῶν συμπήγνυσθαι ξύλων, καὶ μὴ μίαν
μεγίστην διὰ τὸ ἐκ μεγάλων καὶ δυ‖σευρέτων γίνεσθαι καὶ διὰ   f. 18
τὸ βραδέως καὶ δυσκόπως παράγεσθαι. Τὰ δὲ σχήματα κατὰ
65 τάξιν ὑπόκειται.

23. Καὶ δεῖ εἰδέναι ὅτι ὑπὸ τῆς ἔμπροσθεν καὶ μείζονος
χελώνης βασταζόμενος ὁ κριὸς ἐπὶ πλέον ὑψοῦται κατὰ
πρόσωπον τοῦ τείχους, ἐπὶ δὲ τῶν ὄπισθεν ταπεινοῦται· καὶ γὰρ
ἀνωφερῶς κινούμενος σφοδροτάτην ἐπὶ τὰ ἀνώτερα τῶν τειχῶν
5 ἀποτελεῖ τὴν πληγήν· ἐπὶ δὲ τὰ κάτω συγκύπτων ἀσθενεστάτην
καὶ ἔκλυτον, ἐνίοτε δὲ καὶ ἐπισφαλῆ. ‖ | f. 18v

24. ⟨Ἐ⟩ν ἁπάσαις δὲ ταῖς χελώναις ἧλοι πλατυκέφαλοι, ὡς   Wes 229
προείρηται, ἄνωθεν ἐμπησσέσθωσαν πρὸς τὰ τῆς στέγης πλάγια
καὶ κατωφερῆ μέρη ἄχρι τοῦ ἡμίσους αὐτῶν, καὶ τὸ διὰ μέσου
ἀνεστηκὸς ἀναπληρούσθω πηλοῦ λιπαροῦ καὶ κολλώδους μετὰ

24: 1–22 ⟨Ἐ⟩ν – ὧν: cf. Apollod. 156:3–158:1.

50 παρεξέχειν Sch ‖ 54 τύχωσι VB: τύπτωσι Sch ‖ 60 Post δὲ add. δεῖ Wes

tortoise far from the wall. For if the ram is shorter in length and
the tortoise is nearer the wall, it will not be able to withstand the
heavy objects hurled down and striking it, on account of the
flatness of the roof, but will be broken or destroyed at the joint-
fittings and become dangerous to itself and those attacking with
the ram. The ridge-pole above, which is held by the previously
mentioned slanting one-piece timbers, must project forward to
the face of the wall, in order to have a front covering on it and
<thus> intercept objects sent against the ram. For if the very
large stones thrown from the wall and the beams that are descending evenly parallel <to the wall>, equally weighted and
balanced, should encounter the uncovered ram as it attacks the
wall, either the ram itself will sway and be destroyed or it will
throw and kill the men moving it. Such is the front tortoise that
holds the suspended sections of the ram at intervals. The second
tortoise is lower in height and smaller. And behind them are two
others smaller still, which are necessary for a secure approach.
These tortoises must be numerous and small, as we said earlier,
so they can be moved forward without great labor and assembled
from small beams, rather than one very big <tortoise>, because
this would require large and difficult to find materials and be
moved into position slowly and with difficulty. The drawings are
below in sequence.

<fig. 11>

23. You should be aware that the ram, lifted up by the forward
and larger tortoise, is higher at the face of the wall, lower toward
the rear. For if directed upward it delivers a very forceful blow
against the upper parts of the wall; but if it strikes against the
lower parts, <it delivers> a very weak blow, dissipated and sometimes even destabilizing.

24. In all the tortoises flat-headed nails, as mentioned previously, should be driven from above to half their <length> into
the sloping and descending parts of the roof. And the raised area
in between should be filled with greasy and viscous clay soft-

5 τριχῶν μεμαλαγμένου καὶ ἀδιασχίστου συντηρουμένου. Πρὸς
δὲ τοὺς τροχοὺς τοὺς βαστάζοντας τὴν χελώνην ἐπὶ τὰ κάτω
ζυγὰ σφῆνας εὐμεγέθεις ὑποθεῖναι ἀφ’ ἑκατέρων τῶν μερῶν
ὑπεμβαίνοντας, ὥστε ἀντέχειν πρὸς τὸ τοῦ ὕψους μέγεθος· αἱ
γὰρ τῶν τροχῶν περόναι μόναι καὶ μάλιστα αἱ περὶ ἕκαστα τὰ
10 ζυγὰ διερχόμεναι δίκην ἀξόνων, βραχεῖαι οὖσαι, οὐ
δυνήσονται βαστάσαι τὴν χελώνην, οὐδὲ ἀσφαλῶς αὐτὴν
ἱσταμένην ἕξομεν πρὸς τὴν μέλλουσαν γίνεσθαι τοῦ κριοῦ
ἐπικίνησιν. Ὑποβάλλονται δὲ κάτωθεν οἱ σφῆνες, οὐ μόνον τὸ
τοῦ ὕψους ἀντεχόμενοι βάρος, ἀλλὰ καὶ τὴν τῶν τροχῶν
15 κωλύοντες παρακίνησιν· ὅταν δὲ θελήσωμεν ἐπικινῆσαι τὴν
χελώνην, τοὺς κάτω τεθέντας ὑποχαυνώσομεν σφῆνας. Καὶ δεῖ
εἰδέναι ὅτι τὰ λίθινα τείχη τάχιον ἐνσείεται καὶ ῥήγνυται τῶν
πλινθίνων· διὰ γὰρ τὸ χαῦνον καὶ μαλακὸν τῆς πλίνθου ἡ ἐκ
τοῦ κριοῦ γινομένη πληγὴ ἀσθενής ἐστι καὶ ἔκλυτος, βαθύνουσα
20 τὴν πλίνθον καὶ λακκίζουσα ⟨μᾶλλον⟩ ἢ ῥηγνύουσα καὶ
διασπῶσα· ὁ δὲ λίθος πρὸς τὴν τοῦ σιδήρου σκληρότητα
ἀντίτυπος ὢν ⟨ . . . ⟩ ‖ Ι   f. 19

25. ⟨Ο⟩ἱ δὲ περὶ Ἡγήτορα τὸν Βυζάντιον τὸν μέγιστον κριὸν   Wes 230
πηχῶν ἑκατὸν εἴκοσι κατὰ μῆκος ἐποίουν, ἐκ δὲ πτέρνης κατὰ
μὲν πάχος ποδιαῖον, εἰς δὲ πλάτος παλαιστῶν πέντε· ἐπὶ δὲ τὸ
ἔμπροσθεν ἄκρον συνῆγον αὐτὸν εἰς πλάτος ποδιαῖον καὶ πάχος
5 τριπάλαιστον· ἕλικας σιδηρᾶς τέσσαρας ἀποτεινομένας ἐπὶ
πήχεις δέκα ἔμπροσθεν προσηλοῦντες, καὶ ὅλον ὑποζωννύοντες
τρισὶ σχοινίοις κατὰ πάχος γυρόθεν ὀκταδακτύλοις, καὶ
βυρσοῦντες αὐτὸν κύκλῳ, ἀνελάμβανον κατὰ μέσον ἐκ τριῶν
μὲν διαλειμμάτων, βασταγμάτων δὲ τεσσάρων. Τὰ δὲ σχοινία
10 τὰ ἐκ τῶν ὀνίσκων τῶν ἐκ τῆς κριοδόχης ἀνέχοντα καὶ
ἐπιφέροντα τὸν κριὸν τὰς ἀρχὰς εἶχον ἁλύσεσι σιδηραῖς
πεπλεγμένας. Ἐποίουν δὲ καὶ ἐπιβάθραν ἐπὶ τῇ προφορᾷ τοῦ
κριοῦ σανίδος ἔμπροσθεν ἐφηλωθείσης καὶ δίκτυον

25: 1–29 ⟨Ο⟩ἱ – τετρακισχιλίων: cf. Ath. Mech. 21:2–26:5.

24: 16 ὑποχαυνώσομεν Wes: ὑποχαυνώσωμεν VB ‖ 20 μᾶλλον add. Wes (cf. Apollodorus
157:7–8) ‖ 22 < . . . > Wes (cf. Dain, 30)   **25:** 12 πεπλεγμένας Wes (cf. Ath. Mech. 25:1):
πεπλεγμέναις VB

ened with hairs and <so> kept from cracking. Against the wheels
that hold up the tortoise one should place below the lower beams
very large wedges that go in under on both sides, to hold up the
massive height. For the pins of the wheels alone, and especially if
they are short, going through each beam-<pair> like axles, will
not be able to lift the tortoise, nor will we keep it standing securely at the coming movement of the ram. The wedges inserted
below not only hold up the weight of the high <structure>, but
also prevent the slipping of the wheels. Whenever we wish to
move the tortoise, we shall loosen the wedges positioned below.
You should be aware that stone walls are more quickly shaken
and shattered than brick ones. For because of the porousness and
softness of the brick, the blow coming from the ram is weak and
dissipated, hollowing and pitting the brick rather than shattering
and breaking it. But stone, being correspondingly resistant to the
hardness of iron < ... >

25. The <men> of Hegetor of Byzantium made the largest
ram, 120 *pecheis* in length, its butt-end 1 *pous* thick, 5 *palaistai*
wide; at the front end they narrowed it to 1 *pous* wide and 3
palaistai thick. They nailed in front four iron coils that extended
10 *pecheis,* girding the whole thing with three ropes 8 *daktyloi* in
circumference and covering it around with ox-hide and suspended
it in the middle at three intervals from four suspension <points>.
The ropes from the reels of the ram holder, which hold up and
swing the ram, were entwined at the front end with iron chains.
They also made a scaling-ladder on the forward end of the ram,
a board being nailed in front and a plaited net of considerable

πεπλεγμένον ἐπὶ πάχος ἱκανὸν κατὰ διάστασιν δακτύλων
15 τεσσάρων, ἢ καὶ πλείω τὰς ὀπὰς ἔχον, πρὸς τὸ εὐκόλως
ἀναβαίνειν ἐπὶ τὸ τεῖχος. Ἀνήρτων δὲ αὐτὸν καὶ ἐκίνουν ἐπὶ
ὀκτατρόχου χελώνης, κατὰ μὲν τὸ τοῦ σχαρίου κάτωθεν μῆκος
πήχεις ἐχούσης τεσ|σαρακονταδύο, τὸ δὲ πλάτος εἰκοσιοκτώ.   Wes 231
Καὶ τὰ ἐπὶ τοῦ σχαρίου πρὸς ὕψος πηγνύμενα κατὰ τὰς γωνίας
20 τέσσαρα σκέλη ἐκ δύο ἕκαστα συνημμένων ξύλων ἐποίουν,
μῆκος ἔχοντα ἀνὰ πηχῶν κδ΄ ‖ καὶ πάχος παλαιστῶν πέντε, κατὰ   f. 19v
δὲ πλάτος πηχυαῖα· ἄνωθεν δὲ τῆς κριοδόχης θωράκιον
ἐπήγνυον οἱονεὶ περίφραγμα, ὥστε πρὸς αὐτὸ ἀσφαλῶς
δύνασθαι ἑστάναι τοὺς ἐποπτεύοντας τὰ κατὰ τοῦ κριοῦ ἀπὸ
25 τῶν ἐναντίων βαλλόμενα. Τὸν δὲ τοιοῦτον κριὸν ἐξαχῶς | Wes 232
ἐκίνουν, καθαιροῦντες ἀπὸ ἑβδομηκονταπήχους ὕψους, καὶ
πρὸς τὰ πλάγια πάλιν ἐπὶ πήχεις ἑβδομήκοντα παρασύροντες·
ἐκινεῖτο δὲ ὑπὸ ἑκατὸν ἀνδρῶν προσφερόμενος· τὸ δὲ
κινούμενον σύμπαν βάρος ταλάντων ἦν ὡσεὶ τετρακισχιλίων.
30 Καὶ τὸ σχῆμα ὑπόκειται.
    26. Καὶ δεῖ εἰδέναι ὅτι τῶν κριῶν οἱ μὲν ὑπὸ πλήθους ἀνδρῶν
οἰακίζονται κατά τινας τῶν πάλαι μηχανικῶν, οἱ δὲ ἐξ
ἀντισπάστων ἐφέλκονται, καὶ ἕτεροι ἐπὶ κυλίνδρων
προωθοῦνται. Ἔστιν δὲ ὅτε αὐτοὺς καὶ δι᾽ ὀνίσκων
5 περιστρεφομένων τήν τε προσαγωγὴν καὶ ἀναστροφὴν
ποιουμένους τὴν πλῆξιν ἀπεργάζεσθαι. Ἔξεστι δὲ τῷ τεχνίτῃ
πρὸς τὰ τῶν κριῶν μεγέθη καὶ τὴν ἀνήκουσαν τοῦ ἔργου χρείαν
ἐπινοεῖν καὶ τὴν κίνησιν. ‖   f. 20, 20v
    27. ⟨Ἐ⟩ὰν θελήσωμεν τὸ σύμπαχον τῶν τειχῶν καταμαθεῖν
καὶ τὰς γινομένας τῶν πολεμίων πράξεις καὶ τὸ πλῆθος ἐκ τῶν
ὄπισθεν σκοπῆσαι, ἐργασίας καὶ συσκευὰς ἡμερινάς τε καὶ
νυκτερινὰς ἔνδον τοῦ τείχους περὶ τὴν πόλιν πραττομένας
5 θεάσασθαι, σκοπὸν κατασκευάσομεν τοιοῦτον. Δύο ξύλα
τετράγωνα ἑτεροπλατῆ λαβόντες, πλάτος ἔχοντα ἀνὰ δακτύλων
δώδεκα, τὸ δὲ πάχος ἀνὰ ὀκτώ, ὀρθὰ ἐπιστήσομεν τὸ μὲν ἓν

26: 1–4 κριῶν – προωθοῦνται: cf. Ath. Mech. 10:1–2.   **27:** 1–92 ⟨Ἐ⟩ὰν – ὠρθωμένον: cf.
Apollod. 161:9–164:4.

---

20 ξύλων VB: σκελῶν Sch

thickness with the openings at intervals of 4 *daktyloi* or even more, for easily climbing onto the wall. They mounted and moved it on an eight-wheeled tortoise whose undercarriage below had a length of 42 *pecheis* and a width of 28. And they made the four legs on the undercarriage, which were attached at the corners upward, each from two beams joined together, with a length of about 24 *pecheis,* a thickness of 5 *palaistai,* and a width of 1 *pechys.* Above the ram holder they affixed a breastwork, like a fence, so that those watching out for objects launched against the ram by the enemy could stand securely on it. They moved such a ram in six directions, creating destruction from a height of 70 *pecheis* and sweeping it to the sides in turn over a distance of 70 *pecheis.* It was brought forward and moved by a hundred men. The entire weight moved was about 1,000 talents. The drawing is below.

<fig. 12>

26. You should be aware that some of these rams are managed by large numbers of men, according to certain ancient engineers, others are dragged by block and tackle, still others pushed forward on rollers. Sometimes they effect their percussion going backward and forward by means of turning reels. The craftsman can also contrive the movement according to the sizes of the rams and the requirement<s> pertinent to the task.

27. If we wish to examine closely the thickness of walls and to inspect the activities of the enemy and their numbers behind the wall, and to view the labors and schemes taking place day and night inside the wall around the city, we shall construct a scout-ladder as follows. Taking two squared beams with unequal sides, about 12 *daktyloi* wide and 8 thick, we shall stand them upright,

μεταξὺ δύο κατὰ κρόταφον κειμένων ἤτοι κατὰ πάχος,
ἑτεροπλατῶν καὶ αὐτῶν ὄντων, ἀποκεχωρισμένων δὲ ἀπ᾽
10 ἀλλήλων ὅσον κατὰ πάχος χωρηθῆναι τὸ | ὀρθόν· ὡσαύτως δὲ   Wes 233
κα ὶ τὸ ἕτερον πρὸς ἄλλα δύο ἴσα τε καὶ ὅμοια καὶ ὁμοίως
κείμενα· ἀπεναντίον δὲ τῶν κειμένων δύο διπλῶν κατὰ μέσον
ἄλλο πρὸς τῇ γῇ τιθέσθω ἀντικείμενον καὶ συμβαλλόμενον τοῖς
κειμένοις διπλοῖς πρὸς τοῖς ἐφεστῶσι δυσὶν ὀρθοῖς· καὶ
15 σχηματιζέσθω ἡ βάσις καθάπερ ἦτα λιτὸν ἐκ πλαγίων
διπλόγραμμον· ἀπ᾽ ἄκρων δὲ τῶν κειμένων δύο διπλῶν
τέσσαρα παραστήσομεν ξύλα, δύο ἐφ᾽ ἑκάστῳ, ἀντιβαίνοντα
ἄνωθεν καὶ ἐπιστηρίζοντα τὰ ἐφεστῶτα ὀρθά· ταῦτα δὲ τὰ ὀρθὰ
δεχέσθωσαν κατὰ μέσον δύο ἕτερα ξύλα, πλάτους ὄντα ἀνὰ
20 δακτύλων ὀκτώ, κατὰ δὲ πάχος ἀνὰ ἕξ, ἀπ᾽ ἀλλήλων ἀπέχοντα
ποδῶν οὐκ ἔλασσον τριῶν. Ταῦτα δὲ τὰ τέσσαρα τρυπάσθωσαν
|| ἐπ᾽ εὐθείας πρὸς ἄλληλα, καὶ συμπερονάσθωσαν τὰ μὲν ὀρθὰ   f. 21
πρὸς τὸ δίμοιρον αὐτῶν ἐπὶ τὰ ἄνω, τὰ δὲ ἐμβαλλόμενα ἐπὶ τὸ
ἕκτον αὐτῶν μέρος τὸ πρὸς τὰ κάτω. Κατερχέσθωσαν δὲ ἀπὸ
25 τῶν ὀρθῶν καὶ πάλιν ἀνερχέσθωσαν ὑπὸ περόνης εὐλύτως
φερόμενα· τρυπάσθωσαν δὲ καὶ αὐτὰ πάλιν ἀπὸ τῆς περόνης
ἐπὶ τὸ δίμοιρον αὐτῶν, καὶ ἔστι πρὸς τὸ ἐπίλοιπον ἕκτον μέρος·
δίμοιρον δὲ τοῦ ὅλου μήκους ἐνταῦθα νόει τὸ μεταξὺ τῶν
τρημάτων πρὸς τὰ ἄκρα γινόμενον, τουτέστι τὸ πρὸς τὰ δύο ἕκτα,
30 ἅπερ ποιοῦσι τρίτον μέρος τοῦ ὅλου μήκους. Ταῦτα τοίνυν
κατερχόμενα κατὰ μέσον δεχέσθωσαν κλίμακα ἐλαφρὰν
πεπερονημένην δυσὶ περόναις πρὸς τὰς ῥηθείσας τρή|σεις. Οἱ   Wes 234
δὲ τὴν κλίμακα ποιοῦντες μηροὶ ἔστωσαν κατὰ πλάτος
δακτύλων μὴ ἔλασσον ἕξ, ἐπὶ δὲ πάχος τεσσάρων. Ἀπὸ δὲ τῆς
35 κάτω περόνης τῆς ἐπὶ τῶν ὀρθοστατῶν διεκβληθείσης ἐπὶ τὸ
ἀναχθὲν ἕκτον μέρος τῶν καταχθέντων ἕλκυστρον ἐμβαλλέσθω
βαθμίδα τινὰ περιλαμβάνον ἢ σχοινίων δεσμὸν ἢ πρὸς κρίκους
σιδηροῦς διὰ τὴν ἕλξιν ὑπεμβαῖνον· ξύλον δέ ἐστι περικαμπές
τε καὶ εὔτονον, μήκους ὡσεὶ ποδῶν ὀκτὼ πρὸς τὸ ἱκανῶς ἑλκύειν
40 καὶ κατάγειν διὰ μέσου τῶν ὀρθίων τὸ ἀναχθὲν ἕκτον μέρος· τὸ
δὲ ἐγκλιθὲν ὅλον σὺν τῇ κλίμακι εἰς ὕψος ἀνάγει μετάρσιον.

27: 8 κρόταφον Wes: κότραφον VB || 12 ἀπεναντίον Wes: ἀπεναντίων VB || 13 ἄλλο Wes:
ἄλλῳ VB || 15 λιτὸν Wes || 27 ἔστι Sch: ἔτι VB

one of them between two others that lie on their side, that is, on their thick <side>; these also have unequal sides and are separated from one another enough to leave room for the upright on its thick <side>. And the other <upright> is likewise put between two other beams that are of equal size and form and lying similarly. Another beam should be placed on the ground at the midpoint opposite the two pairs of beams that lie flat, at right angles to and joined with the two pairs that lie flat at the point where the two uprights stand on them. The base should take the form of an uncial *eta* with double lines on the sides. From the ends of the two pairs that lie flat we shall place four posts, two on each <side>, which go up against and support the vertical uprights. Placed between these uprights should also be two other beams, about 8 *daktyloi* wide and 6 thick, no less than 3 *podes* apart. These four <beams> should be drilled on a straight line with respect to one another, and the uprights should be pinned two-thirds of the way up and the <beams> that are being inserted at one-sixth up from their bottom. <The inserted beams should be able to> move down from the uprights and up again, carried freely on a pin. They should also be drilled again up from the pin two-thirds of their <entire length>, <so> there is one-sixth part remaining. Understand that the area there between the drill holes is two-thirds of their whole length compared to the ends, that is, compared to the two one-sixth portions, which form a third of the whole length. These beams that come down should then receive between them a lightweight ladder pinned by two pins at the aforementioned holes. Let the sidebars that form the ladder be at least 6 *daktyloi* wide and 4 thick. From the bottom pin that is inserted through the uprights on the elevated sixth part of the <beams> that have been lowered, a handle should be inserted that connects to a rung or a loop of rope or goes in under iron rings for dragging. This <handle> is a curved and strong post, about 8 *podes* long, for adequately dragging up and bringing down through the middle of the uprights the elevated sixth part; it raises up high into the air the entire inclined part <of the structure> together with the ladder. It will, therefore,

Συμβήσεται οὖν, τοῦ μέρους τούτου ‖ ὑπὸ τοῦ ἑλκύστρου ἐπὶ τὸ
κάτω ἑλκομένου, ὑπὸ τοῦ ἑτέρου παραδόξως εἰς ὕψος ἀρθῆναι
τὸν κατάσκοπον, καὶ ὀρθὴν τὴν κλίμακα διαμένειν διὰ τὸ δυσὶν
45   ἐπεζεῦχθαι περόναις. Δεῖ δὲ τὸ κάτωθεν μέρος ὑπὸ τοῦ
ἑλκύστρου κρατούμενον, εἰ δυνατόν, πρὸς τὴν στάσιν
ἐπέχεσθαι· εἰ δὲ μή, ὑπὸ πλαγίων διερχομένων ξύλων ἢ
στροφωματίων παρεξοχαῖς ἐγκλειόμενον κατὰ τὸν τῆς στάσεως
καιρὸν ἀτρεμεῖν. Καὶ δεῖ εἰδέναι ὅτι τὸ ὑπερανέχον τρίτον
50   μέρος τῶν ὀρθῶν πρὸς ἀσφάλειαν τῶν ἐγκλινομένων ἀνίσταται·
τὸ δὲ ἀνώτερον ἕκτον μέρος τῶν ἐγκλινομένων, ἤτοι τὸ τοῦ μέσου
αὐτῶν τέταρτον (ὡς ἀνωτέρω ἐδηλώθη) εἰς ὑποστήριξιν τῆς
δισσῶς ἄνωθεν πεπερονημένης ἐλαι‖φρᾶς κλίμακος· τὸ δὲ
κατώτατον αὐτῶν ἕκτον, διὰ τὴν τοῦ ἑλκύστρου πρὸς αὐτὸ
55   ἐμβολήν, ἐπὶ τῇ γινομένῃ σφοδρᾷ κάτωθεν ἕλξει, ἅμα δὲ καὶ
ἐπ᾽ ἀναφορᾷ τοῦ λοιποῦ πενταπλασίου καὶ τῆς κλίμακος,
παρείληπται. Ἔστω δὲ καθ᾽ ὑπόθεσιν τὸ ὕψος τῶν ἑστώτων
ὀρθίων, ἕως τοῦ διμοίρου αὐτῶν, ὅσον ἐστὶ τὸ ὕψος τοῦ τρίτου
μέρους τοῦ τείχους· καὶ ἀπ᾽ αὐτοῦ ἄχρι τοῦ διμοίρου τῶν
60   ἐγκλινομένων, ἤτοι ἐπὶ τῇ πρώτῃ περόνῃ τῆς συμβολῆς τῆς
κλίμακος, ὅσον ἐστὶ τὸ τοῦ τείχους ἥμισυ· καὶ αὐτὴ δὲ ἡ κλῖμαξ,
ὅσον τὸ ἥμισυ· τὸ δ᾽ ἐκ τῶν τριῶν συντιθέμενον ὕψος τρίτῳ
μέρει ὑπὲρ τὸ τεῖχος ἀνάξει τὸν κατάσκοπον. Καὶ ἔστι φανερόν.
‖ Ἐπεὶ γὰρ τὸ τοῦ τείχους ὕψος σπιθαμῶν ἢ ποδῶν ἢ πηχῶν ἢ
65   τινων ἄλλων καταμετρούντων ὑπετέθη ἑξήκοντα, τὰ πρὸς τῇ
βάσει ὀρθὰ ἑστῶτα ἀνὰ τριάκοντα ἔστωσαν· πρὸς δὲ τὸ ὕψος
τῶν εἴκοσι τὴν περόνην δεχέσθωσαν· δίμοιρον δὲ τὰ εἴκοσι
τῶν τριάκοντα. Καὶ τὰ ἀπὸ τῶν ὀρθῶν κατερχόμενα ἀνὰ
τεσσαρακονταπέντε κατὰ μῆκος γινέσθωσαν· ἀπὸ δὲ τῆς
70   ῥηθείσης περόνης ἐπὶ τῇ τῆς κλίμακος πρώτῃ συμβολῇ
ἐναπολαμβανέσθωσαν τριάκοντα· δίμοιρον δὲ ταῦτα τῶν
τεσσαρακονταπέντε, ὡς ἀνωτέρω προδέδεικται. Ἔστω δὲ καὶ
ἡ κλῖμαξ ἀπ᾽ αὐτῆς τῆς συμβολῆς ἐπὶ τὸ λοιπὸν αὐτῆς ὕψος
ἑτέρων τριάκοντα· τὸ δὲ ἐκ τῶν τριῶν ὑψῶν κατ᾽ ἀριθμὸν
75   συναγόμενον ποιεῖ ὀγδοήκοντα· ταῦτα δὲ τῶν ἑξήκοντα τρίτῳ
μέρει ὑπερέχουσι· τρίτον ἄρα τὰ κʹ τῶν ξʹ. Γινέσθω δὲ καὶ

---

76 ὑπερέχουσι Sch: ὑπερέχωσι VB

follow that when this part is drawn down by the handle, the observer is wondrously raised upward by the other <end> and the ladder remains upright because it is bound fast by two pins. The lower part must be secured into vertical position, if possible controlled by the handle; if not, it must remain stable while in vertical position, locked on the projections either by beams running through horizontally or by pivots (?). You should be aware that the top third of the uprights rises up to steady the beams that incline, the upper sixth of the beams that incline, that is, the one-fourth of their central section (as was clarified above), to prop up the lightweight ladder which is doubly pinned at the top; their lowest sixth, through the insertion of the handle into it, is used for forcefully dragging from below and simultaneously bringing up the remaining five-sixths and the ladder. Hypothetically let the height of the vertical uprights as far as their two-thirds point be as much as the height of one-third of the wall; and from here to the two-thirds point of the beams that incline, that is, to the first pin of the joint of the ladder, be as much as one-half of the wall. And the ladder itself should be as much as one-half. And the height composed of the three parts will elevate the observer above the wall by one-third. And this is clear. For when the height of the wall has been assumed as 60 *spithamai* or *podes* or *pecheis* or some other unit of measure, the uprights standing on the base should be about 30 units. They should receive the pin at the height of 20; for 20 is two-thirds of 30. And the beams that come down from the uprights should be about 45 units in length. From the aforementioned pin to the first joint of the ladder, 30 units should be encompassed. This is two-thirds of 45, as was shown above. The ladder from the joint itself to its remaining height should be another 30 units. The combination numerically of the three heights makes 80. This exceeds 60 by a third; 20 then is one-third of 60. And a covering of

προστέγασμα ἐπὶ τὸ ἀνώτατον μέρος τῆς κλίμακος ἐκ βύρσης | Wes 236
παχείας τε καὶ εὐτόνου ὡς ἀσπίδος περικαμφθείσης, ἢ ῥάχιν
ὀξεῖαν κατὰ μέσον δεχόμενον καὶ κλίσιν ἐξαρκοῦσαν ἐπὶ τὰ
80 πλάγια, πρὸς τὸ ἀπὸ τόξου ἢ σφενδόνης φυλάττεσθαι τὸν
κατάσκοπον. Οὐ μικρὰν δὲ βοήθειαν παρέξουσι καὶ σχοινία
λεπτὰ εὔτονα, ἐπὶ τοὺς μηροὺς τῆς ἄνωθεν ἐλαφρᾶς κλίμακος
περιειλημμένα, καὶ τετανυσμένα ἄχρι τῆς τῶν περονῶν
συμβολῆς, μήπως ἡ τοῦ ὕψους παράτασις ἢ λιθοβόλου τυχοῦσα
85 ‖ πληγὴ ῥῆξιν ἢ σπάσιν ἐπὶ τοῖς ξύλοις ποιήσηται καὶ πτωματίσῃ   f. 22v
τὸν κατάσκοπον. Εἰς δὲ τὴν τοῦ σκοποῦ ὀρθίαν καὶ
ἀπαρέγκλιτον στάσιν μέγιστον συμβάλλονται καὶ σχοινία
τέσσαρα ἐπὶ τὰ ἄκρα τῶν ὀρθοστατῶν προσδεδεμένα καὶ | Wes 237
ἀπεκτεταμένα ἀπ' ἐναντίας ἀλλήλων, εἰ ἐνδεθήσεται σιδηροῖς
90 ἢ ξυλίνοις πασσάλοις μακρόθεν τῇ γῇ ἐμπησσομένοις, ἵνα μὴ
διὰ τὸ ὕψος ἀκροβαρῆσαν περινεύσῃ τὸ ἔργον. Καὶ τὰ σχήματα
ὑπόκειται, τό τε κείμενον καὶ τὸ ὠρθωμένον. ‖   f. 23

    28. ⟨Γ⟩ίνεται δὲ ἁπλουστέρα ἡ τοῦ αὐτοῦ σκοποῦ βάσις ἐκ
τριῶν μόνων ξύλων κατὰ πλάτος ⟨πρὸς⟩ τῇ γῇ τιθεμένων, δύο
μὲν πλαγίων ἀπ' ἀλλήλων διεστώτων, καὶ ἑτέρου κατὰ μέσον
ἀπεναντίον συμβεβλημένου, ὡς ἦτα λιτὸν ἀπλόγραμμον
5 ἐσχηματισμένων· ἐπάνω δὲ τῶν πλαγίων ὑπὸ γλωσσίδος κατὰ
μέσον τὰ ὀρθὰ ἐφίστανται· ἐκ δὲ τῶν ἄκρων τὰ πρὸς αὐτὰ
ἀντιβαίνοντα δ΄.

    29. ⟨Γ⟩ίνεται δὲ καὶ ἄλλως· ἐκ τριῶν ξύλων δύο μὲν πρὸς τῇ γῇ
κειμένων, ἀπ' ἀλλήλων δὲ μικρὸν ἀποκεχωρισμένων ὅσον κατὰ
πλάτος εἰσδέξασθαι τὰ ὀρθά· τούτων δὲ τῶν κειμένων διαλόξως
| ἄνωθεν ἀνακεχαραγμένων, καὶ ἑτέρου ἴσου τε καὶ ὁμοίου καὶ   Wes 238
5 ὁμοίως κάτωθεν ἀνακεχαραγμένου ἐπ' αὐτῶν κατὰ τὴν θέσιν
ἐφαρμοζομένου, μεταξὺ δὲ τῶν δύο καὶ ἐφ' ἑκάτερα τοῦ
ἐπιτεθέντος λοξοῦ τὰ ὀρθὰ κατὰ πλάτος ἐμβάλλονται· ἀπ'
ἄκρων δὲ τῶν κειμένων ἀντιβαίνοντα δύο ἐπὶ τὰ πλάτη τῶν
ὀρθῶν καὶ δύο ἀπὸ τοῦ λοξοῦ ἐπὶ τὰ πάχη διαλόξως· ἀλλ'
10 οὐδετέρα τούτων ἐστὶν ἀσφαλεστάτη ὡς ἡ προειρημένη. Τὴν
δὲ ἀπ' ἀλλήλων διάστασιν ⟨τῶν⟩ τιθεμένων πλαγίων καὶ τῶν

---

85 πτωματίσῃ Sch: πτώσῃ V: πώσῃ B: σπάσῃ Wes ‖ **28:** 2 πρὸς add. Sch ‖ 4 λιτὸν Wes ‖
29: 11 τῶν add. Wes

thick and strong ox-hide should be <placed> in front at the top of the ladder, like a curved shield, or one with a sharp ridge in the middle and a sufficient inclination to the sides, to protect the observer from bow and sling. And slender, strong ropes will provide no small assistance when bound around the sidebars of the lightweight ladder on top, stretched as far as the joint of the pins, lest the extension of the height or the chance blow of a stone thrower break or convulse the beams and cause the observer to fall. Four ropes will also contribute greatly to the straight and unwavering vertical position of the scout-ladder, when bound to the tops of the uprights and stretched opposite one another, if they are fastened by iron or wooden stakes driven deeply into the earth some distance away, lest due to the height the structure grow top-heavy <and> sway. And the drawings are below, both the flat and the upright view.

<fig. 13.>

28. The base of the same scout ladder is simpler, <if constructed> of only three beams placed on their wide side on the ground, two <beams> on the sides at a distance from each other, and another joined in the middle at right angles, <the three> forming as it were an uncial *eta* written with single lines. The uprights stand on the middle of the side <beams> under a tongue-like strap. From the ends four <braces> go up to them.

29. There is also another way. Of three beams, two lie on the ground, separated a little from each other, enough to receive the uprights on their wide side. Those that lie <on the ground> are cut on top at an angle, and another, equal and similar and similarly cut on its bottom, is fitted in position onto them. And between the two and at either end of the imposed diagonal beam, the uprights are inserted on their wide side. From the ends of the beams that lie <on the ground> two <braces> go up to the wide sides of the uprights, and two from the diagonal beam at an angle to their thick sides. But neither of these is very secure compared to the one mentioned earlier. And the craftsman will determine the distances from one another of the <beams> placed

ὀρθῶν ὁ τεχνίτης διορίσει, πρὸς τὴν τοῦ ὕψους σκοπήσας
σύνθεσίν τε καὶ συμμετρίαν· ὡσαύτως δὲ καὶ τὰ μεγέθη τῶν
ξύλων τῆς τε βάσεως καὶ τοῦ ὕψους ἐπὶ τὰς τρεῖς διαστάσεις
15 κατὰ ἀναλογίαν ἐπαυξήσει τε καὶ μειώσει. ‖   f. 23v

    30. Διάδης μὲν οὖν καὶ Χαρίας οἱ Πολυείδου τοῦ Θετταλοῦ
μαθηταί, οἱ συστρατευθέντες Ἀλεξάνδρῳ τῷ Μακεδόνι
μηχανικοί, πρῶτοι τά τε τρύπανα καὶ τὰς διαβάθρας καὶ τοὺς
φερομένους διὰ τροχῶν ξυλίνους πύργους ἐξεῦρον· καὶ τοὺς
5 μὲν ἐλάσσονας αὐτῶν πηχῶν πρὸς ὕψος ἐποίουν ἑξήκοντα, τὴν
δὲ βάσιν ἐτετραγώνιζον, ἑκάστην πλευρὰν τοῦ τε μήκους καὶ
πλάτους ἀνὰ πηχῶν τιθέντες δεκαεπτά, δεκαστέγους αὐτοὺς
ποιοῦντες, ἐπὶ δὲ τῇ ἀνωτάτω στέγῃ συναγωγὴν ἰσοτετράγωνον
ἀπολαμβάνοντες, κατὰ ἀναλογίαν τοῦ τῆς βάσεως πέμπτου
10 μέρους τοῦ λεγομένου ἐμβαδοῦ, ἤτοι τοῦ | ὑπὸ τῶν τεσσάρων   Wes 239
πλευρῶν περιοριζομένου χωρίου, ὡς ἐφεξῆς δηλωθήσεται. Τοὺς
δὲ μείζονας καὶ ἡμιολίους τούτων πεντεκαιδεκαστέγους
ἐποίουν, ὕψος δὲ πηχῶν Ϟʹ· καὶ ἔτι τοὺς διπλασίους
εἰκοσαστέγους πρὸς ὕψος πηχῶν ρκʹ· ἑκάστην δὲ πάλιν πλευρὰν
15 τῆς τῶν διπλασίων βάσεως ἀνὰ πηχῶν κδʹ ἔγγιστα. Καὶ μείζονάς
τε καὶ ἐλάσσονας κατὰ ἀναλογίαν κατεσκεύαζον, ἐπὶ τὰς τρεῖς
διαστάσεις τὰ ξύλα αὐξάνοντες ἢ μειοῦντες, τουτέστι κατά τε
μῆκος πλάτος τε καὶ πάχος· ὡσαύτως δὲ καὶ τὰς τῶν στεγῶν
διαιρέσεις πρὸς τὴν τοῦ ὕψους κατεμέριζον συμμετρίαν.
20 Ἑξατρόχους αὐτούς, ἐνίοτε δὲ καὶ ὀκτατρόχους πρὸς ‖ τὸ   f. 24
ἔξογκον τοῦ μεγέθους ἐποίουν· ἐπὶ πάντας δὲ ἀεὶ τὸ τῆς βάσεως
πέμπτον μέρος ἄνωθεν ἐπετίθουν.

    31. Ὁ δὲ Ἀπολλόδωρος, σεμνότερον πρὸς πόδας
κατασκευάζων τὸν πύργον, ὑφημιόλιον αὐτὸν τῶν ἑξήκοντα
πηχῶν καὶ τετράτροχον δηλοῖ, ποδῶν πρὸς ὕψος ἐμφαίνων
ἑξήκοντα· ὅθεν καὶ αὐτὸς ἑκάστην τὴν περὶ τὴν βάσιν πλευρὰν
5 κατὰ μῆκος ποδῶν ἐποίει δεκαέξ, δίχα τῆς ποδιαίας ἐπὶ τὰ ἄκρα

30: 1–4 Διάδης – ἐξεῦρον: cf. Ath. Mech. 10:10–12. 4–19 καὶ – συμμετρίαν: cf. Ath. Mech.
11:3–12:10. **31:** 1–32 Ὁ – καλείσθωσαν cf. Apollod. 164:8–165:10.

30: 1 Πολυείδου Mar: Πολυΐδου VBP ‖ 5 ὕψος B: ὕψους V ‖ 13 ὕψος B: ὕψους V ‖ 16 τε
Sch: δὲ VB ‖ 22 ἐπετίθουν VB: ἀπετίθουν Sch

on the sides and of the uprights by considering the composition and commensurability of the height; in a similar manner will he increase and decrease the sizes of the beams of the base and of the height proportionally for the three dimensions.

<fig. 14>

30. Diades and Charias, the students of Polyeides the Thessalian, engineers who campaigned with Alexander of Macedon, first invented borers and drop-bridges and wooden towers carried on wheels. They used to make the smaller of these 60 *pecheis* in height and the base square, setting each side, length and width, at about 17 *pecheis,* making them ten stories; on the top story they contracted it equally on all sides, in a proportion of one-fifth of the so-called area of the base, that is, the place delimited by the four sides, as will be shown in what follows. They made some others larger than these, one and a half times <as large> and fifteen stories, 90 *pecheis* high; and even double, twenty stories, to a height of 120 *pecheis;* <they used to make> each side in turn of the base of the doubled ones approximately 24 *pecheis.* And they constructed them larger and smaller, proportionally increasing or decreasing the timbers for the three dimensions, that is, in length, width, and depth; in a similar manner they partitioned the divisions of the stories commensurably with the height. They made them on six wheels, sometimes even on eight on account of the very massive size; but for all they always imposed at the top one-fifth of the base.

31. And Apollodorus, constructing his tower smaller, <reckoning> in *podes,* makes clear it is two-thirds of 60 *pecheis* and four-wheeled, indicating 60 *podes* in height. Whence he made each side around the base 16 *podes* in length (apart from the 1-*pous*

παρεξοχῆς, πλάτους ποδὸς ἑνὸς καὶ δακτύλων τεσσάρων, κατὰ
δὲ πάχος δακτύλων δώδεκα, διπλᾶ τὰ κάτω ζυγὰ ποιῶν, ὅπου
οἱ τροχοὶ πρὸς τὸ μέσον, οἱ δὲ μεσοστάται ἐπὶ ταῖς παρεξοχαῖς
ἐμβάλλεσθαι μέλλουσι. Ταῦτα τὰ δύο καὶ δύο ζυγὰ κατὰ πάχος
10 ἐτίθει, καὶ μεταξὺ πρὸς ἕκαστα δώ|δεκα δακτύλων μεσόχωρον   Wes 240
εἴτε καὶ μεῖζον ἐπὶ τὰ πλάτη διϊστῶν, ὀρθοὺς ἐπὶ τὰ ἄκρα τοὺς
μεσοστάτας ἐμβάλλει μέχρι τοῦ ἐδάφους κατερχομένους, οὕς
τινες σκέλη τοῦ πύργου ὠνόμασαν, ποδῶν πρὸς ὕψος ἀνὰ δεκαὲξ
ὄντα, πλάτους ποδὸς ἑνὸς καὶ δακτύλων τεσσάρων, κατὰ δὲ
15 πάχος ἀνὰ δακτύλων δώδεκα· ταῦτα πρὸς τοῖς κειμένοις διπλοῖς
διὰ κανονίων περιτομίδων τε καὶ χελωνίων, ἤτοι ἡμισφαιρίων
περὶ τὸ μέσον ἐγγεγλυμμένων καὶ ὡς γρονθαρίων τινῶν
ἐκκεκομμένων, παρομοίων τοῖς ἐπὶ τῶν στρο|λφίγγων τῶν θυρῶν   f. 24v
τιθεμένοις, περὶ τὴν προσήλωσιν ἀσφαλίζεται, ἵνα μένωσιν
20 ὀρθά. Τοῖς ὀρθίοις τούτοις σκέλεσι μεσοστάταις οὖσιν ἀπὸ τῶν
κειμένων διπλῶν ἐπὶ τὰ ἀντικείμενα διπλᾶ ἕτερα ξύλα ἴσα ὄντα
κατὰ μῆκος ὡς ἀντιζυγίδας ἐτίθει, ἰσοτετράγωνον τὸ τοῦ πύργου
σχηματίζων σχάριον, ἤτοι τὴν βάσιν ἐξ ἴσου περιορίζων, ἵνα
οἱ ῥηθέντες τέσσαρες μεσοστάται ἴσον ἀπ' ἀλλήλων
25 πανταχόθεν ἀπέχωσιν· ἐφ' ἑκάστῳ δὲ τῶν τεσσάρων δύο
παρίστανεν ξύλα ἀριθμῷ ὄντα ὀκτώ, ἰσοπλατῆ τούτων καὶ
ἰσοπαχῆ, ὕψους ἀνὰ ποδῶν ἐννέα, ἐφεστῶτα δὲ καὶ
παριστάμενα τῶν μεσοστατῶν ἐφ' ἑκάτερα ἐπὶ τὰ κείμενα
διπλᾶ καὶ προσηλούμενα καὶ αὐτὰ ἀσφαλῶς (ὡς προείρηται)
30 πρός τε τὰ ζυγὰ καὶ τοὺς μεσοστάτας· καὶ οὕτως τὰ τρία
συνίστανεν ἐν τάξει ὀρθοστάτου ἑνὸς κατὰ μέσον
ὑπερανέχοντος. Ταῦτα δὲ τὰ ὀκτὼ παραστάται καλείσθωσαν.

32. Καὶ ἐπεὶ δυσεύρετοί εἰσι διὰ τὸ τοῦ πλάτους μέγεθος οἵ τε
μεσοστάται καὶ παραστάται, ἀνάγκη τοῖς περὶ Διάδην καὶ
Χαρίαν ἕπε|σθαι καὶ ἰσοτετράγωνα ἀνὰ δώδεκα δακτύλων τὰ   Wes 241
σκέλη κάτωθεν ποιεῖν, ἄνωθεν δὲ ἐλάσσονα· ἐξαιρέτως δὲ τὰ
5 παριστάμενα, καὶ μάλιστα πρὸς κατασκευὴν μεγέθους τοιούτου
πύργου σύμμετρα τυγχάνοντα.

32: 3–4 καὶ – ἐλάσσονα: cf. Ath. Mech. 12:2–4.

31: 16 περιστομίδων Sch

projection at the ends), 1 *pous,* 4 *daktyloi* wide and 12 *daktyloi* thick, making the bottom timbers double, where the wheels are going to be inserted in the middle of them and the center-stanchions <inserted> on the projections. These double timbers he placed on their thick sides and between each <pair>, leaving open a gap of 12 *daktyloi* or even more in breadth, he inserts the center-stanchions upright at the ends; these, which some call the tower's "legs," go down as far as the bottom. They are 16 *podes* high, 1 *pous,* 4 *daktyloi* in width, about 12 *daktyloi* thick. These are secured to the horizontal double <timbers> at the point of fastening with little crossbars, angle braces, and shell-caps, that is, hemispheres hollowed out in the center and like some cutout little fists, similar to those placed on door pivots, to keep them upright. And at these upright legs that are center-stanchions, he placed, from the double horizontal timbers to the opposite double timbers, other timbers equal in length as transversals, forming the equal-sided undercarriage of the tower, that is, equally delimiting the base in order that the aforementioned four center-stanchions be equidistant from one another at all points. Next to each of the four <center-stanchions> he stood two <other> stanchions, eight in <total> number, with width and thickness equal to the others, 9 *podes* high. These stand next to the <center->stanchions on either side and stand on the horizontal double timbers and are also nailed securely (as mentioned above) to the timbers and the center-stanchions. And so he stood the three in order together with one upright in the middle taller <than the others>. Let these eight be called side-stanchions.

32. And since the center-stanchions and the side-stanchions, on account of their great width, are hard to find, it is necessary to follow the <men> of Diades and Charias and make the lower legs about 12 *daktyloi* square, but those above smaller, especially the side-stanchions, and above all commensurate for the construction of a tower of such size.

33. Πρὸς αὐτὰ δὲ πάλιν ἄνωθεν ὁ προρρηθεὶς ‖ Ἀπολλόδωρος
ὁμοίως τοῖς κάτω ζυγὰ καὶ ἐπιζυγίδας ἐτίθει ἐλάσσονας τῷ
μήκει ποδὸς ἄχρι, καὶ ἕως τῆς ἀνωτάτω στέγης πρός τε μῆκος
καὶ πλάτος ἐκ τῶν τιθεμένων ἀνὰ πόδα ἀφῄρει, ἵνα συναγωγὴν
5   ἄνωθεν ὁ πύργος λάβῃ, μήπως ἀκροβαρήσας περινεύσῃ, ἀλλ᾽
ἀσφαλῆ τὴν στάσιν ἐκ τοῦ κάτωθεν πλάτους τῆς ἕδρας ἔξῃ. Τῶν
δὲ στεγῶν αἱ μὲν περίπτεροι ἔστωσαν, αἱ δὲ περιδρόμους κύκλῳ
ἔχουσαι πλάτους ὡσεὶ ποδῶν τριῶν· χρειώδεις γάρ εἰσιν εἰς τὴν
τῶν ἐμπρησμῶν ἐκβοήθησιν. Καθ᾽ ὃ δὲ διέστηκεν ἐπὶ τὰ πλάτη
10   τὰ κάτω ζυγὰ τὰ τοὺς μεσοστάτας δεξάμενα ἐπὶ τὰ ῥηθέντα
δωδεκαδάκτυλα ἢ καὶ μείζονα μεσόχωρα, τῷ τεχνίτῃ ἐμφαίνων
ἐντέλλεται τροχοὺς ἐμβάλλειν τέσσαρας ἐξ εὐτόνων ἀξόνων
συμπεπερονημένους καὶ σιδηροῖς πετάλοις ψυχρηλάτοις
συνδεδεμένους, τὴν διάμετρον ἔχοντας ἤτοι τὸ ὕψος ποδῶν ὡσεὶ
15   τεσσάρων ἥμισυ· συμπερονᾶσθαι δὲ ὁτὲ τοὺς αὐτοὺς τροχοὺς
καὶ διὰ σιδηρῶν βραχέων ἀξόνων, διά τε τὸ ἐπικείμενον βάρος
καὶ τὸ ἔξογκον τοῦ μεγέθους· καὶ τοὺς μὲν δύο πρὸς ἕκαστα μόνα
τὰ δύο ξύλα ἀσφαλίζεσθαι, τοὺς δὲ λοιποὺς δύο πρὸς τὰ ἐξ
ἐναντίας ἀντικείμενα αἴροντας ἀπὸ τῆς γῆς καὶ ǀ ἀνέχοντας τὰ
20   διπλᾶ ξύλα, ἵνα εὐστρόφως οἱ τροχοὶ καὶ ἀπαρεμποδίστως
κυλίωνται καὶ ὅλον συγκινῶσι τὸ τοῦ πύργου σύμπηγμα.

34. Οὕτως οὖν τῆς κατασκευῆς ‖ συνισταμένης ηὑρίσκοντο οἱ
πρῶτοι μεσοστάται τρίτῳ ἑαυτῶν μήκους μέρει ἐπὶ τῇ ἀνωτέρᾳ
στέγῃ ἀνέχοντες. Ὅθεν παραστάτας ἐπὶ τὰ ἀνώτερα ζυγὰ πάλιν
ἐτίθει ὑπερέχοντας τοῦ μεσοστάτου, καὶ πρὸς αὐτὸν ἄλλον
5   συνεχόμενον ὑπὸ τῶν παραστατῶν, καὶ οὕτως κατὰ πᾶσαν
στέγην τετραμερῶς συμπλέκων τὸν πύργον ἐστήριξεν. Καὶ τὸν
μὲν πρῶτον μεσοστάτην οὐκ ἐποίησε τοῖς παραστάταις τούτοις
ἴσον, ἵνα μὴ αἱ συμβολαὶ αὐτῶν ἐγγὺς ἀλλήλων ὦσιν, ἀλλ᾽
ἀντιπαραλλάσσῃ πᾶς ἁρμὸς ἀφεστηκὼς πρὸς τὸν ἕτερον, καὶ
10   τῇ τῶν παρακειμένων συνοχῇ καὶ ἑνότητι ἰσχὺν λαμβάνῃ. Καὶ
κλίμακας δὲ πρὸς τὰς ἐπιζυγίδας διὰ τὴν ἀνάβασιν παρετίθει

33: 1–**34:** 20 Πρὸς – πύργωμα: cf. Apollod. 165:11–167:9.

33: 12 τέσσαρας ἐξ εὐτόνων V: τέσσαρας ἐξ εὐτόνου B: δι᾽ ἐξευτόνων Sch ‖ 15 ὁτὲ Sch:
ὅτε VB

33. And upon these <uprights> the aforementioned Apollodorus in turn placed above timbers like those below and cross-timbers, shorter in length up to a *pous*. And up to the top story he decreased the <stories> placed there by a *pous* in length and width, in order that the tower might be contracted above, lest in any way it become top-heavy <and> sway, but rather that it might stand securely due to the width of the lower base. And some of the stories are surrounded by ledges, others have galleries around them of about 3 *podes* in width; for these are needed for protection against burning. Where the lower timbers that receive the center-stanchions are separated in breadth by the aforementioned gaps of 12 *daktyloi* or even more, Apollodorus indicates <and> bids the craftsman to insert four wheels pinned from strong <wooden> axles and secured with cold-forged iron plating — the wheels have a diameter, that is, a height, of about 41/2 *podes;* <and> sometimes that the same wheels are pinned also with short iron axles on account of the imposed weight and very massive size and these are secured two to each individual pair of timbers, but the remaining two to the opposite timbers on the other side, raising from the earth and holding up the double timbers, so that the wheels may roll easily and without hindrance and move the whole superstructure of the tower.

34. Therefore, when the construction is arranged in this way, the first center-stanchions are found to rise above the next story by a third part of their length. Whence <Apollodorus> in turn placed side-stanchions on the upper timbers, taller than the center-stanchion, and on top of this <center-stanchion> another one, encompassed by the side-stanchions; and thus weaving at the four corners on every story he stabilized the tower. And he did not make the first center-stanchion equal to these side-stanchions, lest their joints be near one another, but rather that every connection might alternate, separate with respect to the other, and obtain strength by the joining and unity of the side-stanchions. And on the cross-timbers he placed ladders for ascending

τὸ ἕτερον ἐκ τοῦ ἑτέρου πλευροῦ διαγωνίως χωριζούσας.
Ἠσφαλίζετο δὲ τὸν πύργον καὶ σχοινίοις ἄνωθεν κατὰ τὰς
γωνίας δεδεμένοις καὶ κατὰ μέσον ἔξω ἐπισυρομένοις,
15 πλατυτέραν ἐν σχήματι βάσιν τῷ πύργῳ ἐμποιῶν οἱονεὶ ἕδραν,
περιδεδεμένοις πασσάλοις περόνας ἔχουσιν ἢ σιδηροῖς ἥλοις
καὶ κρίκοις, πλαγίοις πρὸς τὴν ἀπότασιν ἐμπησσομένοις, οὐ
μικρὰν βοήθειαν διὰ τῆς τῶν σχοινίων τάσεως πρὸς ὑποστήριξιν
τῷ πύργῳ παρεχόμενος. Οὕτως ἐξ ὀλίγων καὶ μικρῶν ξύλων μέγα
20 καὶ ἰσοϋψὲς τῷ τείχει κατεσκεύαζε πύργωμα, ‖ ⟨μ⟩ήτε στεγῶν   f. 26, 26v
διαιρέσεις ἢ | ὕψη σημάνας, μήτε τῆς ἄνωθεν συναγωγῆς τὸ   Wes 243
πέμπτον μέρος δηλώσας.

35. Εἰ δέ τις ἀπορῶν ἐπιζητοίη τοῦτο, ἐκ τῆς κάτωθεν βάσεως
λήψεται διὰ τοῦ ὑποτεθέντος ἐφ᾽ ἑκάστῃ πλευρᾷ ἀριθμοῦ. Ἐπεὶ
γὰρ ἡ πλευρὰ ποδῶν ἐδόθη δεκαέξ, πολλαπλασιαζομένη δὲ ἐπὶ
τὴν ἑτέραν καὶ ἰσομήκη αὐτῆς ποιεῖ τὸ ὅλον ἐμβαδὸν ἤτοι τὸ
5 ἔνδον τοῦ τετραπλεύρου χωρίον ποδῶν σνς´, καὶ ἔστι τούτων
τὸ πέμπτον ποδῶν να´ πέμπτον ἔγγιστα· ζητῶ ποῖος ἀριθμὸς ἐφ᾽
ἑαυτὸν ἢ ἐπὶ τὸν ἰσομήκη αὐτοῦ πολλαπλασιαζόμενος τοῦτον
ποιεῖ, καὶ εὑρίσκω τὸν ἑπτὰ ἕκτον ἔγγιστα· ἑπτὰ γὰρ ἐπὶ ἑπτὰ
μθ´· καὶ ἑπτὰ ἐπὶ τὸ ἕκτον, τουτέστιν ἐπὶ τὰ δέκα λεπτά, ποιοῦσι
10 λεπτὰ πρῶτα ο´· πάλιν δὲ τὰ ι´ ἐπὶ ζ´ ⟨ποιοῦσιν⟩ ο´· καὶ ἐκ τῶν
συναγομένων λεπτῶν πρώτων ρμ´ τὰ μὲν ρκ´ εἰς πόδας δύο
καταλογίζεσθαι, τὰ δὲ λοιπὰ εἰς τὸ μέρος· ὥστε τὰ πρὸς τῇ
συναγωγῇ τῆς ἀνωτάτω στέγης τιθέμενα ζυγὰ ἀνὰ ποδῶν ἑπτὰ
κατὰ μῆκος καὶ μέρους ἕκτου γινέσθωσαν. Ἀλλὰ καὶ αἱ πρὸς
15 ὕψος ἀπὸ τῆς κάτωθεν βάσεως τιθέμεναι ἐννέα στέγαι ἐπὶ τὴν
τοῦ μήκους καὶ πλάτους ἐπέμβασιν κατὰ τὸν τοῦ τετραπλεύρου
περιορισμὸν ἀνὰ πόδα ἀφαιροῦσαι ἐκ τῶν δεκαέξ, ἑπτὰ ἔγγιστα
καταλιμπάνουσιν. Ἡ αὐτὴ δὲ ἔφοδος | ἐπὶ τῆς ἀνωτάτης τοῦ   Wes 244
πύργου συναγωγῆς καὶ ἐπὶ τρίτου καὶ τετάρτου καὶ ‖ τοῦ   f. 27
20 τυχόντος μέρους ἀεὶ τοῖς ἐπιζητοῦσιν ἔστω.

36. Τὰς δὲ τῶν στεγῶν διαιρέσεις καὶ τὰ πρὸς ὕψος
ἀναστήματα οἱ μὲν περὶ Διάδην καὶ Χαρίαν πρὸς πήχεις

36: 1–9 Τὰς – ἐλάμβανεν: cf. Ath. Mech. 12:6–10.

34: 20 μήτε B: ητε V ‖ **35:** 10 ποιοῦσιν add. Wes ‖ 13 συναγωγῇ Wes: συναγωγῆς VB

<the structure>, which diagonally separated one side from the other. He secured the tower also with ropes tied on top at the corners and in the middle, stretched outward, making a base for the tower broader in form, like a foundation, and bound to stakes with pins or to iron spikes and rings, fixed transversely against the tension. He furnished no little aid for the support of the tower through the tension of the ropes. Thus from a few small beams he constructed a large tower equal in height to the wall. He specified neither the divisions nor the height of the stories, nor indicated the one-fifth contraction on top.

<fig. 15>

35. If someone who is in doubt should seek this, he will obtain it from the lower base through the number proposed for each side. For when the side has been given as 16 *podes,* multiplied by the other side which is its equal, this makes the total area, that is, the inner space of the four-sided figure, 256 <square> *podes,* and one fifth of these *podes* are approximately 51 1/5 *podes.* I ask what number multiplied by itself or by a length equal to it makes this <amount> and I find approximately 7 1/6: for 7 times 7 <is> 49; and 7 times 1/6, that is times 10 minutes <10/60>, makes 70 minutes <70/60>; and again 10 <minutes> by 7 makes 70/60. And from the summed 140 minutes <140/60>, 120 <minutes> are converted into 2 *podes,* and the remainder to the fraction <20/60>. So the timbers set in place for the contraction of the top story should be approximately 7 1/6 *podes* in length. But also the nine stories positioned upward from the lower base, reduced from the <original> 16 *podes* by a *pous* with <each> modulation (?) of length and width in the delimiting of the four-sided <figure>, leave approximately 7 *podes.* And the same method for the uppermost contraction of the tower should always be <employed> for the third and fourth and any part by those who seek it.

36. The <men> of Diades and Charias, counting the divisions of the stories and the elevations upward in *pecheis,* used to place

ἀριθμοῦντες τὴν ἐκ τῆς κάτωθεν βάσεως πρώτην στέγην πηχῶν
πρὸς ὕψος ἐτίθουν ἑπτὰ καὶ δακτύλων δώδεκα· τὰς δ᾽ ἀνωτέρας
5 πέντε ἀνὰ πηχῶν πέντε μόνον· τὰς δ᾽ ὑπολειπομένας ἀνὰ
τεσσάρων καὶ τρίτου, τό τε σύμπαχον τοῦ καταστρώματος τῶν
στεγῶν καὶ τὸ κάτωθεν τοῦ σχαρίου σὺν τῷ ἄνωθεν ἀετώματι
τῷ ὕψει συνηρίθμουν. Ὁμοίως δὲ καὶ ἐπὶ τοῦ ἐλάσσονος πύργου
ἡ διαίρεσις τῶν στεγῶν τὸν αὐτὸν λόγον πρὸς ὕψος ἐλάμβανεν.
    37. Ὁ δὲ ῥηθεὶς Ἀπολλόδωρος, πρὸς πόδας καταριθμῶν τὸν
πύργον, τοὺς ἐκ τῆς βάσεως πρώτους παραστάτας ποδῶν ἐννέα
πρὸς ὕψος ποιεῖ· καὶ εἰ μὲν ἰσοϋψεῖς πάντας βούλεται,
ἑξάστεγον αὐτὸν δηλοῖ καὶ ποδῶν ἓξ μόνων τὴν παρέμβασιν
5 εἶναι· τρίτον δὲ καὶ εἰκοστὸν ἔγγιστα τοῦ ἐμβαδοῦ τῆς βάσεως
ἐπισυνάγει ἄνωθεν ἀνὰ δέκα ποδῶν καὶ τὰ ἀνώτερα τιθεὶς ζυγά.
Εἰ δὲ τὸ πέμπτον τῆς βάσεως ἐπὶ ἑξαστέγου πύργου ἐπισυνάγει
ἄνωθεν, ἑνὸς καὶ ἡμίσεως ποδὸς τὴν τῶν στεγῶν ἐπέμβασιν
τετραμερῶς ἐμφαίνει· εἰ δὲ καὶ δεκάστεγον, ἀνὰ ποδὸς ἑνὸς τὴν
10 παρέμβασιν, ὡς προείρηται, καὶ πέμπτον τῆς βάσεως   Wes 245
ἀπολαμβάνειν ἄνωθεν, ὡς ἂν καὶ τὰ ἀνώ|τερα ζυγὰ ‖ ἀνὰ ποδῶν   f. 27v
ἑπτὰ καὶ μέρους ἕκτου ποιεῖν. Καὶ ἐπὶ μὲν δεκαστέγου τοὺς
κάτωθεν παραστάτας ἀνὰ ποδῶν ἐννέα γίνεσθαι, τοὺς δ᾽ ἐπὶ
ταῖς ἀνωτέραις τέτρασι στέγαις ἀνὰ ποδῶν ἓξ μόνων, τοὺς δ᾽
15 ἔτι ἀνωτέρους ἐπὶ ταῖς ὑπολοίποις τέτρασιν ἀνὰ πέντε καὶ
μέρους.
    38. Οὕτως οὖν οὐ μόνον αἱ κατ᾽ ἀριθμὸν διαφέρουσαι τῶν
πύργων στέγαι πρὸς ἑξήκοντα ποδῶν ὕψος ἰσοϋψεῖς
εὑρεθήσονται, ἀλλὰ καὶ οἱ ἐξ ἀμφοτέρων πρὸς πήχεις καὶ πόδας
κατασκευαζόμενοι πύργοι καὶ κατὰ μέγεθος διαφέροντες
5 σύμμετροι πρὸς ἀλλήλους κατὰ ἀναλογίαν δειχθήσονται. Εἰ
γὰρ ὁ πῆχυς εἰκοσιτεσσάρων κατὰ μῆκός ἐστι δακτύλων, τοῦ
ποδὸς ἑξκαίδεκα ὄντος, ἔχει δὲ ὁ κδ΄ τὸν δεκαὲξ καὶ τὸ ἥμισυ
αὐτοῦ, ἡμιόλιος αὐτοῦ ἐστιν, ὑφημιόλιος δὲ πρὸς πῆχυν ὁ πούς·
ὥστε καὶ αἱ τοῦ ὕψους πήχεις ἑξήκοντα καὶ αἱ τῆς βάσεως τοῦ
10 μήκους δεκαεπτὰ τὴν αὐτὴν ἀναλογίαν πρὸς τοὺς πόδας
ἕξουσιν, ὡσαύτως δὲ καὶ τὴν ἐν λόγοις συμφωνίαν, ὅτι κοινῷ

36: 6 σύμπαχον VBP: σύμπαν πάχος Mar ‖ **38:** 7 τὸν Wes: τῶν VB

the first story on the lower base at a height of 7 *pecheis* 12 *daktyloi;*
and the <next> five higher ones at only 5 *pecheis;* the remaining
ones at 41/3 <*pecheis*>. And they included in their calculation of
the height the entire thickness of the deck of the stories, and the
undercarriage at the bottom and the gable on top. Likewise for
the smaller tower also the division of the stories had the same
ratio with respect to the height.

37. The aforementioned Apollodorus, reckoning his tower in
podes, makes the first side-stanchions on the base 9 *podes* high;
and if he wants them all to be of equal height, he makes clear it
is six stories and the modulation (?) is only of 6 *podes.* And he
encloses on top approximately 23 <minutes> <23/60> of the
area of the base, placing further up timbers of 10 *podes.* And if
he encloses on top one-fifth of the base on the six-story tower,
he indicates that the modulation (?) of the stories at the four
sides is 11/2 *podes.* But if it is a ten-story one, the modulation (?)
is 1 *pous,* as already mentioned, and intercepts on top a fifth of
the base, as this would make the upper timbers about 71/6 *podes.*
And for the ten-story tower, the lower side-stanchions are of 9
podes, those on the next higher four stories of only 6 *podes,* and
those still higher on the remaining four <stories> are 51/4 *podes.*

38. So, therefore, not only will the towers <of Apollodorus>
with different numbers of stories be found equal to 60 *podes* in
height, but even the towers constructed by both groups, by *pecheis*
and by *podes* and differing in size, will be shown to be commensurable with one another in proportion. For if the *pechys* is 24
daktyloi long, the *pous* being 16, but twenty-four is sixteen and
half again of it, then <the *pechys*> is one and one-half times <the
pous>, the *pous* two-thirds of the *pechys.* Thus 60 *pecheis* of the
height and 17 of the length of the base will have the same proportion in *podes,* and so also be harmonious in ratios, because

μέτρῳ ἀμφότεροι μετροῦνται. Ὁ γὰρ τριάκοντα τρὶς μὲν μετρεῖ
τὸν ϛ΄, δὶς δὲ τὸν ἑξήκοντα καὶ πάλιν ὁ ὀκτὼ τρὶς μὲν τὸν κδ΄
μετρεῖ, δὶς δὲ τὸν ιϛ΄· καὶ ἔστιν ὡς ϛ΄ πρὸς ξ΄, οὕτως κδ΄ πρὸς
15 ιϛ΄· καὶ ὡς κδ΄ πρὸς ιϛ΄, οὕτως καὶ οἱ τροχοὶ πρὸς ἀλλήλους κατ'
ἀριθμόν τε καὶ μέγεθος, καὶ ἡ βάσις πρὸς τὴν βάσιν, ὡς καὶ τὰ
τρία πρὸς δύο. Ἐδείχθησαν ἄρα καὶ ‖ οἱ μεⁱτροῦντες πρὸς   f. 28
ἀλλήλους τὸν αὐτὸν τοῖς μετρουμένοις κατ' ἀναλογίαν ἔχοντες   Wes 246
λόγον· ὥστε οὐ μόνον πρὸς συμμετρίαν, ἀλλὰ καὶ συμφωνίαν
20 τῶν φορητῶν πύργων κατασκευὰς οἱ περὶ Ἀπολλόδωρον πρὸς
τοὺς περὶ Διάδην καὶ Χαρίαν εὑρίσκονται ποιοῦντες. Καὶ
φανερὸν ὅτι οἱ πάλαι μηχανικοὶ καὶ πολυμαθέστατοι
ἀρχιτέκτονες ἐπιστημονικῶς καὶ οὐκ ἀλόγως τὰς τῶν
μηχανημάτων κατασκευὰς ἐποίουν.
    39. ⟨Τ⟩οῦ πύργου οὕτως ἐπὶ τῇ κατασκευῇ τελεσθέντος, ἐὰν
μὴ ὁμαλὸς καὶ ἰσοπέδιος ὁ πρὸς τὴν βάσιν ὑποκείμενος εἴη τόπος
ἀλλ' ἀνωφερὴς τυγχάνῃ, ποιήσομεν ὑπόθημα πρὸς τῇ βάσει
τοῦ πύργου τῇ ὁμοίᾳ αὐτοῦ συμπλοκῇ ἐπὶ τῷ ἀνωμάλῳ τῆς γῆς
5 προσερχομένῃ καὶ πλατυνούσῃ τὸν ὑποκείμενον κάτωθεν τόπον,
ὅπως ἐπὶ τῇ συμβολῇ καὶ τῷ κλόνῳ τῆς μάχης ἀκλινὴς πρὸς τὴν
στάσιν ὁ πύργος συντηρῆται. Διαφυλαχθήσεται δὲ πρὸς τὸ μὴ
καίεσθαι ἐκ τῶν πεμπομένων πυροφόρων τριβόλων καὶ
ἀναπτομένων φλογῶν προσηλούμενος σανίσι, μάλιστα μὲν
10 φοινικίναις ἢ ταῖς ἐξ εὐτόνων ξύλων γινομέναις, πλὴν κεδρίνων
πευκίνων τε καὶ κληθρίνων, διὰ τὸ ἔκπυρον αὐτῶν εὔκλαστόν
τε καὶ εὔθραυστον. Ἐπικρεμάσθωσαν δὲ καὶ δέρματα τῷ πύργῳ
ἐπὶ τοῖς ῥηθεῖσιν ἐπὶ τῇ κατασκευῇ περιπτέροις τε καὶ
περιδρόμοις, μὴ προσεγγίζοντα ǀ ταῖς σανίσιν, ἀλλὰ μικρὸν   Wes 247
15 ἔξωθεν ἀπέχοντα διά τε ‖ τὰ πυροβόλα καὶ ὅπως ἀσθενεῖς πρὸς   f. 28v
αὐτὰ καὶ ἔκλυτοι ἐπὶ τῇ τῆς βολῆς ἐνδόσει αἱ τῶν λιθοβόλων
πρὸς τὸ χαῦνον γίνωνται πληγαί. ⟨Π⟩ροσηλούσθω δὲ καὶ ἥλοις
ὁ πύργος ἄνωθεν, ὡς προείρηται καὶ ἐπὶ τῶν χελωνῶν, καὶ πηλοῦ

38: 17 μετροῦντες: cf. Euc. IX:11. **39:** 1–5 ἐὰν – τόπον: cf. Apollod. 173:9–12. 8–12 ἐκ –
εὔθραυστον: cf. Ath. Mech. 17:14–18:1. 8 πυροφόρων τριβόλων: cf. Philo Mech. 94:9–10,
95:8, 100:20–21. 12–30 Ἐπικρεμάσθωσαν – τόπον: cf. Apollod. 173:13–174:7.

20 Ἀπολλόδωρον Wes: διόδωρον VB ‖ **39:** 3 ποιήσομεν Wes: ποιήσωμεν VB ‖ 13 περιπτέροις
Sch: παραπτέροις VB ‖ 17 γίνωνται Wes: γίνονται VB

both are measured by a common measure. For thrice 30 measures 90, and twice <30> 60; and again thrice 8 measures 24, and twice 8, 16. And as 90 is to 60, so 24 is to 16; and as 24 is to 16, so also are the wheels to one another in number and in size, and the base is to the base, as also 3 to 2. The measuring <numbers> then have been shown to mutually have the same ratio proportionally to those being measured. And so the <men> of Apollodorus, in carrying out the construction of his portable towers, will be found not only commensurable but in harmony with <those> of Diades and Charias. And it is clear that the ancient engineers and the very learned master builders carried out the construction of machines scientifically and rationally.

39. When the construction of the tower is thus completed, if the area lying under the base should not be even and level, but happens to slope upward, we shall make a counterplate at the base of the tower with the same intertwined <construction> as it; this comes up against the irregularity of the earth and amplifies the area lying below, so that the tower may be maintained steadfast in position when turbulent battle is joined. It will be guarded against burning from fire-bearing caltrops launched <against it> and from ignited flames if boards are nailed on, especially of palm or others of strong wood, except cedar, fir, and alder, as these easily burn, break, and shatter. Hides should be hung on the tower at the ledges and galleries, which were already mentioned during the construction <account>, not right up against the boards, but a little bit away from them because of the incendiaries and so that the blows of the stone throwers on the hollow space may be weak against these <hides> and dissipated with the slackening of the momentum. The tower should be fitted with nails on top, as was discussed earlier in the case of

λιπαροῦ καὶ κολλώδους ἀναγεμισθήτω ὁ διὰ μέσου τόπος. Εἰς
20 δὲ τὰ προκείμενα τοῖς πυροβόλοις μέρη τοῦ πύργου ἀντὶ
σωλήνων τῶν τὸ ὕδωρ πεμπόντων ἔντερα βοῶν εἰργασμένα
ὡσὰν τεταριχευμένα παρατίθενται ὕδωρ ἐπιχέοντα. Τούτοις
τοῖς ἐντέροις ἀσκοὶ πλήρεις ὕδατος ὑποτίθενται· ἐκθλιβόμενοι
δὲ καὶ πιεζόμενοι ἀναφέρουσι τὸ ὕδωρ. Εἰ δὲ καὶ ἀκρωτήριόν
25 που τοῦ πύργου δυσδιάβατον καίεται, μὴ ἔστι δὲ ὄργανον ὃ
καλεῖται σίφων, κάλαμοι τετρυπημένοι δι᾿ ὅλου ἔσωθεν οἵους
οἱ ἰξευταὶ ἔχουσι πρὸς ἀλλήλους συμβάλλονται, καὶ ὅπου δέῃ
ἐκπέμπουσι τὸ ὕδωρ· ἀσκοὶ γὰρ ὡς καὶ ἐπὶ τῶν ἐντέρων
ὑπόκεινται ἐκφέροντες αὐτὸ διὰ τῶν καλάμων ἐπὶ τὸν
30 ἐμπυριζόμενον τόπον. Οὐ μικρὰν δὲ ὠφέλειαν τῷ πύργῳ
ἐμπαρέξουσι καὶ τύλια ἔξωθεν κρεμάμενα ἀχύροις ὄξει
βεβρεγμένοις γεμισθέντα, ἢ δίκτυα ἐνύγρων βρύων ἢ τοῦ
καλουμένου θαλασσοπράσου, ὡς δυνάμενα | μὴ μόνον ταῖς ἐκ   Wes 248
τῶν πυροβόλων ἀντιμάχεσθαι ἐμπρήσεσιν, ἀλλὰ καὶ πρὸς τὰς
35 τῶν λιθοβόλων ἀντέχεσθαι πληγάς. Καὶ δεῖ εἰδέναι ὅτι πᾶσαι
αἱ ἐκ τῶν πυροφόρων καὶ ἀναπτομένων φλογῶν 〈 . . . 〉 ‖   f. 29
   40. 〈 . . . 〉 μέρη τὸν κριὸν βασταζόμενον ἐπιφέρεσθαι. Ἀπὸ δὲ
τοῦ τρίτου βαθμοῦ τῆς ἄνωθεν κλίμακος ἐπὶ τὸν τῆς ἑτέρας
τρίτον καὶ ἰσοΰψῆ διὰ σανίδων στεγάζονται ἢ βεργῶν
πεπλεγμένων, ἀμφοτέρων δὲ πηλῷ ἐπικεχρισμένων ἢ βύρσαις
5 βοῶν νεοσφαγῶν σκεπομένων διά τε τὰ πυροβόλα καὶ τὰς τῶν
λίθων βολάς. Κατωτέρω δὲ τοῦ | τρίτου βαθμοῦ μετὰ πόδας   Wes 249
δεκαοκτὼ ἢ καὶ εἴκοσι οἱ τυχόντες βαθμοὶ ἄλλην στέγην
λαμβάνουσιν, οὐ πρὸς ὅλον τὸ πλάτος τῶν βαθμῶν· ἀστέγαστος
γὰρ ὁ πρὸς τὴν ἀνάβασιν παραλειφθήσεται τόπος. Χρὴ δὲ τὰς
10 ἐμβαλλομένας περόνας ἐπὶ τοὺς τῶν κλιμάκων μηροὺς πλέον
παρεξέρχεσθαι, ἵνα πλατύτερον τῶν κλιμάκων τὸ χωρίον
στεγάζηται· ἐκεῖ γὰρ ὁ κριὸς ἐνεργήσει μάλιστα ἀπὸ τῆς ἄνωθεν

30–35 Οὐ – πληγάς: Ath. Mech. 18:1–7.   40: 1–44: 45 Ἀπὸ – ἅλωσιν: cf. Apollod. 185:6–
188:9.

25 καίεται Wes: καίηται VB ‖ 26 τετρυπημένοι Wes: τετρυπημένου VB ‖ 31 κρεμάμενα
Wes: κρεμόμενα VB ‖ 36–40: 1 < . . . > Wes (cf. Dain, 30–31) ‖ 9 παραλειφθήσεται Wes:
παραληφθήσεται VB

tortoises, and the area between filled with greasy and viscous clay. At the parts of the tower exposed to the incendiaries the intestines of cattle, prepared as it were pickled in brine, are attached for pouring water, as a substitute for water-shooting pipes. Wineskins full of water are attached to these intestines; when squeezed and pressed they dispense the water. And if somewhere a top part of the tower that is hard to reach should happen to be burning, but no so-called siphon device is available, reeds completely hollowed out inside, such as are used by fowlers, are joined to one another and send the water wherever necessary. For wineskins, when they are attached to the intestines, carry it through the reeds to the burning area. Also of no little protection to the towers will be mattresses hung on the outside filled with chaff soaked in vinegar, or nets of marine moss or so-called seaweed, as these are capable not only of counteracting burning from incendiaries, but even of resisting the blows of stone-throwers. You should be aware that all < . . . > from the fire-bearing <caltrops> and ignited flames < . . . >

40. < . . . > parts (?) the ram in suspension is carried. From the third rung from the top of the ladder to the third <rung> of the other, which is equal in height, the <ladders> are roofed with boards or with plaited branches, and both are smeared with clay or protected with hides of freshly slaughtered cattle against incendiaries or stone shots. Below the third rung, 18 or 20 *podes* down, the rungs there receive another roof, but not over the entire width of the rungs. For the place for climbing upward will be left uncovered. The pins inserted into the sidebars of the ladders must project further out, in order that an area wider than the ladders may be covered. For there the ram will be especially

ἠρτημένος στέγης δυσὶ βαστάγμασιν ἰσοϋψέσι παρὰ μικρόν τι,
ἵνα καὶ οἱ τὸν κριὸν ὠθοῦντες ἐπὶ τοῦ καταστρώματος τοῦ
15 ἐστεγασμένου ἑστῶτες χωρίου ἐπὶ τὰ ἀνώτερα μέρη τῶν τειχῶν
κριομαχῶσιν· εὔθραυστον γὰρ καὶ εὐκατάλυτον πᾶν τὸ
ἀνεστηκὸς καὶ προέχον ὡς ἀπολελυμένον καὶ ἀσύνδετον, οἷαί
τέ εἰσιν αἱ ἐπάλξεις καὶ τὰ προπύργια καὶ ὅσα μὴ πρὸς ἄλληλα
συνεχόμενα ἐπιστηρί|ζονται.   Wes 250

41. Καὶ δι᾽ αὐτοῦ τοῦ κριοῦ τετραγώνου ὄντος δυνήσονται
εὐκόλως ἐπὶ τὸ τεῖχος διέρχεσθαι, ὁμοίως τοῖς ἐπὶ τῶν πύργων
προειρημένοις ⟨γενομένων⟩ ἐπὶ τὰ πλάγια περιφραγῶν. Αἱ γὰρ
κλίμακες αὗται οὐ περιστραφήσονται ‖ ἐπὶ τοὺς μηροὺς   f. 29v
5 παρατρεπόμεναι, ἀλλὰ μενοῦσιν ἀεὶ ἐφεστῶσαι καὶ τὰ αὐτὰ
συντηροῦσαι πρὸς ἀλλήλας διάχωρα. Καὶ ἡ καταγραφὴ
πρόκειται. ‖   f. 30

42. ⟨Π⟩άλιν ἄλλην τάξιν καὶ θέσιν αἱ κλίμακες λαμβάνουσιν
τὴν πρὸς τῷ τείχει ἐπερχομένην, ἴσην οὖσαν καὶ παράλληλον
ἤτοι ὀρθὴν [κατὰ πρόσωπον], καὶ τὰς μὲν βαθμίδας κατὰ
πρόσωπον τοῦ τείχους καὶ ὄπισθεν ἀφορώσας ἔχουσι· τὰ δὲ ἀπ᾽
5 ἀλλήλων διάχωρα ἄνω τε καὶ κάτω οὐχ ὡς αἱ πρῶται ἄνισα
ἔχουσιν, ἀλλ᾽ ἐξ ἴσου τὸ αὐτὸ συντηροῦσι διάστημα. Στέγας
δὲ τὰς αὐτὰς τῶν προτέρων ἔχουσι· παραλλάσσουσι δὲ καὶ κατὰ
τοῦτο. Ἀντὶ γὰρ τοῦ ἑνὸς κριοῦ τοῦ μεταξὺ τῶν προτέρων δύο
κλιμάκων φερομένου δύο ἔξωθεν πρὸς τὰ τῶν μηρῶν πλάγια
10 τιθέμενοι ἐπιφέρονται. Οὗτοι δὲ οἱ κριοὶ κατεργασάμενοί τι ἢ
μετακινήσαντες ἢ λύσαντές τι τῶν προκειμένων τῷ τείχει,
προσεχαλῶντο τὰ ἐκ τῶν ὄπισθεν σχοινία, καὶ | ὁμοῦ τῷ τείχει   Wes 251
αἱ δύο ἐπέρχονται κλίμακες· ἀλλ᾽ ἡ μὲν ἔμπροσθεν ἐπὶ τοὺς
βαθμοὺς αὐτῆς προσεγγίζει τῷ τείχει· ἀφίσταται δὲ ἀπ᾽ αὐτῆς
15 ἡ ἑτέρα, ὅσον καὶ τὸ πρὸς ἀλλήλας κατὰ τὴν ἐπίζευξιν ἀπέχει
διάχωρον, καὶ γίνεται πρὸς τὸ τεῖχος ἐνεργὴς ἀναβάθρα,
καταστρωθεῖσα καὶ περιφραττομένη ἡ ἄνωθεν τῶν κλιμάκων
ἐπίζευξις. Καὶ τὸ σχῆμα ὑπόκειται. ‖   f. 30v

41: 3 προειρημένοις Wes: προειρημένων VB: προσηρτημένων Sch ‖ γενομένων add. Wes ‖
42: 3 κατὰ πρόσωπον secl. Sch ‖ 12 προσεχαλῶντο Sch: προσεχαλῶνται V: προσεχαλῶν B:
προσεχάλων Wes

effective, suspended from the upper roof on two suspension <ropes> of not quite equal height, in order that those thrusting the ram, while standing on the deck of the covered area, may use the ram to attack the upper parts of the walls. For everything that stands up and projects forward is easily broken and knocked down, as it is freestanding and unconnected, such as are the battlements and outworks and all things that are not supported by being secured next to one another.

41. And by means of the ram itself, if it is square, they will be able to pass easily to the wall, when there are fences at the sides like those discussed previously on the towers. For the sidebars of these ladders will not rotate tilting sideways, but they will remain always vertical and maintaining the same intervals to one another. And the depiction is set forth.

<fig. 16>

42. The ladders <can> take on yet another arrangement and position, approaching the wall equal and parallel, that is, upright, and they have the rungs <both> facing the wall and facing back; they do not, as the first ones did, have unequal intervals <between them> above and below, but they maintain the same distance equally. They have the same roofs as the earlier ones. But they differ in this: for instead of the one ram carried between the previous two ladders, two rams are held, set on the outer sides of the sidebars. After these rams are in some way effective in either removing or loosening some of the parts lying on the front of the wall, the back ropes are let down and the two ladders go against the wall simultaneously. But the front one approaches the wall with its rungs; the other stands apart from it by as much as the interval between them at the joined area. And the joined area at the top of the ladders, when decked and fenced, is an effective way to climb to the wall. The drawing is below.

43. ⟨Κ⟩αὶ ἐπὶ ταύτης τῆς θέσεως καὶ ἐπὶ τῆς πρώτης, ἄνευ τῆς
προρρηθείσης δευτέρας τῆς παραλλήλου τῇ θέσει καὶ τάξει
πρὸς τῷ τείχει, τῶν ἐπὶ τῶν κριῶν ἀσχολουμένων οἱ ἐπὶ τῇ στέγῃ
ἑστῶτες καὶ ἄνωθεν προμαχοῦντες θορυβοῦσι καὶ
5 καταπλήττουσι τοὺς προ̣μαχοῦντας πολεμίους· δύο δὲ τοὺς   Wes 252
ὑπερέχοντας ἄνωθεν βαθμοὺς ἐπὶ τῇ τοῦ κριοῦ γενομένῃ κινήσει
βύρσαις περιφράξαντες, προτείχισμα καὶ φυλακὴν ὡς ἐπάλξεις
τείχους ἑαυτοῖς παρέξουσιν.

44. Οὐ μικρὰν δὲ εὐχρηστίαν πρὸς ἀσφαλῆ βοήθειαν καὶ
ὑπηρεσίαν αἱ διπλαῖ παρέξουσι ‖ κλίμακες, ἐὰν καθ’ ἑκάστην   f. 31
τῶν συγκειμένων ἀπὸ τῆς ἰσοϋψοῦς περόνης ἐπὶ τὴν τῆς ἑτέρας
κατέναντι ἰσοϋψῇ, ἤτοι ἐπὶ τὸν ὁμοταγῆ ἑκάστης βαθμόν, κατὰ
5 τὸ αὐτὸ μέτρον ἐπὶ τὸν τῆς ἑτέρας ξύλα ἑτεροπλατῆ ἐπ’ εὐθείας
παραθήσομεν πρὸς τὰ παρεξέχοντα ἄκρα τῶν περονῶν
ὑπεμβαίνοντα καὶ ἀπαράτρεπτα, φυλάττοντα τὰ ἀπ’ ἀλλήλων
τῶν κλιμάκων ἐπὶ τοὺς μηροὺς ἀφεστῶτα διάχωρα, μήτε
ἐπανοίγεσθαι ἐπὶ τῇ τῆς φορᾶς κινήσει δυνάμενα, μήτε τὸ
10 σύνολον ἐπικλείεσθαι. Ἵνα δὲ μὴ ἐκσπῶνται τὰ ξύλα μηδὲ
ἐκπίπτωσι τοῦ κρατουμένου τόπου, χελωνάρια ἐπικαθήμενα ἐπὶ
τοὺς τῶν κλιμάκων μηροὺς προσηλούσθωσαν ὡς τὰ
προειρημένα ἐγγεγλυμμένα ἡμισφαίρια ἢ τὰ κατὰ μέσον
περικεκομμένα γρονθάρια πρὸς τὸ ἐπισφίγγειν καὶ ἐπικρατεῖν
15 τὰ ταῖς περόναις προσπεφυκότα ξύλα. Ὁ δὲ κριός, ὃν κατὰ
μέσον αἱ κλίμακες φέρουσιν, ἐξ ἑκατέρων τῶν πλαγίων κατὰ
τὸ ἔμπροσθεν ἄκρον προσλάβοι ἐπιπήγματα δύο τετρά‖γωνα,   Wes 253
καθάπερ σιαγόνια, ὀρθὰ πρὸς ὕψος ὑπερανεστηκότα τοῦ κριοῦ
πήχεως ἄχρι, εἰς δὲ τὴν προσήλωσιν καὶ κάτωθεν διὰ τὴν τάσιν
20 τοῦ τόνου ἀσφαλιζόμενα. Ταῦτα δὲ τρυπάσθωσαν ἐπ’ εὐθείας
ἀπεναντίον ἀλλήλων πρὸς τὸ μέσον, καὶ ἐπὶ τὰ ἔξωθεν μέρη
τῶν τρημάτων προσηλούσθωσαν στεφάναι στερεαὶ καθάπερ
κρίκοι, δεχόμεναι κατὰ μέσον τὰς λεγομένας χοινικίδας,
ὁμοιουμένας ἐν σχήμασιν ὀστρακίνοις σωληνιδίοις, ‖ ἐκ χαλκοῦ   f. 31v
25 εἰργασμένας ἀπὸ τόρνου ἔσωθεν ἢ ἐξ εὐτόνων ξύλων σιδηροῖς
ἔξωθεν ἐνδεδεμένας πετάλοις, εὐρυτέρας τὰς βάσεις περὶ τὴν
θέσιν ἐχούσας, καὶ κατὰ τὴν περιστροφὴν ὑπὸ τῶν

43: 4 προμαχοῦντες Sch: κριομαχοῦντες VB ‖ 44: 4 ἑκάστης Wes: ἑκάτης VB

43. And with this position and the first (but not the aforementioned second, which is parallel to the wall in position and arrangement), while some men are occupied with the rams, those who stand on the roof and fight in the front line on top raise a clamor and terrify the enemy vanguard. And if they fence with hides the two rungs that project out above where the ram is moved, they will furnish for themselves a rampart and protection like the parapets of a wall.

44. The double ladders will be quite useful in providing unwavering aid and service if at each of the joined <ladders> from the pin at equal height on one to the pin at equal height of the opposite one, that is, on the matching rung of each at the same measured point to the <rung> of the other, we shall place on a straight line planks of unequal width and breadth, which go over the projecting ends of the pins and are immovable; these preserve the intervals that separate the sidebars of one ladder from the other, so they cannot open up during the movement of the <ram->thrust nor close up completely. To keep the planks from being pulled up and falling from the place being controlled, little shell-caps should be placed on the sidebars of the ladders and nailed like the aforementioned hollowed-out hemispheres or the little fists cut out in the middle, for fastening and securing the planks attached to the pins. The ram that the ladders carry between them should receive at the front end on each side two square attachments like cheeks, projecting the distance of a *pechys* straight up above the ram and secured by nailing below also on account of the tension of the spring cord. Let the middle of these <attachments> be drilled at a point on a straight line opposite one another; and onto the outside parts of the holes let strong rims like rings be nailed, which receive in the middle the so-called washers; these are similar in form to small earthenware tubes made inside of bronze with a lathe, or of strong wood bound outside with iron plates, with broader bases around the setting, and during the winding prevented by the nailed rings

προσηλωθέντων κρίκων κωλυομένας τοῦ παρεκπίπτειν τοὺς τῶν
τρημάτων τόπους. Τὰ δὲ τῶν χοινικίδων ἀνακοπέτωσαν στόμια
30 καὶ δεχέσθωσαν κανόνια τετράγωνα ἐπεμβαίνοντα ὡσανεὶ
περιστομίδας, πρὸς τὰ ἄκρα τῶν στομίων παρεξέχοντα· πρὸς ἃ
νεύροις ὠμιαίοις ἢ νωτιαίοις πάντων ζῴων πλὴν συῶν διὰ
μέσου τῶν χοινικίδων διερχομένοις ἐπὶ τῇ τῆς στροφῆς τάσει
διὰ τὸ ἐντόνιον περιειλεῖσθαι, ἢ τοῖς ἐκ νημάτων σηρικῶν
35 ἁδροτέροις μαλάθοις, ἢ καὶ σχοινίοις ἐκ λίνου νηματικοῖς, κατὰ
μέσον εἰσδεχομένοις ξύλον μακρὸν ἐμβαλλόμενον ἐν σχήματι
παλιντόνου ἀγκῶνος ἀντεστραμμένον ὄπισθεν καὶ κατακλεῖδι
κρατούμενον, οἷοί εἰσιν οἱ λιθοβόλοι μονάγκωνες, | οὕς τινες   Wes 254
σφενδόνας καλοῦσιν. Μοχλὸν δὲ ⟨δεῖ⟩ σιδηροῦν ῥιζοκρίκιν
40 ἔχοντα, πρὸς τὰς ῥηθείσας περιστομίδας ἐμβαλλόμενον, βιαίαν
τὴν περιστροφὴν ἐπὶ τῶν χοινικίδων ποιεῖν καὶ σφοδρὰν τὴν
τάσιν ἀπεργάζεσθαι. Ὁ δὲ κριὸς ἀπὸ τῶν κλιμάκων ὠθούμενος
καὶ τῷ τείχει ἐπιφερόμενος ἐπιρρίψει τοῖς τειχοφύλαξιν
ἀπολυθέντα τὸν μονάγκωνα, καὶ πολλὴν ἐργάσεται τῶν
45 ἐφεστώτων ἅλωσιν. Καὶ τὸ σχῆμα καταγέγραπται. || f. 32

45. ⟨Α⟩ὕτη ἡ τοῦ μονάγκωνος κατασκευὴ καὶ πρὸς
καταπαλτικὴν θεωρίαν τοὺς βουλομένους ἐφοδιάσει, πολλὰ
συμβαλλομένη | πρὸς τὸ μακροβολεῖν εὐθυτόνοις τε καὶ   Wes 255
παλιντόνοις ὀργάνοις, ἤτοι λιθοβόλοις τε καὶ ὀξυβελέσιν· ἡ
5 γὰρ τῶν χοινικίδων παράθεσις ἐπιμηκέστερον διὰ τοῦ τόνου τὸ
ὄργανον καὶ περὶ τὴν τάσιν σφοδροτέραν || τὴν ἐξαποστολὴν   f. 32v
ἀπεργάζεται. Ὅσῳ γὰρ κατὰ μῆκος ὁ τόνος παραυξάνεται, ἐπὶ
τοσούτῳ καὶ ἡ τοῦ βέλους ἐξαποστολὴ παρεκτείνεσθαι πέφυκεν,
τῆς τοξίτιδος νευρᾶς πάντα ἀπεργαζομένης καὶ τὴν τῆς
10 ἐξαποστολῆς ὑπομενούσης βίαν, ὅθεν τὴν ταύτης πλοκὴν ἐκ τῶν
εὐτονωτέρων καὶ ἐπιπλέον γυμναζομένων νεύρων τοῦ ζῴου
λέγουσι γίνεσθαι· οἷον ἐλάφου μὲν τῶν ἐν τοῖς σκέλεσι καὶ ποσί,
ταύρου δὲ τῶν ἐπὶ τοῦ αὐχένος· καὶ τὰς μὲν τῶν εὐθυτόνων

44: 32 νεύροις – συῶν: cf. Hero *Bel.* 110. 39–40 Μοχλὸν – ἔχοντα: cf. Hero *Bel.* 110.
45: 9–23 τῆς – ἰσχύος: cf. Hero *Bel.* 109–112.

---

34 διὰ τὸ ἐντόνιον Marsden, 256 adnot. 3: διὰ τὸ εὔτονον VB: δεῖ τῷ ἐντονίῳ Sch ‖ Post
ἐντόνιον add. δεῖ Wes ‖ 39 δεῖ add. Wes

from coming out of the drill holes. The mouths of the washers should be incised and receive square little crossbars that fit on top like clips, projecting over the ends of the mouths. Onto these <crossbars> wrap shoulder or back tendons of any animals except pigs; these run through the middle of the washers <to create> tension when turned by means of the stretcher; or stouter strands (?) of silk threads or even ropes woven from flax. These receive in their midst a long wooden beam inserted in the form of a palintone arm, pulled back and controlled by a retaining pin, like the one-armed stone throwers that some call slings. It is necessary that an iron lever with a ring at the bottom, inserted onto one of the aforementioned clips, create the forceful turn on the washers and increase the tension. When the ram is thrust from the ladders and directed against the wall, it will cast the freed one-arm <beam> at the guards on the wall and will cause great destruction for those standing there. And the drawing is depicted.

<fig. 18>

45. This construction of the one-arm <device> will also furnish interested parties with theoretical information on catapults, as it contributes much for long-range shooting with euthytone and palintone engines, that is stone shooters and missile shooters. For the juxtaposition of the washers makes the engine longer because of the spring cord and thus the discharge more forceful through the tension. For by as much as the spring cord is increased in length, by so much also is the discharge of the missile naturally extended, the bow string tendon doing all the work and sustaining the shock of the discharge; whence they say that this <cord> should be plaited from the more powerful and more exercised tendons of the animal; for example, in the case of the deer from those in the legs and the feet, of the bull those in the neck. And the tendons of the euthytones are rounded in their

νευρὰς στρογγύλας περὶ τὴν πλοκὴν εἶναι, διὰ τὸ πρὸς τὰς τῶν
15 ὀϊστῶν ἐμπίπτειν χηλάς· τὰς δὲ τῶν παλιντόνων πλατείας,
καθάπερ ζώνας, ἐξ ἄκρων ἀγκύλας ἐχούσας, πρὸς ἃς οἱ ἀγκῶνες
ἐμβιβάζονται, ὅπως ὁ λίθος ὑπὸ τοῦ μέσου τῆς τοξίτιδος κατὰ
πλάτος τυπτόμενος καλῶς ἐξαποσταλῇ μὴ παρεκπίπτων πρὸς
τὰ ἄκρα. Τὸν δὲ ἐν τοῖς ἀγκῶσι τόνον καὶ ἐκ τριχῶν φασι
20 γυναικείων πλέκεσθαι· λεπταὶ γὰρ οὖσαι καὶ μακραὶ καὶ πολλῷ
ἐλαίῳ τραφεῖσαι, ὅταν πλακῶσι, πολλὴν εὐτονίαν
λαμβάνουσιν, ὥστε μὴ ἀπᾴδειν αὐτὰς τῆς διὰ τῶν νεύρων
ἰσχύος. Ἀλλὰ περὶ μὲν τούτων νῦν ἅλις. Ἐν γὰρ τῇ βελοποιϊκῇ
πραγματείᾳ λεπτομερῶς | τοῖς ζητητικωτέροις πρὸς κατασκευὴν   Wes 256
25 οὐ μόνον ταῦτα, ἀλλὰ καὶ αἱ τῶν τρημάτων ἐν τοῖς ὀργάνοις
διάμετροι, οἵ τε ἐν τριπλασίονι λόγῳ τῶν ἐν ταῖς βάσεσι
διαμέτρων ὅμοιοι πρὸς ἀλλήλους ‖ δεικνύμενοι κύλινδροι, καὶ   f. 33
ὁ πολυθρύλητος τοῦ κύβου διπλασιασμός, δι' ὧν τὰ μεγέθη
τῶν βελῶν πρὸς τὰ τῶν τυχόντων ὀργάνων διπλάσια ἢ καὶ
30 τριπλάσια γινόμενα ἐπὶ τοῖς αὐτοῖς ἐξαποστέλλονται μήκεσι.
Μαθηματικῶς ἐκεῖ καὶ ὀργανικῶς πάντα τῷ Ἀλεξανδρεῖ
Ἥρωνι πρὸς ἀπόδειξιν διεξήτασται.

   46. ⟨Γ⟩ίνεται καὶ ἑτέρα τῷ εἴδει κλῖμαξ ὑπότροχος, ἀπὸ ξύλων
εὐτόνων τε καὶ ἐλαφρῶν καὶ αὐτὴ κατασκευαζομένη, πρὸς ἣν
ἄλλη ὡς ἐν τάξει ἐπιβάθρας κατὰ μέσον ἄνωθεν ἐμβαλλομένη
ζεύγνυται δι' ἀξονίου, κυλινδρικὰ καὶ λεῖα ἀπὸ τόρνου
5 ἔχοντος τὰ πρὸς τοῖς μηροῖς συμβαλλόμενα ἄκρα, ὅπως εὐλύτως
πρὸς τὴν ἑτέραν καταφερομένη ἐπικλείηται, καὶ πάλιν πρὸς
αὐτὴν ἐπανάγηται πάρορθος ὑπὸ σχοινίων ὄπισθεν κρατουμένη,
ἐπιδιδομένη τε καὶ ἐφελκομένη συμμέτρως διὰ μαγγάνων τῶν
λεγομένων πολυσπάστων, ἤτοι καρείων εὐτρόχων, δύναμιν
10 βιαίαν ἐπὶ τῇ | ἀνέσει καὶ τάσει τῶν σχοινίων ἐμποιούντων διὰ   Wes 257
τῆς τῶν παρακειμένων τροχίλων συμφυοῦς παραθέσεως.
Κωλυμάτια δὲ ἄνωθεν ἐπὶ τῇ ἱσταμένῃ γινέσθωσαν ‖ ἢ   f. 33v
παρεξοχαί τινες, ὄπισθεν ἀναστρεφομένην τὴν ἀνορθουμένην

26–27 οἵ – κύλινδροι: cf. Hero *Bel.* 115.

45: 15 ἐμπίπτειν Sch (cf. Hero *Bel.* 110:3): ἐκπίπτειν VB ‖ 20 μακραὶ Wes: μακρεαὶ VB
‖ 32 Post διεξήτασται vac. quattuor lin. V

plaiting, in order to fit into the notches of the arrows. Those of the palintones are broader like belts, having loops at the ends, into which the arms are placed so that the stone, struck by the middle of the bow string on the broad side, may discharge correctly without falling to the sides. They say that the spring cord in the arms should also be plaited from the hair of women, for these are slender and long and well nourished with oil; whenever plaited, they obtain great power, so as to equal the strength of tendons. But enough now of these matters. For in the *Artillery* treatise not only <are> these issues <discussed> in detail for those who seek more <information> about construction, but also the diameters of the holes in the engines, the spring cylinders <which> are shown to be similar to one another in the triplicate ratio of their base diameters, and the well-known doubling of the cube, through which projectiles, when doubled or even tripled in magnitude in relation to the <magnitudes> of any engines, are discharged over the same lengths. All these things have been detailed and proven therein mathematically and from the engineering perspective by Heron of Alexandria.

46. There is also a different form of ladder with wheels at the bottom, this too constructed of strong and light wood; on top of it another <ladder> is inserted in the middle arranged as a dropbridge, joined by an axle whose ends, which are attached to the sidebars, are cylindrical and smooth, <made> on a lathe, so that when <the upper ladder> is brought down toward the other, it may be easily folded <against it> and in turn may be raised up to it almost straight, controlled by ropes at the back; <it is> let down and pulled up commensurably through pulleys of the so-called pulley systems, that is, smooth-running sheaves, which impart forceful power to the relaxation and contraction of the ropes through the cooperative juxtaposition of the pulley wheels side by side. There should be stops on top of the standing <ladder> or some projections to catch the <ladder> being raised up

ὑποδεχόμεναι, μήπως ἀθρόως ἐπὶ τῇ κορυφῇ τῆς ἑτέρας
15 ἀναχθεῖσα ἐπιβαρήσῃ ὄπισθεν καὶ κατενεχθεῖσα πτῶσιν ἐπὶ
τοῖς ἐργαζομένοις μᾶλλον ἀπειλήσει. Καί, εἰ μὲν μονόξυλος εἴη
ἡ κάτωθεν ἵστασθαι μέλλουσα κλῖμαξ, τὰς βαθμίδας ἐχέτω
μίαν παρὰ μίαν τῶν μηρῶν παρεξεχούσας καὶ τετρημένας ἐπὶ
τῇ ἐξοχῇ, ὅπως διὰ τῶν τρημάτων σχοινίον εὔτονον
20 ἐκτετανυσμένον διερχόμενον ἀδιάκλαστον αὐτὴν φυλάξῃ·
σύνθετος δὲ οὖσα τὴν τῶν προειρημένων κλιμάκων κατασκευὴν
ἐπιδεχέσθω. Ἡ δὲ ἀνάγεσθαι μέλλουσα πρὸς ὅλον αὐτῆς τὸ
μῆκος καταστρωθήτω σανίσι, καὶ σχοινίοις περιειληθεῖσα
στηριχθήτω, ἀσφαλὴς διαβάθρα ἐπὶ τὸ τεῖχος γινομένη·
25 ἀνισταμένη γὰρ αὐτὴ ἐπὶ τῆς ἑτέρας καὶ φερομένη πάρορθος,
ἅμα τῷ τείχει αἱ δύο προσάγονται· καὶ ἡ μὲν κάτωθεν ἱσταμένη,
ἡ καὶ τὰς βαθμίδας πρὸς τὴν ἀνάβασιν ἔχουσα, ἀφιστάσθω τοῦ
τείχους ὅσον σταθμῷ τινι καὶ μέτρῳ τῶν σχοινίων
προσχαλωμένων, τὸ τῆς καταστρωθείσης κατερχόμενον ἄκρον
30 τῷ τείχει ἐπιτεθῇ καὶ ἐπίβασις τοῖς βουλομένοις εἴη· ἱκανὸν δὲ
τὸ πλάτος τῆς τε κλίμακος καὶ ἐπιβάθρας γινέσθω, ὅπως κατὰ
τάξιν πέντε ἢ τέσσαρες ἢ τὸ ἐλάχιστον τρεῖς ἄνδρες στοιχηδὸν
ἀνέρχωνται ἐπὶ τῆς διαβάθρας διερχόμενοι, ὡς ἂν ὁμοψύχως
τοῖς ἐπὶ τὸ τεῖχος ‖ προμαχοῦσιν ┃ ἀντιμαχήσωνται. Περιφραγαὶ   f. 34
35 δὲ ἐκ βυρσῶν ἐφ’ ἑκάτερα τὰ μέρη τῆς τε κλίμακος καὶ   Wes 258
διαβάθρας γινέσθωσαν διὰ τὰ ἐκ πλαγίου ἐπιφερόμενα βέλη.
Δεῖ δὲ τὴν κάτωθεν ἱσταμένην κλίμακα πασσάλοις ἐμπεπηγόσιν
ἀσφαλίζεσθαι καὶ σχοινίοις ἀποτετανυσμένοις ἐπιστηρίζεσθαι
καὶ ὑψηλοτέραν τοῦ τείχους εὑρίσκεσθαι ποδῶν μὴ ἔλασσον
40 τριῶν, ὅπως τὰ ἐκ τοῦ τείχους κατερχόμενα πρὸς τὸ ἀνωφερὲς
ἀδυνατῶσι διέρχεσθαι καὶ ὄλεθρον ἐπὶ τοῖς ἀνιοῦσιν
ἐργάζεσθαι. Κατωφεροῦς δὲ τῆς ἐπιβάθρας ἐπὶ τὸ τεῖχος οὔσης,
προθυμότεροι μᾶλλον οἱ στρατιῶται καὶ εὐτολμότεροι πρὸς τὸ
κατωφερὲς ἔσονται· εἰ δὲ ταπεινοτέρα τοῦ τείχους ἡ κλῖμαξ
45 εἴη, τὰ ἐναντία τούτων ἀποβήσεται. Καὶ τὰ σχήματα
ὑπόκεινται. ‖ ┃   f. 34v

46: 24 ἀσφαλὴς – γινομένη: cf. Philo Mech. 95:42–43.

46: 25 αὐτὴ Wes: αὐτῃ VB ‖ 32 ἐλάχιστον Sch: ἔλασσον VB ‖ 33 ἀνέρχωνται Sch: ἀνέρχονται
VB ‖ 34 ἀντιμαχήσωνται Sch: ἀντιμαχήσονται VB

as it turns backward, lest, when it is suddenly brought up to the top of the other, the weight shift backward and, brought down, it will threaten instead to fall on those operating it. And if the ladder that is going to stand on the bottom is of single-beam construction, it should have rungs alternately projecting beyond the sidebars and be drilled on the projecting parts, so that a strong rope stretched taut may run through the holes and keep it unbroken. If it is composite, it should be constructed like the aforementioned ladders. The ladder that will be raised up should be decked over its entire length with boards and secured with ropes wrapped around it, to become a stable cross-bridge to the wall. For when this <ladder> has been raised up on the other and carried almost straight, the two <ladders> are brought up to the wall together. The one <ladder> that stands below, and also has the rungs for climbing, should stand away from the wall such that, when the ropes are slackened by some amount and gradually, the end of the decked ladder that comes down may be placed on the wall and enable free passage. The width of the ladder and of the drop-bridge should be sufficient to permit five or four or at least three men in a row to go up in good order <and> pass over the cross-bridge, to fight with unanimous spirit against the front-line fighters on the wall. There should be fences of hides on each part of the ladder and on the cross-bridge <to protect> against missiles coming from the sides. The ladder standing below must be secured by stakes driven <into the ground> and supported with ropes stretched <to the stakes>, and it should be no less than 3 *podes* higher than the wall so that objects coming down from the wall will not be able to penetrate to the higher position and injure those climbing up. If the drop-bridge slopes down to the wall, the soldiers will rather be more eager and courageous as they are going down. If the ladder should be lower than the wall, the opposite of this will occur. And the drawings are below.

47. ⟨Γ⟩ενήσεται δὲ εὔχρηστος γέφυρα καὶ μόνη ἡ ῥηθεῖσα
διαβάθρα, ὅταν ἀδυνατῶμεν χωννύειν τάφρους εὐρείας ἢ
βαθείας τε καὶ ὑδάτων μεστάς, εἰ σύμμετρος μήκει πρὸς τὰ τῶν
τάφρων γένηται πλάτη καί, ὡς ἐμάθομεν, εὐλύτως ἐπιζευχθῇ,
5 χωστρίδος ἔμπροσθεν χελώνης πάρορθος ἀνισταμένη, ὑπὸ
σχοινίων ὄπισθεν ἑλκομένη καὶ ἐπιδιδομένη ἢ ὑπὸ τῶν
ῥηθέντων ἄνωθεν πολυσπάστων, ὅταν ἔξογκον ἐπὶ τοσοῦτον τὸ
μέγεθος καὶ ἡ φορὰ τοῦ βάρους τῆς διαβάθρας εἴη· φερομένη
γὰρ ὑπὸ τῆς χελώνης καὶ προσελθοῦσα τῷ ἐμπροσθίῳ χείλει
10 τῆς τάφρου, τὰ ἐκ τῶν ὄπισθεν προσχαλῶνται σχοινία καὶ
κατερχόμενον τὸ ἄκρον πρὸς τὸ ἀπεναντίον ἐπιτίθεται χεῖλος,
καὶ γίνεται ὁδὸς ἀβλαβὴς τοῖς βουλομένοις εὐπροθύμως μετὰ
λαισῶν διέρχεσθαι πηλῷ περὶ τὰ πλέγματα ἐπικεχρισμένων ἢ
τέφρᾳ αἵματι ἀναμεμιγμένῃ καὶ βύρσαις βοῶν νεοσφαγῶν
15 σκεπομένων διά τε τὰ πυροβόλα καὶ τὰ ἐπεγχεόμενα
τεθερμασμένα ὑγρά. Καὶ καθάπερ ἐπὶ τῶν ὀρυκτρίδων
προδέ|δεικται χελωνῶν, οὕτως καὶ τὴν τῶν λαισῶν διάστασιν   Wes 260
ἔλασσον τῶν κ΄ ποδῶν ἀπ᾽ ἀλλήλων ποιεῖσθαι, καὶ ἀπὸ τριῶν
ποδῶν ἄνωθεν τῆς γῆς ἀρχομένους τὴν ἐπὶ τὸ τεῖχος ὀρυγὴν
20 κατεργάζεσθαι. Καὶ τὰ σχήματα ὑπόκεινται. ‖   f. 35

48. ⟨Ο⟩ἱ δὲ περὶ Φίλωνα τὸν Βυζάντιον, πρὸς τὰς τοιαύτας
τάφρους χελώνας προθέμενοι χωστρίδας, πρὸς αὐτὰς σχεδίας
ἐπιζευγνύουσι, καὶ πρὸς ὃ ἂν βούλωνται μέρος τοῦ τείχους τοὺς
στρατιώτας προσάγουσι, σιδηροῦς προσηλοῦντας πασσάλους,
5 οἳ στομωθέντες καὶ ὀξυνθέντες εἰς τὰς συμβολὰς καὶ συμφύσεις
λιθίνων τε καὶ πλινθίνων ὑπεισέρχονται τειχῶν, σιδηραῖς
σφύραις ὑπὸ τῶν ἀναβαινόντων τυπτόμενοι, καὶ ἀγκίστροις
ἅπερ ἐπὶ σχοινίων σὺν τοῖς δικτύοις ἅμα πρὸς τὰς ἐπάλξεις
ἐπιρριπτούντων ἐπιδρασσομένοις, ὥστε μὴ χαλεπαίνειν πρὸς
10 τὴν ἀνάβασιν τοὺς ἐθισθέντας μάλιστα στρατιώτας· τοιαύτη

47: 2–3 ἀδυνατῶμεν – βαθείας: cf. Philo Mech. 97:30–34.   14 τέφρᾳ – ἀναμεμιγμένῃ:
cf. Philo Mech. 99:27.   16–20 Καὶ – κατεργάζεσθαι: cf. Apollod. 144:6–9.   **48:** 2–
4 χωστρίδας – προσάγουσι: cf. Philo Mech. 97:32–33.   4–11 σιδηροῦς – Αἰγύπτιοι: cf.
Philo Mech. 102:19–27.

47: 6 ἢ Wes: ἡ VB ‖ 17 Post διάστασιν add. δεῖ Wes ‖ **48:** 1 Οἱ Wes: ι V: εἰ B

<fig. 19>

47. The aforementioned cross-bridge can also serve as a useful bridge by itself, whenever we are unable to fill in ditches because they are too wide or deep and filled with water, if it should be commensurate in length to the widths of the ditches and, as we have learned, joined loosely <on an axle>, standing almost straight up in front of the filler tortoise; it is dragged up and let down by ropes at the back, or by the previously mentioned pulley systems, whenever the size and burden of the weight of the cross-bridge should be of such great magnitude. For after <the cross-bridge is> carried by the tortoise and reaches the front edge of the ditch, the ropes at the back are slackened and the front comes down <and> is set on the opposite edge. And it becomes a secure passage for those intent on crossing over very eagerly with *laisai* smeared around their plaited parts with clay or with ash mixed with blood and covered with the hides of freshly slaughtered cattle to guard against incendiaries and boiling liquids poured from above. As indicated earlier for the excavating tortoises, in this case too make the interval between the *laisai* less than 20 *podes* and the digging at the wall should begin 3 *podes* above the ground. And the drawings are below.

<fig. 20>

48. The <men> of Philo of Byzantium, bringing forward filler tortoises at such ditches, join rafts to them, and to whatever part of the wall desired bring up soldiers who nail iron stakes, which, being hardened and made pointed, are inserted into the joints and seams of stone and brick walls, hammered with iron mallets by those climbing; and <they used> hooks that are thrown on ropes together with nets to the parapets <and> take hold, so that the most trained soldiers have no difficulty in the climb. For using

48.11–50.4

γὰρ μεθόδῳ Αἰγύπτιοι χρώμενοι τὰς ἀπαρα|σκεύους καὶ Wes 261
ἀνισχύρους πόλεις καὶ ταπεινὰς πρὸς ὕψος πολιορκεῖν ῥᾳδίως
εἰώθασιν. Καὶ τὰ σχήματα ὑπόκεινται. ‖ f. 35v

49. ⟨Δ⟩εῖ δὲ ἐπὶ πάσαις ταῖς κλίμαξι καὶ ταῖς ἐπὶ τῷ τείχει
γινομέναις ἀναβάσεσιν ἢ ἐπιβάθραις σκοπεῖν τὰ
προκαταρτιζόμενα ἐκ λίνου παχέα ἀμφίβληστρα·
ἐπιρριπτόμενα γὰρ καὶ ἀθρόως πάλιν ἐπισυρόμενα τοὺς
5 ἀνερχομένους ἢ ἐπιβαίνοντας ζωγροῦσι καὶ τοῖς ἐχθροῖς
ὑποχειρίους παριστᾶσι. Καὶ πρὸς μὲν ταῖς κλίμαξιν ἀβλαβῆ
τὴν ἀνάβασιν παρεφυλαξάμεθα, ὡς ἐπὶ τῶν ἀγκυρωτῶν
δοκίδων καὶ τῶν κατερχομένων βαρῶν ἀνωτέρω τεχνησάμενοι
διωρίσαμεν. Πρὸς δὲ τὰς ἐπιβάθρας χρὴ δύο ἔμπροσθεν
10 παριστάνειν ξύλα εὐλύτως ἐπιζευγνύμενα κάτωθεν, κατὰ μὲν
πρόσωπον τῶν ἐναντίων ῥᾳδίως καταπίπτοντα καὶ ἀντεχόμενα
ὄπισθεν, ἄνωθεν δὲ πρὸς ὄνυχα ἐκκεκομμένα κατὰ κορυφὴν
συννεύοντα καὶ πρὸς ὀξεῖαν ἐφαρμυζόμενα γωνίαν, | τρίγωνον Wes 262
σχῆμα ‖ σὺν τῇ βάσει τελοῦντα καὶ ἥλους σιδηροῦς ἐκ πλαγίων f. 36
15 δεχόμενα, ὅπως ἐπιρριπτόμενα τὰ ἀμφίβληστρα ἐκεῖθεν
παρεμπλέκηται πρὸς τὴν ἀνάπαλιν ἕλξιν καὶ ἐπισυναγωγὴν
μηκέτι ἀναστρέφοντα. Οἱ δὲ τῷ τείχει ἐπιβαίνειν μέλλοντες
κατὰ πρόσωπον ταῦτα τῶν ἐναντίων καταρριπτοῦντες πρὸς τὴν
ἐπίβασιν ἀνεπηρέαστοι συντηρηθήσονται. Εἰ δέ τινες τῶν ἐπὶ
20 τῆς διαβάθρας ἑστώτων μετὰ στρεπτῶν ἐγχειριδίων πυροβόλων
κατὰ πρόσωπον τῶν πολεμίων διὰ πυρὸς ἀκοντίζουσι, τοσοῦτον
τοὺς τῷ τείχει προεστῶτας πτοήσουσιν, ὥστε τὴν ἀπὸ τῆς μάχης
προσβολὴν καὶ τὴν τοῦ πυρὸς μὴ ὑποφέροντας ῥύμην τάχιον
αὐτοὺς ὑπεκφεύξεσθαι τοῦ τόπου. Καὶ τὰ σχήματα
25 καταγέγραπται. ‖ f. 36v

50. ⟨Δ⟩υνατὸν δέ ἐστι καὶ ἄνευ κλιμάκων ἐπὶ τεῖχος
ἀνέρχεσθαι, ὡς ὁ | Ἀσκρηνὸς Κτησίβιος ὁ τοῦ Ἀλεξανδρέως Wes 263
Ἥρωνος καθηγητὴς ἐν τοῖς ἑαυτοῦ ἐδήλωσεν Ὑπομνήμασι, διὰ
μηχανήματος τοιούτου, καθ' ἅ φησιν Ἀθηναῖος· ὅτι δεῖ

49: 2–6 τὰ – παριστᾶσι: cf. Philo Mech. 95:39–44. 7–8 ἀγκυρωτῶν δοκίδων: Philo Mech.
85: 37–38. **50:** 1–31 ⟨Δ⟩υνατὸν – ἀνατιθέμενον: cf. Ath. Mech. 29:9–31:2.

49: 1 Δεῖ Wes: εῖ V: εἰ B ‖ 20 Post ἑστώτων add. καὶ m. rec. V ‖ **50:** 4 δεῖ Wes: δεῖν VB

such a method the Egyptians were accustomed to besiege readily unprepared, weak cities which had low walls. And the drawings are below.

<fig. 21>

49. With all ladders and ascents on walls, or with drop-bridges, it is necessary to look out for thick casting nets prepared in advance from flax; for when thrown and suddenly dragged back they capture alive those climbing <the ladders> or crossing <the bridges> and put them into enemy hands. We have <already> provided for a secure ascent on the ladders, just as we earlier devised <and> prescribed for use against the poles with anchorlike <hooks> and heavy descending objects. But for drop-bridges it is necessary to set in front two beams joined loosely at the bottom, which fall readily in the direction of the enemy and are held at the back, but are precisely cut in front, converging at the peak and fitted together in a sharp angle, completing with the base beam a triangular form; they have iron nails on the sides, so that the casting nets when thrown are entangled there <and can> no longer be reversed for dragging back and gathering together. Those who are about to mount the wall will be preserved unharmed in their crossing by dropping these <beams> in the direction of the enemy. And if some of those standing on the cross-bridge also use swivel tube, handheld incendiaries to shoot fire in the direction of the enemy, they will so terrify <the defenders> standing on the front of the wall that they will quickly abandon their position, not enduring the attack of battle and the force of fire. And the drawings are depicted.

<fig. 22>

50. One can also mount a wall without ladders by using the following machine, as the Ascrian Ctesibius, the teacher of Heron of Alexandria, made clear in his *Commentaries,* according to Athenaeus. It is necessary to construct a four-wheeled wagon,

5 κατασκευάζειν τετράτροχον ἄμαξαν, περισκεπῆ πάντοθεν
οὖσαν, ἢ κριοφόρον χελώνην, καὶ πρὸς θατέραν τούτων κατὰ
μέσον πηγνύναι δύο ξύλα ὄρθια ἱστάμενα, καὶ ἕτερον πλάγιον
ἑτεροπλατὲς ἄνωθεν πρὸς αὐτὰ κινούμενον κατὰ πλάτος
ἐπιθεῖναι, ἐκκοπὰς ἔχον στρογγύλας ἀφ᾽ ἑκατέρων τῶν μερῶν,
10 καὶ δεχόμενον ὡς αὐλόν τινα ἐπικείμενον σωληνοειδῆ
καμαροειδέσι ξύλοις κατεσκευασμένον, ἐκ πλαγίων δὲ
προσηλωμένον καὶ σανίδας ἔξωθεν καθηλωμένας ἐπιδεχόμενον
ἢ βύρσαις μόναις παχείαις καὶ εὐτόνοις ὡς ἐλαφροτέραις
περιπεφραγμένον, ὥστε χωρεῖν ἄνδρα ἔνοπλον εἰσέρχεσθαι
15 ὄρθιον καὶ ὁτὲ μὲν προπορεύεσθαι, ὁτὲ δὲ ἀναχωρεῖν· οὗ
γενομένου μετεωρίζεσθαι ἄνωθεν τὸν αὐλὸν καὶ μεταφέρεσθαι
πρὸς ὃ ἄν τις ἐθέλῃ μέρος. Τοῦ δὲ ἑνὸς μέρους ἐπὶ τοῦ ἐδάφους
κατερχομένου, τὸ ἕτερον εἰς ὕψος ἀναχθήσεται, διὰ τὸ ἐπὶ τὰς
ἐκκοπὰς τοῦ ἐπικειμένου ξύλου σιδηραῖς ἁλύσεσι πρὸς
20 ἑκατέραν αὐτοῦ πλευρὰν ἐφελκόμενον περι|στρέφεσθαι. Wes 264
Μετεώρου δὲ φερομένου ὅτε τὸ στόμα αὐτοῦ κατὰ τὸ τεῖχος
γένηται, τῆς τετρατρόχου προσαχθείσης χελώνης εἴτε ἀμάξης,
τὸν ἔνδοθεν ὄντα διανοῖξαι τὴν κατέμπροσθεν θύραν καὶ τῷ
τείχει ἔνοπλον ἐπιβῆναι· ὁμοίως δὲ ‖ καὶ πλείονας διὰ τῆς αὐτῆς f. 37
25 τοῦ αὐλοῦ βάσεως ἔνδον τὴν πρόοδον ἔχοντας. Ὑποζώννυται
δὲ ὁ ἐπὶ ταῖς προσηλωθείσαις σανίσιν αὐλὸς πάντοθεν σχοινίοις
εὐτόνοις ἐνδυναμούμενος, καὶ βυρσοῦται δέρμασι διαβρόχοις,
ἵνα ἀπὸ τῶν πυροφόρων φυλάττηται. Μέτρα δὲ τοῦ
προβλήματος τούτου πρὸς τὴν κατασκευὴν μὴ συντετάχεναι τὸν
30 Κτησίβιον, ἀλλ᾽ ὑπόμνημα μόνον ὡς μαθηματικοῖς τοῖς
μεταχειριζομένοις ἀρχιτέκτοσι ταῦτα ἀνατιθέμενον. Ἔξεστι
γὰρ τούτοις τὴν τῶν ὀργάνων μετασκευάζειν συμμετρίαν καὶ
πρὸς τὴν ἀνήκουσαν μεταφέρειν τοῦ τόπου χρείαν. Ἡμεῖς δὲ
γυμνασίας χάριν τοῖς εἰσαγομένοις ἐξεθέμεθα εἰς κατασκευὴν
35 τοῦ προβλήματος συμμετρίαν τοιαύτην.
   51. Γινέσθω τοίνυν τὸ σχάριον τὸ ἐπικείμενον ἐπὶ τῆς
τετρατρόχου ἢ ἑξατρόχου ἀμάξης εἴτε χελώνης κατὰ μὲν μῆκος
πηχῶν δεκαπέντε, ἐπὶ δὲ πλάτος δέκα· αἱ δὲ τῶν τροχῶν

---

12 σανίδας... καθηλωμένας scripsi: σανίσιν... καθηλωμέναις VB ‖ 15 ὁτὲ... ὁτὲ Sch:
ὅτε... ὅτε VB ‖ 27 ἐνδυναμουμένως Sch

covered on all sides, or a ram-carrying tortoise, and on either of them to affix two vertical beams in the center, and to place another beam with unequal sides on top transversely on its wide side, which moves on these, having round notches on either end. And it receives a kind of tube imposed on it, like a pipe, constructed with vaulted beams, nailed at the sides and also receives boards nailed on the outside — or it is fenced only with thick and strong hides, as these are lighter — so that there is room for an armed man to enter standing up straight and to go both forward and backward. This done, <he says> to raise the tube up into the air and transfer it to any desired position. When one part comes down to the ground, the other will be raised up high because it rotates on the notches of the imposed beam, dragged by iron chains to either of its ends. If it is raised in the air, when its mouth reaches the wall — the four-wheeled tortoise or wagon having been deployed — the man inside opens the front door and mounts onto the wall fully armed. In the same way even more men can proceed inside through the same base of the tube. The tube with the nailed boards is girded <and> strengthened all around by strong ropes and is covered with wet hides to be protected from fire-bearing <missiles>. Ctesibius did not draw up measurements for the construction of this problem, but only a note entrusting them to the master builders, as they are mathematicians, who undertake <construction>. For these men can alter the proportion<s> of the engines and make changes in accordance with the specific requirements of the topography. As an exercise we have set forth for beginners such a proportion for construction of the problem.

51. The undercarriage imposed on the four- or six-wheeled wagon or tortoise should be in length 15 *pecheis,* in width 10; the

διάμετροι ἤτοι τὰ ὕψη ἀνὰ πηχῶν δύο ἥμισυ, καὶ τὰ μὲν πρὸς
5 ὕψος ἱστάμενα ὄρθια ἀνὰ πηχῶν γινέσθωσαν εἴκοσι· τὸ δὲ ἐπ᾽
αὐτὰ κινούμενον πλάγιον σὺν τῷ ἐπικειμένῳ αὐλῷ πηχῶν κατὰ
μῆκος τριάκοντα, πλάτος ἔχον κατὰ τὴν βάσιν ποδὸς ἑνὸς
ἡμίσεος, τὸ δὲ πάχος σπιθαμιαῖον· ἵνα, ὃν | λόγον ἔχει τὸ μῆκος   Wes 265
τοῦ σχαρίου πρὸς τὸ πλάτος, τὸν αὐτὸν καὶ τὸ κινούμενον
10 πλάγιον πρὸς τὰ ἱστάμενα ὄρθια· καὶ ὃν πάλιν ἔχει λόγον ‖ τὸ   f. 37v
αὐτὸ κινούμενον πρὸς τὸ μῆκος τοῦ σχαρίου, τὸν αὐτὸν καὶ τὰ
ἱστάμενα ὄρθια πρὸς τὸ αὐτὸ πλάτος· ὡς γὰρ δεκαπέντε πρὸς
δέκα, οὕτως τριάκοντα πρὸς κ΄· καὶ ὡς τριάκοντα πρὸς ιε΄,
⟨οὕτως⟩ κ΄ πρὸς δέκα· ἡμιόλιος δὲ ὁ ιε΄ τοῦ ι΄· ἔχει γὰρ τὸν ι΄
15 καὶ τὸ ἥμισυ αὐτοῦ· ἡμιόλιος ἄρα καὶ ὁ λ΄ τοῦ κ΄· διπλάσιος δὲ
πάλιν ὁ λ΄ τοῦ ιε΄, διπλάσιος ἄρα καὶ ὁ κ΄ τοῦ ι΄. Ὁμοίως δὲ καὶ
τὸ τῆς βάσεως πλάτος πρὸς τὸ αὐτῆς πάχος διπλάσιον. Ἀλλὰ
καὶ αἱ τῶν τροχῶν διάμετροι σύμμετροι πρὸς τὴν καταμέτρησιν
καὶ σύμφωνοι ἐν λόγῳ δειχθήσονται· καὶ γὰρ οἱ δύο ἥμισυ
20 πήχεις τῆς διαμέτρου ἑξάκι μὲν [καὶ ἥμισυ] τὸν ιε΄ μετροῦσι,
τετράκι δὲ τὸν δέκα, καὶ δωδεκάκι μὲν τὸν λ΄, τὸν δὲ κ΄ ὀκτάκι·
καὶ ἔστιν ὡς ὁ ἓξ πρὸς τέσσαρα, οὕτως ὁ τριάκοντα πρὸς κ΄· καὶ
ὡς ὁ ιε΄ πρὸς τὸν ἕξ, οὕτως ὁ ι΄ πρὸς τὸν δ΄· ἡμιόλιος δὲ ὁ ἓξ τοῦ
δ΄· ἔχει γὰρ τὸν δ΄ καὶ τὸ ἥμισυ αὐτοῦ· ἡμιόλιος ἄρα καὶ ὁ ιε΄
25 τοῦ ι΄· διπλασιεφήμισυς δὲ ὁ ιε΄ τοῦ ἕξ· διπλα|σιεφήμισυς ἄρα   Wes 266
καὶ ὁ ι΄ τοῦ τέσσαρα· ὥστε καὶ ἡ τῆς διαμέτρου τῶν τροχῶν
καταμέτρησις σύμφωνος πρὸς τὴν τοῦ μεγέθους κατασκευὴν
εὑρίσκεται, ὡς τὸν αὐτὸν τοῖς μετρουμένοις κατὰ ἀναλογίαν
σῴζουσα λόγον. Καὶ τὸ σχῆμα [δὲ] καταγέγραπται. ‖   f. 38
52. ⟨Ὁ⟩ δὲ αὐτὸς αὐλὸς ἐνεργέστερος πρὸς πολιορκίαν
γενήσεται, εἰ μεῖζον κατὰ μέγεθος ἐπὶ τὸ ἔμπροσθεν στόμιον
εἴη, καὶ ὑπὸ δύο κλειομένων θυρίδων τὴν ἐξέλευσιν ἔχοι, ὥστε
καὶ δύο ἐνόπλους ἄνδρας τοὺς τῷ τείχει ὁμοῦ ἐπιβαίνειν
5 μέλλοντας παρὰ μέρος ἑστῶτας ἐπ᾽ ἀλλήλους εἰσδέχεσθαι. Αἱ
δὲ τοῦ αὐτοῦ στομίου θύραι ἔξωθεν καταπληκτικαὶ διὰ γλυφῆς
ἐκφανοῦς καὶ πολυχρώμου γραφῆς σὺν τῷ ἐμπροσθίῳ μέρει τοῦ
αὐλοῦ γινέσθωσαν, δράκοντος ἢ λέοντος πυροφόρον

51: 8 ἔχει B: ἔχῃ V ‖ 14 οὕτως add. Wes ‖ 20 ἑξάκις Wes ‖ καὶ ἥμισυ secl. Wes ‖ 21 τετράκις Wes ‖ δωδεκάκις Wes ‖ ὀκτάκις Wes ‖ 29 δὲ secl. Sch ‖ **52:** 3 ἔχοι Wes: ἔχει VB

diameter of the wheels, that is, their heights, about 21/2 *pecheis* and the standing uprights about 20 *pecheis;* the transverse beam moving on them with the imposed tube should be 30 *pecheis* in length, having at the base a width of 11/2 *podes,* a thickness of 1 *spithame,* in order that the ratio between the length and width of the undercarriage be the same as that between the moving transverse beam and the uprights. And in turn the ratio between the same moving <beam> and the length of the undercarriage should be the same as that between the uprights and the width. For as 15 is to 10, so 30 is to 20; and as 30 is to 15, so 20 is to 10; 15 is 11/2 times 10, for it has 10 and half of it; and 30 then is 11/2 of 20. And in turn 30 is twice 15 and then 20 is twice 10. Likewise the width of the base is twice its thickness. But the diameters of the wheels will also be shown commensurable in measurement and harmonious in ratio; for the 21/2 *pecheis* of the diameter multiplied by 6 measure 15 and by 4, 10 and by 12, 30 and by 8, 20. And as 6 is to 4, so 30 is to 20. And as 15 is to 6, so 10 is to 4; 6 is 11/2 of 4, for it has 4 and half again of 4; 15 then is 11/2 of 10; and 15 is 21/2 times 6 and 10 then is 21/2 times 4. Thus the measurement of the diameter of the wheels also is found harmonious to the magnitude of the construction, as preserving the same ratio proportionally to the <numbers> being measured. And the drawing is depicted.

<fig. 23>

52. The same tube will be more effective for besieging, if its front opening should be larger in size and is exited through two doors that close, so as to accommodate two armed men, in turn standing beside each other, who are going to mount the wall together. The doors of this same opening, together with the front part of the tube, should have a frightening facade with deep carvings and polychrome painting, depicting a fire-bearing

ἐπιφερόμεναι προτομὴν εἰς κατάπληξιν καὶ φόβον τῶν ἐναντίων
10   προσερχομένην, ‖ ὅπως καὶ πρὸ τῆς ἐπιβάσεως πτοηθέντες οἱ
τῷ τείχει προεστῶτες ἀπὸ τῶν μεταπυργίων ἐκφύγωσιν. Καὶ δεῖ
Ι εἰδέναι ὅτι, εἰ μὲν ἐπ᾽ εὐθείας ἰσοϋψὴς ὁ αὐλὸς ἐπὶ τοῖς ὀρθίοις
κείμενος ξύλοις τῷ τείχει προσέρχεται, ἐπ᾽ εὐθείας καὶ τὴν
ἐπίβασιν δηλώσει· εἰ δὲ ἀνώτερος τοῦ τείχους ἐπὶ τῇ θέσει
15   εὑρίσκεται, μικρὸν καταχθεὶς ἔμπροσθεν καὶ ἐπικύψας τὴν
ἐνέργειαν τελέσει· εἰ δὲ ταπεινότερος τοῦ τείχους ἐπὶ τὸ ὕψος
τύχῃ, παρεκβληθεὶς ἐπιπλέον ἔμπροσθεν καὶ προσαχθεὶς
πάρορθος, ἐκ τοῦ ἐλάσσονος καὶ ὄπισθεν μέρους ὑπὸ τῆς
ἁλύσεως καταγόμενος ἀνωφερῶς τε μικρὸν προκύψας ἐπὶ τὸ
20   τεῖχος, καὶ τὴν πρὸς τὸ μεῖζον ὕψος τοῖς βουλομένοις ἐπιβαίνειν
ἀναπληρώσει χρείαν. Καὶ τὸ σχῆμα ὑπογέγραπται. ‖
   53. ⟨Τ⟩ὰς ἐκ τῶν πλοίων ἀγομένας μηχανάς φησιν ὁ Ἀθηναῖος,
ἅς τινες σαμβύκας καλοῦσιν ἐκ μεταφορᾶς τῶν μουσικῶν
ἐσχηματισμένας ὀργάνων, ἐμφερεῖς οὔσας ἐπὶ τῇ καμαρικῇ
κατασκευῇ τῷ προειρημένῳ αὐλῷ, μὴ ἔχειν τι ἄξιον γραφῆς διὰ
5   τὸ πᾶσιν εὐγνώστους εἶναι καὶ φανεράς. Αἱρετώτερον δέ ἐστι
μηδὲ γενέσθαι Ι πολλάκις αὐτὰς ἢ παραλόγως καὶ ἀσυμμέτρως
κατασκευασθῆναι. Καὶ γὰρ οἱ ἐν τῇ περὶ Χίον πολιορκίᾳ
εἰκαστικῶς τοῦ σκοποῦ ἀστοχήσαντες καὶ ὑψηλοτέρας τῶν
πύργων τὰς σαμβύκας προσενεγκόντες, τοὺς ἐπ᾽ αὐτὰς
10   ἀναβάντας ὑπὸ τοῦ πυρὸς ἀπολέσθαι ἐποίησαν, μὴ δυνηθέντας
ἐκ τοῦ ὕψους τοῖς πύργοις ἐπιβῆναι· χαλάσαι τε οὐκ ἦν δυνατὸν
οὐδενὶ τρόπῳ· εἰ δὲ μή, κατεστρέφετο τὰ πλοῖα, ἔξω βάρους τοῦ
ἄνωθεν ἐπικειμένου φορτίου φερομένου. Διὸ καὶ ἐπάγει μὴ
ἀπείρους τῆς ὀπτικῆς εἶναι πραγματείας τοὺς ταῖς τοιαύταις
15   μηχαναῖς χρῆσθαι μέλλοντας· καὶ ὅτι, ἐπάν τινες τῶν
ἀρχιτεκτόνων ἐνθάλασσον ἑλεῖν προαιρῶνται πόλιν,
ὑποζυγώσαντες δυσὶ πλοίοις πρὸς ὕψος τιθέασι τὸ μηχάνημα,
καὶ ἐν ταῖς γαλήναις εἰώθασιν αὐτὸ τοῖς τείχεσι προσάγειν.

53: 1–15 ⟨Τ⟩ὰς – μέλλοντας: cf. Ath. Mech. 27:7–28:6. 15–43 ἐπάν – ἐπίβασιν: cf. Ath.
Mech. 31:3–33:2.

---

10 προσερχομένην Wes: προσερχομένη V: προσερχομένης B ‖ **53:** 2 ἅς τινες Wes: ἅστινας
VB ‖ 12 ἔξω βάρους Wes: ἐξωβαροῦς VB

figurehead of a dragon or lion; this leads to terror and fear among the enemy, so that those standing on the front of the wall, terror-stricken even before the wall is mounted, flee from the curtain walls. One should be aware that if the tube lying on the upright beams is brought forward straight and equal to the height of the wall, it will reveal that the passage to the wall is a straight one. Should it be found higher than the wall in position, if it is lowered in front slightly and tipped forward, it will fulfill its function. But should it be lower in height than the wall, if it is turned further sideways in front and brought on an angle, <then> brought down at the lesser and rear part by the chain and tipped a little upward toward the wall, it will fulfill its purpose for those intent on mounting to a greater height. And the drawing is delineated.

<fig. 24>

53. Athenaeus says the machines deployed on ships (which some call *sambucas,* <a name> fashioned by comparison to musical instruments, being similar in vaulted construction to the aforementioned tube) have nothing worthy of description as they are well known and obvious to everyone. Oftentimes it is preferable that they not be made at all, rather than be constructed without calculation and incommensurably. For those at the siege of Chios, missing the mark in their conjecture and bringing up the *sambucas* higher than the towers, caused those who went up in them to perish by fire, as they were unable to mount the towers on account of the height. And it was in no way possible to lower the *sambucas;* otherwise the ships would capsize, the weight imposed on top being <then> carried outside the <center of> gravity. Wherefore he urges those who are going to use such machines to familiarize themselves with the treatise on optics. And <he says> that, whenever some master builders propose to capture a coastal city, they put up the machine after joining together two ships and usually bring it to the walls in calm weather. But if the ships should be

Ἀλλ' εἰ μὲν ὑπὸ ἐναντίου ἀνέμου τὰ πλοῖα καταληφθῶσι καὶ
20   τεθραυμένον ὑποδύῃ πρὸς αὐτὰ κῦμα, ἀναδύνει καὶ
περιτρέπεται ἀνθελκόμενον τὸ στηριχθὲν ἐπὶ τὰ πλοῖα
μηχάνημα· τὰ γὰρ πλοῖα οὐ τὴν αὐτὴν καὶ ὁμοίαν ἀεὶ ποιοῦνται
κίνησιν, ἀλλὰ τὸ μὲν αὐτῶν πρὸς τῇ τοῦ κύματος κορυφώσει
ἐνίοτε τυγχάνει, τὸ δὲ ἐπὶ τῇ κατα|δύσει· ‖ ὅθεν σπαρασσόμενα   Wes 269
25   ἐνθραύονται τὰ μηχανήματα, ὑπὸ τῆς αὐτεπιβουλεύτου   f. 39v
μηχανῆς ἀνθελκόμενα, τοὺς δὲ πολεμίους πρὸς εὐτολμίαν
μᾶλλον καὶ θάρσος καθιστᾶσι. Καὶ ἐπείπερ ἐστὶν εὐκινησία
περὶ τὴν ἀνθρωπίνην ψυχήν, οὐ μόνον τὰ καλῶς ὑφ' ἑτέρων
εὑρημένα δεῖ ἡμᾶς εἰδέναι, ἀλλὰ καὶ αὐτούς τι προσευρίσκειν
30   τῶν εἰς ὠφέλειαν συντεινόντων, πεφιλοτιμήμεθα πρὸς τὴν τοῦ
μηχανήματος ὑποστήριξιν ἐφευρόντες τοῦ ἐφαρμόζεσθαι κατὰ
μέσον τῆς ἐπιζεύξεως τῶν δύο πλοίων τὸ λεγόμενον πιθήκιον,
βάρος τι ὂν κατὰ μὲν μέγεθος ἐμφερὲς τῷ σχήματι, ἐκκρεμὲς δὲ
κάτωθεν ὂν καὶ ἐπιβρῖθον διὰ τὸ ἰσόρροπον, ὅπως τοῦ
35   θαλασσίου κλύδωνος πάντοθεν σαλεύοντος καὶ κλονοῦντος τὰ
πλοῖα,|ὀρθὸν καὶ ἀπαράπτωτον διασώζηται τὸ μηχάνημα. Πρὸς   Wes 270
δὲ τοὺς ἀνέμους καὶ τὰ ἐμπαράσκευα ἐξ ἑτοίμου ἔχειν τὰ πρὸς
πολιορκίαν ἀμυντήρια· μικρὰς παρασκευάζειν ἑλεπόλεις ὡς
θωράκιά τινα πυργοειδῆ ἢ ἐπιβατήρια κατὰ τὸ ὕψος σύμμετρα
40   καὶ εὐπρόχειρα ὄντα, ἵνα, ὅταν τὰ πλοῖα ἐγγὺς τοῦ τείχους
γένωνται, τότε διὰ σχοινίων ἢ τῶν προρρηθέντων πολυσπάστων
τὰ τοιαῦτα ἀνίστωνται μηχανήματα τὴν ἐπὶ τὸ τεῖχος
ὁδοποιοῦντα ἐπίβασιν.

    54. Ἐνεργὴς δὲ πρὸς τὴν τοιαύτην χρείαν καὶ ὁ προρρηθεὶς
αὐλὸς φανήσεται σύμμετρος ὢν τῷ μεγέθει [εἰ] πρὸς τὰ
ἐπιζευχθέντα | πλοῖα, ⟨ἐὰν⟩ ἐπὶ τῶν ὀρθίως ἐστηριγμένων   Wes 271
ἐπανάγηται ξύλων μετακινούμενος, ὡς προδέδεικται, ἢ ἐπὶ τοῦ
5   λεγομένου καρχησίου δυνάμενος ἐπ' αὐτοῦ τὰς ἓξ ποιεῖσθαι

54: 5–6 καρχησίου – γέρανοι: cf. Ath. Mech. 35:4–37:2.

---

20 τεθραυσμένον Wes ‖ ὑποδύῃ Wes: ὑποδύει VB ‖ 32 πιθήκιον Wes: πιθίκιον VB ‖ 37 Post
ἀνέμους add. δεῖ Wes ‖ τὰ¹ Wes: τὸ VB (cf. Ath. Mech. 33:1) ‖ 42 ἀνίστωνται Wes: ἀνιστ^ᾶν
VB (cf. Ath. Mech. 33:3) ‖ **54:** 2 εἰ secl. Wes ‖ 3 ἐὰν add. Wes

caught by an adverse wind and a breaking wave slip against them, the machine fastened on the ships rides up and, pulled apart, overturns. For the <joined> ships do not always make the same and similar movement, but sometimes one of them is at the crest of the wave, the other in the valley. Hence the machines are shattered <and> break up, pulled apart by their self-destructive design, and instill greater courage and boldness in the enemy. And <he says> that since there is agility in the human spirit, we ought not only to know the fine discoveries of others, but even ourselves ought to devise some beneficial contributions; <that> we are proud of our discovery for supporting the machine, whereby we fit in the middle, where the two ships are joined, the so-called little ape, a kind of weight corresponding in size to the design, which is suspended at the bottom and presses down to create equilibrium, so that when the sea's wave surges all around and tosses the ships, the machine is kept upright and does not fall over. Against the winds have ready too equipment prepared as defenses for besieging; and prepare small siege towers such as towerlike breastworks, or landing bridges commensurate with the height <of the wall> and easy to handle, in order that, whenever the ships should be near the wall, then such engines may be raised up by ropes or the aforementioned pulley systems <and> provide passage to the wall.

54. The aforementioned tube will also appear effective for such a function, when commensurate in size with the joined ships, if it be raised on beams fixed upright <and> moves as discussed earlier, or atop the so-called universal joint, able to make the six

κινήσεις, καθάπερ καὶ αἱ λεγόμεναι γέρανοι· ἢ καὶ ἐπὶ
κατακλεῖδος ἐπάνω στύρακος ἐπικειμένης, τοῦ στύρακος δι᾽
ἐργάτου τὴν περιστροφὴν πρὸς ὕψος καὶ ταπείνωμα
ποιουμένου. Οὕτως οὖν καὶ Δᾶμις ὁ Κολοφώνιος ἐπὶ στυράκων
10 τὰς σαμβύκας ἐτίθει, ὡς ὁ μηχανικὸς Βίτων ἐν τοῖς αὐτοῦ
πολιορκητικοῖς ὑπομνήμασι. Τὰ δὲ ῥηθέντα ἐσχηματισμένα
πάντα ἔκκειται. || f. 40, 40v

55. ⟨Γ⟩ινέσθω σχεδία μῆκος ἔχουσα μικρῷ μεῖζον τοῦ πλάτους
τοῦ μέλλοντος γεφυροῦσθαι ποταμοῦ, καὶ καταστρωθήτω
σανίσι ξυλοιπυρίοις ἐμπησσομέναις, ἵνα μὴ κατὰ διαφόρους   Wes 272
κινήσεις τοῦ ποταμίου ῥεύματος ἀπελαύνηται καὶ διασπωμένη
5   ῥηγνύηται. Καὶ τὰ μὲν πλείονα τῆς σχεδίας ξύλα σχοινίοις
προσδεδεμένοις καὶ ἥλοις ξυλίνοις ἀραιοῖς καταπεπηγόσιν
ἀσφαλιζέσθωσαν· τὸ δὲ κατὰ πρόσωπον τῶν πολεμίων
ἐπέρχεσθαι μέλλον ὅλον μῆκος τῆς σχεδίας σὺν τοῖς ἐφ᾽
ἑκάτερα δυσὶ πλαγίοις προτείχισμα ἐχέτω ξύλινον γιγγλυμωτὸν
10 ὕψους ποδῶν ιβ´· γίνεται δὲ κατὰ πῆξιν ὀρθίων ἑστώτων ξύλων
στρογγύλας τρήσεις κάτωθεν ἐπιδεχομένων καὶ ὑπὸ λείων
περονῶν συμβεβλημένων ἐπὶ πλαγίαις σανίσι προσηλωμέναις
ἔξωθεν, ἵνα ἐπισυρομένων καὶ πλαγιαζομένων τῶν ὀρθῶν
εὐλύτως κατερχόμενον συγκαταπίπτῃ καὶ τὸ προτείχισμα.
15 Κρεμάσθωσαν δὲ καὶ δέρματα ἢ ῥάκη ἐπὶ ταῖς σανίσι μικρὸν
παρεξέχοντα ἔξωθεν· καὶ κλίμακες ἔνδον ἐπικείσθωσαν τοὺς
ἄνωθεν μηροὺς πεπερονημένους πρὸς τοῖς ὀρθίοις ξύλοις
ἔχουσαι, τετρημένοις καὶ αὐτοῖς ἄνωθεν οὖσι, τοὺς δὲ κάτωθεν
ἐπὶ τοῦ καταστρώματος σχοινίοις προσδεδεμένους, ἵνα
20 παρορθίων ἀνθεστηκότων τῶν κλιμάκων ὀρθὸν διαμένῃ
ἀπαντώμενον τὸ προτείιχισμα. Οὕτως οὖν οἱ ἐπὶ τῶν κλιμάκων   Wes 273
ἑστῶτες εὐπροθύμως ἀντιμαχήσονται κατὰ πρόσωπον τῶν
πολεμίων ὑψηλότεροι ὄντες, προπύργια εἰς φυλακὴν ἑαυτῶν καὶ

7–10 κατακλεῖδος – ἐτίθει: cf. Bito 57–61. **55: 1–57: 11** ⟨Γ⟩ινέσθω – ὑπόκειται: cf. Apollod.
189:4–193:5.

---

9 Δᾶμις Wes: δάμις VB ‖ 11 ὑπομνήμασι Sch: ὑπεμνημᾱτ᾽ VB: ὑπεμέμνητο Wes ‖ **55: 3**
ἐμπησσομέναις Wes: ἐμπησσομένης VB ‖ 9 γιγγλυμωτὸν Sch: γιγγλυμωτὸν VB ‖ 10 πῆξιν
Wes: πτῆξιν VB ‖ 23 ὄντες B: ὄντες ? in macula V

movements atop it, like the so-called cranes, or even on the bracket imposed on a <screw->shaft, the <screw->shaft rotating up and down through a capstan. Thus then did Damis of Colophon put *sambucas* on shafts, as the engineer Biton <says> in his poliorcetic commentaries. All the <devices> that have been discussed are illustrated here.

<figs. 25 and 26>

55. A raft should be a little longer than the width of the river that is going to be bridged and should be decked with boards, held <loosely> with wooden pegs (?), in order that it may not be driven away by the different movements of the river's current and shattered <and> broken. The majority of the beams of the raft should be secured with ropes bound <to them> and with a few firmly set wooden nails. The entire length of the raft that will face the enemy, together with the two sides at either end, should have a hinged wooden rampart, 12 *podes* high. This rampart involves affixing vertical beams, which receive round holes at the bottom and are joined by smooth pins to horizontal boards that are nailed on the outside, in order that when the uprights are drawn back and placed horizontal, the rampart too may easily come down and fall. Hides or patchwork material should be hung on the boards, projecting outward a little. And let ladders be set inside with their sidebars pinned on top to the upright beams, which are themselves also drilled on their upper parts, but below <the sidebars> are bound on the deck with ropes, in order that when the ladders stand against <the beams> diagonally, the rampart may remain upright since it meets with them. Thus therefore those who stand on the ladders will fight eagerly when facing the enemy, because they are higher up, having in

ἀσφάλειαν ἐκ τοῦ προτειχίσματος ἔχοντες. Μὴ ἐνούσθω δὲ ὅλον
25 ἀνιστάμενον τὸ προτείχισμα, ἀλλὰ πρὸς μέρη τινὰ ἀσύνδετον
ἔστω, ἵνα, ἐὰν ἀνάγκη κατὰ τὴν προσβολὴν γένηται, τὸ μὲν
αὐτοῦ ἵσταται, τὸ δὲ καταπίπτῃ· εἰ δὲ χρεία γένηται καὶ ὅλον
καταπεσεῖν, πάσας τὰς ὑπαντώσας κλίμακας καὶ ἀντεχούσας
ἐπὶ τῷ προτειχίσματι λύσαντες ἐκ τῶν κάτωθεν μερῶν
30 ὑποσυροῦμεν ἐπὶ τοῦ καταστρώματος ἐπιθέντες. Ταύτην δὲ τὴν
σχεδίαν πασσάλοις τῇ γῇ ἐμπεπηγόσι μακρόθεν διὰ σχοινίων
ἀποκρατοῦντες ἀσφαλισόμεθα· καὶ ἐκ τοῦ πρὸς ἡμᾶς χείλους
τὸ ἓν αὐτῆς ἄκρον κατὰ μικρὸν ‖ ἐπιδιδόντες ἀπελάσομεν   f. 41
ἄνωθεν, τοῦ ἀποκρατοῦντος αὐτὴν ἀπολυομένου σφηνός. Καὶ
35 οὕτως κατὰ μικρὸν ἡ σχεδία παρέρχεται ὑπὸ τῆς τοῦ ὕδατος
κατα|φορᾶς καθάπερ θύρα διανοιγομένη, τοῦ στρατεύματος   Wes 274
πλήρης οὖσα· καὶ μετέρχεται τὸ ἓν αὐτῆς ἄκρον ἐπὶ τὸ χεῖλος
τοῦ ποταμοῦ τὸ πρὸς τοὺς πολεμίους. Καὶ ἐπεὶ μακροτέρα τοῦ
ποταμίου πλάτους ὑπετέθη, οὐ δύναται ὑπὸ τοῦ ῥεύματος πρὸς
40 κατάρρουν πάλιν ἀντιστρέφεσθαι. Τοῦ δὲ προτειχίσματος
ἔνδοθεν ἐπὶ τῷ καταστρώματί εἰσιν ἀφεθέντα τρυπήματα πρὸς
μέρη τινὰ καὶ μέχρι τῆς γῆς διερχόμενα, πρὸς ἃ πάσσαλοι
ξύλινοι ἐπιμελῶς πήγνυνται καὶ προσδέδεται κρυφίως ἡ σχεδία.
Καὶ ἔστι τὸ σχῆμα τοιοῦτον. ‖   f. 41v

56. 〈Ἐ〉πελθόντος δὲ τοῦ ἑνὸς τῆς σχεδίας ἄκρου ἐπὶ τὸ
ἐναντίον χεῖλος τοῦ ποταμοῦ καὶ πρὸς τῇ γῇ ἀσφαλισθέντος
ἔνδον τοῦ προτειχίσματος, ὡς προείρηται, τότε ἀπολύεται ἐξ
ἄκρου καὶ τὸ ἕτερον, καὶ πάλιν ἡ τοῦ ῥεύματος καταφορὰ
5 πλαγίαν αὐτὴν ἐπιπέμπει καὶ παρατίθησι πρὸς τὸ ἕτερον χεῖλος
τοῦ ποταμοῦ ὅλην κατὰ μῆκος ἐφαρμόζουσα, τοῦ πλήθους
συνηγμένου καὶ ἑτοίμου ὄντος πρὸς τὴν τῆς μάχης
ἀντιπαράταξιν. Οἱ δὲ ἐπὶ ταῖς κλίμαξιν ἀναβάντες ὡς ἐπὶ
τείχους ἑστῶτες καὶ τεθαρρηκότες ἀντιμαχήσονται. Ὅταν δὲ
10 ἀποστρέψῃ τοὺς πολεμίους ἡ ἀπὸ τοῦ προτειχίσματος
καταπλήττουσα συμβολή, λύονται τὰ κάτωθεν τῶν κλιμάκων
δεσμά, καὶ πλαγιάζει κατ' ὀλίγον ὅλος ὁ τοῖχος τοῦ

---

30 ὑποσυροῦμεν Sch: ὑποσύρωμεν VB ‖ 32 ἀσφαλισόμεθα Sch: ἀσφαλισώμεθα VB ‖ **56:**
9 ἀντιμαχήσονται Wes: ἀντιμαχήσωνται V: vocabulum in B prorsus corruptum (cf. Apollod.
192:3)

the rampart outworks for their safety and security. The rampart should not stand as a unified whole, but be in unconnected sections, in order that, if it should be necessary during the attack, one part of it stands, another part may fall. But if it should be necessary for the whole thing to fall, after freeing from the lower parts all the ladders that meet with and brace themselves on the rampart, we shall draw it back, placing it on the deck. We shall secure this raft by controlling it through ropes on stakes driven into the ground some distance away. And gradually releasing one end of it, the upper one, from the river bank on our side, we shall propel it away, when the wedge that controls it is set free. And thus the raft, filled with troops, gradually passes across, being opened like a door by the downward rush of the water. And one end of it reaches the enemy's bank of the river. And since the raft is assumed to be longer than the width of the river, it cannot be turned further downstream by the current. Openings are left on the deck behind the rampart at certain points and they go through to the ground; into them wooden stakes are carefully set, and the raft is secured invisibly. The drawing is such as follows.

<fig. 27>

56. When one end of the raft reaches the opposite bank of the river and is secured behind the rampart to the land, as stated above, then the other end is also released and in turn the downward rush of the current sends the raft diagonally and places it on the other bank of the river, fitting the whole thing lengthwise. And the mass <of troops> is gathered together and ready for engagement in battle. And the men who have mounted on the ladders, as if standing on a wall, and taking courage, will offer battle. Whenever the terrifying encounter from the rampart turns back the enemy, the lower bindings of the ladders are freed, and the whole wall of the rampart is slowly placed flat, that is to say, as

προτειχίσματος ὑποσυρομένων δηλονότι τῶν κλιμάκων καὶ
ἐπιπιπτόντων τῷ κατα|στρώματι· καὶ γίνεται ὁδὸς ὅλον τὸ   Wes 275
15   μεσόχωρον τοῦ καταπίπτοντος προτειχίσματος· καὶ οὕτως
διηνεκὴς ἡ διάβασις ἔσται. Τρυπάσθω δὲ κρυφίως καὶ κάτωθεν
τὸ προτείχισμα ἐπὶ ταῖς κατὰ πρόσωπον προσηλωθείσαις
πλαγίαις σανίσιν, ὥστε ἀκοντίζειν καὶ τοξεύειν ἐπὶ τοὺς
πολεμίους καὶ ἐκ τοῦ κάτωθεν μέρους, ἀφανῶν [δὲ] τῶν
20   μαχομένων ὄντων, διπλῇ τε μάχεσθαι τάξει κατὰ πρόσωπον·
πρὸς μόνην δὲ τὴν ἄνωθεν τοὺς πολεμίους ἀφορᾶν τε καὶ
διαμάχεσθαι.

57. ⟨Ἐ⟩πεθέμην καὶ ὡς ὀρθογραφεῖται τὸ σχῆμα, ἵνα φανερὰ
καὶ ἡ τῶν κλιμάκων γένηται θέσις καὶ ἡ τοῦ προτειχίσματος.
Τὴν δὲ | δὴ σχεδίαν ἐκ τοῦ πρὸς ἡμᾶς χείλους ἀπολυομένην,   Wes 276
καὶ ὥσπερ θύρας διανοιγομένην ἐπὶ τῇ καταφορᾷ τοῦ ποταμίου
5   ῥεύματος, βοηθεῖν δεῖ, μήπως ἀθρόως ἐπιπολὺ αὐτὴν ἐνσείουσα
προσκρούσῃ καὶ θρύψῃ ἐπὶ τὸ ἕτερον χεῖλος τοῦ ποταμοῦ τὸ
πρὸς τοὺς πολεμίους ὅθεν χρὴ χαλινοῦν αὐτὴν καὶ ἀναχαιτίζειν
ἀπὸ τοῦ πρὸς ἡμᾶς χείλους ἀποκρατοῦντας, τὴν δὲ τῶν σχοινίων
ἐπίδοσιν κατὰ μικρὸν ποιεῖσθαι, ὅπως πραέως καὶ κατ' ὀλίγον
10   διερχομένη ἐπὶ τὸ ἕτερον τοῦ ποταμοῦ χεῖλος ἀκινδύνως
ἐπιτεθήσεται. Καὶ τὸ σχῆμα ὑπόκειται. ‖   f. 42

58. ⟨Τ⟩αῦτα τοίνυν τὰ πρὸς ἀναγραφὴν καὶ σχηματισμὸν κατ'
ἐκλογὴν συνταχθέντα πολιορκητήρια μηχανήματα οἱ τῶν
στρατευμάτων ἐξάρχοντες μετὰ λόγου καὶ συνεχοῦς μελέτης
ἐπιμελῶς κατεργαζόμενοι, τὴν θείαν διὰ παντὸς ἐνοπτριζόμενοι
5   δίκην, ἐπὶ δικαιοσύνῃ καὶ εὐσεβείᾳ κεκοσμημένοι καὶ τῇ
κραταιᾷ χειρὶ συνεργίᾳ τε καὶ συμμαχίᾳ τῶν θεοστέπτων καὶ
φιλοχρίστων ἀνάκτων Ῥώμης ἐνδυναμούμενοί τε καὶ
φρουρούμενοι, εὐχερῶς τὰς τῆς Ἄγαρ μάλιστα λήψονται
πόλεις, αὐτοὶ μηθὲν ἀνήκεστον ὑπὸ τῶν θεολέστων ἐχθρῶν
10   πάσχοντες.

58: 9–10 μηθὲν – πάσχοντες: cf. Philo Mech. 104:42–43.

---

19 δὲ secl. Wes ‖ 57: 1 Ἐπεθέμην Β: πεθέμην V: vid. Apollod. 193:1 Ὑπεθέμην ‖ 58: 4
ἐνοπτριζόμενοι Wes: ἐνοπριζόμενοι VB

the ladders are drawn back and fall on the deck. And the entire gap created by the falling rampart becomes a passageway and thus the crossing will be continuous. Let the rampart be drilled invisibly <to the enemy> down lower on the horizontal boards that are nailed in front, so that <one can> hurl spears and shoot arrows at the enemy also from this lower section, those fighting there being invisible, and so that <one can> fight in double rank in front, while the enemy have in view and fight against only the upper <rank>.

57. I have added the drawing as sketched in upright view, in order that the placement of the ladders and the rampart may be clear. One has to be careful of the raft when freed from our bank and being opened like doors at the downward rush of the river's current, lest <the current>, suddenly shaking the raft quite extensively, strike and break it against the other bank of the river on the enemy's side; hence it is necessary to bridle and check it, controlling it from our bank and gradually releasing the ropes, so that gently and slowly proceeding to the other bank of the river it will be set against it without harm. And the drawing is below.

<fig. 28>

58. If army commanders carefully complete with logic and continuous diligence these siege machines, which have been selectively compiled for description and illustration, and always contemplate divine justice, being honored for their fairness and reverence, and strengthened and guarded by the powerful hand and cooperation and alliance of the God-crowned and Christ-loving emperors of Rome, they will easily capture cities, especially those of Agar and themselves suffer nothing fatal from the God-damned enemy.

⟨ΓΕΩΔΑΙΣΙΑ⟩

1. ⟨Ἐ⟩πειδὴ οὐκ ἔξεστι τοὺς πολιορκεῖν βουλομένους ὕψη
τειχῶν πόρρωθεν καὶ διαστήματα ἐξ ἀποστημάτων, πλάτη τε
ποταμῶν ἐν τῇ ἀναμετρήσει παραλογίζεσθαι, ἀλλ' ἐμπειρίᾳ
γραμμῶν ἠσκημένους καὶ γνώσει διοπτρικῆς ἰθυφανείας τὴν
5   ἐπίσκεψιν ποιεῖσθαι πρὸς τὸ ἰσοστασίους ἑλεπόλεις τοῖς τείχεσι
καὶ σύμμετρα ζεύγματα ταῖς σχεδίαις πρὸς τὰ τῶν ποταμῶν
πλάτη ἐπαγαγεῖν, ἵνα ὡς ἐν γεφύρᾳ ἢ διαβάθρᾳ ‖ ἀβλαβῶς τὸ   f. 42v
στράτευμα κατὰ τάξιν διαπερᾶται· ὅτι πολλοὶ πολλάκις
μείζονα ἢ ἐλάσσονα ὧν ἔχρην κατασκευάσαντες μηχανήματα
10   καὶ προσενεγκάμενοι (ὡς καὶ ἐν τῷ πρὸ τούτου δεδήλωται
συντάγματι), τοὺς ἐπ' αὐτὰ προκινδυνεύειν μέλλοντας ὑπὸ τῶν
ἐναντίων ἀπολέσθαι ἐποίησαν, αἰσθήσει ἀλογίστῳ καὶ εἰκασίᾳ
παραπεισθέντες· ὅθεν ἐσκεψάμεθα τὴν μετὰ λόγου δύναμιν τῆς
διοπτρείας καὶ τὸ ἐν πολλοῖς αὐτῆς βιωφελέστατον πράγμασιν,
15   ἐκ τῶν προγενεστέρων καὶ πολυμαθεστάτων τὰ ἁπλούστερα
συλλεξάμενοι, ψιλαῖς ἐφόδοις γραμμικαῖς διορίσαι καὶ ἐπ'
ὀλίγων διαγραμμάτων τὰς ἀποδείξεις ποιήσασθαι, ὅπως, ἐκτὸς
βέλους τῶν πολεμίων ἑστῶτες, δυνώ‖μεθα ὕψη, μήκη τε καὶ   Vin 350
διαστήματα πρὸς ἀλήθειαν ἀψευδῶς καταριθμεῖν. Ἡ δὲ σκέψις
20   τοὺς φιλομαθοῦντας οὐ πρὸς στρατηγικὴν μόνην ἐπιστήμην
ἐφοδιάσει, ἀλλὰ καὶ πρὸς ὑδάτων ἀγωγάς, τειχῶν τε
κατασκευὰς καὶ λιμένων περιγραφὰς χρειωδεστάτη φανήσεται,
πρὸς [τε] γεωδαισίαν τε καὶ τὴν τῶν οὐρανίων θεωρίαν οὐ
μικρὸν συμβαλλομένη. Καὶ χρή, τό τε μῆκος καὶ τὸ παλιλλογεῖν

1: 1 ἔξεστι – βουλομένους: cf. Hero *Dioptr.* I:10.   2 διαστήματα ἐξ ἀποστημάτων: cf. Hero
Dioptr. II:10.   3 ἀναμετρήσει παραλογίζεσθαι: cf. Hero *Dioptr.* II:18.   6–7 σύμμετρα –
ἐπαγαγεῖν: cf. Afric. *Cest.* VII:15.   8–12 πολλοὶ – ἐποίησαν: cf. Hero *Dioptr.* II:14–17.   17–
18 ἐκτὸς βέλους: cf. Hero *Dioptr.* II:20.   21–22 ὑδάτων – λιμένων: cf. Hero *Dioptr.* II:3;
XVII:1.   23 οὐρανίων θεωρίαν: cf. Hero *Dioptr.* II:5.

Tit. ΓΕΩΔΑΙΣΙΑ Vin: om.VP ‖ **1:** 1 Ἐπειδὴ Vin: πεὶ δὲ V: ἐπεὶ δὲ P ‖ 19 Ἥδε Vin ‖ 23 τε secl.
Vin ‖ γεωδαισίαν Vin: γεωδεσίαν VB

<Geodesia>

1. Since those intent on conducting a siege must not mis-calculate in the measurement of heights of walls from afar, of intervals from distances, and of widths of rivers, they must make their investigation trained in the expertise of mathematical figures and in knowledge of dioptric direct viewing so they can bring up siege towers equal in height to the walls, and platforms fastened on rafts commensurate with the widths of the rivers, so that the army may cross in good order safely as if on a bridge or drop-bridge. For many have often constructed and deployed machines larger or smaller than needed, since they were led astray by thoughtless perception and estimation (as was made clear in the previous treatise), causing the men about to risk their lives on them to be destroyed by the enemy. Hence, having collected the simpler <material> from earlier and most learned <writers>, we have planned to define the rational potential of dioptrics and its great usefulness in <daily> life in many matters, with plain linear methods, and to create proofs on the basis of a few diagrams, so that standing outside the range of the enemy, we may be able truthfully <and> without error to compute heights and lengths and intervals. The examination will supply those who are eager to learn not only with knowledge for generals, but will appear most useful also for aqueducts, construction of walls, and outlines of harbors, making no small contribution to mensuration and contemplation of the heavens. And it is necessary to avoid

25 ἀποφυγόντας, τὸ μὲν περὶ τὰς λέξεις ἀσαφὲς καὶ δύσφραστον
τῶν πάλαι ἐπιστημόνων εὐκρινῆσαι καὶ πρὸς τὸ ἰδιωτικώτερον
μεταβαλεῖν, τὸ δὲ περὶ τὰς ἀποδείξεις μαθηματικῶς εἰρημένον
πλάτος τῶν λόγων συνόψει εὐλήπτων περιελεῖν, καὶ τὸ ὑψηλὸν
τῆς περὶ τὰ νοήματα θεωρίας ἐπὶ τὸ ταπεινὸν καὶ
30 αἰσθητικώτερον κατενεγκεῖν, εὐσύνοπτον τὴν πραγματείαν
εὐεπιβόλοις ἀνδράσι ποιουμένους καὶ τοῖς τυχοῦσιν ἴσως σχολῇ
ταύτην μεταχειριζομένοις, ἐξαιρέτως δὲ τοῖς ὁπωσοῦν
γεωμετρίαν ἐπεσκεμμένοις. ‖ | f. 43

  2. ⟨...⟩ καὶ ΓΔ βάσιν· ὁμοίως δὲ καὶ τὸν ⟨λόγον⟩ τῆς ΑΒ πρὸς   Vin 354
τὴν ΒΔ· καὶ ἐν ᾧ πάλιν λόγῳ ἐστὶν ἡ ΒΔ πρὸς θατέραν τῶν ΔΓ,
ΔΗ, ἐν τῷ αὐτῷ καὶ ἡ ΑΒ ⟨πρὸς θάτερον⟩ τῶν ΘΗ, ΕΓ ὑψῶν. Χρὴ
δέ ποτε τὸν προϊστάμενον κατὰ κάθετον κάμακα πρὸς μείζονα
5 ὕψη καὶ ὑδραγώγια, κατὰ τὸ Θ σημεῖον πρὸς τύλον τινὰ
κρεμαστὴν ἐπιδέχεσθαι δίοπτραν τὴν καὶ λυχνίαν καλουμένην.
Μετρήσας δὲ τὰς ΔΓ, ΔΗ, τῶν ἐλασσόνων τριγώνων βάσεις πρὸς
ἡμᾶς οὔσας, καὶ εὑρὼν αὐτὰς κατὰ μῆκος, ἔχω καὶ τὰς ΓΕ, ΗΘ
ἐγνωσμένας, ὡς τῆς διόπτρας καὶ | τοῦ κάμακος ὕψει ἐνούσας·   Vin 356
10 καὶ εἰ δεκαπλασίαν τὴν βάσιν τοῦ ὕψους εὕρω, δεκαπλασίαν
καὶ ὅλην τὴν ΔΒ τῆς ΑΒ ἀποφανοῦμαι. Δύναμαι δὲ καὶ ὅλην
τὴν ΔΒ εὑρεῖν, ὡς ἐπὶ τοῦ μήκους καὶ πλάτους ἐμάθομεν· καὶ
εὑρὼν αὐτὴν ὀργυῶν ρκ′, δώδεκα καὶ τὴν ΑΒ ἀποφανοῦμαι,
ὅπερ ἐστὶ τὸ ζητούμενον τοῦ τείχους ὕψος ἐπὶ τὸ τοῦ προμαχῶνος
15 ἄκρον, ὡς [τοῦ] ἀπὸ τοῦ ⟨ἐπὶ⟩ ἐδάφους τῶν θυρῶν ὑποτεθέντος
Β πρὸς τὸ ἐπὶ μέρους τινὸς τοῦ τεθρίππου σημειωθὲν Α. Περὶ δὲ
μοιρῶν καὶ μορίων, ἱκανῶς τοῖς ἐπιζητοῦσι διὰ τῶν
ἀριθμητικῶν ἄνωθεν διεξήλθομεν μεθόδων. ‖   f. 43v
  3. ⟨Δ⟩είξομεν δὲ καὶ πῶς δύο σημείων πόρρω ἀφ᾽ ἡμῶν

---

30 εὐσύνοπτον τὴν πραγματείαν: cf. Hero *Metrica proem* 1:7. **2:** 4 κάμακα: cf. Afric. *Cest.*
VII:15. 5 ὑδραγώγια: cf. Hero *Dioptr.* VI: 120. 6 δίοπτραν – λυχνίαν: cf. Afric. *Cest.* VII:15.
3: 1–3 δύο – σημείοις: cf. Hero *Dioptr.* X:1–2; XIII:27–28.

---

28 εὐλήπτων VP, –ων per compendium V: εὐλήπτως leg. Müller: εὕληπτον Vin ‖ 31
εὐεπιβόλοις Vin: εὐεπιβούλοις VP ‖ **2:** 1 < ... > Vin (cf. Dain, 31) ‖ τὸν P: τὸ V ‖ λόγον add.
Vin ‖ 3 πρὸς θάτερον add. Vin ‖ 5 ὑδραγωγίαν Vin ‖ 7 τῶν ἐλασσόνων τριγώνων Vin: τοῦ
ἐλάσσονος τριγώνου VP ‖ 9 ὕψει ἐνούσας P: ὕψη μὲν οὔσας Vin ‖ 15 τοῦ secl. Vin ‖ ἐπὶ
add. Vin

length and repetition, to render distinct what is unclear and difficult in the diction of knowledgeable men of former times, and
to translate it into a more familiar style, but also to remove the
breadth employed mathematically in proofs by summary of the
words that are easy to grasp, to bring down to a low and more
sensible level the height of their theory concerning these concepts, making the treatise easy to survey for shrewd men and
those who happen to take it by chance in hand as time permits,
but especially for those who in any way have studied geometry.

2. < ... > and the base ΓΔ; likewise also the ratio of AB to BΔ;
and in turn the ratio that BΔ has to either ΔΓ or ΔH, in the same
ratio also is AB <to either> of the heights ΘH <or> EΓ. It is
necessary at times, for greater heights and for aqueducts, for the
pole that stands perpendicular in front at point Θ to receive a
dioptra<-target>, the <one> also called a lamp, which hangs on
a peg. And having measured ΔΓ <and> ΔH, which are the bases
of the smaller triangles within our reach and finding their length,
I have ascertained too ΓE and HΘ, as the height of the dioptra
and of the pole. And if I find the base is ten times the height, I
shall conclude also that the whole of ΔB is ten times AB. I am
<then> able to find also the whole of ΔB, as we learned for
length and width. And finding it of 120 *orgyai,* I shall conclude
that AB is 12, which is the sought height of the wall at the top of
the merlon, like <the distance> from <point> B assumed at the
bottom of the doors to point A noted on some part of the
quadriga. We have discussed above through arithmetic methods
units and fractions sufficiently for those who seek <this>.

<fig. 29>

3. We shall also demonstrate how to take the interval be-

δοθέντων καὶ ὁρωμένων, τὸ μεταξὺ διάστημα λαμβάνειν τὸ πρὸς διαβήτην, μὴ προσεγγίσαντας τοῖς δοθεῖσι σημείοις.

Ἔστωσαν τὰ ὁρώμενα σημεῖα τὰ Α, Β, ἐπὶ τῆς τῶν καγκέλλων
5 σκοπούμενα διαστάσεως, τὸ μὲν Α ἐπὶ τοῦ τρίτου, τὸ | δὲ Β ἐπὶ   Vin 358
τοῦ ἐνάτου. Στήσας οὖν τὴν διόπτραν ἐπὶ τῆς ἄνω νύσσης πρὸς
τῷ Γ σημείῳ, καὶ πρὸς τὴν θέσιν τοῦ ἐπιπέδου τῶν δοθέντων
σημείων τὸ τύμπανον καταστήσας, διάγω δύο εὐθείας διὰ τῶν
ὀπῶν τοῦ κανόνος, ἐπὶ μὲν τοῦ τρίτου τὴν ΓΑ, ἐπὶ δὲ τοῦ ἐνάτου
10 τὴν ΓΒ. Καὶ μετρῶ μίαν τούτων διὰ κανόνος, ἢ καὶ ὡς ἀνωτέρω
προδέδεικται. Καὶ εὑρὼν αὐτὴν ὀργυῶν τυχὸν π΄, τέμνω ταύτην
πρὸς ὃ ἂν θελήσω μέρος. Ἔστω ἡ τομὴ κατὰ τὸ δέκατον μέρος
τὸ πρὸς τῇ νύσσῃ ἐπὶ ὀργυὰς η΄ κατὰ τὸ Δ σημεῖον. Καὶ
μεταστήσας πρὸς αὐτὸ τὴν διόπτραν, διάγω εὐθεῖαν διὰ τοῦ
15 κανόνος τὴν ΔΕ τέμνουσαν ὁμοίως τὴν ΓΒ κατὰ τὸ δέκατον
μέρος ἐπὶ τὸ Ε. Ἔσται ἄρα καὶ αὐτὴ ἡ ΔΕ δέκατον μέρος τῆς
ΑΒ διαστάσεως· ὡς γὰρ ἡ ΑΓ πρὸς τὴν ΓΔ καὶ ἡ ΒΙ˙ πρὸς τὴν ΓΕ,
οὕτως καὶ ἡ ΑΒ πρὸς τὴν ΔΕ ἔσται. Ἀλλὰ καὶ ὡς ἡ ΔΕ πρὸς τὴν
ΕΓ, οὕτως καὶ ἡ ΑΒ πρὸς τὴν ΒΓ. Μετρήσας δὲ καὶ τὴν ΕΔ || f. 44
20 πρὸς ἡμᾶς οὖσαν, καὶ εὑρὼν αὐτὴν ὀργυῶν δ΄, ἐγνωσμένην καὶ
τὴν ΑΒ ἔχω, ὡς δεκαπλασίαν, μ΄ ὀργυῶν οὖσαν. Ὥστε τὸ μεταξὺ
ζητούμενον τῶν Α, Β σημείων διάστημα ὀργυῶν εὕρηται μ΄.

4. ⟨Ἔ⟩στιν δὲ καὶ ἄλλως τὸ μεταξὺ τῶν δοθέντων δύο σημείων
ἐπιγνῶναι διάστημα, κατὰ τὸ νῦν ἐκκείμενον διάγραμμα. | Vin 360

Νοείσθω καθ᾽ ὑπόθεσιν τὸ μὲν Α σημεῖον κατὰ τὸ πλάτος τοῦ
ἱππικοῦ πρὸς τὸ ἀριστερὸν μέρος τῆς σφενδόνης σκοπούμενον,
5 τὸ δὲ Β ἐπὶ τὸ δεξιόν. Ἵστημι οὖν τὴν διόπτραν πρὸς τὸν
καλούμενον ἁπλοῦν, ὀλίγον ἀπέχουσαν ἐξ ἐναντίας τῆς ἄνω
νύσσης, ὡς ἐπὶ τὸ Γ σημεῖον, ὥστε τὴν ὄψιν πρὸς τὴν τῶν
δοθέντων σημείων εὐθυωρίαν μηδὲν παρεμποδίζεσθαι.
Καταστήσας δὲ τὸ τύμπανον πρὸς τὴν θέσιν τοῦ ἐπιπέδου τῆς
10 βάσεως τῆς σφενδόνης, διάγω δύο εὐθείας διὰ τοῦ κανόνος,
πρὸς μὲν τὸ ἀριστερὸν πέρας τὴν ΓΑ, πρὸς δὲ τὸ δεξιὸν τὴν ΓΒ.
Καὶ μίαν τούτων, ὡς προείρηται, μετρήσας καὶ εὑρὼν αὐτὴν

4: 1–2 ⟨Ἔ⟩στιν – διάστημα cf. Hero *Dioptr.* X:26–27; 37.

3: 13 τὸ¹ Vin: τῷ VP ‖ 15 ΓΒ P: ΒΓ V ‖ **4:** 6 ἁπλοῦν P: ἄπλουν Vin

tween two given points distant from us and visible, on the horizontal plane, without approaching the given points.

Let the visible points be A and B, viewed across the distance of the starting gates, A at the third <gate>, B at the ninth. After standing the dioptra at the upper turning post, at point Γ, and setting the disc to the position of the plane of the given points, I draw two straight lines through the <sight->holes of the sight-rod, ΓA on the third <gate>, ΓB on the ninth. And I measure one of these with the sight-rod, that is as was shown above. And finding it perhaps 80 *orgyai*, I divide this at whatever part I wish. Let the division be at one-tenth of the way from the turning post, 8 *orgyai* at point Δ. And after moving the dioptra to this <point>, I draw a straight line ΔE with the sight-rod, which likewise divides ΓB at the tenth part, at E. This <line> ΔE then will be one-tenth of the distance AB; for as AΓ is to ΓΔ, and BΓ to ΓE, so also will AB be to ΔE. But also as ΔE is to EΓ, so also AB is to BΓ. And having measured also EΔ which is within our reach, and finding it of 4 *orgyai*, I also can determine AB as it is ten times this, which is 40 *orgyai*. So the interval sought between the points A and B has been found to be of 40 *orgyai*.

<fig. 30>

4. It is possible also in another manner to determine the interval between two given points according to the diagram now set forth.

Let the point A be imagined hypothetically seen at the width of the hippodrome to the left part of the *sphendone*, B to the right. I then stand the dioptra at the so-called undivided area, slightly distant from the upper turning post opposite, <for example> at point Γ, so as not to obstruct the line of sight along the straight course between the given points. Having set the disc to the position of the plane of the base of the *sphendone*, I draw two straight lines with the sight-rod, to the left extremity ΓA, to the right ΓB. Having measured one of these, as described before,

ὀργυῶν τυχὸν ρκϛ΄, μετέρχομαι ἐπὶ τὸ ἕτερον τοῦ κανόνος
ἀγγεῖον· καὶ ἀκινήτων πάντων τῶν ἐν τῇ διόπτρᾳ μενόντων,
15 ἀνανεύω μικρὸν τὸ τύμπανον, καὶ λαμβάνω ἐπ᾽ εὐθείας τῆς
ΒΓ, ὡς πρὸς μέρος αὐτῆς ὀκτωκαιδέκατον ἐπὶ τὰ εὐώνυμα τοῦ
ἁπλοῦ πρὸς ζ΄ ὀργυάς, σημεῖον τὸ Δ· ὁμοίως δὲ καὶ ‖ ἐπὶ τὰ δεξιὰ   f. 44v
ἐπ᾽ εὐθείας τῆς ΑΓ, τὸ Ε, καὶ ἐπιζευγνύω τὴν ΕΔ. Καὶ ἐπεὶ
ὀκτωκαιδέκατόν ἐστι μέρος ἡ ΕΓ τῆς ΓΑ, καὶ ἡ ΔΓ τῆς ΓΒ,
20 ὀκτωκαιδέκατον καὶ τὸ τῆς ΔΕ διάστημα πρὸς τὸ τῆς ΑΒ ἔσται.
Ὡς γὰρ αἱ ἐλάσσονες πλευραὶ τῶν σχηματιζομένων δύο
ἀντικορύφων τριγώνων εἰσὶ πρὸς τὰς μείζονας, οὕτως καὶ ἡ τοῦ
ἐλάσσονος βάσις πρὸς τὴν τοῦ μείζονος ἔσται. Μετρήσας δὲ
τὴν ΔΕ τοῦ ἐλάσσονος τριγώνου βάσιν, ὡς πρὸς ἡμᾶς οὖσαν,
25 καὶ εὑρὼν αὐτὴν ὀργυῶν τυχὸν δύο ἥμισυ, ἔχω καὶ τὴν ΑΒ
ἐγνωσμένην, ὡς ὀκτωκαιδεκαπλασίαν ὑπάρχουσαν· ὥστε πάλιν
τὸ μεταξὺ τῶν Α, Β σημείων διάστημα, Ι κατὰ τὸ πέλμα, τοῦ   Vin 362
πλάτους τοῦ ἱππικοῦ πρὸς τῇ βάσει τῆς σφενδόνης, εὕρηται
ὀργυῶν με΄. ‖   f. 45
    5. ⟨Δ⟩υνατὸν δέ ἐστι μὴ μόνον τὸ μεταξὺ τῶν δοθέντων δύο
σημείων λαμβάνειν διάστημα, ἀλλὰ καὶ τὴν θέσιν ἀνευρίσκειν
τῆς τὰ σημεῖα ἐπιζευγνυούσης εὐθείας, μὴ προσεγγίσαντάς τινι
τῶν δοθέντων σημείων.
5   Ἔστωσαν τὰ ὁρώμενα σημεῖα τὰ Α, Β, τὸ μὲν Α πρὸς ἓν τῶν
τοῦ εὐρίπου ἑπτὰ τμημάτων, ἐπὶ τῆς τῶν στηθέων σκοπούμενον
βάσεως, τὸ δὲ Β πρὸς τὸ ἐπὶ τοῦ βασιλικοῦ καθίσματος ἔδαφος,
ἢ μιᾶς τῶν ἐφ᾽ ἑκάτερα ἐν τοῖς δρομεῦσι κατὰ τοὺς γυμνικοὺς
ἀγῶνας καλουμένων παρασκευῶν. Καταστήσας οὖν τὴν
10 διόπτραν πρὸς τὴν τῆς κάτω νύσσης ἀντιπεριαγωγήν,
ἀπεναντίον τοῦ Β, κατὰ τὸ Γ σημεῖον, διοπτεύω διὰ τοῦ κανόνος,
ἕως ἐπ᾽ εὐθείας τὸ ῥηθὲν Α ἐξ ἄκρου θεάσομαι. Καὶ μετελθὼν
πρὸς τὸ πλάγιον τῆς διόπτρας τὸ ἐπὶ τῇ νύσσῃ, μικρὸν ἀνανεύω
τὸ τύμπανον, καὶ διάγω εὐθεῖαν καταντικρὺ τῆς τῶν βαθμίδων

5: 1–2 ⟨Δ⟩υνατὸν – διάστημα: cf. Hero *Dioptr.* X:1–3; XIII: 26–27.   2 τὴν θέσιν: cf. Hero
Dioptr. X:3; XIII: 26.

---

14 ἀγγεῖον Vin: αὐγεῖον VP ‖ 17 ἁπλοῦ   Vin ‖ 5: 11 ἀπεναντίον VP: ἐπ᾽ ἐναντίον Vin ‖
διοπτεύω Vin: διοπτρεύω VP

and finding it to be perhaps 126 *orgyai*, I move to the other housing of the sight-rod. And with all the other parts of the dioptra remaining unmoved, I tilt the disc up a little and I take point Δ along the <prolongation of> line BΓ, at for example 1/18th of its length, to the left of the undivided area, that is, at 7 *orgyai*; likewise also to the right on <the prolongation of> the line AΓ, point E, and I join EΔ. And since EΓ is 1/18th of ΓA, and ΔΓ <is 1/18th> of ΓB, the interval ΔE will be 1/18th of AB. For as the smaller sides of the two triangles, depicted joined at the apex, are to the larger, so also will the base of the smaller be to that of the larger. And having measured the base ΔE of the smaller triangle as being within our reach, and finding this to be perhaps 21/2 *orgyai*, I have ascertained too AB, as 18 times this. So in turn the interval between points A and B, in the arena, <the interval> of the width of the hippodrome at the base of the *sphendone*, has been found to be 45 *orgyai*.

<fig. 31>

5. It is possible not only to take the interval between two given points, but also to find the position of a straight line joining the points, without approaching either of the given points.

Let the visible points be A and B, A at one of the seven sections of the *euripos*, viewed at the base of the balustrades, B on the ground by the imperial *kathisma*, or by one of what are called among the runners in the athletic contests pavilions, on either side <of it>. So having set the dioptra at the counterturn of the lower turning post, opposite B at point Γ, I sight with the sight-rod until I see on a straight line the previously mentioned <point> A from the extremity. And moving to the side of the dioptra toward the turning post, I tilt the disc up a little and I draw a straight line ΓΔ directly down from the flight of stairs, observed,

15 ἀναβάθρας τὴν ΓΔ, | ὡς ἐπὶ τὸ ἔδαφος τῶν προεστώτων στηθέων   Vin 364
παρατηρουμένην κατὰ τὸ Δ σημεῖον, πρὸς ὀρθὰς οὖσαν τῇ ΑΓ
ἐν ὀρθῇ γωνίᾳ τῇ πρὸς τὸ Γ. Καὶ παράγω τὴν διόπτραν ἐπὶ τῆς
ΓΔ, ἕως ἐπ᾽ εὐθείας τὸ Β σημεῖον ἐπόψομαι. Τετάχθω ἡ διόπτρα
κατὰ τὸ Ε· ἡ ἄρα ΒΕ ‖ τῇ μὲν ΓΔ πρὸς ὀρθάς ἐστι, τῇ δὲ ΑΓ   f. 45v
20 παράλληλος. Δύναμαι δὲ τὸ ἀπὸ τοῦ Γ ἐπὶ τὸ Α, καὶ τὸ ἀπὸ τοῦ
Ε ἐπὶ τὸ Β λαβεῖν διάστημα, ὡς πολλάκις τριγωνίσας τὸ σχῆμα
ὑπεθέμην. Καὶ εἰ μὲν ἴσην εὕρω τὴν ΓΑ τῇ ΕΒ, ἴσον καὶ τὸ ΓΕ
διάστημα τῷ ΑΒ ἀποφανοῦμαι. Εἰ δὲ μίαν αὐτῶν μείζονα τῆς
ἑτέρας, ἀφαιρῶ τὴν ὑπεροχὴν ἐκ τῆς μείζονος, καὶ οὕτως
25 ἐπιζευγνύω τὴν ἐλάσσονα· οἷον, εἰ εὕρω τὴν ΓΕ τοῦ πλάτους
ὀργυῶν δώδεκα, τὴν δὲ ΓΑ ϛ΄, καὶ πα΄ τὴν ΕΒ, τὰς ὑπερεχούσας
ὀργυὰς ἐννέα ἀπὸ τοῦ Γ ἐπὶ τὸ Ζ ἀφαιρῶ, καὶ οὕτως ἐπιζευγνύω
τὴν ἐλάσσονα διὰ τῆς ΖΕ ἴσης οὔσης καὶ παραλλήλου κατὰ
τὴν θέσιν τῇ ΑΒ. Εἰ μὲν γὰρ ἴση ἦν ἡ ΑΓ τῇ ΒΕ, δώδεκα ἂν
30 ὀργυῶν καὶ τὸ τῆς ΑΒ διάστημα, ὡς τὸ τῆς ΓΕ, ὑπῆρχεν· ἐπεὶ δὲ
ὑπερέχουσα ἡ ΓΑ τῆς ΕΒ εὑρέθη ὀργυὰς ἐννέα, ταύτας ἡ ΖΕ
ἀπολαμβάνει, καὶ τὴν πρὸς τὸ Γ ὀρθὴν ὑποτείνει γωνίαν. Ἔστιν
δὲ καὶ ἡ ΓΕ βάσις ὀργυῶν δώδεκα, ὥστε ιε΄ ἡ ΖΕ ἔσται, ὡς κατὰ
δύναμιν δυσὶ ταῖς περὶ τὴν ὀρθὴν ἐξισουμένη πλευραῖς. Τῶν
35 αὐτῶν ἄρα ὀργυῶν ‖ καὶ τὸ ἀπὸ τοῦ Α διάστημα ἐπὶ τὸ Β ἔσται.   f. 46
Ὥστε εὕρηται οὐ μόνον τὸ μεταξὺ τῶν Α, Β σημείων κατὰ
μέγεθος διάστημα, ἀλλὰ καὶ ἡ θέσις τῆς τὰ σημεῖα
ἐπιζευγνυούσης εὐθείας, καθὼς καὶ τὸ προκείμενον ὑπετέθη
διάγραμμα. | Vin 366

6. ⟨Κ⟩αὶ τὴν μὲν εὐθυμετρίαν οὕτως ἐπιγνωσόμεθα· τὰ δὲ ὑπὸ
τῶν εὐθυγράμμων τε καὶ περιφερογράμμων σχημάτων
περιεχόμενα ἐπίπεδα χωρία μετρηθήσεται τρόπῳ τοιῷδε.
Ἐπὶ μὲν τετραγώνων ἰσοπλεύρων τε καὶ ἑτερομήκων τὴν τοῦ
5 μήκους δεῖ πλευρὰν ἐπὶ τὴν τοῦ πλάτους πολλαπλασιάζειν, ἢ
καὶ ἀνάπαλιν, καὶ τὸν ἐκ τῶν δύο πλευρῶν γινόμενον ἐπίπεδον
ἀριθμὸν τὸ τοῦ σχήματος ἐμβαδὸν ἀποφαίνεσθαι, ἤτοι τὸ ὑπὸ
τῶν τεσσάρων ‖ πλευρῶν περιοριζόμενον χωρίον, ὡς ἐπὶ τοῦ   f. 46v
ῥηθέντος δειχθήσεται διαγράμματος. Ἐπεὶ γὰρ ἡ ΑΓ ὀργυῶν

---

23 τῷ P: τοῦ V ‖ 26 ΕΒ Vin: ΕΔ VP ‖ 30 ΑΒ Vin: ΑΕ VP

for example, at the bottom of the front balustrades at point Δ perpendicular to AΓ in a right angle at Γ. And I move the dioptra along ΓΔ until I see point B on a straight line. Let the dioptra be stationed at E. Then BE is perpendicular to ΓΔ, parallel to AΓ. I am able to take the interval from Γ to A, and that from E to B as I have often proposed by constructing the triangular figure. And if I find ΓA equal to EB, I shall conclude that the interval ΓE is equal to AB. And if I find one of these larger than the other, I subtract the excess from the greater one, and so I join the smaller; for example, if I find ΓE of 12 *orgyai* in width, ΓA 90, and EB 81, I subtract the excess 9 *orgyai,* from Γ to Z, and so I join the smaller through ZE, which is equal and parallel in position to AB. For if AΓ is equal to BE, the interval AB would be 12 *orgyai,* as is that of ΓE. When ΓA is found to exceed EB by 9 *orgyai,* ZE removes these <9> and subtends the right angle at Γ. The base ΓE is 12 *orgyai* so that ZE will be 15, its square being equal to the <sum of> the squares of the two sides at the right angle. The interval from A to B then will consist of these <15> *orgyai.* So not only is the interval between points A and B found in size, but also the position of the straight line joining the points, as the diagram set forth here also demonstrates.

<fig. 32>

6. We will determine thus linear measurement; but plane surfaces contained by rectilinear and curvilinear figures will be measured in the following way.

For square and oblong quadrilaterals it is necessary to multiply the sides, the length by the width, or also vice versa, and to conclude that the area of the figure is the square number from the two sides, that is, the surface delimited by the four sides, as will be shown by the aforesaid diagram. For when AΓ is 90 *orgyai,*

10 ἐστιν ∠΄, δώδεκα δὲ ἡ ΓΕ, ἐπ᾽ ἀλλήλας πολλαπλασιαζόμεναι
,απ᾽ ποιοῦσιν, ὅπερ ἐστὶ τὸ ὅλον τοῦ ἑτερομήκους χωρίον· ὁ
αὐτὸς δὲ τρόπος καὶ ἐπὶ ἰσοπλεύρων τετραγώνων γινέσθω.
Παρομοίαν δὲ καὶ φανερὰν ἕξουσι τὴν ἀναμέτρησιν καὶ οἱ
καλούμενοι ῥόμβοι, ὡς ἐκ τετραγώνων ἰσοπλεύρων διαστροφῆς
15 γινόμενοι, καθάπερ καὶ τὰ ῥομβοειδῆ ἐκ τῶν ἑτερομήκων· καὶ
γὰρ τὰς πλευρὰς ὡρισμένας ἔχουσι, καὶ μίαν τῶν διαγωνίων
δοθεῖσαν. Ὁ μὲν γὰρ ῥόμβος ἐκ δύο ἰσοσκελῶν σύγκειται
τριγώνων, τὸ δὲ ῥομβοειδὲς ἐκ δύο ὀξυγωνίων ἢ ἀμβλυγωνίων,
ὡς ἐπὶ τοῦ αὐτοῦ διαγράμματός ἐστιν ἰδεῖν, τὸ ὑπὸ τῆς ΖΕ καὶ
20 ΑΒ ἐξ ἑτερομήκους διαστροφῆς ἐπὶ τὸ ῥομβοειδὲς
μετασχηματισθέν, καὶ ὑπὸ μὲν τῆς ΖΒ διαγωνίου εἰς δύο
τρίγωνα ὀξυγώνια διαιρούμενον, ὑπὸ δὲ τῆς ΑΕ εἰς δύο
ἀμβλυγώνια. Τὰ | δὲ τῶν τριγώνων χωρία ἐξ ἡμισείας τῶν ἐξ   Vin 368
αὐτῶν ἀναγραφομένων τετραγώνων ἀπαριθμεῖν χρή· ἐπεὶ καὶ

6: 13–18 φανερὰν – ἀμβλυγωνίων: cf. Hero *Metrica* I:14:10–15.

6: 13 ἀναμέτρησιν: in marg. V: Τὰ γὰρ πρὸς ἀναμέτρησιν καὶ σχηματισμὸν πόρρωθεν
κατὰ μεγέθ(η) ἐπιγινωσκόμενα χωρία στρατηγικὴν ἐπιστήμην πρὸς πολιορκίαν τε καὶ
μάχης ἀντιπαράταξιν τακτικῶς ἐφοδιάζειν εἴωθε· καὶ γὰρ ὁ τῶν στρατῶν ἐξάρχων πρὸς
τὰ τῶν τετραγώνων ἢ ἑτερομήκων χωρίων ἐπιστήσας μεγέθη, ὁπόσους ὁπλίτας κατὰ
πεζικὴν τάξιν ψιλούς τε καὶ πελταστὰς ἢ δορατοφόρους τε καὶ ἀκροβολιστὰς ἱππέας
κατὰ φαλαγγαρχίαν εἰσδέξονται· τῶν τε ῥομβοειδῶν πρὸς τὰ τῆς ἴλης ἐντάγματα ὁπόσους
ζυγοῦντας ἅμα καὶ στοιχοῦντας ἐκ περιττοῦ ἀριθμοῦ· ἢ ζυγοῦντας μὲν καὶ μὴ στοιχοῦντας
ἢ καὶ ἀνάπαλιν ἐξ ἀρτίου καὶ ὡς ὑπὸ τοῦ μέσου ζυγοῦ τῶν πλαγιοφυλάκων εἰς δύο
τεμνομένων ἔμβολα ἤτοι σφηνοειδῆ κατὰ μέτωπον σχήματα πρόσω μὲν κατὰ ἰλάρχην,
κατὰ δὲ οὐραγὸν ὄπισθεν, καὶ ὅπως δεῖ τὴν φάλαγγα πρὸς τὰς τῶν τόπων θέσεις κατὰ
δεξιόν τε καὶ λαιὸν καταλοχίσαι (καταλοχήση V) κέρας ἀντιπορείας χάριν ἢ
ὑπερκεράσεως (ὑπερκεράσεως V) τῶν πολεμίων· καὶ ἐπεὶ κατὰ βάθος ὁ λόχος ἀνὰ ὀκτὼ ἢ
δώδεκα ἀνδρῶν διὰ τὴν διμοιρίαν κατά τινας τάττεται, πλεόνων δὲ ὁτὲ (ὅτε V) καὶ
ἐλασσόνων κατὰ ἄρτιον ἀριθμὸν πρὸς τὸ τῶν πεζῶν καὶ τῶν ἱππέων πλῆθος ἄχρι μονάδος
διαιρούμενον· ἔστω οὖν ὁ λόχος ἀνὰ ις΄, ὅλη δὲ ἡ φάλαγξ μυρίων ἑξάκις χιλίων τπδ΄,
ὥστε ,ακδ΄ εἰσὶν οἱ κατὰ μέτωπον τῆς φάλαγγος ἀφωρισμένοι λοχαγοί· δῆλον δὲ ὅτι
τεταγμένοι μὲν ἤτοι ὡς ἀπὸ πηχῶν δ΄ ἀ||φεστῶτες ,δϛ΄ κατὰ τὸν περιορισμὸν ἕξουσι,
στάδια ὄντα ι΄ καὶ πήχεις ∠ϛ΄, πεπυκνωκότες δὲ ὡς ἀπὸ δύο πηχῶν στάδια ε΄ καὶ πήχεις
μη΄, κατὰ δὲ πῆχυν ἕνα συνησπικότες δύο ϛ΄ καὶ πήχεις κδ΄, τοῦ σταδίου ρ΄ ὀργυῶν ὄντος,
τῆς δὲ ὀργυᾶς πηχῶν δ΄, καὶ τοῦ πήχεως σπιθαμῶν β΄, δακτύλων δὲ κδ΄· ταῦτα συνιέντες
οἱ τῶν στρατευμάτων ἡγούμενοι, τὰς δὲ τῶν τόπων θέσεις κατὰ σχῆμα καὶ μέγεθος
ἐκλεγόμενοι πόρρωθεν εὐτάκτως τε καὶ ἀνεπισφαλῶς τὰς πορείας ποιήσονται, ἔν τε
πολιορκίαις καὶ ἀντιπαρατάξεσι τοὺς ἐναντίους καταγωνιζόμενοι.

and ΓE is 12, multiplied together they make 1,080, which is the whole surface of the oblong. Let the same method also be used for squares. The so-called rhombi will have similar and clear measurement[2] as being <a result of> the twisting of squares <fig. 33a>, as also the rhomboids <from twisting> of oblongs. For they have the sides defined and one of the diagonals given. For the rhombus is composed of two isosceles triangles, the rhomboid from two acute or two obtuse <triangles>, as is to be seen in the same diagram <figs. 32 and 34>, the figure being reformed from an oblong to a rhomboid by the twisting of ZE and AB, and divided into two acute triangles by the diagonal ZB, and by AE into two obtuse triangles. It is necessary to calculate the surfaces of the triangles from one-half of the quadrilaterals described

---

[2] [Marginal scholion] For the areas observed from a distance by size for measurement and representation customarily supply in good order knowledge for generals on both siege warfare and direct confrontation. For the commander of armies knows, in terms of the sizes of square and rectangular areas, how many hoplites in infantry order and light-armed troops and targeteers or mounted spear carriers and bowmen the areas will receive per *phalangarchia;* and of rhomboids, for the insertions of the squad, how many by rank and file in odd number, or by rank and not file or vice versa in even <number>; and, with the flank guards separated into two by the middle rank, how many beak formations, that is, wedge shaped in front, by squad commander forward, by squad-closer behind; and how it is necessary to divide up the phalanx with regard to the local topography by right or left wing for a countermovement or wing-envelopment of the enemy. And when the rank is arranged eight men deep, or twelve for the "double quarter" according to some, but sometimes more and less, by even number divisible to unity for the number of infantry and cavalry, let then the rank be 16, the whole phalanx 16,384, so the file leaders stationed at the face of the phalanx number 1,024. It is clear that drawn up <in standard formation>, that is, 4 *pecheis* apart, they will have 4,096 <*pecheis*> at the boundary, which is 10 *stadia* and 96 *pecheis;* but compacted to 2 *pecheis* apart they will have 5 *stadia* and 48 *pecheis;* but shield to shield at 1 *pechys* apart they will have 21/2 <*stadia*>, and 24 *pecheis.* <For> the *stadion* is 100 *orgyai,* the *orgya* 4 *pecheis,* and the *pechys* 2 *spithamai,* but 24 *daktyloi.* And knowing these things the leaders of expeditions, selecting from local topography by form and size from a distance, will make their marches in good order and steadfastly, prevailing over the enemy in sieges and direct confrontations.

25 πᾶν τετράγωνον ὑπὸ τῆς διαγωνίου εἰς δύο τέμνεται τρίγωνα,
τὸ δὲ πεντάγωνον εἰς τρία, τὸ ἑξάγωνον εἰς τέσσαρα, καὶ ἐφεξῆς
ὁμοίως ἡ διαίρεσις γινέσθω. Καὶ εἰ μὲν ‖ τὸ ἐμβαδὸν τοῦ   f. 47
τετραγώνου ‚α΄ εὑρίσκηται, φ΄ τὸ τοῦ τριγώνου ἔσται. Ὅτι δὲ
καὶ πᾶν τὸ νοήσει τε καὶ αἰσθήσει καταλαμβανόμενον τρίγωνον
30 τὰς τρεῖς γωνίας δυσὶν ὀρθαῖς ἴσας ἔχει, δῆλον ἐνταῦθά ἐστιν·
εἰ γὰρ πᾶν τετράγωνον τέτρασιν ὀρθαῖς ἴσας ἔχει τὰς γωνίας,
ὑπὸ δὲ τῆς διαγωνίου εἰς δύο ἀφορίζεται τρίγωνα καὶ γωνίας
ἕξ, τὰς μὲν ὀρθάς, τὰς δὲ κατὰ τὸ μᾶλλον καὶ ἧττον ὀξυνομένας
τε καὶ ἀμβλυνομένας, αὗται δὲ αἱ ἓξ ἐπὶ παντὸς τετραγώνου
35 τέτρασιν ὀρθαῖς ἴσαι εἰσίν, ἑκάτερον ἄρα τῶν ἀφοριζομένων
δύο τριγώνων τὰς τρεῖς γωνίας δυσὶν ὀρθαῖς ἴσας ἕξει· ὅθεν
καὶ πᾶν τὸ αἰσθήσει τε καὶ φαντασίᾳ καταληφθῆναι δυνάμενον.
Περὶ δὲ μετρήσεως τραπεζίων τε καὶ τραπεζοειδῶν
καλουμένων, ὡς ἀπὸ τῆς τῶν γωνιῶν τεταγμένων ἰσότητος, καὶ
40 λοιπῶν τεταγμένων τε καὶ ἀτάκτων σχημάτων, Ἀρχιμήδης καὶ
Ἥρων ἐν τῇ καθολικῇ πραγματείᾳ τοῖς ἐντελεστέροις
ἀπέδειξαν· ἡμεῖς δέ, τοὺς εἰσαγομένους πρὸς τὰ μαθήματα
ἐρεθίζειν βουλόμενοι, μετρικὰς ὑπομνήσεις ἠνθολογήσαμεν,
ἀφορμὰς ὑποθέσεων διὰ τὸ εὐπρόθυμον παρεχόμενοι· καί, τὸ
45 δὴ λεγόμενον κατὰ τὴν παροιμίαν "ἐν πίθῳ μανθάνειν αὐτοὺς
τὴν κεραμείαν" προϋπεθέμεθα. ‖ | f. 47v

7. ⟨Κ⟩ύκλου δὲ διάμετρον καὶ τὴν πρὸς αὐτὴν γινομένην   Vin 370
περίμετρον, καὶ τὸ ὅλον χωρίον μετὰ διόπτρας εὑρήσομεν, ἐπὶ
τοῦ κέντρου τοῦ κύκλου ἑστῶτες, μὴ προσεγγίσαντες τῇ
περιφερείᾳ.

5 Ἔστω τοίνυν τὸ τοῦ κύκλου κέντρον τὸ Α σημεῖον, καθ' ὃ τὴν
δίοπτραν ἵστημι· καὶ καταστήσας τὸ ἐν αὐτῇ τύμπανον πρὸς
τὴν θέσιν τοῦ ἐπιπέδου ὑφ' οὗ μέλλει ὁ ἐκ τῆς διοπτρείας
καταγράφεσθαι κύκλος, λαμβάνω σημεῖον διὰ τῶν ὀπῶν τοῦ
κανόνος ἐπ' εὐθείας τὸ Β, καὶ ἀπὸ τοῦ αὐτοῦ σημείου
10 κυκλοτερῶς περιάγω τὸ τύμπανον σὺν τῷ κανόνι διὰ τῆς

45–46 ἐν – κεραμείαν: cf. Pl. *Grg.* 514E.

---

32 ἀφορίζεται Vin: ἀφαιρίζεται VP ‖ 39 τεταγμένων Vin: τετραμμένων VP

from them. And since every quadrilateral is cut into two triangles by the diagonal, the pentagon into three, the hexagon
into four, let the <further> division be similar in sequence. And
if the area of the quadrilateral should be found to be 1,000, that
of the triangle will be 500. This is herein clear, that every triangle
conceived in concept and reality has three angles equal to two
right angles: for if every quadrilateral has its angles equal to four
right angles, <and> it is partitioned into two triangles and six
angles by the diagonal (the right angles and the greater and smaller
acute and obtuse angles), and these six are in every quadrilateral
equal to four right angles, then each of the two partitioned triangles will have three angles equal to two right angles <fig. 33b>.
And so it is for every triangle able to be conceived in reality and
imagination. Concerning measurement of so-called trapezia and
trapezoids, as classified from the equality of the angles, and the
remaining regular and irregular figures, Archimedes and Heron
in the general treatise have explained for the more accomplished.
But we, wishing to motivate those being introduced to mathematics, have culled suggestions on measurement, furnishing starting points for the subjects to promote eagerness. And we have
assumed as a basis the proverbial saying "they learn pottery on
the pot."

7. We shall find the diameter of a circle and its circumference
and its complete surface with a dioptra, standing at the center of
the circle, not approaching its perimeter.

Let then the center of the circle be point A, at which I stand
the dioptra. And setting the disc on it to the position of the plane
by which the circle is to be described with dioptrics, I take a
point B through the <sight->holes of the sight-rod on a straight
line; and from the same point I turn the disc with the sight-rod

ἐπικειμένης τῷ τόρμῳ χοινικίδος, ἢ στύρακος ἐν τῇ διόπτρᾳ
τυχόντος, ἕως πάλιν ἐπὶ τοῦ αὐτοῦ σημείου κατὰ τοῦ δοθέντος
ἐπιπέδου ἡ περιαγωγὴ γένηται, ἀφ᾽ οὗ καὶ ἤρξατο φέρεσθαι.
Ἐν δὲ τῇ κυκλοτερεῖ ταύτῃ περιφορᾷ κατοπτευθήσεται σημεῖά
15 τινα τὰ τὸν κύκλον περιορίζοντα, πρὸς λίθους ἢ θάμνους ἤ τινας
ἄλλους εὐθεωρήτους σκοπούς, οἷά εἰσι τὰ Β, Γ, Δ, Ε, Ζ, Η, ⟨Θ,⟩ Ι,
Κ, Λ, Μ, Ν, Ξ, Ο, Π· καὶ ταῦτα ἐπὶ τῷ περιορισμῷ τοῦ κύκλου
σημειωσάμενος, μετρῶ τὸ ἀπὸ τοῦ Α ἐπὶ τὸ Β διάστημα, ἤτοι τὸ
ἀπὸ τοῦ κέντρου ἐπὶ τὴν περιφέρειαν, ὡς ἐπὶ τοῦ μήκους καὶ
20 πλάτους ἐμάθομεν· καὶ εὑρὼν αὐτὸ ὀργυῶν τυχὸν ρε΄, ἔχω καὶ
τὴν ὅλην τοῦ κύκλου διάμετρον σι΄, | ὡς διπλασίαν τῆς ἐκ ‖ τοῦ   Vin 372
κέντρου. Ὅτι δὲ πάσης διαμέτρου τριπλασιεφέβδομός ἐστιν ἡ   f. 48
περίμετρος, δήλη ἐστὶν χξ΄ καὶ αὐτὴ οὖσα, ὡς τρὶς τὸν σι΄
ἔχουσα καὶ τὸ ἕβδομον αὐτοῦ. Ἀλλ᾽ ἐπεὶ πάλιν τὸ ἐκ τῆς
25 διαμέτρου καὶ τοῦ τετάρτου τῆς περιμέτρου ἴσον ἐστὶ τῷ τοῦ
κύκλου ἐμβαδῷ, καθά φησιν Ἀρχιμήδης ὅτι, "Πᾶς κύκλος ἴσος
ἐστὶ τριγώνῳ ὀρθογωνίῳ, οὗ ἡ ἐκ τοῦ κέντρου ἴση ἐστὶ μιᾷ τῶν
περὶ τὴν ὀρθὴν γωνίαν, ἡ δὲ περίμετρος τῇ βάσει," τὸ δὲ ἀπὸ
τῆς διαμέτρου καὶ τῆς ὅλης περιμέτρου τετραπλάσιον τοῦ
30 κύκλου· αἱ ἄρα τῆς διαμέτρου ὀργυαὶ σι΄, ἐπὶ τὰς ρξε΄ τοῦ
τετάρτου τῆς περιμέτρου πολλαπλασιαζόμεναι, γίνονται
χιλιάδες λδ΄, καὶ χν΄· ὅπερ ἐστὶ τὸ τοῦ κύκλου ἐμβαδόν· τὰ γὰρ
σ΄ ἐπὶ τὰ ρ΄ χιλιάδας κ΄ ποιοῦσι· ἐπὶ δὲ τὰ ξ΄, δώδεκα· καὶ ἐπὶ
τὰ ε΄, ͵α΄· καὶ πάλιν τὰ ι΄ ἐπὶ τὰ ρ΄, ͵α΄· ἐπὶ δὲ τὰ ξ΄, χ΄· καὶ ἐπὶ
35 τὰ ε΄, ν΄· ὥστε εὕρηται ἡ μὲν ἀπὸ τοῦ κέντρου τοῦ κύκλου ρε΄, ἡ
δὲ διάμετρος σι΄, καὶ ἡ περίμετρος χξ΄· τὸ δὲ ἐμβαδόν, ἤτοι τὸ
ὅλον χωρίον ἀπό τε τῆς διαμέτρου καὶ τοῦ τετάρτου τῆς
περιμέτρου, ὀργυῶν χιλιάδων λδ΄, καὶ χν΄. ‖   f. 48v, 49
Εὐχερέστερον δὲ καὶ ἄνευ διόπτρας τὴν τοῦ κύκλου διάμετρόν
40 τε καὶ περίμετρον καὶ τὸ ὅλον χωρίον ἐπιγνωσόμεθα, ἀπὸ
σχοίνου τινὸς κατὰ μῆκος δοθείσης. Ἔστω οὖν ἡ δοθεῖσα

7: 15–16 λίθους – σκοπούς: cf. Afric. *Cest.* VII:15.   26–28 Πᾶς – βάσει: cf. Archim. *Circ.*
I:232:1–3.

7: 16 Θ P, om. V (cf. V f. 48v: Θ, in pictura) ‖ 16–17 Ι Κ P: Κ Ι V ‖ 17 τοῦ κύκλου Vin: τῷ
κύκλῳ VP

around in a circle by means of the cylinder resting on the stud, or perhaps by a <screw->shaft in the dioptra, until it comes around again to the same point in the given plane from which it also began to be moved. In this circular turn some points will be observed that delimit the circle, at stones or shrubs or some other easily observed markers, such as B, Γ, Δ, E, Z, H, <Θ>, I, K, Λ, M, N, Ξ, O, Π. And having marked these at the boundary of the circle, I measure the interval from A to B, that is, from the center of the circle to the perimeter, as we learned for length and width. And finding this perhaps 105 *orgyai,* I also have the entire diameter of the circle as 210, as being double the radius. As the circumference is 3 1/7 times the entire diameter, this is clearly 660, as containing 3 times 210 and 1/7 of it. But since in turn the <product> of the diameter and 1/4 of the circumference is equal to the area of the circle (as Archimedes says, "Every circle is equal to a right triangle, of which the radius is equal to one of <the sides> at the right angle, the circumference to the base"), the <product> of the diameter and the whole circumference is 4 times <the area of> the circle. The 210 *orgyai* of the diameter then, multiplied by the 165 of the 1/4 of the circumference are 34,650, which is the area of the circle. For the 200 <multiplied> by the 100 make 20,000; and by the 60, 12,000; and by the 5, 1000; and again the 10 by 100, 1,000; and by the 60, 600; and by the 5, 50. So that the radius of the circle has been found to be 105, the diameter 210, and the circumference 660; the area, that is, the entire surface, <derived> from the diameter and 1/4 of the circumference, 34,650 *orgyai.*

<fig. 35>

More easily even and without a dioptra will we determine the diameter and circumference and entire surface of the circle, with

σχοῖνος ὀργυῶν κατὰ μῆκος λε΄, ἢ ὅσον ἄν τις κατὰ γνώμην
ἕληται· καὶ πρὸς μὲν τὸ ἓν ἄκρον κρίκον σιδηροῦν μετὰ ἥλου
ἐχέτω, τοῦ ἥλου ἐν τάξει κέντρου τῇ γῇ ἐμπησσομένου, ὡς διὰ | Vin 374
45 τοῦ ἑτέρου ἄκρου τὴν κυκλοτερῆ περιγραφὴν κατὰ τάξιν
ἀποτελεῖσθαι, ἕως ἀφ᾽ οὗ ἤρξατο σημείου, ἐπὶ τοῦ αὐτοῦ πάλιν
ἡ σχοῖνος τετανυσμένη περιαχθῇ· ὥστε ἡ ἐν ἀρχῇ καὶ ἡ ἀπ᾽
ἀρχῆς καὶ ἡ ἐπ᾽ ἀρχὴν τριαδικῶς ἐπὶ τῇ τοῦ κύκλου περιγραφῇ
θεωρηθήσεται· ἐν ἀρχῇ μὲν αὐτὸ τὸ κέντρον περὶ ὃ τὸ ἄκρον
50 τῆς σχοίνου ἐπὶ τοῦ ἥλου διὰ τοῦ κρίκου περιάγεται· ἀπ᾽ ἀρχῆς
δὲ τὸ ἕτερον τῆς σχοίνου ἄκρον τὸ περὶ τὴν ἐπ᾽ ἀρχὴν κατ᾽
ἴσην διάστασιν κυκλοτερῶς ἐπὶ τὰ Β, Γ, Δ, Ε, Ζ, Η, Θ σημεῖα
περιαγόμενον. Οὕτως οὖν τοῦ κύκλου δηλωθέντος, εὑρεθήσεται
μὲν ἡ διάμετρος ὀργυῶν ο΄, ὡς διπλασία τῆς ἐκ τοῦ κέντρου,
55 τῆς δὲ διαμέτρου τριπλασιεφέβδομος ἡ περίμετρος ὀργυῶν σκ΄
τυγχάνουσα, καὶ τὸ ἀπὸ τῆς διαμέτρου καὶ τοῦ τετάρτου τῆς
περιμέτρου, γων΄, ὅπερ ἐστὶ τὸ τοῦ κύκλου ἐμβαδόν· αἱ γὰρ ο΄
τῆς διαμέτρου ἐπὶ τὰς ν΄ τοῦ τετάρτου τῆς περιμέτρου, γφ΄
ποιοῦσιν, καὶ ἐπὶ τὰς ε΄, ‖ τν΄· ὥστε ἀπὸ τῆς δοθείσης σχοίνου   f. 49v
60 τῶν λε΄ ὀργυῶν, εὕρηται ἡ μὲν τοῦ κύκλου διάμετρος ὀργυῶν
ο΄, κ΄ δὲ καὶ σ΄ ἡ περίμετρος, καὶ γων΄ τὸ περιεχόμενον
χωρίον. ‖   f. 50

8. ⟨Τ⟩ὰ δὲ στερεὰ τῶν σχημάτων οὐχ ὡς τὰ ῥηθέντα ἐπίπεδα
πρὸς δύο μόνον θεωρηθήσεται διαστάσεις, ἀλλ᾽ ἀνάγκη ἐπὶ
τρεῖς· ἐπεὶ καὶ πᾶν σῶμα τριχῇ ἐστι διαστατόν, μῆκος ἔχον
πλάτος τε καὶ πάχος, ταὐτὸ δὲ εἰπεῖν βάθος ἢ ὕψος· τὸν γὰρ ἐκ
5 τοῦ μήκους καὶ πλάτους γινόμενον ἐπίπεδον ἀριθμὸν ἐπὶ τὴν
τρίτην τοῦ ὕψους ποιοῦντας διάστασιν, τὰ στερεὰ τῶν
σχημάτων ἀπαριθμεῖν. | Vin 376

Καὶ πρότερον μὲν ἐπὶ κυβικοῦ σχήματος ἡ ἀναμέτρησις
γινέσθω διὰ τὸ ἴσον πάντῃ τῶν διαστάσεων· κύβος γάρ ἐστι
10 σχῆμα στερεὸν ὑπὸ ἓξ τετραγώνων ἴσων περιεχόμενον, ἐπὶ

8: 3–4 σῶμα – ὕψος: cf. Hero *Deff.* 11.   9–10 κύβος – περιεχόμενον: Euc. XI *def.* 5.

---

44 ἐμπηξομένου Vin ‖ 58 ν΄ Vin: νε΄ VP ‖ 8: 7 Post σχημάτων add. δεῖ Vin

a rope of given length. Let then the given rope be of 35 *orgyai* in length, or however long one might judge preferable. At one end let it have an iron ring with a nail, the nail fixed in the ground in the center position, so as to complete in good order with the other end the delineation of the circle, as from the point where it began the rope, stretched taut, is brought around again to the same <point>. So the rope in the beginning and from the beginning and with respect to the beginning will be seen from three perspectives in the delineation of the circle. In the beginning there is the center itself around which the end of the rope on the nail is drawn by means of the ring; from the beginning there is the other end of the rope which is drawn around in a circle at a distance that is equal with respect to the beginning on points B, Γ, Δ, E, Z, H, Θ. Thus when the circle has been made manifest, the diameter will be found of 70 *orgyai,* as double the radius, and the circumference 220 *orgyai* as being 31/7 of the diameter, and the <product> of the diameter and 1/4 of the circumference is 3,850, which is the area of the circle. For the 70 of the diameter <multiplied> by the 50 of 1/4 of the circumference, make 3,500 and by the 5, <make> 350. So from the given rope of 35 *orgyai* the diameter of the circle has been found, 70 *orgyai,* the circumference 220, and the contained surface 3,850.

<fig. 36>

8. Solid figures, unlike the previously discussed planes, will be viewed not in two dimensions only, but necessarily in three — in as much as every body is extended in three <dimensions>, having length, width, and thickness or, to say the same thing, depth or height — for <it is necessary> to calculate solid figures by multiplying the square number derived from the length and width by the third dimension of height.

And let <our> first measurement be on the cubic figure since all its dimensions are equal. For a cube is a solid figure

πλευραῖς μὲν ιβ΄, γωνίαις δὲ ὀρθαῖς η΄, καὶ ἐπιπέδοις ϛ΄, ἐν τρισὶ
διαστάσεσι κατ᾽ ἰσότητα θεωρούμενον· ὅθεν καὶ τοὺς
ἁρμονικοὺς ἐν συμφωνίᾳ καὶ θείους λόγους οἱ Πυθαγόρειοι ἐπὶ
τοιούτου δεικνύουσι σχήματος, ἁρμονίαν τὸν κύβον
15   ἐπονομάζοντες. Τὸ δὲ τοῦ σχήματος στερεὸν εὑρεθήσεται
οὕτως· εἰ γὰρ ἡ βάσις τοῦ κύβου μονάδων κη΄ κατὰ μῆκος εἴη,
τῶν αὐτῶν καὶ κατὰ πλάτος ἔσται, καὶ πρὸς ὕψος ὁμοίως· τὰς
δὲ τοῦ μήκους κη΄ ἐπὶ τὰς τοῦ πλάτους ποιοῦντες, τὸ τῆς βάσεως
ἐπίπεδον μονάδων ἕξομεν ψπδ΄· καὶ τοῦτο πάλιν ἐπὶ τὰς τοῦ
20   ὕψους κη΄ πολλαπλασιάζοντες, συνάγομεν μονάδας δισμυρίας,
‖ καὶ χιλιάδα ⟨καὶ⟩ ↗νβ΄· ἅσπερ ἀποφανούμεθα τὸ τοῦ κύβου   f. 50v
στερεόν. Εἰ δὲ ἐπὶ τοῦ αὐτοῦ κύβου ἰσοΰψῆ κύλινδρον
ἐπινοήσομεν ἐγγραφόμενον καὶ σφαῖραν μέσον
περιλαμβάνοντα, ὥστε κατὰ τὸν μέγιστον αὐτῆς κύκλον τῆς τοῦ
25   κυλίνδρου ἐφάπτεσθαι ἐπιφανείας, δειχθήσεται ἡ τοῦ κύβου
βάσις πρὸς τὴν τοῦ κυλίνδρου λόγον ἔχουσα ὃν ἐν ἐλαχίστοις
καὶ πρώτοις ἀριθμοῖς ὁ ιδ΄ πρὸς τὸν ια΄· ὡσαύτως δὲ καὶ τὰ ϛ΄
τοῦ κύβου ἐπίπεδα πρὸς τὴν ἐπιφάνειαν τοῦ κυλίνδρου σὺν ταῖς
δυσὶ βάσεσιν ἔσονται, καὶ τὰ δ΄ ἄνευ τῶν βάσεων, καὶ τὸ
30   στερεὸν πρὸς τὸ στερεὸν ἔσται· ἡ δὲ τοῦ κυλίνδρου ἐπιφάνεια
ἄνευ μὲν τῶν βάσεων ἴση ἐστὶ τῇ ἐπιφανείᾳ τῆς
ἐμπεριλαμβανομένης ὑπ᾽ αὐτοῦ σφαίρας, σὺν δὲ ταῖς βάσεσιν
ἡμιόλιος αὐτῆς ὁ κύλινδρος εὑρεθήσεται κατά τε τὴν
ἐπιφάνειαν καὶ τὸ στερεόν.
35   Ἡ δὲ τοῦ κυλίνδρου βάσις ἐπιγνωσθήσεται ἔκ τε τῆς διαμέτρου
καὶ τοῦ τετάρτου τῆς περιμέτρου, ὡς ἀνωτέρω προείρηται. Ἐπεὶ   Vin 378
γὰρ ἐδόθη κη΄ ἡ διάμετρος, πη΄ ἡ περίμετρος ἔσται
τριπλασιεφέβδομος οὖσα· καὶ ἔστι τὸ τέταρτον αὐτῆς κβ΄· τὰ
οὖν κη΄ ἐπὶ τὰ κβ΄ ποιοῦσι τὸ ἐμβαδὸν τῆς βάσεως χιϛ΄· ἔστι δὲ

---

11 πλευραῖς – ϛ΄: cf. Nicom. Ar. II:26:2.   26–27 ἐλαχίστοις – ἀριθμοῖς: cf. Euc. VII:21.   27
ιδ΄ – ια΄: cf. Archim. Circ. I:234:19–20; Hero Metrica I:26.   32–34 σὺν – στερεόν: cf. Archim.
Sph. Cyl. I:130:5–9; Method. II:438:25–27; Hero Metrica II:11.

---

11 πλευρὰς … γωνίας … ὀρθὰς Vin ‖ ἐπιπέδοις scripsi: ἐπίπεδα VP ‖ 13 Πυθαγόρειοι Vin:
πυθαγόριοι VP ‖ 21 χιλιάδα Vin: χιλιάδας VP ‖ καὶ add. Vin ‖ 28 σὺν Vin: καὶ VP

contained by six equal squares, on twelve edges, with eight right angles and six planes, viewed in three dimensions equally. Whence the Pythagoreans demonstrate by such a figure ratios that are harmonic in agreement and divine, naming the cube "harmony." The volume of the figure will be found thus. For if the base of the cube should be 28 units in length, it will be the same in width and likewise in height. And multiplying the 28 of the length by those of the width, we shall have the plane of the base 784 units, and multiplying this in turn by the 28 of the height we obtain 21,952. This we shall conclude is the volume of the cube. And if we shall imagine a cylinder of equal height inscribed in the same cube and comprehending a sphere in its interior, so that <the sphere> at its maximum circumference touches the surface of the cylinder, the base of the cube will be shown to have the ratio of 14:11 with respect to the base of the cylinder, <to express it> in numbers that are least and prime <to one another>. So also the six planes of the cube will be <similar> to the surface of the cylinder with the two bases, and four without the bases, and so will the volume be to the volume. The surface of the cylinder without the bases is equal to the surface of the sphere comprehended by it, but with the bases the cylinder will be found 11/2 times the <sphere> in surface and volume.

<fig. 37>

The base of the cylinder will be determined from the diameter and 1/4 of the circumference as was discussed above. For when the diameter has been given as 28, the circumference will be 88, being 31/7 of it. And 1/4 of it is 22. And thus the 28 <multiplied> by the 22 make the area of the base 616. The base of the cube is

40 καὶ ἡ βάσις τοῦ κύβου ψπδ΄· ὡς ἐν ἐλαχίστοις καὶ πρώτοις
ἔφημεν ἀριθμοῖς, ὁ ιδ΄ πρὸς τὸν ια΄· ὁ γὰρ ψπδ΄ ἔχει τὸν χις΄ ‖   f. 51
καὶ τὸ τέταρτον αὐτοῦ τὰ ρνδ΄, καὶ ἔτι τὸ μδ΄, ὅπερ ἐστὶ ιδ΄.

Οὕτως οὖν καὶ αἱ ἀπὸ τῆς βάσεως τοῦ κύβου ἀνεστηκυῖαι
τέσσαρες ἐπιφάνειαι πρὸς τὴν κυλινδρικὴν ἐπιφάνειαν ἔσονται,
45 καὶ τὰ ἓξ ἐπίπεδα πάλιν τοῦ κύβου πρός τε τὴν τοῦ κυλίνδρου
ἐπιφάνειαν καὶ τὰ τῶν βάσεων ἐπίπεδα, καὶ τὸ στερεὸν πρὸς τὸ
στερεόν· αἱ γὰρ τῆς βάσεως τοῦ κύβου τέσσαρες πλευραὶ ἐπὶ
τὰς κη΄ τοῦ ὕψους γίνονται ͵γρλς΄· καὶ αἱ πη΄ τῆς περιμέτρου
τῆς βάσεως τοῦ κυλίνδρου ἐπὶ τὰς τοῦ ὕψους κη΄, ͵βυξδ΄· καὶ
50 εἰσὶν ἐν τῷ αὐτῷ λόγῳ.

Ὡσαύτως καὶ τὰ ἓξ ἐπίπεδα τοῦ κύβου, ͵δψδ΄ γινόμενα, πρός
τε τὴν τοῦ κυλίνδρου ἐπιφάνειαν σὺν ταῖς ἐν τῇ ἕδρᾳ καὶ τῇ
ἐφέδρᾳ βάσεσι, τῶν ͵γχ϶ς΄ συναγομένων.

Ὁμοίως δὲ καὶ τὸ στερεὸν τοῦ κύβου, ἀπὸ τοῦ ἐπιπέδου τῆς
55 βάσεως τῶν ψπδ΄ ἐπὶ τὰς τοῦ ὕψους κη΄, ͵β καὶ ͵α϶νβ΄
εὑρισκόμενον, πρὸς τὸ τοῦ κυλίνδρου τὸ ἀπὸ τῶν χις΄ τῆς
βάσεως ἐπὶ ǀ τὰς αὐτὰς τοῦ ὕψους κη΄, ἃ ͵ζσμη΄ γινόμενον·   Vin 380
ὥστε ἐν τῷ αὐτῷ λόγῳ πάντοθεν τὸν κύβον περὶ τὸν
ἐγγραφόμενον ἰσοϋψῆ κύλινδρον θεωρεῖσθαι.

60 ⟨Ὅ⟩τι δὲ ἡμιόλιός ἐστιν ὁ κύλινδρος τῆς ἐγγραφομένης ἐν αὐτῷ
σφαίρας, δείξομεν οὕτως· ἐπεὶ γὰρ ἡ τοῦ κυλίνδρου ἐπιφάνεια
σὺν τοῖς ἐπιπέδοις τῶν βάσεων ͵γχ϶ς΄ ὑπάρχει, ἃ δὲ καὶ ͵ζσμη΄
τὸ στερεόν· δειχθήσεται ‖ καὶ ἡ τῆς σφαίρας ἐπιφάνεια, ἔκ τε
τῶν πη΄ τῆς περιμέτρου τοῦ ἐν αὐτῇ μεγίστου κύκλου καὶ τοῦ   f. 51v
65 ὕψους τοῦ ἄξονος τῶν κη΄, ͵βυξδ΄ γινομένη· τὸ δὲ στερεὸν αὐτῆς
ἀπὸ τῆς βάσεως τοῦ μεγίστου κύκλου τῶν χις΄ ἐπὶ τὸ δίμοιρον
τοῦ ἄξονος, ἤτοι ἐπὶ τὰς ιη΄ δίμοιρον, χιλιάδων ια΄ γινόμενον
καὶ υ϶η΄ διμοίρου. Καὶ ἔστιν ἡ ἐπιφάνεια πρὸς τὴν ἐπιφάνειαν,
καὶ τὸ στερεὸν πρὸς τὸ στερεόν, ὡς προείρηται, ἐν λόγῳ ἡμιολίῳ·
70 ὥστε δύο τριτημόρια ἡ σφαῖρα εὕρηται τοῦ περιλαμβάνοντος

60–61 ἡμιόλιός – σφαίρας: cf. Archim. *Sph. Cyl.* I:130:5–9; *Method.* II:438:25–27.

---

40 Post ψπδ΄ add. ἔστιν οὖν ἡ βάσις τοῦ κύβου πρὸς τὴν βάσιν τοῦ κυλίνδρου Vin
52 σὺν ταῖς ἐν Vin: καὶ ταῖς σὺν VP ‖ 53 ἐφέδρᾳ Vin: ἐφ΄ ἕδρᾳ VP ‖ 55 τὰς Vin: ταῖς VP ‖ 58
περὶ VP: πρὸς Vin ‖ 68 διμοίρου VP: δίμοιρον Vin

784, <a ratio of> 14:11, as we have said, in the numbers that are least and prime <to one another>. For the 784 contains the 616 and 1/4 of it, <namely> 154, and further 1/44, which is 14.

Such then too will be the four surfaces rising from the base of the cube <in relation> to the cylindric surface, and the six planes in turn of the cube to the surface of the cylinder and the planes of its bases, and the volume to the volume. For the four edges of the base of the cube <multiplied> by the 28 units of the height arc 3136; and the 88 of the circumference of the base of the cylinder multiplied by the 28 of the height 2,464; and they are in the same ratio.

So also the six planes of the cube, being 4,704, <are proportional> to the surface of the cylinder with the bases on the bottom and top, which is 3,696 in total.

Likewise the volume of the cube <derived> from the plane of the base of 784 multiplied by the 28 units of the height, being found as 21,952, <compared> to that of the cylinder <derived> from the 616 of the base multiplied by the same 28 of the height, is 17,248. So in the same ratio in all aspects is the cube viewed around an inscribed cylinder of equal height.

That the cylinder is 11/2 times the sphere inscribed inside it we shall demonstrate as follows. For since the surface of the cylinder with the planes of its bases is 3,696, the volume is 17,248. And the surface of the sphere will be shown, <derived> from the 88 <units> of the circumference of the largest circle in it and the height of the axis of 28, to be 2,464. The volume of <the sphere, derived> from the base of the largest circle of 616 units, <multiplied> by 2/3 of the axis, that is, by 182/3, is 11,4982/3. And the surface is proportional to the surface and the volume to the volume, as has been said, in the ratio of 11/2:1. So the sphere has

αὐτὴν ἰσοΰψοῦς κυλίνδρου. Πᾶσα δὲ σφαιρικὴ ἐπιφάνεια τοῦ
μὲν ἐμβαδοῦ τοῦ μεγίστου αὐτῆς κύκλου τετραπλασία ἐστί, τῆς
δὲ περιμέτρου τοσαυταπλασία, ὅσον καὶ ὁ ἐν αὐτῇ ἄξων κατὰ
μῆκός ἐστιν· τὰ γὰρ ‚βυξδ΄ τετραπλάσια μέν εἰσι τῶν χις΄,
75 ὀκτωκαιεικοσαπλάσια δὲ τῶν πη΄.

[Ἔστι δὲ καὶ πᾶσα σφαῖρα τετραπλασία κώνου τοῦ βάσιν μὲν
ἔχοντος τὸν μέγιστον τῆς σφαίρας κύκλον, ὕψος δὲ ἴσον τῇ ἐκ
τοῦ κέντρου τῆς σφαίρας. Καὶ γὰρ ἡ τῆς κωνικῆς βάσεως   Vin 382
περίμετρος, πη΄ οὖσα, ἐπὶ τὴν τοῦ ἄξονος ἡμίσειαν, ⟨ὡς⟩ πρὸς
80 ὕψος ⟨τὴν⟩ ἀπὸ τοῦ κέντρου ιδ΄, ‚ασλβ΄ ποιεῖ. Καὶ αἱ τοῦ
ἐμβαδοῦ τῆς βάσεως αἱ χις΄ ἐπὶ τὰς αὐτὰς ιδ΄ τῆς τοῦ ἄξονος
ἡμισείας, ‚ηχκδ΄· ὥστε τὸ ἡμισφαίριον, κατά τε τὴν ἐπιφάνειαν
καὶ τὸ στερεόν, ἴσον τοῖς δυσὶν εὕρηται ‖ κώνοις, ἡ δὲ σφαῖρα   f. 52
τέτρασιν.]
85 ⟨Κ⟩ῶνος δέ ἐστι σχῆμα στερεὸν ἀπὸ βάσεως κυκλικῆς πρὸς ἓν
σημεῖον μετέωρον συνεστώς. Κατὰ δὲ Εὐκλείδην, "ὅταν,
ὀρθογωνίου τριγώνου μενούσης μιᾶς πλευρᾶς τῶν περὶ τὴν
ὀρθὴν γωνίαν, περιενεχθὲν ⟨τὸ⟩ τρίγωνον εἰς τὸ αὐτὸ πάλιν
ἀποκατασταθῇ ὅθεν ἤρξατο φέρεσθαι, τὸ περιληφθὲν σχῆμα
90 κῶνος καλεῖται· κἂν μὲν ἡ μένουσα εὐθεῖα ἴση ᾖ τῇ ⟨λοιπῇ τῇ⟩
περὶ τὴν ὀρθὴν περιφερομένη, ὀρθογώνιος ἔσται ὁ κῶνος· ἐὰν
δὲ ἐλάττων, ἀμβλυγώνιος· ἐὰν δὲ ᾖ μείζων, ὀξυγώνιος." —
"Ἄξων δέ ἐστι τοῦ κώνου ἡ μένουσα εὐθεῖα περὶ ἣν τὸ τρίγωνον
στρέφεται." — "Βάσις δὲ ὁ κύκλος ὁ ὑπὸ τῆς περιφερομένης
95 εὐθείας γραφόμενος."

⟨Ε⟩ὑρίσκεται δὲ καὶ πᾶς κύλινδρος τριπλάσιος κώνου τοῦ τὴν
αὐτὴν αὐτῷ βάσιν ἔχοντος καὶ ὕψος ἴσον. Ἐπεὶ γὰρ ἡ τοῦ
κυλίνδρου ἐπιφάνεια ‚βυξδ΄ ἐστίν, τὸ δὲ στερεὸν ἃ ‚ζσμη΄, (ἡ
δὲ τοῦ κώνου ἐπιφάνεια ἐκ τῆς αὐτῆς περιμέτρου τῶν πη΄ καὶ

71–72 Πᾶσα – ἐστί: cf. Archim. Sph. Cyl. I:120:15–16; Hero Metrica I:proem.   76–78 Ἔστι
– σφαίρας: cf. Archim. Sph.Cyl. I:124:15–17; Method. II:438:22–25.   85–86 ⟨Κ⟩ῶνος –
συνεστώς: cf. Hero Deff. 83.   86–92 ὅταν – ὀξυγώνιος: cf. Euc. XI def. 18.   93–94 Ἄξων
– στρέφεται: cf. Euc. XI def. 19.   94–95 Βάσις – γραφόμενος: Euc. XI def. 20.   96–97 πᾶς
– ἴσον: cf. Archim. Method. II:458:15–16; Euc. XII:10; Hero Metrica I:proem.

76–84 secl. Vin ‖ 77 τῇ Vin: τὸ VP ‖ 79 ὡς add. Vin ‖ 80 τὴν add. Vin ‖ ποιεῖ Vin: ποιοῦσιν VP
‖ 81 τὰς αὐτὰς Vin: τῶν αὐτῶν VP ‖ 88 τὸ add. Vin ‖ 90 λοιπῇ τῇ add. Vin

been found to be 2/3 of a cylinder of equal height that compre-
hends it. Every spherical surface is 4 times the area of its largest
circle, as many times its circumference as the length of its axis.
For the 2,464 <units> are 4 times 616 and 28 times 88.

<fig. 38>

[Every sphere is 4 times a cone with a base <equal to> the
greatest circle of the sphere, but a height equal to the radius of
the sphere. For the circumference of the conic base being 88,
multiplied by half of the axis, that is, the radius of 14 <units> in
height, makes 1,232. And the 616 of the area of the base multiplied by the same 14 of half the axis make 8,624. So the hemisphere, in surface and volume, has been found equal to two cones,
the sphere to four.]

A cone is a solid figure constructed from a circular base to a
single point above. According to Euclid: "When, one side of those
about the right angle in a right-angled triangle remaining fixed,
the triangle is carried round and restored again to the same position from which it began to be moved, the figure so comprehended is called a cone. And if the straight line that remains fixed
be equal to the remaining <side> that is carried around the right
angle, the cone will be right-angled; if less, obtuse-angled; if
greater, acute angled." "The axis of the cone is the straight line
that remains fixed <and> about which the triangle is turned."
"The base is the circle described by the straight line that is carried around."

Every cylinder is found to be 3 times the cone that has the
same base as it and equal height. For when the surface of the
cylinder is 2,464, the volume is 17,248, (the surface of the

[137]

100 τοῦ τρίτου μέρους τοῦ ἄξονος τῶν θ´ γ´´, ωκα´ καὶ τρίτου ἐστίν)
ἐκ δὲ τῶν χις´ τοῦ ἐμβαδοῦ τῆς βάσεως ἐπὶ τὸ αὐτὸ τρίτον τοῦ
ἄξονος, ͵εψμθ´ ⟨καὶ⟩ τρίτου τὸ στερεὸν εὑρίσκεται, καὶ εἰσὶ πρὸς
ἀλλήλους ἐν λόγῳ τριπλασίῳ· τριτημόριον ἄρα τοῦ ἰσοϋψοῦς
κυλίνδρου ὁ κῶνος ἀποδέδεικται. | Vin 384

105 ⟨Τ⟩ριπλάσιον δὲ καὶ τὸ πρίσμα παραλληλεπίπεδον ‖ ὂν τῆς   f. 52v
πυραμίδος εὑρίσκεται τῆς βάσιν τὴν αὐτὴν αὐτῷ ἐχούσης καὶ
ὕψος ἴσον.

Καὶ ἔστι τὸ κέντρον τοῦ βάρους τοῦ κυλίνδρου κατὰ τὴν
διχοτομίαν τοῦ ἄξονος· ὡσαύτως δὲ καὶ ἐπὶ τοῦ πρίσματος
110 ἔσται. Τὸ δὲ τοῦ κώνου κέντρον ἐπὶ τοῦ ἄξονος ⟨σημείου⟩ τοῦ
διαιρεθέντος οὕτως, ὥστε τὸ πρὸς τῇ κορυφῇ τμῆμα τριπλάσιον
εἶναι τοῦ λοιποῦ· ἡ αὐτὴ ἄρα τοῦ ἄξονος διαίρεσις καὶ ἐπὶ τῆς
πυραμίδος γινέσθω.

Πυραμὶς δέ ἐστι σχῆμα στερεὸν ἐπιπέδοις περιεχόμενον ἀπὸ
115 τοῦ τῆς βάσεως ἐπιπέδου πρὸς ἑνὶ σημείῳ συνεστώς, ἢ τὸ ἀπὸ
βάσεως τριγώνου ἢ τετραγώνου ἢ πολυγώνου πρὸς ἓν σημεῖον
μετέωρον συνεστώς. - Πρίσμα δέ ἐστι σχῆμα στερεὸν ἐπιπέδοις
περιεχόμενον, ὧν δύο δὴ τὰ ἀπεναντίον ἴσα τε καὶ ὅμοιά ἐστι
καὶ παράλληλα, τὰ δὲ λοιπὰ παραλληλόγραμμα.

9. ⟨Ἔ⟩στω οὖν ἐπὶ παραλληλογράμμου καὶ ἑτερομήκους
οἰκήματος, ἢ δεξαμενῆς ὁμοιοσχήμου, ὡς ἐπὶ τῆς Ἀετίου
κινστέρνης, τὴν τοῦ στερεοῦ ἀναμέτρησιν δηλοποιῆσαι.
Ῥάδιον δὲ μᾶλλον ἐπὶ τῆς Ἄσπαρος, διὰ τὸ ἴσον τῶν περὶ τὴν
5 βάσιν διαστάσεων, πλινθικοῦ τοῦ ‖ σχήματος ὄντος. Πλινθὶς   f. 53
δέ ἐστι σχῆμα στερεὸν ὑπὸ ἓξ ἐπιπέδων περιεχόμενον, ἴσον τὸ
τῆς βάσεως μῆκος καὶ τὸ πλάτος ἔχουσα, ἔλασσον δὲ τὸ ὕψος·
εἰ γὰρ ἴση καὶ πρὸς ὕψος ὑπῆρχεν, κύβος ἂν ἦν, εἰ δὲ μείζων,
δοκὶς ἐσχηματίζετο· δοκὶς γάρ ἐστιν ἡ μεῖζον τὸ ὕψος τοῦ τῆς

105–107 ⟨Τ⟩ριπλάσιον – ἴσον: cf. Euc. XII:8.   108–12 Καὶ – λοιποῦ: cf. Archim. *Method.*
II:432:27–433:2.   114–15 Πυραμὶς – συνεστώς: cf. Euc. XI *def.* 12.   117–19 Πρίσμα –
παραλληλόγραμμα: cf. Euc. XI *def.* 13.   9: 5–7 Πλινθὶς – ὕψος: cf. Hero *Deff.* 113.   9–10
δοκὶς – ἔχουσα: cf. Hero *Deff.* 112.

---

102 καὶ add. Vin ‖ 110 σημείου add. Vin ‖ 119 Post παραλληλόγραμμα vac. quattuor lin. V ‖
9: 3 κινστέρνης Vin: κιγστέρνης VP, et infra 11, 13

cone <is derived> from the same circumference of 88 <units> and 1/3 of the axis, 91/3, which is 8211/3), and from 616 <units> of the area of <the cone's> base <multiplied> by the same 1/3 of its axis, the volume is found to be 5,7491/3 and they are in a ratio of 3:1 to each other. The cone then has been proven <to be> 1/3 of a cylinder of equal height.

<fig. 39>

The parallelepipedal prism is found to be 3 times a pyramid that has the same base as the prism and equal height.

And the center of gravity of the cylinder is at the bisection of its axis; in like manner will it also be for the prism. The center <of gravity> of the cone is at the point where the axis is divided such that the section at the top is three times the remainder; the same division of the axis then should also be used for the pyramid.

A pyramid is a solid figure contained by planes constructed from the plane of the base to one point, or constructed to one point above from the base of a triangle, quadrilateral or polygon. A prism is a solid figure contained by planes two of which, namely those that are opposite, are equal, similar and parallel, while the rest are parallelograms.

<fig. 40>

9. Let us then use a parallelogram-shaped and oblong construction or reservoir similar in form, for example, the cistern of Aetius, to make clear the measurement of the solid. It is rather easier with that of Aspar because of the equal dimensions of its base, the figure being a plinth. A plinth is a solid figure contained by six planes, having the length and width of the base equal, the height smaller. For if it was also equal in height, it would be a cube, if greater it would form a *dokis*. For a *dokis* has the height

10 βάσεως μήκους καὶ πλάτους ἔχουσα. Ὑποκείσθω δὲ τοίνυν ἡ | Vin 386
βάσις κατὰ μῆκος τῆς τοῦ Ἄσπαρος κινστέρνης ὀργυῶν ο´,
πλάτος ὁμοίως τὸ αὐτὸ ἔχουσα, καὶ ὕψος ὀργυῶν ιβ´. Ζητῶ οὖν
εὑρεῖν πόσων ὀργυῶν ἐστι τὸ τῆς κινστέρνης στερεόν, καὶ πόσων
κεραμίων ὑγροῦ ἐστι χωρητική. Πολλαπλασιάζων δὲ τὰς τοῦ
15 μήκους ο´ ἐπὶ τὰς αὐτὰς ο´ τοῦ πλάτους, ἔχω τὸ κατὰ τὴν βάσιν
ἐπίπεδον ὀργυῶν ͵δϡ´· ταύτας οὖν πάλιν ἐπὶ τὰς τοῦ ὕψους ιβ´
πολλαπλασιάζω, καὶ γίνονται χιλιάδες νη´, καὶ ω´. Καὶ ἐπεὶ τὰ
μήκει τετραπλάσια δυνάμει ἑξκαιδεκαπλάσιά εἰσι, στερεῷ δὲ
τεσσαρακαιεξηκονταπλάσια, ἔστι δὲ ἡ ὀργυὰ κατὰ μῆκος
20 δακτύλων Ϟϛ´, ὁ δὲ πῆχυς κδ´, τετραπλασία ἄρα κατὰ μῆκος
τοῦ πήχεώς ἐστι, καὶ ἔστι τὸ τῆς βάσεως μῆκος πηχῶν σπ´· ἐκ δὲ
τούτων εὑρίσκεται τὸ ἐπίπεδον πηχῶν χιλιάδων οη´, καὶ υ´· καὶ
γὰρ τὰ ιϛ´ ἐπὶ τὰ ͵δϡ´ χιλιάδας ποιοῦσιν οη´, καὶ υ´· ἐκ δὲ τούτων
πάλιν τὸ στερεὸν γίνεται πηχῶν χιλιάδων τρισχιλίων καὶ ψξγ´,
25 καὶ σ´· οὕτως οὖν τὰ ξδ´ ἐπὶ τὰς νη´ χιλιάδας καὶ ω´, ‖ ποιοῦσι. f. 53v
Καὶ ἐπεὶ πάλιν τὰ μήκει ἑξαπλάσια δυνάμει
ἑξκαιτριακονταπλάσια δείκνυνται, στερεῷ δὴ
ἑξκαιδεκακαιδιακοσιαπλάσια ἔσονται· ἔστι γὰρ ὁ ποῦς ιϛ´
κατὰ μῆκος δακτύλων, ἕκτον ὀργυᾶς ὑπάρχων· ὅθεν πάλιν τὸ
30 κατὰ τὴν βάσιν μῆκος ποδῶν γίνεται υκ´· τὸ δὲ ἐπίπεδον
χιλιάδων ρος´, καὶ υ´· καὶ τὸ ὅλον στερεὸν ποδῶν μυριάδων
χιλίων καὶ σο´, καὶ ω´. Τὰ γὰρ λϛ´ ἐπὶ ͵δϡ´ ποιοῦσι χιλιάδας
ρος´, καὶ υ´· καὶ τὰ σιϛ´ ἐπὶ τὰς νη´ χιλιάδας καὶ [τὰ] ω´,
μυριάδας χιλίας καὶ σο´, καὶ ω´. Καὶ ἐπεὶ ὁ στερεὸς ποῦς, κατὰ
35 τὴν τῶν μηχανικῶν διατύπωσιν, ἀπὸ τῶν ιϛ´ τοῦ μήκους
δακτύλων κυβιζόμενος, ͵δϞϛ´ εὑρίσκεται, οἱ δὲ ιϛ´ καθ᾿ ἑαυτοὺς
τέσσαρας οὐγκίας ὕδατος παρὰ μικρὸν ἀπολαμβάνουσι,
πεντή|κοντα δὲ δάκτυλοι μετὰ ἑνὸς καὶ πέμπτου οὐγκιῶν ιβ´ Vin 388
Ἰταλικῶν λίτραν περιέξουσιν· οἱ δὲ σνϛ´ τοῦ ἐπιπέδου λίτρας

34–35 ὁ στερεὸς – διατύπωσιν: Hero De Mensuris 23:1.

18 ἑξκαιδεκαπλάσιά scripsi: εξ και δεκαπλασια V (in ras.): ἑξ καὶ δεκαπλάσιά P:
ἐκκαιδεκαπλάσιά Vin ‖ 22 οη´ Vin: ο´ VP ‖ 23 οη´ Vin: ο´ VP ‖ 24–25 ψξγ´, καὶ σ´ Vin: να´
καὶ ϡιβ´ VP ‖ 27 ἐκκαι– Vin ‖ 28 ἑξ καίδεκα καὶ διακοσιαπλάσια VP:
ἐκκαιδεκακαιδιακοσιαπλάσια Vin ‖ 33 τὰ secl. Vin ‖ 38 πέμπτου Vin: τρίτου VP ‖ 39 δὲ VP:
δὴ Vin

greater than the length and width of the base. Let the base then be assumed as the length of the cistern of Aspar, 70 *orgyai,* having likewise the same width, and a height of 12 *orgyai.* I seek then to find of how many *orgyai* the volume of the cistern consists, and how many *keramia* of liquid it is capable of holding. Multiplying the 70 of the length by the same 70 of the width, I have the plane on the base as 4,900 <square> *orgyai.* These then in turn I multiply by the 12 of the height and there are 58,800. And since the quadrupling in first power is in second power 16 times, but in third power 64 times, <and> the *orgya* is in length 96 *daktyloi,* the *pechys* 24, then <the *orgya*> is four times as long as the *pechys* and <thus> the length of the base is 280 *pecheis.* From these the plane is found <to consist> of 78,400 <square> *pecheis.* For the 16 <multiplied> by the 4900 make 78,400, and from these in turn the volume is of 3,763,200 <cubic> *pecheis.* So then the 64 <multiplied> by the 58,800 make <them>. And since again the sextupling in first power is shown in second power as 36 times, they will be 216 times in third power. For the *pous* is 16 *daktyloi* in length, being 1/6 of an *orgya.* Whence in turn the length at the base is 420 *podes,* the plane is 176,400 and the whole volume is 12,700,800 <cubic> *podes.* For the 36 multiplied by the 4,900 make 176,400; and the 216 multiplied by the 58,800 make 12,700,800. And since the cubic *pous,* in the system of engineers, cubed from the 16 *daktyloi* of length, is found to be 4,096, but the 16 contain in themselves not quite 4 *oungiai* of water, then the 51 1/5 *daktyloi* will constitute a liter of 12 Italian *oungiai;* and

40 ε΄, καὶ οἱ τοῦ στερεοῦ ͵δϛ΄ λίτρας π΄. Εὑρίσκεται ἄρα ὁ στερεὸς
πούς ὑγροῦ χωρητικὸς πρὸς μέτρον κεραμίου λιτρῶν Ἰταλικῶν
π΄· ὥστε, ὅσων στερεῶν ποδῶν ἡ δεξαμενὴ κατηρίθμηται,
τοσούτων καὶ κεραμίων ὑγροῦ ἐστι χωρητική. Ὡσαύτως δὲ καὶ
πρὸς τὸ τυχὸν μέρος τοῦ βάθους σημειούμενοι, τὸν τοῦ ὕδατος
45 ὄγκον ἐξαριθμησόμεθα.

⟨Κ⟩υλινδρικοῦ δὲ τοῦ σχήματος ὄντος, τὸ τοῦ κύκλου ἐμβαδόν,
‖ ὡς προέφημεν, λαμβάνειν, καὶ τοὺς κατὰ τὴν βάσιν   f. 54
εὑρισκομένους πόδας ἐπὶ τὸ ὕψος ποιεῖν· τὸν δὲ γινόμενον
ἀριθμόν, ἐπὶ μὲν δεξαμενῆς, κατὰ τὸν τοῦ ὕδατος ὄγκον
50 ἀποφαίνεσθαι. Ἐπὶ δὲ ὁμοιοσχήμου οἰκήματος, δίχα τῆς
ἐπικειμένης ἄνωθεν ἀετώσεως, σῖτον, κριθήν τε καὶ ὄσπρια καὶ
ὅσα ἐκ τῶν εἰδῶν τοῦ διωρισμένου ποσοῦ πρὸς μεδίμνους,
μοδίους τε καὶ χοίνικας καὶ τὰ εὐτελέστερα τῶν μερῶν
θεωροῦνται, κατὰ σταθμὸν καὶ μέγεθος, ἐκ τοῦ
55 κατασκευαζομένου στερεοῦ ποδὸς ἀνασκοποῦντας, ἐπαριθμεῖν.

10. ⟨Ἐ⟩πιγνωσόμεθα δὲ καὶ πηγῆς ἀπόρρυσιν κατὰ Ἥρωνα
ὅση τίς ἐστιν.

Ἀλλ' εἰδέναι μέντοι χρὴ ὅτι οὐκ ἀεὶ ἡ αὐτὴ διαμένει
ἀνά‖βλυσις· ὄμβρων μὲν γὰρ ὄντων, ἐπιτείνεται, διὰ τὸ ἐπὶ τὰς   Vin 390
5 κορυφὰς τῶν ὀρέων τὸ ὕδωρ πλεονάζον βιαιότερον
ἐκθλίβεσθαι· αὐχμῶν δὲ ὄντων, ἀπολήγει. Αἱ δὲ γεννητικαὶ
πηγαὶ οὐ παρὰ πολὺ τὴν ἀνάβλυσιν ἔχουσιν. Δεῖ οὖν
περιλαβόντας τὸ πᾶν τῆς πηγῆς ὕδωρ, ὡς μηδαμόθεν ἀπορρεῖν,
σωλῆνα ‖ μολιβοῦν τετράγωνον ποιῆσαι πολλῷ τῆς ῥύσεως   f. 54v
10 κατὰ τὴν ὑποδοχὴν μείζονα, καὶ ἐναρμόσαι αὐτὸν δι' ἑνὸς
τόπου, ὥστε δι' αὐτοῦ τὸ τῆς πηγῆς ὕδωρ ἀπορρεῖν. Δεῖ δὲ τὸν
σωλῆνα πρὸς τὸν ταπεινότερον κεῖσθαι τῆς πηγῆς τόπον, ὡς
ῥαδίαν ἔχειν τὴν ἀπόρρυσιν· τὸν δὲ ταπεινότερον τόπον διὰ
διόπτρας ἐπιγνωσόμεθα. Φανερὸν δὲ τὸ ἀπορρέον ὕδωρ ἐν τῷ
15 περιστομίῳ τοῦ σωλῆνος πρὸς ὕψος γενήσεται. Ἔστω οὖν πρὸς

10: 3–35 Ἀλλ' – χορηγίαν: cf. Hero *Dioptr.* XXXI. 6–7 γεννητικαὶ πηγαὶ: cf. Proc. *Theol. Plat.* V:142:3.

43 Post τοσούτων add. ὀγδοηκοντάκις Vin ‖ 47 προέφαμεν Vin ‖ Post προέφημεν add. δεῖ Vin ‖ 55 Post ἐπαριθμεῖν vac. quinque lin. V ‖ **10:** 4 μὲν Vin: τε VP (cf. Hero *Dioptr.* XXXI:2) ‖ 6 ἀπολήγει Vin: ἀπολήγειν VP ‖ γενναῖαι Vin (cf. Hero *Dioptr.* XXXI:7) ‖ 7 ἔχουσιν scripsi: ἔχωσιν VP: ἴσχουσι Vin (cf. Hero *Dioptr.* XXXI:8)

the 256 of the plane, 5 liters, and the 4,096 of the volume, 80 liters. Then the cubic *pous* is found to have a liquid capacity equal to a *keramion* of 80 Italian liters. So by as many cubic *podes* as the reservoir has been measured, so many *keramia* of liquid also can it hold. Likewise also noting down for any portion of depth, we shall calculate the amount of water.

<fig. 41>

When the figure is a cylinder, take the area of the circle as we have said above and multiply the <square> *podes* found in the base by the height. One concludes that the resulting number is the amount of water in the case of a reservoir. In the case of a similarly shaped building, apart from <any> gable situated on top, one reckons, by weight and volume, wheat, barley, legumes, and such things as are evaluated according to the forms of the quantity in question by *medimnoi, modioi,* and *choinikes* and smaller measures, looking to the cubic *pous* constructed.

10. We shall also determine what the quantity of the discharge of a spring is, following Heron.

But one should be aware, however, that they do not always gush up at the same <rate>. For when there are rains, <flow> increases, because the excess water at the mountaintops is forced out more powerfully; when there are droughts, it ceases. Productive springs do not greatly check their flow. It is necessary then that, after enclosing all the water of the spring so that it discharges nowhere, we make a quadrangular lead pipe much larger than the flow at the receiving point, and fit it in one place so that the water of the spring flows out through it. And it is necessary that the pipe be situated at the lower part of the spring, so as to easily receive the discharge. And we shall determine the lower part with the dioptra. The discharging water will become obvious with regard to its height in the mouth of the pipe. Let it be

ὕψος δακτύλων τριῶν· ἐχέτω δὲ καὶ πλάτος τὸ στόμιον
δακτύλων ἕξ· τρεῖς δὲ ἐπὶ ἕξ ποιοῦσι δεκαοκτώ. Ἀποφανούμεθα
ἄρα τὴν τῆς πηγῆς ἀνάβλυσιν δακτύλων εἶναι ιη΄.

⟨Ἀ⟩λλ᾽ εἰδέναι χρὴ ὅτι οὐκ ἔστιν αὔταρκες τὸ γνῶναι ὅσον ἡ
20 πηγὴ χορηγεῖ ὕδωρ, τὸ εὑρεῖν τὸν ὄγκον τῆς ῥύσεως, ἀλλὰ καὶ
τὸ τάχος· ταχυτέρας μὲν γὰρ τῆς ῥύσεως οὔσης, πλέον
ἐπιχορηγεῖται τὸ ὕδωρ, βραδυτέρας δὲ ἔλαττον. Ὅθεν χρή, ὑπὸ
τὴν τῆς πηγῆς ῥύσιν τάφρον ὀρύξαντας, τηρῆσαι ἐξ ἡλιακοῦ
ὡροσκοπίου πόσον διὰ τῆς ὥρας ὕδωρ ἐν τῇ τάφρῳ ἀπορρεῖ,
25 καὶ οὕτως τὸ ἐπιχορηγούμενον ὕδωρ δι᾽ ὅλης τῆς ἡμέρας
στοχάσασθαι ὅσον [κατὰ τὸν ὄγκον] ἐστίν. Ὥστε οὐκ
ἀναγκαῖόν ἐστι τὸν τῆς ῥύσεως ὄγκον ἐπιτηρεῖν [ἀλλὰ καὶ τὸ
τάχος]· διὰ γὰρ τοῦ ὡριαίου χρόνου φανερὰν ἕξομεν καὶ τὴν
τοῦ ὕδατος ἡμερήσιον χορηγίαν. ‖ Εἰ γὰρ πᾶν νυχθήμερον ∣   f. 55
30 ἰσημερινῶν ἐστιν χρόνων τξ΄, ὡρῶν δὲ κδ΄, ἑκάστη ὥρα   Vin 392
ἰσημερίας χρόνους ιε΄ περιέξει, πλείους δὲ ὁτὲ καὶ ἐλάσσονας
ἡ καιρική. Καὶ ἐπεί, χειμῶνος μὲν ὄντος, ἐπὶ πλέον ἡ ῥύσις
γίνεται, θέρους δὲ ἐπ᾽ ἔλαττον, ἐὰν διὰ τῆς τυχούσης ὥρας τὸ
ἐν τῇ τάφρῳ καταρρέον ὕδωρ κ΄ τυχὸν στοχασώμεθα κάδων,
35 τετρακοσίων ἄρα καὶ π΄ τὴν τῆς πηγῆς χορηγίαν διὰ τοῦ
νυχθημέρου ἀποφανούμεθα.

11. ⟨Ἐ⟩πεὶ οὖν τὰς ἐν τῇ γῇ ἐπαγγελθείσας διοπτρικὰς ἀνωτέρω
διεξήλθομεν χρείας, δι᾽ εὐχρηστίαν τῆς τοιαύτης διόπτρας
ἱκανοὶ ἐσόμεθα καὶ ἐπὶ τὴν τῶν οὐρανίων ἀναχθῆναι θεωρίαν,
ἡλίου τε μέγεθος καὶ σελήνης δι᾽ αὐτῆς διακρίνοντες, τά τε
5 ἀπ᾽ ἀλλήλων τῶν ἀστέρων διαστήματα, ἀπλανῶν τε πρὸς
ἀπλανεῖς καὶ πλανήτας ἐπισκέπτεσθαι, καὶ πλανήτων πρὸς
πλανωμένους καὶ ἀπλανεῖς. Ἐκ γὰρ τῆς ἐν τῷ τυμπάνῳ
καταγραφῆς τῶν τξ΄ μοιρῶν καὶ τῶν μεταξὺ ἐγχαρασσομένων
λεπτῶν τὰ ζητούμενα μεγέθη συνορᾶν δυνησόμεθα. ‖ Ὅταν οὖν   f. 55v

---

11: 1–22 ⟨Ἐ⟩πεὶ – διαστήματα: cf. Hero Dioptr. XXXII.

---

26 κατὰ τὸν ὄγκον secl. Vin ‖ 27–28 ἀλλὰ καὶ τὸ τάχος secl. Vin ‖ 31 δὲ ὅτε καὶ VP: μὲν ὁτέ,
ὁτὲ δὲ καὶ Vin ‖ 34 στοχασώμεθα Vin: στοχασόμεθα VP ‖ 35 π΄ Vin: κ΄ VP ‖ 36 Post
ἀποφανούμεθα vac. quinque lin. V ‖ 11: 6 ἐπισκέπτεσθαι Vin: ἐπισκέπεσθαι VP ‖ 8
ἐγχαρασσομένων Vin: ἐγχωρουμένων VP

then 3 *daktyloi* high; let the mouth also have a width of 6 *daktyloi;* 3 times 6 make 18. We shall conclude then that the spring gushes up 18 <square> *daktyloi* .

<fig. 42>

One must realize that to know how much water the spring produces, it is not sufficient to find the <cross-sectional> amount of the flow, but also the speed. For when the flow is faster, it produces more water, when slower, less. And so it is necessary, after digging a ditch beneath the flow of the spring, to watch with the sundial for how much water per hour discharges into the ditch, and so to estimate how much water is produced in a whole day. With this method it is unnecessary to watch for the <cross-sectional> amount of the flow. For through an hour's time we shall have clear also the daily production of water. For if every day-night cycle consists of 360 equatorial time degrees, but 24 hours, each hour of equatorial time will comprise 15 time degrees, the seasonal hour sometimes more and less. And since, when it is winter, the flow is more, but in summer less, if through any hour we estimate the water flowing into the ditch as perhaps 20 *kadoi,* we shall conclude then the production of the spring throughout the day-night cycle as 480 <*kadoi*>.

11. Since therefore we have discussed in what precedes the promised dioptric applications on the earth, we shall be ready to be led up also to contemplation of the heavens through the use-fulness of such a dioptra, determining the magnitude of the sun and moon through it, and to observing the distances of stars from each other, of fixed stars in relation to fixed stars and planets, and of planets in relation to other planets and fixed stars. For from the engraving of the 360 degrees on the disc and the minutes inscribed between them we shall be able to see the magni-

10 βουλώμεθα δύο ἀστέρων τὴν μεταξὺ διάστασιν ἐπισκέψασθαι
πόσων ὑπάρχει μοιρῶν, παρεγκλινοῦμεν τὸ πρὸς ἡμᾶς μέρος τοῦ
τυμπάνου, πρὸς ὕψος τὸ ἕτερον ἀνανεύοντες, ἄχρις ἂν διὰ τοῦ
αὐτοῦ ἐπιπέδου ἀμφοτέρων τῶν ἀστέρων τὰς θέσεις
ἐπισκεψώμεθα· καὶ ἀκινήτων πάντων τῶν ἐν τῇ διόπτρᾳ
15 μενόντων, περιστρέψομεν τὸν ἐπὶ τῷ τυμπάνῳ κανόνα, ἕως ἕνα
  | τῶν ἀστέρων διὰ τῶν δύο ὀπῶν θεασώμεθα. Καὶ   Vin 394
σημειωσάμενοι τὴν μοῖραν ἢ τὸ λεπτόν, καθ᾽ ὃν ἂν τόπον τὸ
μοιρογνωμόνιον ὑπάρχῃ, περιστρέψομεν αὖθις τὸν κανόνα,
ἄχρις ἂν διὰ τῶν δύο ὀπῶν καὶ τὸν ἕτερον ἐπισκεψώμεθα, τὴν
20 κατὰ τὸ μοιρογνωμόνιον ὁμοίως σημειούμενοι μοῖραν· καὶ
μετρήσαντες ἐπὶ τοῦ τυμπάνου τὰς μεταξὺ τῶν σημείων μοίρας,
τὰ ἀπ᾽ ἀλλήλων τῶν ἀστέρων ἀποφανούμεθα διαστήματα.

    Διοπτεύσαντες δὲ κατά τινα τόπον τοῦ ζῳδιακοῦ ἕνα τῶν
ἀστέρων, εἰ μὲν κατὰ μῆκος ἐπὶ τὰ προηγούμενα, ὡς ἀπ᾽
25 ἀνατολῶν ἐπὶ δυσμάς, τὸν ἕτερον ἐπιζητοῦμεν ἐπὶ τὰ δεξιὰ
ἡμῶν· τὸν ἐν τῷ τυμπάνῳ κανόνα περιστρέφοντες, τοῦτον
διοπτεύομεν· εἰ δὲ πρὸς τὰ ἑπόμενα, ὡς ἀπὸ δύσεως ἐπὶ τὸ
μεσουράνημα, ἢ τὸν ὡροσκόπον, ἐπὶ τὰ εὐώνυμα. Ἡγούμενα
δὲ καλεῖται ζῴδια τὰ ἀπὸ Κριοῦ || ἐπὶ Ἰχθύας, Ὑδροχόον,   f. 56
30 ⟨Αἰγόκερων,⟩ Τοξότην τε καὶ τὰ ἑξῆς· ἑπόμενα δέ, τὰ ἀπὸ Κριοῦ
ἐπὶ Ταῦρον, Διδύμους, Καρκῖνόν τε καὶ τὰ λοιπά.

    Καὶ εἰ μὲν κατὰ μῆκος τοῦ ζῳδιακοῦ τὴν ἀπόστασιν
ἐπισκεπτόμεθα, οὐχ ὡς ἔτυχεν διοπτεύσομεν, ἀλλ᾽ ἐπὶ
ἰσημερινῆς γραμμῆς παράλληλον τὴν διόπτραν ἱστῶντες· εἰ δὲ
35 κατὰ πλάτος τὴν ζήτησιν ποιούμεθα, ὡς ἀπὸ βορρᾶ ἐπὶ νότον ἢ
ἀνάπαλιν, ἐπὶ μεσημβρινῆς. Αὗται δὲ αἱ γραμμαὶ ἐν τῷ
ἀξιαγάστῳ βασιλικῷ πρὸς νότον παρακυπτηρίῳ ⟨ἐν⟩ τοῖς
Βουκολέοντος ὑφ᾽ ἡμῶν ἐγχαραχθεῖσαι ἐπὶ τῶν πρασίνων
ἔκκεινται κοσμηταρίων· τὴν δὲ τούτων εὕρεσιν ἐν τῇ Θέσει τῶν
40 ἡλιακῶν ἀνεγράψαμεν ὡροσκοπίων.

    Ὅταν οὖν βουλώμεθα, ἐπὶ τοῦ διορίζοντος τὸ ὑπὲρ γῆν καὶ

---

16 θεασώμεθα P: θεασόμεθα V || 18 ὑπάρχῃ Vin: ὑπάρχει VP || 30 Αἰγόκερων add. Vin || 34
ἰσημερινῆς Vin: μεσημβρινῆς VP || 36 μεσημβρινῆς Vin: ἰσημερινῆς VP || 37 ἐν add. Mango,
49 adnot. 3 || τοῖς VP: τοῦ Vin

tudes we are seeking. Whenever then we wish to observe the distance between two stars in number of degrees, we shall incline downward the part of the disc closest to us, tilting the other part upward until we observe in the same plane the positions of both stars. And with all the <other> parts of the dioptra remaining unmoved, we shall turn the sight-rod on the disc, until we see one of the two stars through the two <sight->holes. And having noted the degree or minute at the place where the degree indicator might be, we shall again turn the sight-rod until we observe the other star through the two <sight->holes, noting likewise the degree at the degree indicator. And after measuring on the disc the degrees between the points, we shall conclude the distance of the stars from each other.

After sighting one of the stars in some region of the zodiac, if for the longitude in the direction of the leading <signs>, as from east to west, we seek the other to our right; turning the sight-rod on the disc, we sight this <star>. If in the direction of the following <signs>, as from the west to the meridian, or to the ascendant, to the left. The leading <signs> is the name given to those zodiac signs from Aries to Pisces, Aquarius, <Capricorn>, Sagittarius, and the others in turn; the following <signs> is the name given to those from Aries to Taurus, Gemini, Cancer, and the rest.

And if we observe the distance for longitude in the zodiac, we shall sight not at random but setting the dioptra parallel to the equator; but if we make the investigation for latitude, as from north to south or vice versa, <we set it parallel> to the meridian. These lines lie engraved by us on the green architraves (?) in the admirable imperial terrace balcony (?) which faces south near Boukoleon's. We have recorded how to find these lines in <our> *Positioning of Sundials*.

Whenever, therefore, we wish to take visually the tropical, equa-

ὑπὸ γῆν ἡμισφαίριον, πρὸς ἀνατολὰς ἢ δυσμάς, αἰσθητῶς τά τε
τροπικὰ καὶ ἰσημερινὰ καὶ τὰ μεταξὺ μηνιαῖα λήψεσθαι
σημεῖα, πρὸς | ἰσημερινὴν γραμμὴν τὴν διόπτραν ἱστῶντες   Vin 396
45 παράλληλον, τὸν κανόνα διϊθύνομεν, καὶ διὰ τῶν δύο ὀπῶν πρὸς
ἀνατολήν τε καὶ δύσιν ἐπ' εὐθείας διοπτεύοντες, ταῦτα ἐπὶ τοῦ
καθ' ἡμᾶς ὁρίζοντος τεκμαιρόμεθα· ἔνθα ὁ ἥλιος, ἐπὶ τὴν
πρώτην τοῦ Κριοῦ ἢ τοῦ Ζυγοῦ ὅταν παραγένηται μοῖραν,
ἐαρινάς τε καὶ μετοπωρινὰς ἰσημερίας ποιεῖται. Καὶ ἐπεὶ
50 παράλληλον τῷ ὁρίζοντι τὸ τύμπανον παρατέθειται, || f. 56v
ἀριθμήσαντες ἀπὸ τῆς θέσεως τοῦ μοιρογνωμονίου ἐπὶ τὰ
βόρεια μοίρας λβ΄β΄΄, καὶ πρὸς αὐτὰς τὸν κανόνα ἰθύναντες,
τὰ θερινὰ τροπικὰ ληψόμεθα· ἐκεῖ γὰρ ὁ ἥλιος, ἐπὶ τὴν πρώτην
τοῦ Καρκίνου γινόμενος μοῖραν, θερινὰς ποιεῖται τροπάς. Τὰ
55 δὲ μεταξὺ μηνιαῖα σημεῖα ἀπὸ τοῦ ἰσημερινοῦ διὰ δεκαεξ καὶ
κη΄ ληψόμεθα μοιρῶν, καὶ ἀνάπαλιν ἀπὸ τοῦ ἰσημερινοῦ ἐπὶ
τὰ νότια τὰς αὐτὰς μοίρας ἀριθμοῦντες, καὶ πρὸς αὐτὰς τὸν
κανόνα παράγοντες, τά τε χειμερινὰ τροπικὰ καὶ τὰ μεταξὺ
μηνιαῖα καθορᾶν δυνησόμεθα. Καὶ ἐκεῖ διὰ τῶν ρπ΄ τοῦ
60 ἡμικυκλίου μοιρῶν τὰ κατὰ διάμετρον ζῴδια ἐπὶ τοῦ ὁρίζοντος
ἀνατέλλει τε καὶ δύνει· Καρκίνου γὰρ ἀνατέλλοντος Αἰγόκερως
δύνει, Ὑδροχόου δὲ δύνοντος ἀνατέλλει Λέων.

Ἐβουλήθην σκοπῆσαι πόσας μοίρας ἀφέστηκεν ἐπὶ τὰ
ἡγούμενα τῶν ζῳδίων ὁ λαμπρὸς τῶν Ὑάδων, ὁ καὶ Λαμπαύρας,
65 τοῦ ἐπὶ τῆς Καρδίας τοῦ Λέοντος, καλουμένου δὴ Βασιλίσκου.
Καὶ περὶ δευτέραν ὥραν νυκτερινὴν πρὸς ἀνατολὰς διοπτεύσας,
| καί, ὡς ἐκφανῆ, τὸν ἐπὶ τῆς Καρδίας τοῦ Λέοντος λαβών,   Vin 398
ἐσημειωσάμην τὴν μοῖραν ἐπὶ τοῦ τυμπάνου καθ' ἣν τὸ
μοιρογνωμόνιον ὑπῆρχεν· καὶ περιστρέψας ἐπὶ τὰ ἡγούμενα τὸν
70 κανόνα, διώπτευσα ἐπὶ τοῦ Ταύρου τὸν Λαμπαύραν, τὴν πρὸς
αὐτὸν μοῖραν ὁμοίως σημ||ειωσάμενος· καὶ μετρήσας ἐπὶ τοῦ   f. 57
τυμπάνου τὰς μεταξὺ τῶν σημείων μοίρας, εὗρον π΄ ἔγγιστα·
ὅσας καὶ οἱ ἀστέρες ἀμφότεροι ἀπ' ἀλλήλων ἀπέχουσιν. Ὁ
γὰρ Βασιλίσκος, σὺν τῷ ἐπικινήματι τῶν ἀπὸ τοῦ Πτολεμαίου
75 χρόνων, ι΄ ϛ΄ μοίρας ἐπὶ τοῦ Λέοντος νῦν εὑρίσκεται ἐπέχων·

---

47 ὁρίζοντος P: ὁρίζοντες V ‖ 59 ἐκεῖ Vin: ἐπεὶ VP ‖ 65 δὴ Vin: δὲ VP

torial, and monthly points in between on the <circle> bounding the hemisphere above the earth and <that> below the earth, at the <points where the sun> rises and sets, setting the dioptra parallel to the equator, we direct the sight-rod and sighting through the two <sight->holes to east and west on a straight line, we mark these points on our horizon. These are where the sun, when it is in the first degree of the Ram or Libra, makes spring and autumn days of equal length. And when the disc has been set parallel to the horizon, counting from the position of the degree indicator to the north 32²/3 degrees and guiding the sight-rod to them, we shall take the summer tropical points. For there the sun, being in the first degree of Cancer, creates the summer solstices. And the monthly points between we shall take at 16 and 28 degrees from the equator, and vice versa from the equator to the south counting the same number of degrees, and leading the sight-rod to them, we shall be able to view the winter tropical points and the monthly points between. And at 180 degrees around the hemisphere the diametrically opposite signs rise and set on the horizon. When Cancer rises, Capricorn sets, Aquarius sets while Leo rises.

I wished to see by how many degrees, in the direction of the leading <signs> of the zodiac, the bright <star> of the Hyades, namely Lampauras, was distant from the <star> on the Heart of Leo, called Regulus. And about the second hour of the night after sighting the dioptra to the east and, when the <star> on the Heart of Leo is clearly visible, taking its position, I noted the degree on the disc at which the degree indicator lay; and having turned the sight-rod in the direction of the leading <signs>, I sighted the dioptra on Lampauras in Taurus, noting likewise its degree. And having measured on the disc the degrees between the signs, I found approximately 80; the two stars are so many <degrees> from each other. For Regulus, with the onward movement of the time since Ptolemy, is found to have now 10¹/2

καὶ ὁ λαμπρὸς τῶν Ὑάδων ἐπὶ τοῦ Ταύρου κ´ β´´. Ἀριθμήσας
δὲ τὰς ι´ Ϛ´ τοῦ Λέοντος ἐπὶ τὰ ἡγούμενα, Καρκίνου τε καὶ
Διδύμων ἀνὰ λ´, καὶ ἐπὶ τοῦ Ταύρου θ´ γ´´, τὰς αὐτὰς π´ εὗρον·
ὡσαύτως δὲ καὶ ἐπὶ τὰ ἐπόμενα, ὡς ἀπὸ τοῦ Ταύρου ἐπὶ τὸν
80   Λέοντα.

Πάλιν δὲ περὶ τὸ μεσονύκτιον διοπτεύσας ἀπὸ τοῦ ἐπὶ τῆς
Καρδίας τοῦ Λέοντος, ἐπὶ τὰ ἐπόμενα, τὸν Ἀρκτοῦρον τὸν καὶ
Βοώτην καλούμενον, ἐπὶ τοῦ Ζυγοῦ, βορειότερον δὴ ὄντα τοῦ
ἰσημερινοῦ μοίρας λ´ καὶ μίαν, ἐσημειωσάμην, καὶ εὗρον διὰ
85   μέσου μοίρας νδ´ ἔγγιστα· ὅσας καὶ ὁ Ἀρκτοῦρος ἐπὶ τὰ ἐπόμενα
τοῦ Βασιλίσκου ἀπέχει. Ὁ γὰρ Ἀρκτοῦρος νῦν ε´ μοῖραν τοῦ
Ζυγοῦ, σὺν τῷ ἐπικινήματι, ἐπέχει· καὶ εἰσὶ τοῦ μὲν Λέοντος
ἐπὶ τὰ ἐπόμενα, ιθ´ Ϛ´, τῆς Παρθένου λ´, καὶ ε´ τοῦ Ζυγοῦ· ὅσαι
καὶ ἐν τῷ τυμπάνῳ ἔγγιστα ἠρίθμηνται.

90   Ὁ αὐτὸς ἄρα τρόπος καὶ ἐπὶ τῶν λοιπῶν ἀπλανῶν τῶν πρώτου
καὶ δευτέρου μεγέθους ὄντων, καὶ ἐπὶ τῶν ε´ πλανήτων ἀεὶ
γινέσθω. Τὴν δὲ τῆς σελήνης ἀπόστασιν, οὐ μόνον πρὸς
πλανήτας καὶ τοὺς τῶν ἀπλανῶν ἐκφανεῖς, τοὺς ὁμοίαν πρὸς
αὐτὴν ‖ κεκτημένους ἢ ἐναντίαν κρᾶσιν ἐπισκοπεῖν χρή, ἀλλὰ   f. 57v
95   καὶ ‖ πρὸς τὰ νεφελοειδῆ λεγόμενα συστήματα, οἷον περὶ τὴν   Vin 400
Φάτνην, ἢ τὸν Πλόκαμον, ἢ τὰς ἐπὶ τοῦ διχοτομήματος τοῦ
Ταύρου, Πλειάδας καλουμένας, ἢ τὰς ἐπὶ τῶν Κεράτων διὰ τὸ
σχῆμα τοῦ Υ στοιχείου Ὑάδας ὡς ὑετῶν καὶ ὄμβρων
παραιτίους. Ἐπιτηρεῖν δὲ χρὴ μάλιστα τὴν σελήνην, καὶ περὶ
100   ἃς ποιεῖται πρὸς τὸν ἥλιον φάσεις ζ´, εἰ συνεγγίζει τούτων, ἢ
μοιρικῶς πρὸς αὐτὴν οἱ ἀστέρες σχηματίζονται, ἢ συνοδικὰς
φάσεις πρὸς ἥλιον ποιοῦνται. Ταῦτα οὖν οἱ περὶ τὴν διοπτρείαν
καὶ τὰ φαινόμενα ἐπεσκεμμένοι, τὰς δὲ ἐποχὰς ἐκ τοῦ προχείρου
λαμβάνοντες κανόνος, οὐ μόνον τὰ τῶν ἀστέρων ἀποφανοῦνται
105   διαστήματα, ἀλλὰ καὶ ἀέρων καταστήματα καὶ ἀνωμαλίας,
δυσκρασίας τε καὶ εὐκρασίας, διὰ τῶν κατ᾽ ἔτος γινομένων
ἐπισημασιῶν τῶν ἀστέρων συνιέντες, προγνώσονται.

83 δὴ Vin: δὲ VP ‖ 100 εἰ VP: ἢ Vin

degrees in Leo; and the bright <star> of the Hyades 202/3 degrees in Taurus. Having counted the 101/2 of Leo in the direction of the leading <signs>, about 30 <each> for Cancer and Gemini, and 91/3 in Taurus, I found the same 80; it is likewise in the direction of the following <signs>, that is, from Taurus to Leo.

Again at midnight after sighting from the <star> on the Heart of Leo in the direction of the following <signs>, I noted Arcturus, also called Bootes, in Libra, being 31 degrees north of the equator; and I found between them about 54 degrees. So many <degrees> is Arcturus distant from Regulus in the direction of the following <signs>. For Arcturus now is at the fifth degree in Libra, with the onward movement. And there are 191/2 degrees for Leo in the direction of the following <signs>, for Virgo 30, and 5 for Libra; approximately so many have also been counted on the disc.

Let the same method then always be used also for the other fixed stars of the first and second magnitude and for the five planets. It is necessary to consider the distance of the moon, not only to the planets and the most visible fixed stars, the ones that possess both similar and dissimilar astrological temperaments as the moon, but also to the so-called nebular systems, like those around the Manger or the Lock, or even those in the bisection of Taurus, the so-called Pleiades, or the Hyades in the Horns, <so named> because they resemble the letter *upsilon,* which produce rains and storms. It is particularly necessary to observe the moon, especially concerning which of its seven phases it is making with respect to the sun, if it approaches these <stars> or the stars are configured with it <i.e., the moon> to the degree, or are making their synodic phases with respect to the sun. Those with a knowledge of dioptrics, when they have considered these phenomena too and taken the positions from the handy sight-rod, not only will conclude the distances of the stars, but will also know in advance the conditions and irregularities of the airs, good and bad atmospheres, understanding these through the annual indications of the stars.

Parangelmata Poliorcetica

Title: As noted in the Introduction (2), the rubricator failed to add the notice of author and title in the extensive space left at the head of the first folio of Vat. gr. 1605. A later hand (Dain, *Tradition*, 13, suggests 14th–15th century) has added Ἡρων(ος) (sic) — προοίμ(ιον). Another hand (Devreesse, in a letter to Dain, ibid., 33, suggests Allatius) has added in the upper left corner "1605 Heronis Poliorcetica." Barocius titles the work "De machinis bellicis," Martin Πολιορκητικά, Wescher Πολιορκητικά, Schneider Παραγγέλματα Πολιορκητικά. Schneider's title is now the most frequently cited one.

Chapter 1. Introduction

The Anon. Byz. describes the difficulty of the subject, particularly as the result of the method, both verbal and pictorial, of his sources, lists his major sources, and describes his own method of presentation.

3 **καταγραφῆς:** The term appears in five instances in Apollod. (158:10, 160:2, 170:9, 182:3, and 186:2, four of which are attested in the tenth-century Paris. suppl. gr. 607) at the end of a verbal description and to introduce an accompanying drawing; the Anon. Byz. uses it in a similar manner at **11**:6 (drawn from Apollod. 186:2) and also uses the verb (τὸ σχῆμα καταγέγραπται) at **44**:45, **49**:25 and **51**:29. For the use of the term in the tacticians as "*dessin, tracé*," see A. Dain, *Histoire du texte d'Élien le Tacticien* (Paris, 1946), 49–51 and 65 n. 1; on its use in the mid-tenth-century *Sylloge tacticorum* to refer to a diagram of an infantry square, see E. McGeer, "The Syntaxis Armatorum Quadrata: A Tenth-Century Tactical Blueprint," *REB* 50 (1992), 227. See also Mugler, *Dictionnaire*, s.v., and E. M. Bruins, *Codex Constantinopolitanus* (Leiden, 1964), III, 208.

4 **ἀγνωσία:** The reading, I suggest, is sound, used as in Pseudo-Dionysius, *De mystica theologia* I:1: εἰς τὸν γνόφον τῆς ἀγνωσίας . . . καθ᾽ ὃν ἀπομυεῖ πάσας τὰς γνωστικὰς ἀντιλήψεις, II:1 δι᾽ ἀβλεψίας καὶ ἀγνωσίας ἰδεῖν καὶ γνῶναι τὸ ὑπὲρ θέαν καὶ γνῶσιν. For its function in the Anon. Byz.'s view of the drawings in his source manuscripts, see

[153]

the Introduction, 9–10. See also below, **1**:39 on σχηματισμός.

5 **σχημάτων**: The term is that used in Apollod.'s introduction (137:7–8: σχήματα πολλὰ καὶ ποικίλα διέγραψα) and frequently in his text. On the nature of the original technical illustrations in Apollod.'s text versus those preserved in the extant manuscripts see below, **27**:92. On the Anon. Byz.'s own approach, the σχηματισμός, see the Introduction, 8–14 and below **1**:39. On σχῆμα see also Downey, "Architects," 116.

7–8 **κατασκευὴν καὶ τεκτόνευσιν**: Marsden, *Treatises*, 44, suggests that for Heron of Alexandria and Philo Mech. κατασκευή refers to "the complete construction of a piece of artillery from the drawing board to the finished product." The Anon. Byz.'s use of τεκτόνευσις here may then be pleonastic, as the reversal of the terms below (**1**:36) also suggests, but perhaps also emphasizes the practical nature of his focus.

9 **μηχανικῶν**: The terms μηχανικός, ἀρχιτέκτων and τεχνίτης are all used by the Anon. Byz. and by Ath. Mech.; Apollod. uses only τεχνῖται once and τέκτων once. The Anon. Byz. uses μηχανικοί exclusively of his classical sources or other ancient "engineers." His use of ἀρχιτέκτονες is often similar in time frame (cf. **2**:14–15 κατὰ τοὺς πάλαι ἀρχιτέκτονας), although he also describes them as πολυμαθέστατοι (**38**:22) and μαθηματικοί (**50**:30, where they are also said to be able to alter the dimensions of a siege device in terms of local topography), adjectives not found in his sources. Whether these descriptions apply only to the ἀρχιτέκτονες "of old" or reflect a contemporary perspective on their level of education is uncertain. He does use πολυμαθέστατος again in the *Geodesia* (**1**:15) of his ancient sources for that treatise. The uses of ἀρχιτέκτων at *De cer.* 701:4 and Anna Comnena, *Alexiad* III:4:3 suggest the the term was used in the middle Byzantine period of individuals with significant education. Downey, "Architects," 109, suggests that μηχανικός was by the time of Procopius the term used for highly skilled individuals with both theoretical education as well as practical skills, and superior to the ἀρχιτέκτων, who was a "chief of carpenters or builders." C. Mango, *Byzantine Architecture* (New York, 1974), 24, argues that while μηχανικός is usually translated as "engineer," he was more properly "an architect having a grounding in mathematics." He further suggests "We may imagine that, as time went on, the *architektones* sank to

the level of the craftsman." The Anon. Byz. also says (**26**:6, **29**:12) that the τεχνίτης is capable of altering the dimensions of siege engines to the requirements of local topography, passages perhaps influenced by Ath. Mech. (19:1–2: Ἀλλὰ τοιαῦτα μηχανήματα ἔξεστι μετασκευάζειν τῷ τεχνίτῃ ἐμβλέποντι εἰς τοὺς τόπους τῶν προσαγωγῶν). The reliance on classical sources makes isolation of contemporary usage difficult. I have used "engineer," "master builder," and "craftsman" respectively in the translation.

10 Ἀπολλοδώρου: Apollodorus of Damascus, the chief engineer in Trajan's Dacian Wars and architect of the famous bridge over the Danube, banished and executed by Hadrian. For editions and translations of his *Poliorcetica* see the Bibliography. For a recent view that some two-thirds of the text of the *Poliorcetica* attributed to him are later additions, particularly those portions describing impractical devices, and that the remaining third was not written by Apollod. himself, see Blyth, "Apollodorus," passim.

10 Ἀδριανόν: The text of Apollod. is presented as a response to a letter of request received from an unnamed emperor, addressed only as δεσπότης. It has been argued (T. Reinach, "A qui sont dediées les Poliorcétiques d'Apollodore?" *Revue des études grecques* 8 [1895], 198–202; R. T. Ridley, "The Fate of an Architect: Apollodorus of Damascus," *Athenaeum* 67 [1989], 551–65, specifically 560, and Blyth, "Apollodorus," 149–53) and seems quite likely that this δεσπότης was Trajan, not Hadrian. The basis on which the Anon. Byz. has opted for Hadrian is unknown. For an example of apparent corruption of Τραιανέ to Ἀδριανέ in the dedication of Aelian's *Tactica*, see A. Dain, *Histoire du texte d'Élien le Tacticien* (Paris, 1946), 19 and n. 1.

11 Ἀθηναίου: His date is not certain, but probably 1st century B.C. and a contemporary of Vitruvius, chapters of whose 10th book on military engines are quite similar to sections of Ath. Mech. (see Marsden, *Treatises*, 4–5 with references to opposing views). For editions and translations of his Περὶ μηχανημάτων see the Bibliography.

12 Μάρκελλον: Most likely C. Claudius Marcellus, Augustus' nephew and son-in-law, who died in 23 B.C. (see Marsden, *Treatises*, 5).

12 Ἀγησιστράτου: Dated by Marsden, *Development*, 206 with discussion of other views, to the second quarter of the first century B.C. On the use of Agesistratus' work by Ath. Mech. and Vitruvius see Marsden, *Treatises*, 4–5. The Anon. Byz.'s mention here of the use by Ath. Mech. of Agesistratus and below by Biton of different earlier engineers may be intended to set his own use of the classical sources in the tradition of poliorcetic writing.

13 ὑπομνήματα: The title of Ath. Mech.'s work is Περὶ μηχανημάτων (Schneider, *Athenaios*, 8; Marsden, *Treatises*, 4).

13 Βίτωνος: His work, titled Κατασκευαὶ πολεμικῶν ὀργάνων καὶ καταπαλτικῶν (Marsden, *Treatises*, 12, 66), is dated by Marsden, *Treatises*, 6, 78 n. 1, with a discussion of other views, to ca. 240 B.C. See also M.J.T. Lewis, "When was Biton?" *Mnemosyne* 7 (1999), 159–68, who suggests 156 or 155 B.C. For text, translation, and commentary see Marsden, *Treatises*, 61–103. Biton is cited again below by name at **54**:10.

13 Ἄτταλον: Marsden, *Treatises*, 6, 78 n. 1 suggests Attalus I of Pergamum, based on his dating of Biton; but for other views see Garlan, *Recherches*, 167 n. 8, and M.J.T. Lewis (as in previous note).

15 < . . . >: Wescher in his note (198 n. 7), followed by Schneider in both text and note (5 n. 2: "offenbar verstümmelt"), posited a lacuna here, based on the absence of references to Heron of Alexandria and Philo Mech. whose works are cited subsequently. Wescher in his note suggests reading: . . . μηχανικῶν · ⟨τὰ Ἥρωνος Ἀλεχανδρέως⟩ βελοποιϊκά, καὶ τὰ ⟨Φίλωνος⟩ πρὸς . . . . Βελοποιϊκά is attested in titles of works by Heron and Philo Mech. (Marsden, *Treatises*, 18, 106), and is used below (**45**:23) specifically in reference to that of Heron. Philo Mech.'s overall work is titled Μηχανικὴ σύνταξις, which was originally arranged in nine books of which the fourth was titled βελοποιϊκά and the eighth πολιορκητικά (see Marsden, *Treatises*, 156). The Anon. Byz. most frequently cites from the latter. On the formation of a "corpus" of classical poliorcetic authors, as seen in Paris. suppl. gr. 607 (dated late 9th–early 10th century by Wescher, ca. 925–950 by Dain, later by Müller; see also Marsden, *Treatises*, 11–12), and consisting of the works of Ath. Mech., Biton, Apollod., and Heron of Alexandria *(Bel., Cheiroballistra, Dioptra)* and in other versions Philo Mech., see Dain, "Stratégistes," 379–81.

17 **διαιτητικά**: Cf. below, **3**:49–51 on dietary preparations for cities under siege, διὰ ... βρώσεως ... καὶ ... διαίτης and the related scholion on the "epimonidian" compound, derived from Philo Mech. On the husbanding and distribution of foodstuffs while under siege, cf. *De obsid.* 48:12ff.

19 **τεχνολογίαν**: For τεχνολογεῖν, "to prescribe the rules of an art," see Aristotle, *Rhetorica* 1354b17 and on τεχνολογία as "technical treatise" see D. Λ. Russell, *Longinus' On the Sublime* (Oxford, 1964), 60 n. on 1:1. The Anon. Byz. here uses it not of a treatise, but of the system used in such treatises, on which see Basil, *Adversus Eunomium libri tres* I:9 (PG 29:532C): Οὔτε γὰρ ἴσμεν τεχνολογίας λέξεων and Iamblichus, *De vita Pythagorica* 182: εἶναι δὲ τὸν καιρὸν μέχρι μέν τινος διδακτόν τε καὶ ἀπαράλογον καὶ τεχνολογίαν ἐπιδεχόμενον; see also George the Monk, *Chronicon*, ed. C. de Boor, 2 vols. (Leipzig, 1904; repr. Stuttgart, 1978, with corrections by P. Wirth), 1:13. Martin renders "la méthode d'exposition générale," Schneider "nach der ... üblichen Ausdruckweise."

21–22 **ἀσυνήθη ... ὀνόματα**: The wording is taken directly from the preface of Apollod. (138:14–15). Nevertheless, it is a consistent part of the Anon. Byz.'s method to simplify vocabulary (see the Introduction, 5–8).

22 **βίβλῳ**: See on **δέλτῳ** at **2**:21.

25–28 **Μόνα ... παραθέμενοι**: The Anon. Byz. indicates that he has gathered his added material "from the remaining <writers>" and he uses, in addition to Apollod., Ath. Mech., Heron, and Philo Mech. extensively and Biton more sparingly in the text. However, he also adds clearly contemporary material, for example, the tortoise called *laisa* (see below on **2**:4) as well as material not found in extant classical sources (e.g., the wheeled ladder described in chap. 46), which may or may not be contemporary. See Dain, *Tradition*, 16 n. 2, for a list of new or otherwise unattested items. The sentence lacks a main verb.

26–27 **ἐπεργασιῶν ... ἐπενθυμημάτων**: The terms (see ἐπενθυμημάτων repeated below at **3**:7 with ταυτολογιῶν and ἐπαναλήψεων) may reflect an acquaintance, direct or more likely through handbooks, with the rhetorical system found in the Hermogenic *On Invention,* in which ἐργασία ("a working out") is a supporting statement to an epicheireme, the enthymeme and epenthymeme supporting statements and additional supporting statements to an *ergasia*. See *Hermogenis Opera,* ed. H. Rabe (Leipzig, 1913), 148–52, and G. Kennedy, *Greek Rhetoric under the Christian Emperors* (Princeton, N. J., 1983), 90–91. Ἐπεργασία is not found in Hermogenes, but it is attested as a rhetorical term at Porphyry, *ad Iliadem* 17:608:6: ἀλλὰ δεῖ νοεῖν τὰ μὲν διὰ μέσου εἰρημένα, τὰ δὲ κεφαλαιωδῶς ἐξενηνεγμένα ὕστερον τῆς ἐπὶ μέρους ἐπεργασίας τυχόντα κατ' ἐπανάληψιν, notably with ἐπανάληψις, on which see below, **3**:6, and at *Scholia ad Iliadem* 13:203: θαυμαστῶς ⟨δὲ⟩ τῇ ἐπεργασίᾳ ἐχρήσατο ὁ ποιητὴς εἰπὼν "κεφαλὴν κόψεν." On the Anon. Byz.'s method of verbal description see the Introduction, 5–8).

30 **κοινῆς ἐννοίας ἀξιώματα:** Proclus, in explaining the term "axiom" *(In primum Euclidis librum commentarius* 194:9), comments: ταὐτὸν γάρ ἐστιν κατὰ τούτους (i.e., Aristotle and the γεωμέτραι) ἀξίωμα καὶ ἔννοια κοινή. For a discussion of "axioms or common notions," see Heath, *Elements,* 221–22, and Mugler, *Dictionnaire,* at ἀξίωμα. I do not find the specific formulation here attributed to Anthemius elsewhere.

31 **Ἀνθέμιον:** Anthemius of Tralles, the "chief expert" connected with the building of St. Sophia, called by Procopius (*De aedificiis* I:1:50) and Agathias (V:8) μηχανοποιός. See *ODB* I:109.

33 **ἰδιωτείᾳ λέξεων:** Cf. below, **3**:3 τὸ ἰδιωτικόν and *Geodesia* **1**:26 τὸ ἰδιωτικώτερον.

34 **ἁπλότητι λόγου:** As a stylistic term cf. Dionysius Halicarnassensis, *Ars Rhetorica* 9:14:5: τὰς ἁπλότητας τῶν κοινῶν λόγων.

35 **παρὰ … τυχόντων:** From Apollod. 137:10; cf. below, **2**:16–17 ὑπὸ τυχόντων τεχνιτῶν.

39 **σχηματισμὸς καλῶς διορισθείς:** The Anon. Byz. here appears to distinguish by terminology (σχηματισμός vs. σχῆμα, the former term not found in his classical predecessors) his own approach to illustration from that which he finds in his sources and which he judges inadequate for practical construction. See the Introduction, 10–11.

40 **δύσφραστον:** Cf. Ath. Mech., 39:7–10: Διόπερ, ἐὰν κρίνῃς, ἐσχηματογραφημένα πάντα ἔσται τὰ μηχανήματα· καὶ τὸ ἐν τῇ λέξει δύσφραστον ἐπ' αὐτῶν εὔδηλον ἔσται.

Chapter 2. Table of Contents

This "table of contents" is modeled on that in Apollod. (138:18–139:8), with adjustments for the Anon. Byz.'s additions from other sources as well as contemporary material.

1 χελωνῶν: χελώνη = Latin *testudo*. For the first attested Greek use in sieges see Xenophon, *Hellenica* III.1.7 (χελώνη ξυλίνη) on the undermining of the wall of Larisa in 399 B.C. For its debated fifth-century origins see Whitehead, *Aineias,* 196, and generally *RE* III:2229–30.

2 ὀρυκτρίδων: The χελώνη ὀρυκτρίς, a shelter for sappers undermining a wall or tunneling, is described by the Anon. Byz. at chaps. 13–15, drawing on Apollod. 143:6–147:6, who calls them διορυκτρίδες. See also Ath. Mech. 19:3–20:3, Vitruvius X:15:1 (with the note by Callebat and Fleury, *Vitruve, ad loc.),* and Garlan, *Recherches,* 351. See also below **13:5**; it is illustrated on folios 11r and 12v.

2 χωστρίδων: The χελώνη χωστρίς, a shelter for men leveling terrain and filling ditches, thus preparing the way for the advance of siege towers and giving access to the walls. The Anon. Byz. briefly discusses its shape at chap. 11, following Philo Mech. 99:41–44. See also Ath. Mech. 15:13–19:2, Vitruvius X:14 (with the extensive note by Callebat and Fleury, *Vitruve,* 254ff), Lendle, *Schildkröten,* 6–29, and Garlan, *Recherches,* 234–36. The tortoise is illustrated on folio 8r.

3 κριοφόρων: The Anon. Byz. describes the ram-carrying tortoise at chaps. 22–24, following Apollod. 153:8–156:2, and that of Hegetor, the largest in antiquity, in chaps. 25–26, following Ath. Mech. 21:1–25:2. See also Philo Mech. 99:44 and Lendle, *Schildkröten,* 103–21. The device is illustrated on folios 18r and 20r.

3 προτρόχων: The term is found elsewhere only at Ath. Mech. (34:1, 7), used as a substantive to refer to a wheel he recommends placing on any tortoise to permit changes of direction (on which see Lendle, *Schildkröten,* 87ff). The term here, if the reading is correct, would appear to refer to a separate type of tortoise. Martin (449 n. 3), noting its absence in Apollod.'s list and use by Ath. Mech., comments "Héron le Jeune désigne ici, par l'adjectif πρότροχος, la tortue qui a ainsi une roue

de devant"; Schneider, printing προτρόχων, comments in his apparatus, "man erwartet ὑποτρόχων" and translates "und auf Räder gesetzt" relating it to the ram-tortoise. As the term πρότροχος does not appear elsewhere in the Anon. Byz. and the ram-tortoise is described as τετράτροχος, Schneider's suggestion may be correct.

4 λαισῶν: This device, as the νῦν ... ἐφευρεθεισῶν indicates, is a contemporary Byzantine tortoise. The Anon. Byz. describes them below at chaps. 9 and 11 and refers to them in chaps. 17 and 47. See below, chap. 9.

5 ἐμβόλων: In Apollod.'s list they are initially called simply χελωνῶν πρὸς τὰ κυλιόμενα βάρη, later (140:9–10) ἡ δὲ χελώνη ἐμβόλου σχῆμα ἔχουσα. The Anon. Byz. describes them in chap. 7.

5 γερροχελωνῶν: Wicker tortoises are described by the Anon. Byz. in chap. 8, derived from Philo Mech. 99:29–36, and illustrated on folio 7v.

5 τριβόλων: Tripod barriers (not the smaller anticavalry "caltrops" on which see below, 11:19) for use against heavy objects rolled down against besiegers from cities on hills. The Anon. Byz. describes them in chap. 6, following Ath. Mech. 38:2–9. They are illustrated on folio 7v.

6 κριῶν: The Anon. Byz. briefly comments on composite and single-beam battering rams in chap. 21, drawing on Apollod. 159:2–161:8 and in chaps. 25–26, drawing on Ath. Mech. 23:11–26:4. See Lendle, *Schildkröten*, 49–86.

6 ξυλοπυργίων φορητῶν: The Anon. Byz. describes "portable towers" in chaps. 30–39, drawing on Apollod. (164:10–167:9, 173:9–174:7) and Ath. Mech. (10:8–12:11 and 17:14–18:7), with some material lost (on the lacuna see Dain, *Tradition*, 28–31). The illustration appears on folio 26r. Both sources use πύργοι. Ath. Mech. adds the adjective φορητός, on which see Winter, *Fortifications*, 320–21, Callebat and Fleury, *Vitruve*, 243 and Fleury, *Mécanique*, 290. Below the Anon. Byz. uses ξυλίνους πύργους (30:4) and φορητῶν πυργῶν (38:20). For the compound ξυλόπυργος see, for example, *Miracula Demetrii* 188:31, *De cer.* 670:10–11, and Anna Comnena, *Alexiad* XIII:3:12. For discussion of the devices see Lendle, *Texte*, 71–106.

7 **κλιμάκων:** An inflatable hide ladder (drawn from Philo Mech. 102:12–19) is described in chap. 12 and illustrated on folio 9v. A large section of the discussion of ladders, drawing on Apollod. 175:1ff, is lost (on the lacuna see Dain, *Tradition,* 28–31); chapters 40–43 describe ladders used to support rams, drawing on Apollod. 185:7–188:9, illustrated on folios 29v and 30v. Chapter 46 describes a ladder with wheels at the bottom and a "drop bridge" on top that is not found in any extant source and may be a Byzantine innovation (see Dain, *Tradition,* 16 n. 2). For a discussion of ladder systems in Apollod. see Lendle, *Texte,* 1–35.

7–8 **εἴδη διάφορα:** On the shift from the genitives dependent on χρεία ἐστί to the nominatives, an anacoluthon even more pronounced in Apollod., see Martin 450 n. 1 and Blyth, "Apollodorus," 134 and 157–58.

8–9 **προφυλακὴ ... βάρη:** The Anon. Byz. describes in chap. 22 a ram tortoise with a projecting front roof (**22:**48ff) to defend against μέγιστοι λίθοι and πλάγια ξύλα dropped against the ram. For use of projecting beams (κεραῖαι λιθοφόροι) to lift and drop large stones on besiegers, see Marsden, *Treatises,* 51. The *locus classicus* is Archimedes' defense of Syracuse (Polybius, VIII:5: ὄργανα ... προπίπτοντα πολὺ τῆς ἐπάλξεως ταῖς κεραίαις· ὧν τινὰ μὲν ἐβάσταζε λίθους οὐκ ἐλάττους δέκα ταλάντων ... τότε περιαγόμεναι καρχησίῳ πρὸς τὸ δέον αἱ κεραῖαι διά τινος σχαστηρίας ἠφίεσαν εἰς τὸ κατασκεύασμα τὸν λίθον). See also the ⟨Περὶ Στρατηγίας⟩ 13:121–35 and the *De obsid.* 48:4–5, 74:9–11, 82:6–7.

9 **τὰ ... ἀναπτόμενα:** Protection of portable towers against fire is described at the end of chap. 39, drawing on Apollod. (174:1–7) and Ath. Mech. (18:1–7). The phrase ἀναπτομένων φλογῶν, which is not found in the Anon. Byz.'s known sources, occurs below at **15:**16, **39:**9 and 36; the precise nature of the incendiary in each instance is not always clear. See below on πυροβόλος **2:**9. For ἀνάπτω see Trapp, *Lexikon,* s.v.: "(intr.) Feuer fangen, aufflammen, (ent)brennen."

9 **πυροβόλων:** The term is used eight times in the text, including at **14:**15, where it refers to "dry wood shavings spread with liquid pitch or smeared with oil" and at **49:**20 where it refers to the handheld swivel tube for ejecting "Greek fire" (μετὰ στρεπτῶν ἐγχειριδίων πυροβόλων); this second verbal description is further clarified by the illustration on

folio 36r. The Anon. Byz. also uses for incendiaries πυροφόρος (e.g., alone as a substantive at **50:**28 and as an adjective with τρίβολος at **39:**8) and αἱ ἀναπτόμεναι φλόγες (see on τὰ . . . ἀναπτόμενα **2:**9). See commentary on **39:**8 and **49:**20, and generally on pre-gunpowder incendiaries Partington, *History,* 1–21, and A. R. Hall, "A Note on Military Pyrotechnics," in Singer et al., *Technology,* II:374–82.

9 **σκοποί:** These scout-ladders (Lendle, *Texte,* 28 "Spähleiter") are described in chaps. 27–29, drawing on Apollod. (161:9–164:4). For discussion see Lendle, *Texte,* 28–35. They are illustrated on folios 22v and 23r.

10 **διορυγαὶ . . . διάφοροι:** various methods of excavating through walls are described in chaps. 13–20.

11 **διαβάθραι . . . εὐμήχανοι:** Drop-bridges attached to filler-tortoises specifically for use over ditches are described in chap. 47 and illustrated on folio 35r; other similar bridges for use on folding ladders for reaching the top of a wall are described in chaps. 46 and 49, illustrated on folios 34r and 36r. The invention of the drop-bridge is attributed (following Ath. Mech.) to Diades in chap. 30. The Anon. Byz. uses both ἐπιβάθρα and διαβάθρα for the device; for a third alternative see the drop-bridges on a portable tower in Anna Comnena, *Alexiad* XIII:3:9 (Bohemund's siege at Dyrrachium): Πύργος ξύλινος κατεσκεύαστο . . . Ἔδει γὰρ οὕτως κατεσκευάσθαι τὸν μόσυνα τοῦτον, ἵνα διά τινων ὑποβαθρῶν μετεώρων πρὸς τὸ χθαμαλώτερον καταχαλωμένων τὸ τεῖχος τῆς πόλεως ἐκεῖθεν εὐκόλως καταδραμεῖται. For discussion of the device see Lendle, *Texte,* 88–91; Garlan, *Recherches,* 163 and 227–28; Callebat and Fleury, *Vitruve,* 253 n. 8.3; and notes on the chapters cited.

11–12 **δίχα κλιμάκων . . . ἐπιβαίνουσαι:** Chapters 50–52 describe tube-like structures mounted on both wagons and tortoises; they are illustrated on folios 38r and 38v. For discussion see Lendle, *Texte,* 107–16, and Marsden, *Treatises,* 90–94.

12–13 **πολιορκητήρια . . . ἀπαράπτωτα:** See **53:**36 where the latter adjective is repeated and generally chap. 53, where the Anon. Byz. draws on Ath. Mech. (32:3–33:3) to describe the πιθήκιον, a weight for maintaining the stability of ships joined together to support raised gangways for attacks on coastal city walls; illustrated on folio 40r. For discussion see Lendle, *Texte,* 156–60.

14 διαβάσεις: Chapters 55–57, drawing on Apollod. (189:1–193:5), describe the use of rafts for river crossings; they are illustrated on folios 41r and 42r. For discussion see Lendle, *Texte,* 177–83.

15 ἀρχιτέκτονας: See above on **1**:9. For a view of the content of military "architecture," see Leo, *Taktika,* Epilogus, 59–60.

15–19 εὐπόριστα τῇ ὕλῃ . . . εὐδιάλυτα: The list of desirable characteristics is modeled on Apollod., omitting his δύσκαυστα and δύστρωτα, using εὐδιάλυτα for εὔλυτα, and adding εὐσύνθετα (which is found at Apollod. 155:16) πρὸς τὴν χρείαν. Cf. Heron, *Bel.* 90: Γίνεται δὲ τὰ πλεῖστα μέρη τοῦ παντὸς ὀργάνου ἀφαιρετά, ὅπως, ἐὰν δέη μεταφέρεσθαι τὸ ὄργανον, λύσαντες αὐτὸ εὐκόπως μεταφέρωσιν. See also below on **22**:63–64.

16–17 ὑπὸ τυχόντων τεχνιτῶν: See above on **1**:9. For a tenth-century Byzantine example, cf. Leo diac. (16:21) καὶ τὰς ἑλεπόλεις ἐκλογῇ τεχνιτῶν ἐτεκταίνετο, of Nikephoros Phokas preparing for the siege of Chandax.

20–21 στρατηγικὴν ἐπιστήμην . . . ἐφοδιάζειν: The phrase is repeated at *Geodesia* **1**:20–21 and in the scholion at **6**:13. Cf. Leo, *Taktika* I:3: Στρατηγικὴ ⟨τέχνη⟩ δέ ἐστιν στρατηγῶν ἀγαθῶν συνάσκησις ἤγουν μελέτη καὶ γυμνασία μετὰ στρατηγημάτων ἤτοι τροπαίων συναθροισμοῦ.

21 ἐφοδιάζειν: Cf. Apollod. 137:10–138:1 Ταῦτά σοι ἐφωδίασα, δέσποτα . . . and below **45**:2, and *Geodesia* **1**:21 and in the scholion at **6**:13.

21 δέλτῳ: On the use of the term for "codex" and its relation to βίβλος, see Atsalos, *Terminologie,* 106ff.

Chapter 3. Stylistic Issues

The Anon. Byz. combines here his own observations on style and general subject matter with cited material from Porphyry *(Vita Plotini)* and Plato, and with uncited material from Ath. Mech., Heron of Alexandria, and Philo Mech.

1 **ἐξονυχιστής**: For the noun see Demetrakos, *Lexikon,* and Koumanoudes, *Synagoge,* s.v; Souda, Epsilon 1802 defines the verb: ἐξετάζειν τοῖς ὄνυξι. As literary criticism cf. Synesius, *Dion* 267:18, βιβλίον ἐξονυχίζειν and Julian, *Orationes* 7:216a: οὐδὲν θαυμαστὸν ἄνδρα στρατιώτην μὴ λίαν ἐξακριβοῦν μηδ᾽ ἐξονυχίζειν τὰ τοιαῦτα (i.e., philosophical problems).

1 **ἀττικίζουσαν**: On Atticism in the tenth century see R. Browning, "The Language of Byzantine Literature," in S. Vryonis, ed., *The "Past" in Medieval and Modern Greek Culture* (Malibu, Calif., 1978), 103–34, repr. in R. Browning, *History, Language and Literacy in the Byzantine World* (Northampton, 1989), XV, esp. 117–19, and Kustas, *Rhetoric,* 64–66.

2–3 **δεινότητα . . . εὐρυθμίαν**: The list is due to the Anon. Byz. Δεινότης and κάλλος are among Hermogenes' seven qualities of style in the *De ideis,* the former the cornerstone of the system and a component of Attic style (see Kustas, *Rhetoric,* 65).

3 **ἰδιωτικὸν . . . ὕπτιον**: On the former term for "ordinary" as opposed to "professional" style, cf. Aristotle, *Poetica* 1458a21, and "Longinus," Περὶ ὕψους 31.2 with the comments of D. W. Lucas, *Aristotle, Poetics* (Oxford, 1968), 208. On the latter as "flatness of style" see Hermogenes, *De ideis* 2:1:6, 2:4:14, and 2:11:60.

4 **τῶν πάλαι σοφῶν**: Apparently Ath. Mech., who is quoted in what follows.

6–7 **ταυτολογιῶν καὶ ἐπαναλήψεων καὶ ἐπενθυμημάτων**: The Anon. Byz. has added these terms to the recommendations for clarity and conciseness (σαφηνείας . . . συντομίας) given by Ath. Mech. On the Anon. Byz.'s method see the Introduction, 5–8. On the difficult relation between repetition and clarity see Kustas, *Rhetoric,* 70 and 94; on ἐπανάληψις, see *Hermogenis Opera,* ed. H. Rabe (Leipzig, 1913), pp. 423ff; for ἐπενθυμήματα see above on **1**:26–27.

8–9 **διαλεκτικῶν . . . ἀνοίκειος**: For Ath. Mech.'s τῶν δὲ ῥητορικῶν παραγγελμάτων οὐκ οἰκεῖος εἶναι, the Anon. Byz. changing Ath. Mech.'s ῥητορικῶν to διαλεκτικῶν and adding the second phrase, perhaps, as Barocius suggested *(ad loc.),* reflecting Aristotle, *Rhetorica* I:1: Ἡ ῥητορική ἐστιν ἀντίστροφος τῇ διαλεκτικῇ.

13 **καὶ τῶν πραγμάτων**: The phrase is not in the passage of the *Vita Plotini* and is apparently added here by the pragmatically oriented Anon. Byz. to mark the contrast between "concept" and "thing." For the opposite perspective, passages extolling a knowledge of calligraphy, grammar, and orthography, see N. Oikonomides, "Mount Athos: Levels of Literacy," *DOP* 42 (1988), 167–78, esp. 170–71.

13–14 **Τριττὰ ... πράγμασι**: The phrasing is not found specifically in Porphyry or Plotinus, but is found in the sixth-century Neoplatonists on the controversy over the subject of Aristotles' *Categories*. See, for example, Olymp. Phil., *Proll.* 18:25–27: οὐ μία τοίνυν γέγονε δόξα περὶ τοῦ σκοποῦ τῶν Κατηγοριῶν, ἀλλὰ τοσαῦται γεγόνασι δόξαι, ὅσα τὰ ὄντα καθέστηκε· τριττὰ δὲ ταῦτα, ἢ πράγματα ἢ νοήματα ἢ φωναί, καὶ τὰ μὲν πράγματα θεόθεν παράγεται, τὰ δὲ νοήματα ὑπὸ τοῦ νοῦ, αἱ δὲ φωναὶ ὑπὸ τῆς ψυχῆς. εἰς τοσαῦτα τοίνυν καὶ ὁ σκοπὸς μερίζεται. Τῶν ⟨δὲ⟩ διαφόρων αἱρέσεων τοῦτον μεριζουσῶν τρεῖς γεγόνασιν αἱρέσεις περὶ τοῦ σκοποῦ, καὶ ἡ μὲν ἔλεγεν περὶ φωνῶν μόνων διαλέγεσθαι τὸν Ἀριστοτέλη, εἰς ἣν ἦν ὁ Πορφύριος, ἡ δὲ περὶ μόνων πραγμάτων, εἰς ἣν ἦν ὁ Ἑρμῖνος, ἡ δὲ περὶ μόνων νοημάτων, εἰς ἣν ἦν Ἀλέξανδρος; and Elias Phil., *In Cat.* 129:9–11: τριττὰ δὲ τὰ ὄντα, φωναί, νοήματα καὶ πράγματα. Οἱ μὲν οὖν περὶ φωνῶν εἰρήκασι τὸν σκοπόν, ὡς Ἀλέξανδρος καὶ Εὐστάθιος, οἱ δὲ περὶ νοημάτων, ὡς Πορφύριος, οἱ δὲ περὶ πραγμάτων, ὡς Ἑρμῖνος.

19–20 **τὴν κατὰ διάθεσιν ... ἄγνοιαν ... διπλῆν**: The closest statements in Plato are at *Sophist* 229bc: Τὴν ἄγνοιαν ἰδόντες εἴ πη κατὰ μέσον αὐτῆς τομὴν ἔχει τινά. διπλῆ γὰρ αὕτη γινομένη ... Τὸ μὴ κατειδότα τι δοκεῖν εἰδέναι, and *Charmides* 166d: φοβούμενος μή ποτε λάθω οἰόμενος μέν τι εἰδέναι, εἰδὼς δὲ μή, but Plato does not use the phrase κατὰ διάθεσιν in this context. It is, however, widely used in discussions of the "double ignorance" by John Philoponos, for example, *In Aristotelis Analytica Posteriora commentaria* 13(3):191:20–25: Κατὰ διάθεσιν δὲ αὕτη, ὅτι διάκειταί πως κατ' αὐτὴν ὁ ἔχων καὶ οἴεται εἰδέναι ἠπατημένως. διὸ καὶ διπλῆ καλεῖται ἡ τοιαύτη ἄγνοια· οὐδὲ γὰρ οἶδεν ὅτι οὐκ οἶδεν, ἀλλὰ μὴ εἰδὼς καὶ αὐτὸ τοῦτο ἀγνοεῖ, ὅτι ἀγνοεῖ. αὕτη οὖν ἡ κατὰ διάθεσιν ἄγνοια) and cf. Aristotle, *Analytica Posteriora* I:16: Ἄγνοια δ' ἡ μὴ κατ' ἀπόφασιν ἀλλὰ κατὰ διάθεσιν λεγομένη ἔστι μὲν ἡ διὰ συλλογισμοῦ γιγνομένη ἀπάτη, suggesting that the Anon. Byz. has derived the concept from an intermediate source. Curiously similar phrasing is also found in G. Pachymeres, *Paraphrase of Pseudo-Dionysius* (PG 3:1020A): οἴονται τῇ ἑαυτῶν γνώσει τὸ θεῖον εἰδέναι, νοσοῦντες τὴν διπλῆν ἄγνοιαν, δηλονότι τὴν κατὰ διάθεσιν, καὶ τὰ θεῖα ἀγνοοῦντες, καὶ ὅτι ἀγνοοῦσιν οὐκ εἰδότες. Martin *(ad loc.)* argued that the Anon. Byz. misunderstood Plato, because of his use of εἰδέναι instead of οἴεσθαι or similar verb for "supposing" rather than "knowing"; Schneider *(ad loc.)* suggested that there is a corruption of the text. I have retained the reading of the archetype as an apparent error on the part of the Anon. Byz.

22–24 ὁ ἱστοριογράφος Καλλισθένης ... θεῖναι: From Ath. Mech. 7:1–4; for Kallisthenes, Aristotle's grandnephew, who accompanied Alexander as "recorder of deeds" see F. Jacoby, *Die Fragmente der griechische Historiker* (Berlin, 1923; repr. Leiden, 1957), no. 124. For the Byzantine position on the relation of person, style, and subject matter, see Kustas, *Rhetoric*, 145.

26–27 Φιλολάου ... Ἀπολλωνίου: The list replaces one in Ath. Mech. which reads: Straton, Hestiaios, Archytas, and Aristotle. Schneider, *Athenaios*, 53, suggests that the changes are due to the Anon. Byz.'s ignorance of the first three (who are connected with works on mechanics). Martin (260) notes, however, that the Anon. Byz. employs the list in relation to Kallisthenes' dictum on the relation of style and subject, while Ath. Mech. employs his relative to the Delphic dictum to be sparing of time. The changes, then, may relate to this different point of comparison.

Presumably the Anon. Byz. is citing authors whose approach to their subjects is more academic and abstract than he considers appropriate in a treatise on poliorcetics. Martin plausibly conjectures that Aristotle and Isocrates are cited as sources of rhetorical theory, Aristophanes (of Byzantium) and Apollonios (Dyskolos) as grammarians. His suggestion that the Anon. Byz. has confused Philolaus with Philodemus who wrote on rhetoric seems unnecessary. At *Geodesia* Chap. 8 the Anon. Byz. cites Pythagorean views of the cube which may be traced to Philolaus and he is perhaps cited here, following references to Plotinus, Porphyry and Plato, as an example of a more philosophical approach than the Anon. Byz. intends to employ. Philolaus is also cited a number of times by Proclus in the *In primum Euclidis librum commentarius*.

32 μαθηματικός: The characterization is that of the Anon. Byz.

32–33 τὸ Δελφικὸν . . . φείδεσθαι: The dictum is cited from Ath. Mech. 3:4–5; attribution of knowledge of it to Heron and the combination with the following comment are due to the Anon. Byz.

33–34 τὰ τοῦ καιροῦ . . . σοφίας): From Ath. Mech. 4:12–13, where it is said to be τῶν ἀρχαίων φιλοσόφων. For its likely source, Anaxarchus of Abdera (4th century B.C.), see Schneider, *Athenaios,* 52–52.

34–42 τὸ μέγιστον . . . ἐνστάντος: The section is taken with minor variations from Heron, *Bel.* 71–72. Marsden, *Treatises,* 44, notes on ἀταραξία that the theme of "si vis pacem, para bellum" (or "para machinas") was an ancient commonplace. Cf., for another view, the comment of Theo. Sim. 1:4:1: τὴν πόλιν ἐξαπιναίως ἄφρακτον οὖσαν ἐλάμβανε πολεμικῶν τε ὀργάνων χηρεύουσαν διὰ τὸ ἐκ τῆς εἰρήνης ῥαθυμίαν πολλὴν ὑπερεκχεῖσθαι τῆς Θρᾴκης· ἀφύλακτον γὰρ εἰρήνη καὶ προμηθείας οὐκ ἀνεχόμενον.

44 ὀλιγαρκέσιν: The characterization here and below is that of the Anon. Byz.

44 ἐπιμονιδίοις: This spelling, which is that of Vat. gr. 1605 as well as the manuscripts of the Anon. Byz.'s source text Philo Mech., is retained by Wescher and Schneider, changed (to ἐπιμενιδίοις) by Barocius, Martin, and Garlan, *Recherches.* Garlan, ibid., 372, connects it to the Cretan philosopher Epimenides, known for his sobriety and abstinence; a connection to ἐπιμονή is closer to the manuscript evidence. Wescher (277) notes that while Theophrastus (*Historia Plantarum* VII:xii:1) has σκίλλης . . . τῆς Ἐπιμενιδείου καλουμένης, the reading is questionable, as Theophrastus adds ἢ ἀπὸ τῆς χρήσεως ἔχει τὴν προσηγορίαν. For discussion and bibliography see Garlan, *Recherches,* 372, and Dain, *Tradition,* 101–2. The nature of the compound is described in a scholion written at the top, left margin, and bottom of folio 3v, drawn from Philo Mech. (88:26–89:10); it is linked in the manuscript to the text by an asterisk above the word ἐπιμονιδίοις. The scholion is also in ms. B and published by Wescher (277–79), who titles it <Περὶ ἐπιμονιδίου φαρμάκου>. On the σκίλλη see Garlan, *Recherches,* 372.

46 πλησμίοις . . . ἐμποιοῦσιν: Cf. Philo Mech., 89:9–10: φάρμακον·

ἡδὺ γάρ ἐστι καὶ πλήσμιον καὶ δίψαν οὐκ ἐμποιεῖ.

47 **μάλιστα ποιούμεθα πρόνοιαν**: Cf. Heron, *Bel.* 72:9: πᾶσαν πρόνοιαν ποιεῖσθαι.

47–49 **Καὶ ἐπεὶ ... ἐπιστήμη**: Cf. Aristotle, *Topica* 163a:2–3: ἐπιχειρῶν ὅτι τῶν ἐναντίων μία ἐπιστήμη, ὅλως τῶν ἀντικειμένων ἀξιώσειε μίαν εἶναι, and *Analytica Posteriora* 69b:10–12: προτείναντος δὴ μίαν εἶναι τῶν ἐναντίων ἐπιστήμην, ἢ ὅτι ὅλως οὐχ ἡ αὐτὴ τῶν ἀντικειμένων ἐνίσταται, τὰ δ᾽ ἐναντία ἀντικείμενα. Cf. also John Philoponos, *In Aristotelis Analytica Priora commentaria* 13(2):478:27–479:1: Ἐὰν δὲ λέγῃ ἐκεῖνος ὅτι οὐχ ἡ αὐτὴ ἐπιστήμη τῶν ἐναντίων, ἐνστῶμεν οὕτως· τὰ ἐναντία ἀντικείμενα, τῶν ἀντικειμένων μία ἐστὶν ἐπιστήμη, οὐκοῦν τῶν ἐναντίων μία ἐστὶν ἐπιστήμη.

49–52 **οἱ ... διάξουσιν**: On the husbanding and distribution of resources while under siege, see *De obsid.* 48:12ff.

51 **εὐταξίᾳ**: For concern with εὐταξία cf. the preface to Leo, *Taktika* (PG 673D–674A), where the term appears three times.

52–54 **Οὐκ ἀπεικὸς ... καταναλίσκοντας**: Drawn with minor variations from Ath. Mech. 4:9–10.

54–56 **ἀνθηρολεκτοῦντάς ... ψέγοντας**: The Anon. Byz. adds. For ἀνθηρολεκτεῖν see Demetrakos, *Lexikon,* and Trapp, *Lexikon,* s.v.

57–61 **Κάλανον ... εἰώθαμεν**: From Ath. Mech. 5:8–11; for Kalanos, the gymnosophist Sphinas who followed Alexander, called by the Greeks Kalanos, see *RE* X:1544–46. It is notable that a letter from Kalanos to Alexander is preserved by Philo Judaeus, *Quod omnis probus liber sit* (ed. F. H. Colson, *Philo, with an English Translation* [10 vols., London, 1941], IX:64) which has a quotation with a similar beginning, but quite different continuation (Ἑλλήνων δὲ φιλοσόφοις οὐκ ἐξομοιούμεθα, ὅσοι αὐτῶν εἰς πανήγυριν λόγους ἐμελέτησαν).

60 **βιωφελεστάτων**: The Anon. Byz. adds.

Chapter 4. Feints and Deceptions to Begin a Siege
The Anon. Byz. draws here on Philo Mech. 98:14–17 and 98:45–52 for the tactics of feint attacks, continuous attacks in relays at weaker sec-

tions of the walls, and use of noise and trumpets to frighten and confuse the enemy.

2 στρατηγικώτατον ἄρχοντα: For the superlative cf. Anna Comnena, *Alexiad* I:7:4 of her father Alexios and VII:2:5 of Nikephoros Bryennios, and Michael Psellos, *Chronographia* I:24:3 of Bardas Skleros. Below at **58**:3 ἐξάρχοντες is used of the military leaders who will benefit from use of the Anon. Byz.'s work; that latter term is also used in the scholion below at *Geodesia* **6**:13. For the terms see R. Guilland, *Recherches sur les institutions byzantines* (Berlin-Amsterdam, 1967), I:380–404, "Le commandant en chef des armées byzantines," esp. 393 on ἄρχων and *exarque*.

3 αὐτοκρατόρων: The reference is apparently to multiple emperors and thus applicable to much of the first half of the tenth century, but may be used of sequential emperors; see also below, **58**:6–7 θεοστέπτων καὶ φιλοχρίστων ἀνάκτων Ῥώμης.

4 ἀποστάτας: The term is used frequently by Anna Comnena for political "defectors"; see also M. McCormick, *Eternal Victory* (Cambridge, 1986), 187. Presumably that is the sense intended here, although it is difficult to find revolts in the first half of the tenth century requiring sieges. In ca. 922 Bardas Boilas in the citadel (ὀχύρωμα) of Paiperte was taken by John Kourkouas (Theophanes Continuatus, ed. I. Bekker [Bonn, 1838], 403–4), and in 932 the false "Constantine Doukas" was taken in the fort (φρούριον) of Plateia Petra (Theophanes Continuatus, 421); for an example of suppression of the ἀποστασία of the Slavs in the Peloponnese (probably 934), see *De admin.* 50:35–70 and for treatment of defeated defectors see *De cer.* 634:9ff. Martin (276) also suggests Melitene, captured in 934.

4–5 τὰς ... πρότερον: Cf. Leo diac. (11:3–5) of Nikephoros Phokas preparing the siege of Chandax in 961: ἔννοια γοῦν ἐπῆλθεν αὐτῷ, κύκλῳ τὸ ἄστυ περιελθεῖν καὶ ἐς τὸ ἀκριβὲς τοῦτο κατασκοπῆσαι, ἵνα ὅποι παρείκοι προσαγάγῃ τὸν πόλεμον, and Anna Comnena, *Alexiad* XIII:2 of Bohemond at Epidamnus: καὶ κατασκοπήσας τοῦ πολιορκεῖν ἤρξατο.

5–6 καὶ τὴν ... φύλαξιν: Not directly in Philo Mech., but perhaps a summary of Philo Mech.'s recommendation, 96:43–46: βαλόμενος τὸ στρατόπεδον ἔξω βέλους ἐπὶ τοὺς ἀσφαλεστάτους τόπους, περιχαρακώσας κύκλῳ ὡς ἂν ἧ δυνατόν, εἶτα φύλακας καταστήσας ποιοῦ τὴν πολιορκίαν.

7 **καστρομαχεῖν**: See below on **10**:1.

10 **πρὸς τὰ σαθρότερα**: Cf. Philo Mech. 97:13: κατὰ τοὺς ἀσθενεστάτους τόπους ... τὴν πρώτην ποιῆσαι προβολήν.

10–11 **ἐκ διαδοχῆς ... ταγμάτων**: The Anon. Byz.'s paraphrase of Philo Mech.'s ἐκ διαδοχῆς στρατιωτῶν. On the tactic of continuous attack in relays, particularly the technical use of ἐκ διαδοχῆς, see Garlan, *Recherches,* 159ff, with caveats in F. E. Winter, review of Garlan, *American Journal of Archaeology* 80 (1976), 92, and R. K. Sinclair, "Diodorus Siculus and Fighting in Relays," *Classical Quarterly* 16 (1966), 249–55. Similar recommendations are found in Maurice, *Strategikon* X:9, Leo, *Taktika* XV:15–16 (following Onasander (XLII:7), and in the *Sylloge tacticorum* (104:6), and in great detail in Nikephoros Ouranos, *Taktika* 65:100–116, who recommends that the army be divided specifically into three teams, two teams resting while the third presses the siege. The *De re militari* (318:19ff) recommends "no let up by night and day in attacking the wall."

The term τάγματα (Philo Mech. uses it at 96:48: Δεύτερον δὲ λογισάμενος εἰς τάγματα ἢ ἐπαρχίας διαδώσεις τὰ γεώργια) is used here not in the technical sense of the four imperial regiments at Constantinople, but of smaller units of troops, perhaps equal to a βάνδον, a unit of about three hundred men, as frequently in Leo, *Taktika*, e.g., IV:2: Διαιρείσθω τοίνυν ὁ πᾶς ὑπὸ σὲ στρατὸς εἰς τάγματα, ἤγουν τὰ λεγόμενα βάνδα διάφορα, καὶ ἔτι ὑποδιαιρείσθω εἰς δεκαρχίας. On the term in this sense see Dennis, *Treatises,* 263 n. 1, and Dagron, *Traité,* 69 n. 18.

12 **σάλπιγγας**: The tactic is from Philo Mech., and perhaps best explained by Onasander, XLII:17: ἀκουσθεῖσα γὰρ πολεμία σάλπιγξ ἀπὸ τειχῶν ἐν νυκτὶ πολλὴν ἔκπληξιν ἐπιφέρει τοῖς πολιορκουμένοις ὡς ἤδη κατὰ κράτος ἑαλωκόσιν, ὥστε τὰς πύλας καὶ τὰς ἐπάλξεις ἀπολιπόντας φεύγειν, although neither Philo Mech. nor the Anon. Byz. indicate that the trumpeters are actually already on the walls. Leo, *Taktika* XV:20 (following Onasander), also recommends use of trumpets to cause fear, while the *Excerpta Polyaeni* 54:7 (ed. and trans. P. Krentz and E. Wheeler, *Polyaenus, Stratagems of War,* II [Chicago, 1994]) recommends use of trum-

pets all around a besieged city to deceive the besieged into thinking the city has been taken from all sides. See also Garlan, *Recherches,* 397.

14 μεταπυργίων: On the term for "curtain walls," taken from Philo Mech., see Garlan, *Recherches,* 340.

Chapter 5. Objects Rolled Down From Cities on Hills

The Anon. Byz. draws here on Apollod. 139:9–12 (cf. Ath. Mech. 37:5–38:1 and Philo Mech. 94:32–33). The Anon. Byz.'s list omits Apollod.'s ξύλων κορμοί ("tree trunks"), adds κίονες, τρόχοι, and σφόνδυλοι (this last perhaps from Ath. Mech. 37:7), elaborates on Apollod.'s references to wagons and wicker containers, and adds the section on "barrels" and the concluding general reference to containers. The objects listed are illustrated in front of a fortification on a hill on folio 7v, the final four with labels (σφόνδυλος, τετράτροχος ἄμαξα, ἀγγεῖον πεπλεκμένον, ἀγγεῖον κυλινδρικ(όν). The depiction of a column drum, labeled σφόνδυλος, helps clarify the use of the word σφόνδυλος in a poliorcetic context; see Demetrakos, *Lexikon,* s.v. no. 5, and Rochas D'Aiglun, "Athénée," 800 n. 1, who translates as *meule.* See, however, another explanation offered by N. P. Milner, *Vegetius: Epitome of Military Science,* 2nd ed. (Liverpool, 1996), 125 n. 7. The illustration shows a hole in the center of the drum with a rod running through it (presumably to prevent the drum from falling flat while running downhill). See also Lendle, *Texte,* 187.

1 εἰ … δυσβάτων: For Apollod.'s Ἐὰν ἐπ' ὄχθαις ὑψηλαῖς. The word λόφος appears in Apollod. 143:5 at the end of the section, introducing the related illustration. See below on **10:22–23**.

2 τὰ ἄνωθεν … ἐναντίων: The Anon. Byz. adds.

5 ἐκ πλοκῆς διάφορα: For Apollod.'s στρογγύλα.

6 πεπιλημένης: The Anon. Byz. adds.

6–8 καὶ οἷα … ὑγροῦ: The Anon. Byz. adds; for casks to store water during a siege cf. Maurice, *Strategikon* X:4:42–43: δεῖ ἢ πίθους ὀστρακίνους ἢ βούττεις τελείας προευτρεπίζειν καὶ γεμίζειν ὕδατος; and 49–50: ἐν τοῖς πίθοις ἤτοι βουττίοις (= Leo, *Taktika* XV:75).

Chapter 6. Wooden Tripod Barriers

The Anon. Byz. here interposes a solution to the problem of objects rolled against besiegers, drawing on Ath. Mech. (38:2–9), delaying Apollod.'s solution until the next chapter. He is apparently in error, however, in seeing Ath. Mech.'s τρίβολος and Apollod.'s ἔμβολον as separate devices; on the error see Lendle, *Texte,* 134 and n. 149. Blyth, "Apollodorus," 152, also concludes that the two devices have the same function, but suggests that the ἔμβολα in the text of Apollod. are "introduced as something new and more elaborate."

1–2 **τριβόλους . . . ξυλίνους:** Here not the spiked anticavalry weapon (on which see below, **11:**19), but, in the Anon. Byz.'s interpretation of Ath. Mech., large tripodlike structures to repel heavy objects rolled downhill. They are so depicted on folio 7v. The noun is found in Ath. Mech.; the Anon. Byz. adds the adjective. The passages in which the term is used in various military applications are conveniently collected by F. Lammert, *RE* VI:A:2:2413–15.

2 **λαβδαραίας:** The designation "*lambda*-shaped constructions" is added by the Anon. Byz. and is found in tenth-century treatises to describe other military devices. Leo, *Taktika* XI:26, so describes spear-tipped μέναυλα placed against *lambda*-shaped frames and set around a camp to prevent cavalry incursions; the passage is paraphrased by Nikephoros Ouranos, *Taktika* 65:69–70. On the passages see McGeer, "Tradition," 134–35, and M. Anastasiadis, "On Handling the Menavlion," *BMGS* 18 (1994), 1–10, specifically 2–3. At *De cer.* 670:12, 671:1–2 λαβδαρέαι are mentioned, but without description, among the siege equipment for the Cretan expedition of 949; only four such items are specified in this list. Reiske, *De cer.* (I: 670–71), explains "arietes e duobus tignis ad angulum acutum instar Graeci Λ commissis suspensos," but perhaps trebuchets. See also Du Cange, *Glossarium,* at λαμβδαραία.

Chapter 7. Ditch with Wall and Beak Tortoise

The Anon. Byz. draws here on Apollod. 140:3–141.3. For illustration of the ditch with fence, the latter labeled πασσαλοκοπία (a term found in Apollod.'s text at 143:4, τὰ ὑπογεγραμμένα σχήματα τῆς τάφρου, τῆς πασσαλοκοπίας, etc., but oddly not in the Anon. Byz.'s text) see folio

7v, and for the beak tortoise see folios 7v and 8r. For the Anon. Byz.'s "ausführliche, freilich durch Fehlinterpretationen beeinträchtigte Beschreibung der Schnabelschildkröte," see Lendle, *Texte,* 133–35, esp. 134 n. 149. Both the Byzantine text and accompanying illustrations differ significantly from the reconstruction of Apollod.'s device suggested by Lendle.

2–3 ἐκ . . . ἀρχομένους: The Anon. Byz. adds.

3–4 καὶ πρός . . . ἀνέρχεσθαι: The Anon. Byz. adds.

5 τοῖχον: The term is from Apollod.; on its use for any lesser wall see Garlan, *Recherches,* 331 and 391, and Lawrence, *Fortification,* 72.

7 προτείχισμα: The Anon. Byz. adds.

9 νεάκια: The Anon. Byz. adds. Martin, following Du Cange, *Glossarium,* cites parallels for the word in the *De obsid.* and the *Parekbolai* (for both texts see *De obsid.* 49:18 with van den Berg's n.18) and translates "troncs de jeunes arbres"; Schneider renders "Äste." The word is also found at Leo, *Taktika,* Appendix (1104:5–8), and Nikephoros Phokas, *Praecepta militaria* I:120, where McGeer translates "saplings."

10 ἐπ' ἀριστερά: This detail is an addition here and below by the Anon. Byz; thus the wall would be on the troops' left side as they advanced.

11–12 λελοξευμένα . . . κλίσιν: The Anon. Byz. appears (as Martin notes *ad loc.*) to misinterpret Apollod.'s πάσσαλοι . . . λοξούμενοι τῷ αὐτῷ κλίματι ("stakes having the same inclination").

13 κλάδους . . . περιδεσμεῖν: For Apollod.'s κλάδων ἀγκαλίδες περιδέονται. Martin (*ad loc.*) notes that the participle refers to the subject of the infinitive and has κλάδους as its object, yet translates "attacher tout autour des branches d'arbres réunies en fagots." Schneider renders "umwinden sie mit biegsamen Baumzweigen." On ἀπαγκαλίζειν see F. Adrados, *Diccionario griego–espanol* (Madrid, 1986), s.v. doblar, citing only this passage.

13–15 καὶ τὴν . . . ἀναβάσεις: The Anon. Byz. adds.

17–22 τουτέστι . . . τοξικίων: The Anon. Byz. adds. The geometrical descriptions (note συνεστώσας) are characteristic. On the terms see below on **7**:21 and 22.

21 ἐπισκηφθέντων: Martin *(ad loc.)*, whose later manuscript read ἐπὶ συνφισθεισῶν, emended to ἐπισυσφιγχθείσαις (as does Wescher) and reasonably suggested "il est évident, par la description qui précède, que ces tortues doivent être comparées à des proues détachées des navires, renversées à terre de manière à présenter la carène en haut, et serrées les unes contre les autres." This accords well with the illustration of the beak tortoise on folio 8r. Schneider emended to ἐπισκηφθέντων, which seems the simplest. For the prows of ships being used to ram walls, see Philo Mech. 95:23–24: τῶν μεγάλων σκαφίων ἔμβολος εἰς τὸ τεῖχος ἐμβάλῃ; and 99:6–8: Ποιητέον δ' ἐστὶν καὶ ἐμβολὰς εἰς τὰ μεταπύργια τῷ ἀχρειοτάτῳ τῶν μεγάλων σκαφῶν.

22 τοξικίων: The precise nature of the comparison is uncertain; Dain, *Tradition,* 159 n. 2, suggests "Il s'agit d'un nom donné à certains navires."

22–24 μικρὰς . . . φέρεσθαι: The Anon. Byz. adds here, but see the same recommendation below, **13**:35–38, from Apollod.

24–25 καὶ . . . ἥλους σιδηροῦς: Wescher *(ad loc.)* and Schneider *(ad loc.)* detected corruption in the text of Apollod. (140:11–12) that the Anon. Byz. interprets here; Blyth ("Apollodorus," 134 and n. 18) saw the work of a redactor and careless copyist; Lendle *(Texte,* 133 n. 148) attempts to retain the readings. The manuscript readings of Apollod. appear to suggest an alternative, smooth beams for dragging or iron wheels. The Anon. Byz. has suggested a combination of smooth beams and iron nails to secure the device when on the ground.

27–28 ὥσπερ . . . ἅμαξαι: The simile is added by the Anon. Byz. If pressed literally, the comparison would not seem to illustrate clearly a pole that would secure the tortoise in position, as Lendle, *Texte,* 135, argues.

28–29 ἵνα . . . ἐπιστηρίζῃ: For Apollod.'s κατὰ τὴν ὑποστροφὴν ἐρεῖδον.

29–30 καὶ μάλιστα . . . μέλλωσι: The Anon. Byz. adds here, perhaps influenced by Apollod. 142:1: ἀναπαύειν τοὺς φέροντας (cf. below **10**:14–15).

Chapter 8. The Wicker Tortoise

The Anon. Byz. draws here on Philo Mech. 99:29–37 (Ποιοῦνται δὲ αἱ γερροχελῶναι ἐκ τῶν πλεχθέντων γέρρων ἄνωθεν ἐς ὀξεῖαν γωνίαν συγκλεισθέντων πρὸς ἄλληλα, ὡσαύτως δὲ καὶ ἐκ τῶν πρόσθεν; in Philo Mech. they are then covered with hides and set on beams with rollers). For illustration of the device see folio 7v; see also above, **2**:5.

3–4 ἰτεΐνων ... μυρίκης ... φιλύρας: The Anon. Byz. substitutes for Philo Mech.'s γέρρων, apparently reflecting contemporary practice. Cf. *De obsid.* 50:5–6: ἀθροίζειν δὲ καὶ κληματίδας καὶ βέργας ἰτείνας ἢ μυρρινίας πρὸς ποίησιν λαισῶν; and Nikephoros Ouranos, *Taktika* 65:86–88: λαίσας εἴτε ἀπὸ κλημάτων ἀμπελίων, εἴτε ἀπὸ βεργίων ἰτέας, ἢ ἀπὸ μυριχίων.

Chapter 9. The Laisa

For a discussion of the etymology of the term λαίσα and its appearance here and in various other tenth/eleventh-century sources see McGeer, "Tradition," 135–38. *Laisai* are illustrated on folios 8r and 35r.

2–3 ἐν σχήματι τροπικῶν: For ἡ τροπική as "arch" see C. Mango, "On the History of the Templon and the Martyrion of St Artemios at Constantinople," *Zograf* 10 (1979), 4 and n. 16. The *laisai* illustrated on folios 8r and 35r show a rounded arch; for the phrase cf. below, **10**:12–13 ἐν σχήματι ... χελώνης, **17**:12–13 ἐν σχήματι κηπουρικοῦ πλατυλισγίου, and **44**:36–37 ἐν σχήματι παλιντόνου ἀγκῶνος. It is worth noting that Nikephoros Ouranos, *Taktika* 65:88–89, says of the shape of the *laisa*: τὸ δὲ σχῆμα αὐτῶν ἵνα εἰσὶν τροπικῶς οἴκου. ἔστω δὲ τὸ ἐπάνω μέρος οἷον τὸ στέγος αὐτῆς καὶ ὀξύτερον. He adds that they should have two doorways (θυρίδων) with enough room for fifteen to twenty men. On the passage see McGeer, "Tradition," 135. The Anon. Byz. may have smaller versions in mind; the illustration on folio 8r shows 4 men, that on 35r a single man.

Chapter 10. Vine Tortoise

The Anon. Byz. draws here on Apollod. 141:5–143:5. For technical discussion of the vine tortoise and the Anon. Byz.'s interpretations of Apollod., see Lendle, *Texte*, 136–41, and Blyth, "Apollodorus," 134. The frame of the tortoise is illustrated on folio 8r; a modern drawing is given by Lendle, ibid., 139.

1 **καστρομαχίαν**: For Apollod.'s πολιορκία. For the term cf. Theoph., I:379:18–20: παραδεδωκὼς αὐτῷ πρὸς καστρομαχίαν κριόν . . . ἐντειλάμενος αὐτῷ, τὰ μὲν τείχη Χερσῶνος ἐδαφίσαι, *De cer.* 670:10: διὰ τῆς ἐξοπλίσεως καστρομαχίας, with a list of equipment and engines for the Cretan expedition of 949, and J. Haldon, *Constantine Porphyrogenitus, Three Treatises on Imperial Military Expeditions* (Vienna, 1990), C:196–97: βιβλία μηχανικά, ἑλεπόλεις ἔχοντα, καὶ βελοποιϊκὰ καὶ ἕτερα ἁρμόδια τῇ ὑποθέσει ἤγουν πρὸς πολέμους καὶ καστρομαχίας. The Anon. Byz. uses the term here as an aspect of a siege (πολιορκία), specifically the attack on the fortifications. See also above, **4:7**. On κάστρον (castle, citadel of a city, the fortified city as a whole), see *ODB* II:1112, and J. F. Haldon and H. Kennedy, "The Arab-Byzantine Frontier," *Zbornik Radova Vizantološkog Instituta* 19 (1980), 76–116, esp. 94–96 and nn. 56 and 60.

1 **λαός**: For Apollod.'s ὄχλος.

2–3 **πρὸς τὰ πλάτη τῶν ἐμβόλων . . . ἤτοι τῶν χελωνῶν ὄπισθεν**: The Anon. Byz. here interprets, adding the final explanatory phrase, a difficult passage in Apollodorus that seems to suggest that the troops are in the area between the two rear sides of the beak tortoises. The text of Apollod. reads: Ἀκολουθήσει δὲ ὁ ὄχλος ὁ ἐργαζόμενος τῇ πολιορκίᾳ χιτῶνα ἔχων, ὃς ἔσται (Sch. coni. ἕψεται) εἰς τὰ πλάτη τῶν ἐμβόλων. See Lendle, *Texte,* 137, and Lacoste, "Poliorcétiques," 237 n. 3.

4 **ξύλα**: For Apollod.'s κάμακας (vine-poles).

5–10 **ἄνισα . . . ἔστωσαν**: The Anon. Byz. introduces here a characteristic of the design that only appears at the very end of the Apollod. text. Blyth, "Apollodorus," 134 and n. 18, argues that the vertical poles are a later addition to the Apollod. text and at variance with the original design, that the Anon. Byz. has in his description tried to reconcile this irreconcilable confusion.

6–7 **κατὰ δὲ πέντε πόδας**: The text of Apollod. is corrupt here. For discussion of the Anon. Byz.'s interpretation see Lendle, *Texte,* 138, and Lacoste, "Poliorcétiques," 238 n. 2.

11 **ἀναδενδράσιν**: The comparison is added by the Anon. Byz. For

Byzantine examples see Koukoules, *Bios*, V:282.

12–13 ἐν σχήματι ... χελώνης: For Apollod.'s ἵνα τὸ ὑπ' αὐτῶν σχῆμα ᾖ χελώνη. As Lendle, *Texte,* 136, notes, we can only conjecture what type of tortoise Apollodorus had in mind; Lendle opts, based on various similarities, for the ram-tortoise. See his illustration, ibid., 137.

14 ὡς ξίφη: For Apollod.'s στύρακας ("spikes at the butt-end of spears" cf. Kolias, *Waffen,* 199 n. 85). For ξίφος as "point," "spike" see, ibid., 195 n. 67.

15–16 Δέρματα ... λίνα παχέα, ἢ τρύχινα: The text here is problematic. Martin *(ad loc.)* suggested that the Anon. Byz. was reacting to a corruption in the text of Apollod. at 144:2, δέρρεις ἢ λινᾶς ἢ τριχίνας, "linen" skins making no sense. Martin proposed to emend the text of Apollod. with λείας for λινᾶς (thus, "skins, either smooth or hairy"), noting that at 146:4-5 Apollod. speaks of δέρρεις τρίχιναι, but argued that the Anon. Byz. actually wrote λίνα here out of respect for his source. Whether two or three coverings are in question is also unclear. The reading of V is τρυχινα (sic), "ragged," and perhaps the Anon. Byz. uses it, trying to remain close to his source, as equivalent to ῥάκος ("patchwork" = *centones,* on which see the commentary on **13**:21). Notably below at **13**:20–21, where he also paraphrases Apollod. 144:2, the Anon. Byz. writes δέρματα ἢ ῥάκη σκέποντα, ἢ τὰ ἐκ βεργῶν ἢ φοινίκων πεπλεγμένα. Schneider, who prints Δέρματα δέ, ἢ λινᾶ παχέα, ἢ τρίχινα, translates "Häute, Sackleinen oder Filzdeken." On protective body armor made ἐκ λίνου see Kolias, *Waffen,* 152–55.

20–21 ἵνα ... ἐκλύηται: For Apollod.'s ἵνα ἐκλύηται τὰ πεμπόμενα.

22–23 Τὰ δὲ ὑπογεγραμμένα ... ὑπόκεινται: The reference is to the group of illustrations on folios 7v and 8r that depict the devices described in chaps. 5–10. The list in Apollod. (143:3–5) is much more specific: Καὶ ἔστι τὰ ὑπογεγραμμένα σχήματα τῆς τάφρου, τῆς πασσαλοκοπίας, τοῦ ἐμβόλου, τῆς ἀμπέλου, τῆς χελώνης, καὶ τοῦ λόφου σχῆμα.

Chapter 11. Filler Tortoises, Probes for Various Traps

The Anon. Byz. here combines and elaborates on passages from Philo

Mech.: 99:41–44 (filler tortoise as wheeled and covered in front), 85:23–29 (burying pots over which men can safely walk, but which siege engines cause to collapse), 100:4–6 (probing for buried pots and hidden ditches), 100:6–11 (probing for doors and caltrops), 99:11–13 (secretly undermining walls), and 99:18–19 (using smoke against miners). On the χωστρίδες see above, **2:2**, and cf. Anna Comnena, *Alexiad* XI:1:7: τὸν ἐκτὸς τούτων διακείμενον τάφρον ὡς ἐν ῥιπῇ πληρώσαντες κόνεως, ὡς εἰς μίαν ἐπιφάνειαν συναφθῆναι ταῖς ἐφ᾽ ἑκάτερα παρακειμέναις πεδίασιν. The device is illustrated on folio 8r, lower right.

1–2 ⟨Ἐ⟩ὶ . . . κείμεναι: Cf. above, **5:1**. The contrast, not in his classical source, may be the Anon. Byz.'s own; Wescher (209 n. on line 3), however, suggests that there may be a lacuna in the text of Apollod.

2 ὑποτρόχους: For Philo Mech.'s τροχοὺς . . . ἔχουσαι.

4 ἀπὸ τῶν ἐναντίων: The Anon. Byz. adds.

4 πλήττωνται: For Philo Mech.'s τιτρώσκωνται.

5 λαίσας: The Anon. Byz. adds; see above on **2:4** and cf. *De obsid.* 74:18: εἰ δὲ καὶ λαίσας χωστρίδας οἱ ἐχθροὶ ἐπινοήσαιντο.

5–9 χρησίμους . . . ποιησώμεθα: The explanation is not in Philo Mech., and apparently is the Anon. Byz.'s addition.

6 ἐνύδρους καὶ ὑπόμβρους: Philo Mech. twice (82:28, 97:27) uses the clause ἐὰν μὴ ὕπομβρος ᾖ ὁ τόπος; the elaboration is apparently the Anon. Byz.'s own.

7 ἀναγεμίζειν: For the compound see Demetrakos, *Lexikon,* s.v., and cf. below, **12:15, 15:6** and **19:2**.

7 λακκίσματα: Philo Mech. mentions (85:30) among defensive preparations for a siege digging τέλματα and (100:23) besiegers filling them in; the later term is the Anon. Byz.'s substitution. On Philo Mech.'s term see Winter, *Fortifications,* 270–71.

7 ἐξομαλίζειν: Cf. Josephus, *Bellum Judaicum* V:106–108:1: ἐξομαλίζειν τὸ μέχρι τοῦ τείχους διάστημα . . . ἀνεπλήσθη μὲν τὰ κοῖλα καὶ χαραδρώδη τοῦ τόπου.

7–8 τοῖς τείχεσι πλησιάζοντα: Schneider translates "und so geht man bis dicht an die Mauer heran."

12 κεράμια: The term is from Philo Mech.; it appears below in *Geodesia* 9 as a technical unit of liquid measurement. The nontechnical use and context here would seem to justify the translation "clay pots"; I retain *keramia* in the latter passage. On the tactic see Garlan, *Recherches*, 365–66. The Anon. Byz. omits Philo Mech.'s additional comment, σάξαντας τὰ στόματα ψύκει· ἄσηπτον γάρ ἐστι.

12–14 τοῖς μὲν ἀνθρώποις . . . καταδύνειν: The Anon. Byz.'s elaboration with added explanation on the weight of the machines for Philo Mech.'s ὥστε τοὺς μὲν ἀνθρώπους μηθὲν πάσχειν δεινὸν ἐπ᾽ αὐτῶν βαδίζοντας, τὰς δὲ προαγομένας χελώνας καὶ μηχανήματα ἐπ᾽ αὐτῶν καταδύνειν.

14–15 καὶ διασπᾶσθαι . . . κεραμίων: The Anon. Byz. adds.

16–17 μετὰ . . . ἐπιτηδείων: The Anon. Byz.'s elaboration for Philo Mech.'s σειρομάσταις. On σειρομάστης as εἶδος ἀκοντίου see Souda IV:347:21 and Kolias, *Waffen*, 178.

16 ἀκοντίων: The Anon. Byz. chooses the classical term; on ἀκόντιον for μέναυλον see Kolias, *Waffen*, 194. On the latter see also J. Haldon, "Some Aspects of Byzantine Military Technology from the Sixth to the Tenth Centuries," *BMGS* 1 (1975), 11–47, esp. 32–33.

16 λόγχας: On the use of the word for the "point" of a spear see Leo, *Taktika* XX:116 (1044D), XX:188 (1064C), τῶν κονταρίων τὰς λόγχας, and Kolias, *Waffen*, 195.

19 σιδηροῦς τριβόλους: Here the small anticavalry or antipersonnel spiked metal ball (see Dennis, *Treatises*, 263 n. 2), illustrated on folio 8r. The adjective is to distinguish it from the large wooden barrier devices of the same name (see above on 6:1–2). Cf. Leo, *Taktika* VI:27, in a list of infantry equipment: τριβόλους ἀναδεδεμένας διὰ λεπτῶν σφηκωμάτων, καὶ ἐν ἥλωσι σιδηρῷ ἀποκρατουμένας, διὰ τὸ ἑτοίμως συναγαγέσθαι αὐτάς, and Procopius, *De bello gothico* VII:xxiv:16–18.

20 ὑποθέματα: On the tactic see Garlan, *Recherches*, 399 n. 44b.

20 ὑποδήμασι : For Philo Mech.'s ἐνδρομίδας ("a soldier's high boot," LSJ). On the ὑπόδημα in the middle Byzantine period as a high military boot replacing greaves, see Kolias, *Waffen*, 72; McGeer, *Warfare*, 62; and Koukoules, *Bios*, IV:414.

21 γεωργικοῖς: For κηπουρικοῖς in Philo Mech.

22 γριφάνας: The term is added by the Anon. Byz. Cf. Hesychius, gamma, 924:1: ⟨γριφᾶσθαι⟩· γράφειν. οἱ δὲ ξύειν καὶ ἀμύσσειν· Λάκωνες, and *The Oxford English Dictionary*, 2nd ed. (Oxford, 1989–), at "griffaun," "graffane": "a grubbing ax." The illustration on folio 8r shows a tool very similar to a modern rake being used to dig up the caltrops.

24 δικέλλαις:The term is from Philo Mech. and not illustrated in the manuscript. On the Byzantine tool see A. Bryer, "Implements," 70 and fig. 16; A. Harvey, *Economic Expansion in the Byzantine Empire, 900–1200* (Cambridge, 1989), 124; and M. Kaplan, *Les hommes et la terre à Byzance* (Paris, 1992), 48. Cf. *Miracula Demetrii* 154:7–8: τὰς χελώνας καὶ τοὺς μοχλοὺς καὶ τὰς δικέλλας καταλείψαντες ἔφυγον ... οἱ πολέμιοι. See also below, **17:**13 for other implements.

27–29 ἵνα ... ἀπολέσωσι: On methods of counteracting tunneling/ undermining see Polybius XXI:28:11–17 (repeated in *De obsid.* 76:22– 77:16), smoke from burning feathers and charcoal; Anna Comnena, *Alexiad* XIII:3, the siege of Dyrrachium in which the tunnelers are driven off with fire from a resin-sulphur mix on reed tubes; and White-head, *Aineias*, 199 nn. 37:1ff and 37:3. For examples of tunneling/un-dermining as a siege method see, for example, Dahabi, in A. A. Vasiliev, *Byzance et les Arabes*, Fr. ed. by H. Grégoire and M. Canard, 3 vols. [Brus-sels, 1935–68], II.2:242. Dahabi indicates that a Byzantine attempt on Amid in 951 involved "une galerie souterraine d'une longueur de 4 milles," but this failed when discovered by the inhabitants. See also Leo diac. (25:19–26:8), undermining the walls of Chandax in 961 (heavily modeled on Agathias' description of Narses' siege of Cumae); Anna Comnena, *Alexiad* XI:1, undermining the walls of Nicaea, and XIII:3, tunneling to and undermining the walls of Dyrrachium; and esp. Nikephoros Ouranos' recommendation of it above all other methods, *Taktika* 65:139–42.

Chapter 12. Tactics to Induce Capitulation.
The Inflatable Ladder

The Anon. Byz. combines here two separate passages from Philo Mech., the first (96:27–34) on siege tactics ending κλίμακας ἑτοίμους ἔχοντας λάθρα πλησιάσαντας τῷ τείχει, the second (102:12–19) beginning Κατὰ κλοπὴν μὲν νυκτὸς ἢ τὰς σκυτίνας κλίμακας προσθέντας. The illustration on folio 9v shows a ladder with both sidebars and rungs stitched, indicating that in the view of the illustrator the whole device was inflatable; the rope net with hooks over the wall is also clearly shown. A similar rope ladder with hooks is also shown on folio 35v.

1 εὐκόπως πορθεῖν: For Philo Mech.'s λήψεσθαι. The term seems strong given ὑπόφορον below. Rochas D'Aiglun translates with "s'emparer" and Schneider "erobern." For the force of πορθεῖν see Garlan, *Recherches,* 24.

2 ᾿Αθηναῖον: Philo Mech. is said to be "of Byzantium" by Vitruvius, Heron of Alexandria, Eutocius, and the Anon. Byz. himself below at **48:1**. Ath. Mech. (15:13) calls him "Athenian," apparently the source of the contradiction. For discussion see Garlan, *Recherches,* 284, and Schneider, *Athenaios,* 59–60 n. on 15:13.

3 ἀθρόαν: The Anon. Byz. adds.

4–6 εὐάλωτον ... ἕξειν: For Philo Mech.'s ῥᾳδιέστατ' ἂν λάβοις τὸ ἄστυ.

7–8 τῶν πολιτῶν ... ὄντων: The Anon. Byz. adds.

8 ἀνελπίστων: Cf. Thucydides 3:30:2: θάλασσαν ... ἢ ἐκεῖνοί τε ἀνέλπιστοι ἐπιγενέσθαι ἄν τινα σφίσι πολέμιον.

9–10 ὅτε ... τυγχάνουσιν: The Anon. Byz. adds.

11–12 τοῦ πλήθους ... σχολάζοντος: The Anon. Byz. adds.

13 κλίμακας ... δερματίνας: The device is from Philo Mech. who uses σκυτίνας; the illustration of the ladder (folio 9v) retains Philo Mech.'s term, perhaps indicating a similar illustration was in a text of Philo

Mech. available to the Anon. Byz. or his illustrator. While the device seems fanciful, for the use of inflated skins for swimming support see esp. Xenophon, *Anabasis* III:v.9–11: ἃ ἀποδαρέντα καὶ φυσηθέντα ῥᾳδίως ἂν παρέχοι τὴν διάβασιν. For general discussion with classical references see J. Hornell, "Floats and Buoyed Rafts in Military Operations," *Antiquity* 19 (1945), 72–79.

15–16 ὥστε μὴ διαπνεῖν: The Anon. Byz. adds.

16–18 ἐμφυσωμένων γὰρ . . . ἀνάβασιν: The Anon. Byz. adds.

18–19 Εἰ . . . εἴη: The Anon. Byz. adds.

19 στυππίναις: The term is Philo Mech.'s. On the use of flax/linen for netting in Byzantium, see Koukoules, *Bios,* V:331ff. On nets and rope ladders for climbing, cf. Aeneas Tacticus 38:7 (δικτύων συείων ἢ ἐλαφείων ἢ ταῖς ἐκ τῶν σχοινίων κλίμαξι) and Vitruvius X:15.7.3 with Callebat and Fleury, *Vitruve, ad loc.* See also below, **44:35** and **49:3**.

21 δικτυωταὶ . . . τὰ λεγόμενα σάρκινα: The Anon. Byz. adds. For the use of the Latin term (e.g., Caesar, *Bellum Gallicum* II:17, "hanc <i.e., primam legionem> sub sarcinis adoriri"), cf. Maurice, *Strategikon* X:3:9–11 (= Leo, *Taktika* XV:48, and *Problemata* X:11): Ἀντίκεινται δὲ ταῖς τοιαύταις βολαῖς κιλίκια κρεμάμενα ἔξωθεν τοῦ τείχους κατὰ τοὺς προμαχῶνας, σάρκινα, σχοινία εἰλημμένα, πόντιλα κρεμάμενα.

22–23 ἀπὸ . . . δερματίνων: The Anon. Byz. adds.

24 προμαχώνων: The term is from Philo Mech.; see also at *Geodesia* **2:**14 where the same term is taken from Afric., *Cest.*

24–25 καὶ οὕτως . . . διευθετίζωσι: The Anon. Byz. adds.

Chapter 13. Tortoise for Excavating

The Anon. Byz. here draws on Apollod. 143:6–144:11. The device, which protects sappers excavating through walls, is illustrated in position against a curtain wall with merlons and between towers on folio 11r, labeled χελώνη ὀρυκτρίς; two men dressed in calf-high boots, thigh-length tunics (καβάδια), and felt hats (καμελαύκια), each wielding a two-pronged pick, are depicted excavating one side of a similar fortification on folio

11v, with the wooden props and fire depicted on the other side; finally, another similar tortoise labeled χελώνη ὀρυκτρίς πηλῷ ἐπικεχρισμένη is depicted on folio 12v. For the device see also Ath. Mech. 19:3–20:3; Vitruvius X:15:1; Callebat and Fleury, *Vitruve,* 262–63; Garlan, *Recherches,* 351, and above, **2**:2.

1–2 ⟨Τ⟩ὰ ... ἀμπελοχελώναις: The Anon. Byz. adds.

1 ἀνωτέρω προρρηθέντα: See **7**:15ff.

3 διαφόρους: For Apollod.'s πολυτρόπους.

4–5 τὰς λεγομένας ὀρυκτρίδας: Apollod. does not name the device in his description, but does use the phrase χελωνῶν διορυκτρίδων in his table of contents (138:19). Ath. Mech., in his brief description, uses the phrase τῆς ὀρυκτρίδος χελώνης; Anna Comnena, *Alexiad* XIII:2:3, uses ὀρυκτρίδας.

5–9 ταύτας ... οὕτως: The Anon. Byz. adds.

5 διρρύτους: On the term see Trapp, *Lexikon,* s.v., who gives "mit zweiseitig abfallendem Dach, mit Satteldach." It is added here by the Anon. Byz. Such a triangular form is also found in Vitruvius (X:15:1): "Quae autem testudines ad fodiendum comparantur ... frontes vero earum fiunt quemadmodum anguli trigoniorum, uti a muro tela cum in eas mittantur, non planis frontibus excipiant plagas sed ab lateribus labentes, sine periculoque fodientes, qui intus sunt, intuentur." This form of the tortoise is not described or depicted; see below on **13**:7 and cf. ὀξύρρυτος at **22**:11.

7 μονοπτέρους: The term, added by the Anon. Byz., is contrasted with διρρύτους and thus apparently refers to a tortoise with a single slanting roof, like a lean-to, which accords with the Anon. Byz.'s description and the illustrations on folios 11r and 12v. Barocius renders "unicam habentes alam retro," Schneider (note, pp. 21–23) "Pultdach," suggesting a connection with the architectural use of τὸ πτερόν as "'Schwebedecke,' also μονόπτερος ein Gebäude mit einem Dache." Closer parallels for τὸ πτερόν as a defensive barrier may lie with Procopius, *De aedificiis* II:8:14: ὅπερ ἀποκρούεσθαι διὰ σπουδῆς ἔχων οἰκοδομίαν τινὰ τῇ τοῦ περιβόλου ὑπερβολῇ ἑτέραν ἐνῆψε κατ' αὐτὸ μάλιστα τὸ τῶν

σκοπέλων γειτόνημα, προκάλυμμα τοῖς ἐνθένδε μαχομένοις ἀεὶ ἐσομένην. πτερὰ τὴν οἰκοδομίαν καλοῦσι ταύτην ἐπεὶ ὥσπερ ἀποκρέμασθαι τοῦ τείχους δοκεῖ, and with the interesting device described in the *Scholia in Euripidem (scholia vetera) in Phoenissas* 114: ἄλλοι δὲ ἔμβολά φασι τοὺς καθέτας, τὰ νῦν καλούμενα πτερά, ἅπερ ἐστὶ τῇ κατασκευῇ τοιάδε. θύραν κατασκευάσαντες ἴσην κατά τε μῆκος καὶ πλάτος τῇ πύλῃ τοῦ τείχους ἔξωθεν αὐτῆς χαλκᾶ πέταλα καθηλοῦσιν ὡς ὁλόχαλκον τὴν θύραν νομίζεσθαι. ταύτην ἐπάνω τῆς πύλης ἵστασαν οὐχ ἐδραίαν ἀλλῷ ὥσπερ κρεμαμένην. τῶν δὲ πυλῶν κλειομένων καθίεσαν ἄνωθεν τὴν κεχαλκωμένην θύραν, ἥτις μέχρι τοῦ ἐδάφους φθάνουσα ἐκάλυπτε τὰς πύλας ὡς ἂν μηδεμίαν ἐπιβουλὴν γίνεσθαι ἔσθ' ὅτε καὶ πυρὸς προσφερομένου ταῖς πύλαις ξυλίναις οὔσαις. καὶ πολεμίων μὲν πολιορκούντων τάς τε πύλας ἔκλειον καὶ τὰ ἔμβολα καθίεσαν· εἰρήνης δὲ οὔσης διὰ τὸ τὰς πύλας οὔσας μεγάλας δυσχέρειαν παρέχειν ἔν τε τῷ κλείεσθαι καὶ ἀνοίγεσθαι, ταύτας μὲν εἴων ἀνεῳγμένας διὰ παντός, ἑσπέρας δ' ἠρκοῦντο τῷ ἐμβόλῳ διά τινος μηχανήματος αὐτὸ καθιέντες καὶ ἀνέλκοντες. ἔμβολον καλεῖ ἐκ τοῦ ἄνωθεν ἀπὸ τοῦ τείχους ἐμβάλλεσθαι ἔξωθεν τῶν πυλῶν, χαλκόδετον δὲ διὰ τὸ δεδέσθαι καὶ ἠσφαλίσθαι χαλκῷ. The phrase μονόπτερα πλεκτά, ὡς δῆθεν ψιάθιον in Nikephoros Ouranos, *Taktika* 65:95, apparently refers to plaited screens on *laisai.*

8 **τραπεζοειδεῖς ὡς τριγώνους**: The Anon. Byz. adds this description; the phrase seems awkward as the sides of the tortoise would appear to be specifically triangular rather than trapezoidal. Schneider renders "eine unregelmässige Figur, so ziemlich ein Dreieck." For similar geometric influence on description of a tortoise see Anna Comnena, *Alexiad* XIII:3:1: Μικράν τινα χελώνην ... ἐν παραλληλογράμμῳ σχήματι.

10–11 **διὰ ... ἔργου**: The Anon. Byz. adds.

12 **ὁμοίως ... πλάτος**: The Anon. Byz. adds.

13 **λοξῶς**: The Anon. Byz. adds.

13 **πρὸς ὄνυχα**: The phrase here is from Apollod.; the Anon. Byz. adds it again at **13:**19 and at **49:**12 in his own description of a triangular drop-bridge.

13–14 **ὑποτρόχων ἀξόνων**: The Anon. Byz. adds here; only at the end of his description of both the tortoise and the excavating operation does Apollod. mention that the tortoises are wheeled, a mention repeated by the Anon. Byz. at **15**:21. For the view that the oddly positioned addition of wheels as well as the nails and clay covering in Apollod.'s text are due to a later redactor, see Blyth, "Apollodorus," 135.

14 προσεγγίσωσι: For Apollod.'s ἐφαρμόζει: that is, the diagonal cut allows the slanting beam to fit flush against the wall.

15 ὑπόθεμα: The term is from Apollod.; see Marsden, *Treatises,* 160 n. 20, "a strengthening plate fixed beneath," and Marsden, *Development,* 20 and 29. See also below, ὑπόθημα, **39**:3.

16 τὰ ὑποστηρίζοντα: For Apollod.'s τὰ λοξὰ καὶ τὰ ἐρείδοντα.

17–18 ἵνα ... παρεκπίπτῃ ὄπισθεν: For Apollod.'s ὅπως ἅπαντα τὰ ἐπιβαλλόμενα ὀλισθαίνῃ.

18–19 Τὰ ... ἐκκεκομμένα: For Apollod.'s τὰ ἄκρα τῶν ξύλων τούτων.

21 παρασύρωνται: For Apollod.'s ῥέμβηται.

21–22 δέρματα ... πεπλεγμένα: For Apollod.'s δέρρεις ἢ λινᾶς ἢ τριχίνας: see above on **10**:15–16.

21 ῥάκη : Rochas D'Aiglun, "Athénée," 185 n. 1, suggests that ῥάκη = Latin *centones,* citing Caesar, *Bellum Civile* II:9: "Coria autem, ne rursus igne ac lapidibus corrumpantur, centonibus conteguntur," as well as Vegetius IV:15. On *cento* (κέντρων) see Dar.-Sag., *Dictionnaire,* I:1013: "couverture ou vêtement fait de pièces cousues ensemble. ... Les Romains, sachant que la laine brûle difficilement, revêtaient d'épais centons de cette étoffe les galeries d'approche qu'ils employaient dans les sièges." See also *RE* III:1932–33, with references to military uses. The term is also found below at **15**:9 and **55**:15. Cf. also the use of felt (κέντουκλον), e.g., at *De cer.* 670:17 and 671:11 with discussion in Kolias, *Waffen,* 58.

22 φοινίκων: The Anon. Byz. adds; palm is recommended for its resilience by Ath. Mech. (17:14, on a filler tortoise), a passage cited by the Anon. Byz. (**39**:10) and perhaps the source for the recommendation here. Philo Mech. makes similar recommendations (91:4–6, hung on

fortification walls to protect against stone throwers, and 97:24, 98:8, on portable towers). On its properties and geographical range of availability see Lawrence, *Fortification,* 70, 88 n. 3, and 101, and F. Lammert, *Jahresbericht über die Fortschritte der klassischen Altertumswissenschaft* 274 (1941), 57; for references to it in the classical sources see Callebat and Fleury, *Vitruve,* 260 n. 3.2. On availability of wood supplies generally see Dunn, "Exploitation," also, Meiggs, *Trees,* esp. chap. 6, "Timber for Armies."

23 ἑκατέρωθεν: For Apollod.'s πλαγίως.

23–24 ὡσαύτως . . . ἔμπροσθεν: The Anon. Byz. adds these front covers, apparently to protect men putting the tortoise into position.

24–25 Ὅταν . . . ἔμπροσθεν: The Anon. Byz. adds.

29–30 τὰ . . . κατερχόμενα: For Apollod.'s ἡ ὀρυσσομένη γῆ.

30 πρὸς τὸν ἐαθέντα . . . τόπον: For Apollod.'s ποῦ ἀποβληθῇ.

30–32 ἐπὶ . . . δυνήσονται: For Apollod.'s ἀπὸ δὲ τοῦ ὀρύγματος τοσοῦτον ὁ βαθύνων δύναται.

32 ἀπαρεμποδίστως: The Anon. Byz. adds.

32 Ἐγγύτερον: For Apollod.'s Ἔλασσον.

34 οἱ ὀρύσσοντες: The Anon. Byz. adds.

35–38 μικραὶ . . . βαλλόμενα: For Apollod.'s μικραὶ οὖσαι καὶ εὐμετάγωγοι ὦσι, μὴ πολὺ δὲ διεστηκυῖαι, ἵνα μὴ εὐθικτῇ τὰ ἐπιβαλλόμενα.

Chapter 14. Supporting the Excavation.
Burning the Supports to Cause the Collapse.

The Anon. Byz. draws here on Apollod. 145:1–146:3. For a description of excavating through (rather than under) a wall, see Eustathios, *La espugnazione di Thessalonica,* ed. S. Kyriakides (Palermo, 1961), and *The Capture of Thessaloniki,* trans. J. R. M. Jones (Canberra, 1988), 96:1ff. For examples of the use of props that are subsequently burned (although under rather than in the wall), see Leo diac. 25:11–26:8, Nikephoros Ouranos, *Taktika* 65:117–39, and Anna Comnena, *Alexiad* XI:1.

2 διάχωρα: For Apollod.'s ζωθήκας (LSJ: "niche in a wall"). On the latter term, more common in Latin authors, see G. Hermansen, *Ostia: Aspects of Roman City Life* (Alberta, 1981), 23–24.

4 ἀπαρεμποδίστως: The Anon. Byz. adds.

8 ὑποστυλούσθω . . . στυλαρίοις: For Apollod.'s στυλώμασιν ἐρειδέσθω.

10–11 ὑποχαλῶντα τὰ στυλάρια: For Apollod.'s ἐνδάκῃ ὁ στῦλος.

13 ξύλων ξηρῶν ἐσχισμένων: For Apollod.'s σχίδακες.

14 δᾴδων: The term is from Apollod. here and below at **19**:18; see André, "Résine," 87 ("le "bois gras" (δᾷς) . . . tissus du pin gonflés de résine"), and on pine wood see Dunn, "Exploitation," esp. 259.

16 ξύσματα ξύλων ξηρὰ . . . ἐπαλιφέντα: For Apollod.'s ξύσματα ξύλων τεθειωμένα ⟨ . . . ⟩ περιεσπαρμένα, the lacuna in Apollod. posited by Schneider. Schneider, *Apollodoros,* 17, note on Apollod. 145:12, takes Apollod.'s πυροβόλα in this instance to be not fire-arrows but πυρεῖα ("Feuerzeuge"), an interpretation he sees as confirmed by the Anon. Byz.'s additions here. See also below, **19**:9–10. On the Anon. Byz.'s use of τὸ πυροβόλον generically see above on **2**:9. For the form ἐπαλιφέντα see also below, **19**:10 and cf. Athanasius, *Vita Antonii,* PG 26 col. 965:29, ἐπαλιφείς.

17 ὑγρᾷ πίσσῃ: Presumably added by the Anon. Byz., although the source, Apollod., may have a lacuna at this point; see also below at **19**:9–10. For liquid pitch see *De cer.* 673:3 and 677:11: πίσσα λίτραι χιλιάδες ι΄. ὑγροπίσσιον μαγαρικὰ στρογγύλα τ΄, and as one of the materials to be obtained in preparation for withstanding a siege, *De obsid.* 48:19, πίσσαν ὑγρὰν καὶ ξηράν. For discussion see πίσσα ὑγρά, André, "Résine," 95, and on pitch generally, Meiggs, *Trees,* 467–71, and *RE* XIX at "Pech." On the requisitioning of pitch for the Cretan expedition see Dunn, "Exploitation," 268–69. See also below **15**:10 and **19**:10.

Chapter 15. Protective Coverings for Tortoises

The Anon. Byz. here draws on Apollod. 146:4–147:6 with significant changes in the sequence of presentation.

2 **δακτύλων ὀκτώ**: For Apollod.'s ἡμιποδιαῖοι.

2 **καρφία**: The Anon. Byz. adds. Cf. Leo, *Taktika* VI:26: ἥλοις καθηλοῦσθαι . . . ἤγουν καρφίοις. The term is used frequently in the inventory for the Cretan expedition in the *De cer.* (672:12–14) with various descriptive adjectives, and for use with tortoises see *De cer.* 658:22–659:1: περὶ τοῦ ἑτοιμασθῆναι καρφίον ἁρπάγιον κοινοστομαῖον λόγῳ χελωνῶν.

3–4 **ἄχρι . . . ἐχέτωσαν**: For Apollod.'s more general μὴ ὅλοι ὥστε ὑπερεστάναι.

5 **πηλὸν λιπαρόν**: For Apollod.'s λιπαρᾷ γῇ. The Anon. Byz. recommends the same coating against fissures at **24**:4, **39**:18–19, **40**:4 and **47**:13.; Apollod. uses it again at 156:4 and 173:17. The Anon. Byz. is more elaborate and specific in adding κολλώδα, χοιρείων and τραγείων (see **15**:5–6). Cf. Leo, *Taktika,* Appendix, 54 (PG 1117B): αἱ δὲ χελῶναι πηλῷ διαχρίσθωσαν ἄνωθεν. See also Lendle, *Texte,* 100 n. 117.

5–6 **μετὰ τριχῶν χοιρείων ἢ τραγείων**: The Anon. Byz. adds here; cf. Apollod. 156:4: γῆν . . . λιπαρὰν μεμαλαγμένην . . . τριχῶν αὐτῇ μιγεισῶν.

6–7 **ἵνα . . . διασχίζηται**: The Anon. Byz. adds here (cf. Apollod. 157:1: ἵνα τηρήσωσιν ἀρραγάδωτον).

7 **Κρατηθήσεται**: For Apollod.'s κατασχεθήσεται.

9 **Ῥάκη**: See above on **13**:21.

10 **ἄμμος θερμὴ . . . πίσσα . . . ἔλαιον**: The three substances are mentioned by Apollod. For molten pitch (πίσσαν διαλυθεῖσαν πυρί) used against tortoises see ⟨Περὶ Στρατηγίας⟩13:65; for pitch and oil, see Leo, *Taktika,* Appendix, 53 (PG 1116B).

10 **τήλη ἀφεψηθεῖσα**: The Anon. Byz. adds. Schneider suggested (84) that the Anon. Byz. has taken the military use of fenugreek from Josephus, *Bellum Judaicum* III:277:2: τὰς προσβάσεις αὐτῶν ἐπέσφαλλον τῆλιν ἑφθὴν ἐπιχέοντες ταῖς σανίσιν, ἧς ἐπολισθάνοντες ὑπεσύροντο, as the preceding passage of Josephus (ibid., III:274:2–4) contains a reference to boiling oil (ζέον ἔλαιον) being poured from the walls on the Roman besiegers and the comment καὶ τὴν σάρκα φλογὸς οὐδὲν ἔλασσον ἐπεβόσκετο, θερμαινόμενόν τε φύσει ταχέως καὶ ψυχόμενον βραδέως διὰ

τὴν πιότητα. The use of fenugreek in Josephus, however, is to cause the besiegers to slip and fall on their gangways, not to burn their flesh. Leo, *Taktika*, Appendix, 53 (PG 1116B), has πίσσα καὶ ἔλαιον καὶ τῆλις ζέοντα πάντα καὶ ταῖς εἰρημέναις προσχεόμενα κλίμαξι; thus the Anon. Byz. may be reflecting contemporary practice. For a useful collection of references to fenugreek in antiquity *(Trigonella Foenum-graecum,* a genus of leguminous herbs from which about 6% fatty oil can be extracted) see *RE* III:580–82 at *Bockshornklee.*

11–12 ὡς ταχέως ... βραδέως: See above on **15**:10, τήλη.

12–13 παρομοίως ... σάρκας: See above on **15**:10, τήλη.

15 πυροφόρων: See above on **2**:9.

16 ἀναπτομένων φλογῶν: See above on **2**:9.

17–19 Ὡσαύτως ... ἀντιμάχεσθαι: The Anon. Byz. adds.

18–19 δέρμασι ... νεοσφαγῶν: The references to *laisai* and wicker tortoises and this type of protective coating are added here by the Anon. Byz. For the same use of hides see also below, **17**:4, **40**:4–5 and **47**:14. Apollod. (142:1, 146:4, 173:14, 189:11) mentions simply δέρρεις, and once δέρρεις τρίχιναι as protection for various siege machines, while Ath. Mech. (12:11, 18:3, 24:8) uses the phrase ἀγραῖς βύρσαις. For military use of untanned hides see Dar.-Sag., *Dictionnaire,* IV:1:371–72 *(pelles)* and *RE* XIX:369–73 *(pellis).* For Byzantine parallels see *Miracula Demetrii* 148:28–31 τὰς καλουμένας χελώνας, ἅστινας σὺν τοῖς πετροβόλοις δέρρεσιν ἐπισκεπάσαντες ξηραῖς, μεταβουλευσάμενοι πάλιν διὰ τὸ μὴ ὑπὸ πυρὸς ἢ πίσσης καχλαζούσης ἀδικεῖσθαι, δέρρεις νεοσφαγῶν βοῶν καὶ καμήλων ἡμαγμένας ἔτι τοῖς ὀργάνοις ἐκείνοις ἐνήλωσαν, and Leo, *Taktika* XV:30: Εἰσὶ δὲ καὶ πύργοι ἀπὸ ξύλων συγκείμενοι, καὶ διὰ βυρσῶν ἢ ἑτέρας ὕλης ἐπισκεπόμενοι, ὥστε διὰ πυρὸς μὴ φθείρεσθαι; and Appendix, 54: ξύλινοι πύργοι βύρσαις νεοδόρων βοῶν περιφραγκίσθωσαν.

18 διαβρόχοις: Leo, *Taktika,* Appendix, 54 recommends that tortoises be covered on top with clay and that σπόγγοι δὲ ὄξει διάβροχοι ταύταις ἐπιτιθέσθωσαν ἔξωθεν (ἀποτρέποι γὰρ ἂν τὸ ὄξος τὴν τοῦ πυρὸς ἐρωήν). See also below, **50**:27.

20 πόρρωθεν ... τοξοβολιστρῶν: For Apollod.'s μακρόθεν βέλους.

The λιθοβόλος is found in Apollod. (188:6) and Ath. Mech. (18:6), the τοξοβολίστρα is a later term, not found in the classical sources. Cf. Theoph., I:384:11; *De cer.* 670:11 (τοξοβολίστραι μεγάλαι) and 671:16 (μικρὰς τοξοβολίστρας), etc.; Leo, *Taktika* VI:27, where the device with arrows is said to fit in a wagon (Ἑτέρας ἁμάξας ἐχούσας τοξοβολίστρας καὶ σαγίττας αὐτῶν), and ibid.,V:7. On the term see Kolias, *Waffen,* 244–45. The Anon. Byz. uses λιθοβόλος at **27:**84, **39:**35, **44:**38 and **45:**4.

Chapter 16. Bellows-Driven "Flame Thrower"

The Anon. Byz. draws here on Apollodorus 152:7–153:7; on the impracticality of the device, which is illustrated on folio 13r, see Blyth, "Apollodorus," 140. For a similar device see Thucydides IV.100 (an αὐλός, a λέβης filled with charcoal, sulphur, and pitch, and with an iron ἀκροφύσιον, and a bellows). Polybius XXI:28:12–13 (followed by *De obsid.* 76:22ff) describes a related approach to smoking out sappers; the latter device is also found in Leo, *Taktika,* Appendix, 53 (PG 1116C). See also below, **19:**26–29.

2 **προσεγγίζοντα κάτωθεν:** The Anon. Byz. adds.

3 **καὶ ἐπισφαλές:** The Anon. Byz. adds.

5 **φορά** : For Apollod.'s ἐπέρεισις.

5–6 **ὡς φύσει . . . τυγχάνουσα:** For Apollod.'s ἀνωφεροῦς ὄντος. Cf. Aristotle, *Physica* 230b: φέρεται δὲ τὴν μὲν ἄνω φορὰν φύσει τὸ πῦρ. Anna Comnena, *Alexiad* XI:10:4:18 also cites the same passage from Aristotle regarding shooting "Greek fire" horizontally.

7 **ἐπὶ . . . ὁρμῇ:** The Anon. Byz. adds.

7 **οἱ ἔνδον ἐργαζόμενοι:** For Apollod.'s οἱ ταῦτα ποιοῦντες.

8 **συγκαήσονται:** For Apollod.'s συγκαήσεται.

8–9 **κύθρινοι ὀστράκινοι:** The phrase is from Apollod. The container illustrated on folio 13r is labeled ⟨χ⟩ύτρινος.

9 **πετάλων:** For Apollod.'s λεπίσι, as in **16:**11 and **17:**10.

9 **ἐπὶ τοῦ ἔξωθεν μέρους:** The Anon. Byz. adds.

10 **γεμίζονται:** For Apollod.'s πίμπλανται.

10–11 ἀπὸ δὲ τῆς ἔξωθεν ὄψεως: The Anon. Byz. adds.

13 αὐλίσκον: For Apollod.'s σύριγγα. See also below, **19**:29.

15 ὁμοίαν φλογὸς ἀπεργάζονται ἔκκαυσιν: For Apollod.'s πληγὴν ὁμοίαν ἐργάζεται φλογί. Cf. Aristotle, *Problemata* 936a: ἡ δὲ φλὸξ καὶ τὸ ἀπὸ τῶν ἀνθράκων διὰ λεπτότητα εἰσιὸν διαλύει. On the passage of Apollod. see Partington, *History*, 2.

16 ὄξους: The technique is in Apollod. The *locus classicus* is Hannibal (Livy, 21:37); for Byzantine examples see ⟨Περὶ Στρατηγίας⟩ 18:53–56, with n. 1.

16 οὔρου: The Anon. Byz. adds.

17 Καὶ ... ὑπογέγραπται: Cf. Biton, 56:6–7, 61:1, 64:2–3, and 67:3–4: τὸ δὲ σχῆμα οἷόν ἐστιν ὑπογέγραπται.

18 μολιβδουργοί: The reference is in Apollod.; on the methods of lead workers, including blowpipe and bellows, see R. J. Forbes, *Studies in Technology*, VIII (Leiden, 1971), 114–19, and J. O. Nriagu, *Lead and Lead Poisoning in Antiquity* (New York, 1983), 84–91.

Chapter 17. Bow-Drill Used to Bring Down Walls

The Anon. Byz. draws here on Apollod. 148:2–150:3. For discussion of the device, the "Handmauerbohrer," see Lendle, *Texte*, 147–50, and for its impracticality Blyth, "Apollodorus," 140. It is illustrated on folios 14r (with the ἀρίς and the πυελίς labeled) and 14v (on which the handspikes are clearly shown).

2 τρυπάνων: The term is from Apollod. See also above, **11**:17, and below, **30**:3, for different uses of the word, and Winter, *Fortifications*, 72 n. 8. Bryer, "Implements," 79, shows the smaller Byzantine auger (τρυπάνιον).

2–6 ὑπὸ χελωνῶν ... ὑγρά: The Anon. Byz. adds here. See above, **15**:10.

7 τεκτονικοῖς ὀργάνοις: The Anon. Byz. adds. See Lendle, *Texte*, 150 n. 166, for the validity of the simile and Roman industrial uses of such tools.

8 ποδῶν ... πέντε: The text of Apollod. indicates that he sees the

entire device as 5 feet long. For discussion of the difference see Lendle, *Texte,* 148.

8–9 δακτυλιαίαν τὴν διάμετρον ... πάχος γυρόθεν ὡσεὶ δακτύλων τεσσάρων: For Apollod.'s δακτυλιαῖοι τὸ πάχος. The Anon. Byz. here adds the latter dimension using a rough approximation (i.e., 4 for π) for the relation between diameter and circumference, that is, C = 2πr.

10 πέταλον: For Apollod.'s λεπίς.

11–12 πλάτους ... ὀκτώ: Schneider argued *(ad loc.)* that a blade 12 fingers wide is incompatible with a shaft 1 finger in diameter. Lendle, *Texte,*149, notes that the bore holes, according to Apollod. (150:6–151:3), are filled with stakes nearly 3 fingers thick (there are multiple stakes in each bore hole); therefore, a wide blade would be needed to create such holes, justifying the Anon. Byz.'s comparison of it to a garden spade.

12–13 ἐστενωμένον ... πλατυλισγίου: For Apollod.'s οὐραχὸν μέσον ἔχουσα.

13 πλατυλισγίου: Cf. *De cer.* 463:1: ἀξινορύγια καὶ πλατυλίσκια καὶ πτυάρια στιβαρά ("pick-axes and broad spades and heavy shovels"), on which Reiske, *De cer.* II:508 n. 463:1, says "nos appellamus *Spathen."* The precise shape of the tool is uncertain. For λίσγον see A. Harvey, *Economic Expansion in the Byzantine Empire, 900–1200* (Cambridge, 1989), 124, and M. Kaplan, *Les hommes et la terre à Byzance* (Paris, 1992), 48 n. 210 and 275; for λισγάριον Bryer, "Implements," 1070–73. See also Souda Σ542· Σκαφείδιον· τὸ λισγάριον.

14 ἀπὸ τόρνου: The Anon. Byz. adds. The term does not appear in Apollod. or Ath. Mech. (see, however, τετορνευμένοι at Ath. Mech. 23:7). See below on **44:25.**

16 κεφαλοειδῆ παρεξοχήν: For Apollod.'s ἄλλον οὐραχόν. The noun παρεξοχή and the verb παρεξέχειν each occur five times in the *Parangelmata. LSJRS,* s.v., gives on the former "wd. of uncertain meaning." Both appear to be used generically to refer to projecting parts of various structures (see, e.g., **31:6**), and I have so translated.

17 ἐπικεφαλίδα: The Anon. Byz. adds. For the term see Demetrakos, *Lexikon,* s.v., and *LSJRS,* s.v. "perh. *bearing* or *axle-box.*"

21 κανόνια: The rods are depicted on folio 14v.

22 ὡς φρεατίας . . . διεκβληθέντα: The Anon. Byz. adds the simile. Lacoste, "Poliorcétiques," 244 n. 1, comments: "Cette disposition était identique à celle de nos cabestans, ou de nos treuils de haquet." On ἠλακάτη see *Scholia in Thucydidem* 7:25, ὄνευον ("they drew up with windlasses"): μηχανὴ ἐπ' ἄκρων τῶν ἀκατίων πηγνυμένη, ἀφ' ἧς περιβάλλοντες βρόχοις τοὺς σταυροὺς ῥᾳδίως ἐκ τοῦ βυθοῦ ἀνέσπων· ἔστι γὰρ ἡ μηχανὴ ἐπὶ τοσοῦτον βιαιοτάτη, ὥστε καὶ σαγήνην βαρεῖαν ὑπὸ δύο ἀνδρῶν ἀπόνως ἕλκεσθαι. καλοῦσι δὲ τὴν μηχανὴν οἱ τοὺς χαμαιλίχοντας ἕλκοντες ἁλιεῖς ἠλακάτην. ἐρρωμενέστερον δὲ πρὸς τὴν ἀνέλκυσιν καθίσταται, ὅταν καὶ δίκρουν ξύλον πρὸ αὐτῆς τεθείη· ἐπ' εὐθείας γὰρ ἡ ἀντίσπασις τῶν ἀνελκομένων γίνεται. On the windlass with handspikes see Drachmann, *Technology,* 50ff (translating and commenting on the description of Heron, *Mechanics* II:1); Landels, *Engineering,* 10 and 85; and D. Hill, *History of Engineering in Classical and Medieval Times* (La Salle, Ill., 1984), 128. On Byzantine wells and water drawing devices see Koukoules, *Bios,* V:271.

26 εὐκατάφορα: For Apollod.'s εὐόλισθος.

27 τὸ . . . πέταλον: For Apollod.'s ὁ γνώμων τοῦ τρυπάνου.

30–31 ἀνωφερὴς σύντρησις: For Apollod.'s κλίσις.

32 παρεγκεκλιμένην . . . καταφοράν: For Apollod.'s ὄλισθον.

33 κλίσεως· The term is from Apollod. Lammert, "Apollodoros," 311, argues, against Schneider's translation of Apollod. ("Das Bild zeigt, wie der Zusammenbruch aussieht"), "κλίσις ist vielmehr die vorher besprochene Schräge im Ansatze des Bohrers und dadurch der gebohrten Löcher." The illustration on folio 14v shows the borer at an upward angle, but no break or collapse of the wall.

Chapter 18. Positioning of Bore Holes

The Anon. Byz. draws here on Apollod. 150:4–5, adding his own comments on measurement units.

2 πόδα καὶ τέταρτον: On the distance see Lendle, *Texte,* 147 n. 163.

4 σπιθαμὴ . . . τεσσάρων: The Anon. Byz. adds; see the Introduction, 23.

5 ἀπαρχομένους ποιεῖσθαι· Wescher added δεῖ to the text of the *Parangelmata* (including this case) in seven instances, Vincent to the *Geodesia* in two. In all these cases the δεῖ is also lacking in the archetype. An anonymous reader reasonably suggests that the frequent omission is unlikely to be due to scribal error. I have allowed the text of the archetype to stand in six of these cases as ellipsis of δεῖ. On the usage see R. Funk, *A Greek Grammar of the New Testament and Other Early Christian Literature* (Chicago, 1961), 196–97.

Chapter 19. Filling the Bore Holes with Rounded Stakes That Are Set Alight.

The Anon. Byz. draws here on Apollod. 150:6–152:4

2 ἀναγεμίζονται: For Apollod.'s πληρούσθω.

2 ἐκ τῆς ἔξωθεν ... ἔνδον: The Anon. Byz. adds.

3–4 ξύλοις ξηροῖς ἐσχισμένοις: For Apollod.'s σχίδαξι. See above, **14**:16. Cf. Anna Comnena, *Alexiad* IV:4:6: νάφθαν καὶ πίσσαν καὶ ξηρῶν ξύλων σχίδακας.

4 κατὰ πλάτος: For Apollod.'s τὰς πλατύτητας.

5 πασσάλοις: The Anon. Byz. omits Apollod.'s σφηνῶν τρόπον εἰσαγομένοις.

6 πρὸς τὴν βάσιν: The Anon. Byz. adds.

6–7 πρὸς ... ἐστενωμένοις: The Anon. Byz. adds, apparently explaining Apollod.'s σφηνῶν (see above on **19:5**). For this tapering of the stakes see also below, **19:23**.

7–8 κατὰ ... καιρόν: The Anon. Byz. adds.

9–10 ξύλα ... ἐπαλιφέντα: For Apollod.'s ⟨ξύλα⟩ ξηρὰ ἢ τεθειωμένα ἢ πεπισσωμένα.

11 διαλείμματα: For Apollod.'s διάστημα. The term occurs frequently in the *Sylloge tacticorum* for the intervals between infantry units in formation. See also below on **25:8–9**.

12–13 ἔνθα ... σβεννύηται: The Anon. Byz. adds.

15–16 κατὰ μέσον ... διάχωρα: For Apollod.'s τὰ μεταξὺ αὐτῶν χωρία.

16 κατὰ τάξιν ... πρότερα: The Anon. Byz. adds.

18 ἵνα ... σύντρησις: On the nature of the joint channeling see Lendle, *Texte,* 147 n. 163: "Dank der Richtungsänderung der zweiten Bohrserie trafen nun jeweils zwei Bohrlöcher (wohl in etwa 2–3 Fuss Mauertiefe) V-förmig aufeinander und bildeten für die spätere Entzündung des Füllmaterials eine Einheit."

18 πρότερα ... ὑστέρων: The Anon. Byz. adds.

19–20 πελεκημάτων ἢ ῥυκανισμάτων: The Anon. Byz. adds. On the πέλεκυς see Bryer, "Implements," 73–74, "double-bladed hatchet"; on the latter term, which is not in the *TLG,* see Demetrakos, *Lexikon,* s.v., and cf. Biton, 54:2: οὐ γὰρ χρεία ἐπὶ τῶν τοιούτων ἔργων ῥυκανήσεως ἢ λεπτουργίας and *Anthologia graeca* VI.204–6: καὶ πέλεκυν ῥυκάναν τ' εὐαυγέα.

21 ἐπιδρασσόμενον ... ποιεῖται: For Apollod.'s ἐπιβάλλεται.

23 κατὰ τὸ ὅλον ὕψος: The Anon. Byz. adds.

23 μείζονές εἰσι κάτωθεν: For Apollod.'s ἔχουσι ... προβολήν.

24 ἀνέμου ἐμπνέοντος: For Apollod.'s ὑπὸ ἀνέμου.

24 ἐπανάπτεσθαι: For Apollod.'s ἐρεθίζεσθαι.

24–25 Εἰ δὲ νηνεμία ... εἴη: For Apollod.'s εἰ δὲ μή.

27 ἰξευταί: The comparison here, and below (39:26–27) of hollowed reeds used to convey water to put out a fire, is drawn from Apollod. (152:2, 174:6). The comparison extends only to the hollow reeds. On the use of such extendible lime-rods in bird-catching see J. K. Anderson, *Hunting in the Ancient World* (Berkeley, Calif., 1985), 146–47, with mosaic illustrations from the Piazza Armerina, and K. Lindner, *Beiträge zu Vogelfang und Falknerei im Altertum* (Berlin, 1973), esp. 95, on Apollod. On Byzantine uses of ἰξόβεργαι see Koukoules, *Bios,* V:399.

27 χαλκικοῖς: The Anon. Byz. adds. The device is illustrated on folio 15v. For illustrations of the bellows with blowpipe in the text of Apollod. see Schneider, *Apollodoros,* pl. 3. A similar bellows with blowpipe is illus-

trated on folio 13r; see also on **16**:18.

29 αὐλίσκον: For Apollod.'s σύριγγα.

Chapter 20. Use of Rams against Already Weakened Walls

The Anon. Byz. apparently draws here in part on phrases in Apollod. 157:7–9 and 158:1 (on the differences between brick and stone), but the notion of using rams against already weakened brick walls is not in the extant classical sources. On the difficulty of using rams against brick see Winter, *Fortifications,* 71–72.

3 τῷ συμπάχῳ: On the term, found also below at **27**:1 and **36**:6, cf. George the Monk, *Chronicon,* ed. C. de Boor, 2 vols. (Leipzig, 1904; repr. Stuttgart, 1978, with corrections by P. Wirth), 189:18: λίθους ἀκροτόμους καὶ ἀπελεκήτους ἤτοι ἀδαμαντίους καὶ παμμεγέθεις λίαν εἰς τὰ θεμέλια θέμενος ἔχοντα πήχεις ι΄ τὸ σύμπαχον, and see Demetrakos, *Lexikon,* s.v: ὁ παχύς, πυκνὸς τὴν σύστασιν, συμπαγής, ὅθεν τὸ οὐδέτερον ὡς οὐσιαστικὸ τὸ σύμπαχον — ἡ συμπαγὴς σύστασις.

4 τεχνουργήματι: On the term cf. Theo. Sim., II:16:11: διδάξας τοὺς βαρβάρους πρὸς πολιορκίαν τεχνούργημα, Leo diac., 25:13–14: κριὸν Ῥωμαῖοι τὸ τεχνούργημα ὀνομάζουσι, and Souda, Delta 1195:1: Διόπτρα· μηχανικὸν τεχνούργημα.

6 λακκίζουσα: See on **11**:7.

10 κερατίσεις: The term is attested in Achmetis, *Oneirocriticon,* ed. F. Drexl (Leipzig, 1925), 214:10: ἀναλόγως τῆς κερατίσεως.

Chapter 21. Second Table of Contents

This brief transition passage is basically the Anon. Byz.'s own, but perhaps with reference to Apollod. 159:3 (συμβολαί) and 161:7 (μονοξύλους). For composite rams see Apollod. 159:2–161:8. Schneider (33 note) makes the plausible suggestion that a portion of the text may be lost here.

3 ἀρτήσεις: The term is not found in the Anon. Byz.'s classical sources; Apollod. does regularly use ἄρτημα, which the Anon. Byz. changes to βάσταγμα. See below on **25**:9.

5 διαβάθρας: See above on **2**:11.

Chapter 22. Ram Tortoise of Apollodorus

The Anon. Byz. draws here on Apollod. 153:8–156:2. For detailed discussion of the device see Lendle, *Schildkröten*, 103–21; for discrepancies in the text of Apollod. caused by likely interpolations, see Blyth, "Apollodorus," 135 and nn. 21–23. The device is illustrated on folio 18r.

1 πόρτας: The Latin term replacing Apollod.'s πύργον ἢ πύλην. Cf. Leo, *Taktika* XV:4: παρὰ τὰς πόρτας, ἢ εἰς τὰ παραπόρτια τῆς πόλεως; and Nikephoros Phokas, *Praecepta militaria* VI:1: κρατηθῆναι δὲ καὶ τὰς πόρτας τοῦ μὴ ἐξέρχεσθαί τινα.

2 ῥηγνύειν καὶ διασπᾶν: For Apollod.'s σεῖσαι.

3–4 ἄνωθεν ... ἀνέχοντα: For Apollod.'s αἳ τὸ ἄρτημα τοῦ κριοῦ φέρουσιν.

4–5 ἀφ' ὑψηλοῦ ... βασταζόμενος: For Apollod.'s ὑψηλοῦ ... ὄντος τοῦ ἀρτήματος; cf. below on **25**:8–9.

6 πρὸς τὴν κίνησιν: The Anon. Byz. adds.

7 ἐνδυναμοῦται καὶ προσκρούων τῷ τείχει: The Anon. Byz. adds.

8 καὶ ἰσχυράν: The Anon. Byz. adds.

10 εὐπαράγωγος: For Apollod.'s εὐάγωγος.

10–11 τὸ δὲ μῆκος ... ἔλασσον: The Anon. Byz. adds. See Lendle, *Schildkröten*, 110: "Der Anonymus Byzantinus schlägt an der eben zitierten Stelle 24 Fuss (= 7,09 m), kurz davor (225:17) gleiche oder ein wenig kürzere Länge als Höhe ... vor, was der Sache nach wohl zutreffend sein dürfte."

11–12 ἵνα ... εἴη: For Apollod.'s ἵνα ὀξεῖαν τὴν ῥάχιν ἔχῃ, καὶ τὰς πλατύτητας παρορθίους.

11 ὀξύρρυτος: Cf. δίρρυτος at **13**:5.

13 παρεκτρέχῃ: For Apollod.'s παρολισθαίνῃ.

13 Ζυγά: For discussion of the use of the term in Apollod., see Lendle, *Schildkröten*, 108.

13–14 καὶ δύο: The Anon. Byz. adds here and interprets as pairs of beams Apollod.'s ζυγὰ δύο, an interpretation visible in the illustration on folio 18r; both Schneider and Sackur, *Vitruv,* also interpreted Apollod.'s phrase as "Balkenpaare," but for doubts see Lendle, *Schildkröten,* 107–10.

18–19 ὀκτώ . . . ἐφιστάμενα: The Anon. Byz. here interprets Apollod.'s κατὰ τὸν ἀριθμὸν δ΄.

19 συννεύοντα: The Anon. Byz. adds.

22 παρεξέχον . . . αἰτίας: The Anon. Byz. adds.

22–23 καθ᾽ ὃ . . . προσνεύειν: Lendle, *Schildkröten,* 108 n. 121 with illustration and 120, argues that the clause is better taken with what precedes, since the μέσα ζυγά mentioned in what follows here are apparently attached to all the uprights, not just those at the front of the tortoise where the roof is extended.

23 προσνεύειν: An extension of the roof (προστέγασμα) gives added protection to the front end of the ram as it strikes the wall. For reproductions of illustrations of this extension in the manuscripts of Apollod. see Lendle, *Schildkröten,* 104–5. The extension and projecting ridge-pole are visible on folio 18r.

24 ὀρθοστάτας: That is, the eight beams (ξύλα . . . συννεύοντα) that encompass the ridge-pole. Below (**22**:49) they are referred to as παρορθίων.

24 τούτοις: That is, the ὀρθοστάται.

25 παραστάται: The term is from Apollod.; see Lacoste, "Poliorcétiques," 240 n. 1, who comments that amid a variety of uses there is a core sense of "des pièces de renfort, placées contre d'autres pièces."

25–26 ἀντέχοντες καὶ στηρίζοντες: For Apollod.'s ἐρείδοντες.

26 τὰ μέσα ζυγά: See commentary on **22**:22–23.

28–30 Ἀπὸ . . . οὖσι: For discussion of this difficult sentence, particularly the reading τὰ ἔσω, see Lendle, *Schildkröten,* 111–13 (and illustration, 121). See also the suggestion of Lacoste, "Poliorcétiques," 250 n. 1: "Il y a une erreur évidente dans les mss. où on lit: τῶν ἔσω ζυγῶν, au lieu de τῶν κάτω ζυγῶν: il s'agit ici de fourrures destinées à protéger les côtes de la machine, dans la partie correspondante à la hauteur des roues."

30 ἀκλινέσι: The Anon. Byz. adds.

31 τουτέστι τὸ διάστημα: The Anon. Byz. adds.

32 ἀντέχοντας καί: The Anon. Byz. adds.

32–33 τὸ ὅλον ... σύμπηγμα: The Anon. Byz. adds.

33–34 περιτομίδας ... χελωνίων: On the method of securing the beams, which is taken from Apollod., see Lendle, *Schildkröten,* 111–21, *Texte,* 79; and Sackur, *Vitruv,* 36–38.

33 περιτομίδας: The term is from Apollod.; for its likely meaning see Lendle, *Texte,* 79: "Unter περιτομίδες sind offenbar winkelig geschnittene Streben zu verstehen." It is to be distinguished from the περιστομίς at **44**:31.

34 οὐκ ἔξω τομῆς γινομένης: The phrase is from Apollod.; see Lendle, *Schildkröten,* 111, who translates "wobei kein Schnittende (dieser 'Schnittbalken') ausserhalb (der Verbretterung der Maschine) gerät," with discussion at 114–16.

34 χελωνίων: The term is from Apollod. Lendle, *Schildkröten,* 115, renders "Knaggen"; see below on **22**:35–37.

35–37 ὡσανεὶ ... τιθεμένοις: The Anon. Byz. adds. The same simile for the χελώνια occurs again below at **31**:16–19 and **44**:11–14 (as χελωνάρια). Lendle, *Schildkröten,* 112 n. 126, following Sackur, *Vitruv,* 27 n. 1, comments "Dass Eisenbeschläge nach der Art von Türpfannen (die wegen ihren gewölbten Formen zu Recht χελώνια gennant werden konnten) hier nicht gemeint sind." The Anon. Byz.'s interpretation seems to require a translation in the sense of "caps." On pivot sockets lined with bronze inserts in Hellenistic gates see Winter, *Fortifications,* 258.

35 γρονθαρίων: The term appears as a gloss for χελώνια in manuscripts of Apollod.; see Wescher, 178 n. 4. Sophocles, *Lexicon,* citing this use, s.v., gives: "Latin *subgrunda* = γεῖσον"; see also LSJ, s.v. Perhaps the term is used for the portion of a cornice hollowed out to receive a door pivot. Trapp, *Lexikon,* s.v., gives "(kleine) Faust."

38 ὀξυρρύτου: The Anon. Byz. adds.

38–50 Γίνεται . . . τείχους: This section on a lower tortoise with rafters is not found in Apollod. and is apparently the Anon. Byz.'s own addition, influenced in part by Ath. Mech.'s description of Hegetor's ram tortoise, 22:6–9: Ἐπὶ δὲ τῶν ἐπιστυλίων πήγνυνται συγκύπται . . . καὶ ἐπ' αὐτῶν δοκὸς ἐμπήγνυται πλαγία εἰς ἣν πᾶσαι αἱ κορυφαὶ τῶν συγκυπτῶν πήγνυνται, καὶ γίνονται δύο πλευραὶ κεκλιμέναι.

41 συγκύπται: The term occurs in Ath. Mech.'s description of the χωστρὶς χελώνη (18:10), where it is equated with συστάται, and in his description of the ram-tortoise of Hegetor. For discussion of its function and form see Lendle, *Schildkröten*, 27 (who translates as "Dachsparren"); Rochas D'Aiglun, "Athénée," 790, renders with "chevrons."

41 ἀετώματος: ἀετός is found at Ath. Mech. 13:5 and ἀέτωσις at Ath. Mech. 13:3–4. For this form see Souda, Alpha 576:1–2: Ἀετὸς τῶν οἰκοδομημάτων τὸ κατὰ τὸν ὄροφον, ὅ τινες ἀέτωμα καλοῦσιν.

48–49 τῶν προειρημένων παρορθίων μονοξύλων: A reference to the sloping beams of the tortoise which are referred to above as ξύλα . . . συννεύοντα.

50–56 ἵνα . . . διαφθερεῖ: The Anon. Byz. here paraphrases Apollod. 154:6–11.

52–53 μέγιστοι λίθοι: See above on 2:8–9.

53 ἰσοβαρῶς καὶ ἰσοζύγως: The Anon. Byz. adds. For beams on chains dropped on rams cf. Thucydides, II:76 (siege of Plataea): καὶ δοκοὺς μεγάλας ἀρτήσαντες ἁλύσεσι μακραῖς σιδηραῖς ἀπὸ τῆς τομῆς ἑκατέρωθεν ἀπὸ κεραιῶν δύο ἐπικεκλιμένων καὶ ὑπερτεινουσῶν ὑπὲρ τοῦ τείχους ἀνελκύσαντες ἐγκαρσίας, ὁπότε προσπεσεῖσθαί πῃ μέλλοι ἡ μηχανή, ἀφίεσαν τὴν δοκὸν χαλαραῖς ταῖς ἁλύσεσι καὶ οὐ διὰ χειρὸς ἔχοντες, ἡ δὲ ῥύμη ἐμπίπτουσα ἀπεκαύλιζε τὸ προῦχον τῆς ἐμβολῆς.

54 ἀστέγαστον: The Anon. Byz. adds.

57–58 ἡ ἔμπροσθεν χελώνη . . . ἔχουσα: For Apollod.'s ἡ μὲν τὸν ἱστὸν φέρουσα τοιαύτη.

57 βασταγάς: Given Apollod.'s ἡ μὲν τὸν ἱστὸν φέρουσα τοιαύτη, presumably βασταγή refers to what is carried (see Hesychius, 309:1: βασταγή: βάρος, and Trapp, *Lexikon,* s.v., *Gepäck),* while βάσταγμα below at **25**:9 and **40**:13 refers to the suspension system. Barocius, however, renders both terms with *sustentacula* and Schneider with *Gehänge.*

58 ἡ . . . δευτέρα: The second tortoise is illustrated on folio 18r, the others are not. For discussion of Apollod.'s addition of them as a critique of Hellenistic practices, see Lendle, *Schildkröten,* 106–7.

61 ὡς προείπομεν: Said above (**13**:35–38) of the excavating tortoises.

61–62 διὰ τὸ εὐκόπως προσάγεσθαι: For Apollod.'s διὰ τὸ εὐάγωγον καὶ εὐσύνθετον.

63–64 διὰ . . . παράγεσθαι: For Apollod.'s διὰ τὰ ἐναντία τούτοις ἐλαττώματα. The Anon. Byz.'s δυσευρέτων (see also below [**32**:1] δυσεύρετοί εἰσι), a term not found in Apollod. or Ath. Mech., may suggest a somewhat greater concern with the availability of wood than his sources, although Apollod. (139:5) does recommend building machines εὐπόριστα τῇ ὕλῃ (see above, **2**:15–19).

64–65 Τὰ . . . ὑπόκειται: For Apollod.'s Τὰ δὲ σχήματα καὶ τὰ ὄρθια καὶ τὰ κάτω γεγραμμένα παράκειται. On Apollod.'s terminology see below, **27**:92.

Chapter 23. Ramming the Upper Parts of the Wall

The suggestion is added here by the Anon. Byz. The concept of attacking the upper parts of the walls may be derived from Apollod. 185:13–16 (a passage repeated by the Anon. Byz. at **40**:12–16), where rams on ladders are said to have a shorter front hanger to provide them an upward angle, thus giving access to the upper and hence less unified parts of the wall.

Chapter 24. Wheels for the Ram Tortoise

The Anon. Byz. draws here on Apollod. 156:3–158:1.

3 προείρηται: Cf. **15**:1–3, above.

4–5 πηλοῦ . . . μεμαλαγμένου: See above on **15**:5.

5 καὶ ἀδιασχίστου συντηρουμένου: For Apollod.'s ἵνα τηρήσωσιν ἀρραγάδωτον.

8 ὥστε ... μέγεθος: For Apollod.'s οἳ βαστάζουσιν αὐτὴν εὔεδρον.

9–10 καὶ ... οὖσαι: The Anon. Byz. adds.

11–12 ἀσφαλῶς ... ἱσταμένην: For Apollod.'s εὐόλισθον.

13–15 Ὑποβάλλονται ... παρακίνησιν: The Anon. Byz. adds.

18 τὸ χαῦνον: The Anon. Byz. adds.

20 λακκίζουσα: See above, **11:7.**

22 < ... >: Wescher (229:20) suggests that the lacuna contained, in part, material from Apollod. 158:2–161:8 on δέσεις κριῶν. See also Dain, *Tradition,* 30.

Chapter 25. Ram of Hegetor

The Anon. Byz. here draws on Ath. Mech. 21:1–26:5, but with significant changes of order, compressions and omissions; Hegetor's ram is also described by Vitruvius, X:15:2–7. Schneider, *Athenaios,* 61 n. 21:3, comments on the Anon. Byz.'s version: "Was ihm unverständlich war, hat er sich nach seiner Weise zurechtgelegt, oder auch weggelassen." The Anon. Byz. perhaps also wishes to include briefly the largest known ram from antiquity and mentions its length first in his description. For discussion of the two earlier texts with references to the Anon. Byz., see Lendle, *Schildkröten,* 48–86, Callebat and Fleury, *Vitruve,* 263ff, and Fleury, *Mécanique,* 311–16. The device is illustrated on folio 20r; the drawing from Paris. suppl. gr. 607 illustrating the text of Ath. Mech., as well as various modern drawings, are reproduced in Lendle, *Schildkröten,* 49–52.

1 ⟨Ο⟩ἱ ... περί: Ath. Mech. has: Τῆς δὲ ὑπὸ Ἡγήτορος τοῦ Βυζαντίου ηὑρημένης χελώνης. The Anon. Byz.'s expression may simply be a periphrasis for Hegetor; on the usage as denoting either the school associated with the figure named or merely a circumlocution for the figure himself, see W. R. Knorr, *Textual Studies in Ancient and Medieval Geometry* (Boston, 1989), 25 n. 3, and R. Kühner and B. Gerth, *Ausführliche Grammatik der griechischen Sprache,* 3rd ed. (1898; repr. Hannover, 1966),

II:1, p. 269–71. See also below, **32:2, 36:2, 38:**21 and **48:**1.

1 Ἡγήτορα: Known only from the related references in Ath. Mech. (21:2), Vitruvius (X:15:2), and here; he may have been associated with Demetrius Poliorceticus. See *RE* VI:104 (Hegetor, 2) and Callebat and Fleury, *Vitruve,* 263 n. 15.2.1.

2 πηχῶν ἑκατὸν εἴκοσι κατὰ μῆκος: This length is that given by Ath. Mech., while Vitruvius has 104 feet. For doubts about the possibility of a ram beam of 120 *pecheis* see Lendle, *Schildkröten,* 61–62, who suggests a corruption in the text of Ath. Mech. from 70 to 120 cubits; Fleury, *Mécanique,* 318–20, Meiggs, *Trees,* 168–69; and Callebat and Fleury, *Vitruve,* 263.

2 πτέρνης: On the term as "butt-end" see Landels, *Engineering,* 96 and 117, and Marsden, *Treatises,* 166 and 173.

3–5 εἰς δὲ πλάτος … τριπάλαιστον: Ath. Mech. (23:11–24:2) has ἐκ δὲ πτέρνης πάχος μὲν ποδῶν β′, πλάτος δὲ ε′ παλαιστῶν· εἰς ἄκρον δὲ συνῆκται αὐτοῦ τὸ μὲν πάχος ποδιαῖον, τὸ δὲ πλάτος τριπαλαιστιαῖον. The Anon. Byz.'s dimensions are approximately the same as those given by Vitruvius; see Fleury, *Mécanique,* 319 n. 3.

5 ἕλικας: For an illustration of these protective iron bands ("eiserne Windungen"), see Lendle, *Schildkröten,* 63, who describes their function: "um das an der Spitze besonders gefährdete Holz vor Beschädigungen … zu schützen."

7 τρισί: On the number see Lendle, *Schildkröten,* 63 n. 78.

7 σχοινίοις: For Ath. Mech.'s ὅπλοις. Vitruvius (X:15:6) makes clear that the ropes are placed along the entire length of the ram and bound by smaller wrappings; for discussion and illustration see Lendle, *Schildkröten,* 63–64.

7 κατὰ πάχος γυρόθεν: That is, "circumference," the phrase added by the Anon. Byz.; see Schneider, *ad loc.,* and Lendle, *Schildkröten,* 64 n. 79.

8–9 ἀνελάμβανον … βασταγμάτων δὲ τεσσάρων: For Ath. Mech.'s καὶ διαλαμβάνεται κατὰ μέσον ἐκ τριῶν διαλημμάτων ἁλύσεσι παχείαις. Διαλημμάτων (LSJ, *"windings* of a chain") is the reading of Paris. suppl. gr. 607; other manuscripts of Ath. Mech. have διαλειμμάτων, and presumably the Anon. Byz. had the latter reading. Rochas D'Aiglun, "Athénée," 792 n. 1, translates the text of the Anon. Byz.: "il le suspendait par le milieu par quatre points de suspension, qui laissaient entre eux trois intervalles." See also on the passage Lendle, *Schildkröten,* 64. On διάλειμμα see above on **19**:11.

9 **βασταγμάτων**: The term βάσταγμα is not used by Ath. Mech. or Apollod. (the latter uses ἄρτημα). See Trapp, *Lexikon,* s.v., and above on **22**:57 (βασταγή).

10 **ὀνίσκων . . . κριοδοχῆς**: The mechanism is described in somewhat more detail by Ath. Mech.; for a reconstruction of its operation see Lendle, *Schildkröten,* 58–60. The illustration on folio 20r shows two methods of holding the ropes, cylindrical rods at the rear, pulley wheels at the front. The illustrations in Paris. suppl. gr. 607, folio 23, and Vindob. phil. gr. 120, folio 32v, show only pulley wheels.

12 **ἐπιβάθραν**: The term and the description are from Ath. Mech. and here refer to a net suspended vertically on a board at the front of the ram to allow troops to climb to the breach in the wall created by the ram, as illustrated on folio 20r. Lendle, *Schildkröten,* 66, and Schneider translate "Stiege," De Rochas "échelle." The word is used elsewhere by the Anon. Byz. in the more usual sense of a drop-bridge or *pont-volant:* see on **2**:11.

17 **σχαρίου**: The term is from Ath. Mech.; for discussion see Lendle, *Schildkröten,* 51: "das gesamte Grundgestell der Maschine"; Callebat and Fleury, *Vitruve,* 254 n. 14:1:2; and Marsden, *Treatises,* 84. Dain, *Tradition,* 20 n. 1, comments that the use of σχάριον for ἐσχάριον consistently in Vat. gr. 1605 is one of the indications that the Anon. Byz. was using a manuscript tradition of the poliorcetic corpus followed also by Vindobonensis phil. gr. 120, rather than that of Paris. suppl. gr. 607.

23 **οἱονεὶ περίφραγμα**: The Anon. Byz. has added the simile.

25–26 **ἑξαχῶς ἐκίνουν**: Ath. Mech. (26:1–2) explains: Κινήσεις δὲ τὸ ἔργον λαμβάνει ἕξ· τὴν εἰς τὸ ἔμπροσθεν καὶ τὴν εἰς τὸ ὀπίσω, καὶ τὰς εἰς τὰ πλάγια, καὶ τὴν ἀνάνευσιν καὶ τὴν ἐπίνευσιν; for discussion see Lendle, *Schildkröten,* 67–68. See also D'Ooge, *Nicomachus,* 238 n. 4, on the six categories in Neo-Pythagorean arguments and below, **54**:5–6.

28 ἐκινεῖτο: For Ath. Mech.'s οἰακίζεται. See below, **26:2**.

28 προσφερόμενος: The Anon. Byz. adds, perhaps to explain the need for a hundred men, a number that seems excessive for operating the ram once in place, but that would be needed to move it into position. See Lendle, *Schildkröten,* 69 n. 86.

29 ταλάντων . . . τετρακισχιλίων: For doubts about the weight see Lendle, *Schildkröten,* 69 n. 87.

Chapter 26. Historical Methods of Moving Rams

A summary passage on battering rams with items drawn mainly from Ath. Mech. (particularly from his history of the origin of the battering ram, which he in turn drew from Agesistratus), as noted below.

1 ὑπὸ πλήθους ἀνδρῶν: Cf. Ath. Mech. 9:15–10:2: Γῆρας . . . ὁ Καρχηδόνιος . . . τὸν κριὸν . . . οὐκ ἐκ ἀντισπάστων εἷλκεν, ἀλλ᾽ ὑπὸ πλήθους ἀνδρῶν προωθούμενον ἐποίησε. On Geras of Carthage, known only from the references in Ath. Mech. and Vitruvius, see Callebat and Fleury, *Vitruve,* 241 n. 2.4, and W. Kroll, *RE,* suppl. VI:73.

2 οἰακίζονται: The verb is found at Ath. Mech. 26:4; the Anon. Byz. substituted ἐκινεῖτο for it above at **25:28**.

3 ἀντισπάστων: The term is from Ath. Mech., for example, 13:10–14:1: Ἴστα δὲ καὶ κριοδόχην ἐν αὐτῇ, ἐφ᾽ ἧς καὶ τὸν κύλινδρον ἐπετίθει (i.e., Diades), δι᾽ οὗ προωθούμενος ὁ κριὸς δι᾽ ἀντισπάστων ἐνήργει τὴν χρείαν.

3 κυλίνδρων: Cf. Ath. Mech. 10:4–5: Μετὰ ταῦτα (i.e., the invention of Geras of Carthage) δὲ ἐποίησάν τινες ἐπὶ κυλίνδρων προωθούμενον τὸν κριὸν καὶ οὕτως ἐχρῶντο.

6 τεχνίτῃ: The Anon. Byz. adds; see above on **1:9**.

Chapter 27. Scout-Ladder of Apollodorus

The Anon. Byz. here follows and greatly elaborates on Apollod. 161:9–164:4. For discussion of the device with illustrations see Lendle, *Texte,* 28–35; on its impracticality as well as the Anon. Byz.'s failure to understand the design in Apollod.'s text see Blyth, "Apollodorus," 140–41 and

n. 31. It is illustrated in the manuscript on folio 22v and the base alone on 23r. The version of Apollod. is illustrated in Paris. suppl. gr. 607, folio 36 (reproduced by Schneider, *Apollodoros,* pl. 6, fig. 23, and Wescher, 163, fig. 65).

6 **τετράγωνα**: "Squared," that is, with four faces at right angles.

6 **ἑτεροπλατῆ**: With faces of unequal width. See Lacoste, "Poliorcétiques," 256 n. 1.

6–7 **πλάτος . . . ὀκτώ**: The Anon. Byz. adds the dimensions; see Lendle, *Texte,* 29.

12–14 **ἀπεναντίον . . . ὀρθοῖς**: For Apollod.'s μεταξὺ δὲ αὐτῶν ἄλλο ἐντίθεται ξύλον ἐπὶ τοῦ ἐδάφους πρὸς ὀρθὰς τῷ πρώτῳ κειμένῳ.

15–16 **ἦτα λιτὸν . . . διπλόγραμμον**: The simile is added by the Anon. Byz. and see below, **28**:4. On the use of λιτός for "uncial" see Atsalos, *Terminologie,* 217ff. For its implications for the Anon. Byz.'s date see the Introduction, 4.

17–18 **ἀντιβαίνοντα . . . ἐπιστηρίζοντα**: A periphrasis for Apollod.'s ἀντήρειδες ("stanchions").

21 **τὰ τέσσαρα**: That is, the two uprights and the two swing-beams.

30–31 **Ταῦτα . . . κατερχόμενα**: A periphrasis for Apollod.'s κηλώνια ("swing-beams," "swipes"). The Anon. Byz. also uses ἐμβαλλόμενα and ἐγκλινόμενα for these beams; as his aim is to avoid technical terms, it seems best to translate literally, although the term "swing-beams" or "swipes" would simplify the translation.

34–41 **Ἀπὸ . . . μετάρσιον**: The Anon. Byz. here interprets the brief comment in Apollod. on the handle (162:10–11: κατὰ δὲ τὸ ἄλλο ἕλκυστρον ξύλον ποδῶν μὴ πλεῖον ἡ΄ τὸ μῆκος). For discussion see Lendle, *Texte,* 31, who sees the Anon. Byz.'s view as essentially correct.

35–36 **τὸ ἀναχθὲν ἔκτον μέρος**: That is, when the swing-beams are lowered, the bottom sixth is raised.

44–45 **διὰ . . . περόναις**: The Anon. Byz.'s interpretation of Apollod.'s διὰ τὸ διπλοῖς κηλωνίοις ἐπεζεῦχθαι: see Lendle, *Texte,* 32.

45–49 Δεῖ . . . ἀτρεμεῖν: The Anon. Byz. adds. The meaning of στροφωμάτιον is difficult. The primary meaning is "hinges," but perhaps here = στρόφιγξ, "pivot pins," "axles" (so LSJ at στρόφωμα II). Barocius renders "verticulis" and Schneider "Zapfen."

53 δισσῶς: On the Anon. Byz.'s interpretation of how the ladder is secured to the swing beams, see Lendle, *Texte*, 32.

57ff Ἔστω . . . : The Anon. Byz.'s dimensions for the device differ from and are considerably more elaborate than those of Apollod., so as to produce a ladder higher by 5 feet. For doubts about its practicality see Lendle, *Texte*, 33–34.

77–80 ἐκ βύρσης . . . πλάγια: For Apollod.'s θυρεοῦ τρόπον. The illustration shows two different forms of shield, both long, one semicircular at the top, straight on the bottom, the other pointed at both ends. While here a special-purpose device, more generally on the Byzantine long shield see Kolias, *Waffen*, 91.

81–86 Οὐ μικρὰν . . . κατάσκοπον: The Anon. Byz. adds. The concept of protecting the legs of the ladder with ropes is not found in Apollod. and may be a Byzantine innovation.

86–87 Εἰς . . . συμβάλλονται: The Anon. Byz. adds.

89 ἀπεκτεταμένα . . . ἀλλήλων: The Anon. Byz. adds.

92 τό τε κείμενον καὶ τὸ ὠρθωμένον: The terms are from Apollod. (163:3 and cf. 156:1–2 and 193:2), whose original work contained technical drawings no longer faithfully represented in any of the extant manuscripts of his text. On their nature in the original, "Grundriss . . . Aufriss," "ground plan . . . elevation," see Sackur, *Vitruv*, 19–21; Lendle, *Texte*, 34, 182; idem, *Schildkröten*, 109; and Blyth, "Apollodorus," 133 and n. 16 and 144 and n. 39. The illustrations in Vat. gr. 1605 (folio 22v) show the scout-ladder in two positions, one fully raised, the other partially so, with the swing-beams parallel to the ground. This suggests that the Anon. Byz. and/or the artist did not understand or does not use the terms technically; the translation attempts to retain this latter interpretation. The illustration of Apollod.'s σκοπός in Paris. suppl. gr. 607, folio 36 (reproduced by Schneider, *Apollodoros*, pl. 6, and Wescher, 163, fig.

65), is also not a ground plan or elevation. See also below, **57:**1.

Chapters 28–29. Additional Bases for the Scout-Ladder

The bases described here are not found in Apollod. and are apparently an addition of the Anon. Byz. The first with single planks on either side is depicted on folio 23r.

4 ἦτα λιτόν: See above, on **27:**15–16.

5 γλωσσίδος: For the term see Trapp, *Lexikon,* s.v.

29:12 τεχνίτης: On adaptation by the craftsman see above on **1:**9.

13 συμμετρίαν: See below on **38:**19.

14 τρεῖς διαστάσεις: Cf. below, **30:**17–18.

Chapter 30. Portable Siege Towers

The portable towers of Diades and Charias are described in chaps. 30, 32, and 36; they are also found in Ath. Mech. 10:10–12:10 and Vitruvius X:13:3ff. The Anon. Byz. has material not found in either of his predecessors. Sackur, *Vitruv,* 98ff, advanced the theory that he used a now lost source called by Sackur "Athenaeus Minor." However, Dain, *Tradition,* 19, reasonably suggests that: "les ajouts ne sont pas tels que notre auteur n'ait pu les donner de son propre cru." Lammert, "Apollodoros," 331, concludes that "der Anonymus Byzantinus kannte nur den Athenaeus Major." See also Lendle, *Texte,* 76 n. 103, who characterizes Sackur's theory as "unhaltbare." For discussion of the towers of Diades and Charias see Sackur, ibid., 106ff; Lendle, *Texte,* 71–77; Callebat and Fleury, *Vitruve,* 242ff; Garlan, *Recherches,* 226–28; and Fleury, *Mécanique,* 289–92.

The towers of Apollod. are described in chaps. 31, 33–34, 37, and 39, following the text of Apollod. (164:8–167:9 and 173:9–174:7), with the Anon. Byz. inserting his own mathematical comments in chaps. 35 and 38. For detailed discussion of Apollod.'s tower see Lendle, *Texte,* 77–101, and Sackur, *Vitruv,* 26–30. The tower of Apollod. is illustrated on folio 26r.

1 Διάδης . . . καὶ Χαρίας: On Alexander's engineers see *RE* V:305 (Diades, 2), III:2:2133 (Charias, 11), suppl. VI:26–27, and Schneider, *Athenaios,* 57 n. 10:10

1 Πολυείδου τοῦ Θετταλοῦ: On Philip of Macedon's engineer see Ziegler, *RE* XXI:2:1658–59 (Polyidos, 6); Callebat and Fleury, *Vitruve,* 242; Schneider, *Athenaios,* 57 n. 10:9; and Garlan, *Recherches,* 237.

3–4 πρῶτοι ... ἐξεῦρον: Ath. Mech. (10:10–12) has Διάδης ... φησιν ἐν τῷ μηχανικῷ αὐτοῦ συγγράμματι εὑρηκέναι τούς τε φορητοὺς πύργους καὶ τὸ λεγόμενον τρύπανον καὶ τὸν κόρακα καὶ τὴν ἐπιβάθραν. Vitruvius (X:13:3) has "Diades scriptis suis ostendit se invenisse." Garlan, *Recherches,* 227–28, notes that at best Diades could have devised new models of the drop-bridge and portable tower, which were known and used before he worked.

3 τρύπανα: For Diades' "borer," an iron-pointed beam on rollers, moved by a windlass, for piercing walls, see Schneider, *Athenaios,* 58 n. 14:4; Garlan, *Recherches,* 238 with illustration; Lendle, *Texte,* 132; Callebat and Fleury, *Vitruve,* 250 n. 13:7:1; and Fleury, *Mécanique,* 297–99. It is different from the τρύπανον of Apollod., a handheld drill, on which see above, **17:2.**

3 διαβάθρας: For Ath. Mech.'s ἐπίβάθραν; the Anon. Byz. uses the two terms interchangeably. See above on **2:11.**

4 φερομένους διὰ τροχῶν ξυλίνους πύργους: Ath. Mech. has φορητοὺς πύργους. On the device and terminology see above on **2:6.**

5–7 τὴν δὲ βάσιν ἐτετραγώνιζον ... τιθέντες: Ath. Mech. has πύργον ... δεῖ γενέσθαι ... τὸ δὲ πλάτος ἔχοντα πήχεις ιζ'.

8 ἰσοτετράγωνον: On the term see Sophocles, *Lexicon,* s.v.

9–10 πέμπτου μέρους ... ἐμβαδοῦ: On the "contraction" Ath. Mech. (11:5–6) has συναγωγὴν δὲ τοῦ πλάτους εἰς τὸ ἄνω τὸ πέμπτον μέρος, Vitruvius (10:13:4) "Turrem autem minimam ait <i.e., Diades> oportere fieri ne minus altam cubitorum LX, latitudinem XVII, contracturam autem summam imae partis quintam." The Anon. Byz. presents a contraction of area rather than of the width, and, as is clear in his numerical example in chap. 35, *to* one-fifth rather than *of* one-fifth, that is, he sees the area of the top story as one-fifth the area of the bottom story. For the consequences of this incorrect interpretation see Sackur, *Vitruv,* 34 n. 1 and 106ff. For a contraction similar to that of the Anon. Byz. see Diodorus Siculus, 20:91:4, the *helepolis* of Demetrius, in the siege of

Rhodes, whose base had a reported area of 4,300 square feet, its upper story 900.

11–12 Τοὺς δὲ μείζονας ... πεντεκαιδεκαστέγους: A fifteen-story tower of Diades and Charias is not mentioned by either Ath. Mech. or Vitruvius. See Schneider, *Athenaios,* 58 n. 11:9.

15 κδ´ ἔγγιστα: Ath. Mech. has κγ´ϛ´ (231/2).

17–18 τουτέστι ... πάχος: The Anon. Byz. adds.

19 συμμετρίαν: See below, **38**:19.

20 Ἐξατρόχους ... ὀκτατρόχους: The wheels of Diades' and Charias' towers are not mentioned by Ath. Mech. or Vitruvius. Ath. Mech. (18:16) does describe a χωστρὶς χελώνη as ὀκτάτροχος, a term also used by the Anon. Byz. at 15:3 and apparently reused here. See Lendle, *Texte,* 73, and Schneider, *Athenaios,* 58 n. 12:11.

Chapter 31. Apollodorus' Tower

1 σεμνότερον: On the sense "smaller" see *De admin.* 53:265; E. Dawes and N. Baynes, *Three Byzantine Saints* (Crestwood, N.Y., 1977), 74–75; and Nikephoros Phokas, *Praecepta militaria* I:96–97, III:11, IV:37.

5–6 δίχα ... παρεξοχῆς: For Apollod.'s κατὰ δὲ τὰ ἄκρα ἀποχωροῦντα ὡς πόδα.

8 μεσοστάται: For the "center-stanchions" and "side-stanchions" (παραστάται), which together constitute the composite uprights supporting each story, see Garlan, *Recherches,* 226 n. 7, and Sackur, *Vitruv,* 26–30.

12–13 οὕς ... ὠνόμασαν: The Anon. Byz. adds. Ath. Mech. (11:6, 12:2) reports this usage by Diades and Charias.

16 κανονίων περιτομίδων τε καὶ χελωνίων: The terms are from Apollod.; see above on **22**:33 and Lendle, *Texte,* 79.

16–19 ἤτοι ... τιθεμένοις: The Anon. Byz. adds the simile for the χελώνια; see above on **22**:35–37.

20 Τοῖς ὀρθίοις ... οὖσιν: For Apollod.'s Κατὰ δὲ τοὺς ὀρθοστάτας.

21–22 ἴσα ὄντα κατὰ μῆκος: That is, the base is a square.

22 ἀντιζυγίδας: The term ἀντιζυγίς does not appear in his classical sources, but is used here by the Anon. Byz. to represent the timbers placed at right angles to the double timbers to complete the lower base. Apollod. (165:14) simply calls them ἕτερα ξύλα. For views on their nature and number in Apollod. see Lendle, *Texte*, 80–81, and Sackur, *Vitruv*, 28 n. 1. Trapp, *Lexikon*, s.v., has "(Ersatz–)Verbindung."

24–25 ἴσον ... ἀπέχωσιν: This phrasing suggests that the Anon. Byz. does not see the uprights of the tower leaning inward to accommodate the progressively shorter timbers; see below on **33:2–3.**

32 παραστάται: See above on **31:8.**

Chapter 32. The Tower of Diades and Charias

1 δυσεύρετοί εἰσι: Cf. the recommendation (taken from Apollod.) for use of εὐπόριστα τῇ ὕλῃ at **2:**15 and see above on **22:**63–64.

2 τοῖς περί: See above, **25:**1.

Chapter 33. Apollodorus' Tower

2 ἐπιζυγίδας: See Lendle, *Texte*, 80–81, on Apollod. 165:12: "Zwar ist klar, dass mit ἐπιζυγίδες Querbalken gemeint sind, welche die Verbindung zwischen den ζυγά herstellten."

2–3 ἐλάσσονας τῷ μήκει ποδὸς ἄχρι: For Apollod.'s ἐλάττονες τῶν κάτω τῷ μήκει πόδα. The method by which the tower's uprights converged to allow for the progressive shortening of the upper horizontal timbers is not completely clear in either Apollod. or the Anon. Byz. On the problem in the text of Apollod. see Lacoste, "Poliorcétiques," 260 n. 1, and Lendle, *Texte*, 80. Sackur, *Vitruv*, 34 n. 1, concluded on Apollod. that "die Eckständer um dieses Mass natürlich vom Lot abweichen müssen"; for such an approach see Diodorus Siculus XX.91.4: κίονες ... συννενευκότες πρὸς ἀλλήλους of a tower built by Demetrius for the siege of Rhodes. On the Anon. Byz. Sackur suggests, "Man kann sich deswegen nicht des Verdachts erwehren, dass der Byzantiner senkrechte Pfosten annimmt, die in jedem Stockwerk absetzen (wie es auch das

Bild zeigt)," a view he characterizes as "einen allerschlimmsten Fehler, der es zu einer vollständigen Unsinnsdarstellung macht." Lacoste (ibid.) however, saw the Anon. Byz.'s approach, although not stated in Apollodorus, as "d'ailleurs parfaitement rationnelle."

7 περίπτεροι ... περιδρόμους: The terms are taken from Ath. Mech. (11:8, 13:7,10). For the former as "narrow ledges" for fighting fires see Lendle, *Texte,* 72–73; on the latter as "inner galleries," ibid., 75 and n. 102. See also Garlan, *Recherches,* 227, and Callebat and Fleury, *Vitruve,* 245 n. 13:5:1 and below, **39:**13–14.

8–9 εἰς τὴν ... ἐκβοήθησιν: Cf. Ath. Mech. 12:5–6: εἰς τὴν ἐκβοήθησιν τῶν ἐμπυρισμῶν.

12–15 τροχοὺς ... ἥμισυ: On the passage see Blyth, "Apollodorus," 136–37 and nn. 26 and 27; Lendle, *Texte,* 40 n. 40 and 82. The phrase λεπίσι ψυχρηλάτοις occurs four times in Ath. Mech., at 17:2 of the τριπήχεις wheels of a χελώνη χωστρίς. Blyth suggests that the Anon. Byz. "must have found these words or something very like them in his text of the [i.e., Apollod.'s] *Poliorcetica.* They may have been a marginal gloss that did not get into the main tradition." Lendle, ibid., 82, argues that wheels of such large size would be too close together to allow for a stable structure and also could scarcely have been accommodated under the structurally important crossbeams. He suggests that the reading δ′ may be an error for δύο. As the archetype manuscript has τεσσάρων, it seems best to allow it to stand in the text.

20 ἀπαρεμποδίστως: Cf. above on **13:**32.

21 σύμπηγμα: From Apollod. 166:6. LSJ, s.v., gives "superstructure," "framework."

Chapter 34. Apollodorus' Tower

4 πρὸς αὐτόν: The text here seems to describe another center-stanchion at the next higher level placed on top of the lower center-stanchion (αὐτόν). The illustration on folio 26, however, shows the outer side-stanchion placed on top of the lower center-stanchion, the center-stanchion on top of the lower inner side-stanchion, etc., as the tower legs work inward to allow for the progressively shorter cross beams and the narrowing of the whole structure.

11 **κλίμακας:** On placement of the ladders see Lendle, *Texte,* 86–87.

17 **πλαγίοις**: That is, slanted away from the tower to prevent being pulled out by the tension; so Lendle, *Texte,* 84.

19 **ἐξ ὀλίγων καὶ μικρῶν ξύλων**: The phrase is from Apollod.; for his stress on use of small and readily available materials, in contrast to the long timbers used by Hellenistic engineers, see Lendle, *Texte,* 77–78. See also above, **2**:15 19 and **22**:63–64.

20–22 ⟨μ⟩ήτε . . . **δηλώσας**: The Anon. Byz. adds. See Sackur, *Vitruv,* 107, who suggests that Apollod.'s intent is to require no calculation by the craftsman other than a shortening of the timbers by 1 foot at each story. For adaptation by the craftsman, however, see above on **1**:9.

Chapter 35. Numerical example added by the Anon. Byz.

On the error here of the contraction as one of area rather than width, as well as *to* one-fifth rather than *of* one-fifth see Sackur, *Vitruv,* 34 n. 1 and 109f, and above on **30**:9–10.

6 **να′ πέμπτον**: On the value 1/5 for the contraction, see above, **30**:9–10.

8 **ἑπτὰ ἕκτον ἔγγιστα**: The value is an approximation for an irrational number. The calculation for the approximation should be 7 1/6 x 7 1/6 = 49 + 7/6 + 7/6 + 1/36 = 51 13/36; see Schneider, 51 n. 1. The multiplication of the two fractions by each other (1/6 x 1/6) is omitted. For methods of approximating square roots of non-square numbers, see Heron, *Metrica* I:8, E. M. Bruins, *Codex Constantinopolitanus* (Leiden, 1964), III:191–92, and Heath, *History,* II:51–52 and 323–26, etc. For use of sexagesimal fractions in such calculations, see Heath, *History,* I: 60–63.

9–10 **λεπτά** . . . **λεπτὰ πρῶτα**: On the use of "minutes" (λεπτά or πρῶτα λεπτά) in the sexagesimal system of fractions, see Heath, *History,* I:45.

12 **εἰς τὸ μέρος**: The fractional remainder (140/60 = 2 and 20/60) would be 1/3 rather than 1/5.

16 **ἐπέμβασιν**: The term is not found in Apollod. or Ath. Mech. It also occurs, together with παρέμβασις, below in chap. 37. Barocius trans-

lates both terms with "super adiectione"; Schneider renders the former with "den Raum … verringern" and the latter once "Verkürzung" in chap. 37. LSJ, ἐπέμβασις 2 has "pl., *steps*." The terms appear to refer to the progressive decrease in size of the timbers delimiting the area of each story. I have translated with "modulation" based on Vitruvius (IV:3:3), who speaks of a "modulus, qui Graece *embater* dicitur, cuius moduli constitutione ratiocinationibus efficuntur omnis operis distributiones," that is, a rhythm in pacing or spanning. Παρέμβασις below is apparently used in a similar fashion.

Chapter 36. Diades and Charias

2 οἱ μὲν περί: See above on **25**:1.

6–8 τό τε σύμπαχον … συνηρίθμουν: The observation is not found in the Anon. Byz.'s sources and is apparently his own; for its correctness and discussion of the calculations in the preceding passage, see Lendle, *Texte*, 76, and Sackur, *Vitruv*, 110–11.

7 ἀετώματι: See above on **22**:41.

Chapter 37. Apollodorus' Portable Siege Tower

4 ποδῶν ἒξ … παρέμβασιν: The Anon. Byz. adds; the timbers would decrease from 16 feet in length to 10 feet, the area from 256 to 100 square feet, as the tower rose to six stories. On παρέμβασις see above, **35**:16.

5 τρίτον δὲ καὶ εἰκοστὸν ἔγγιστα: 23/60 is the closest sexagesimal approximation to 100/256 (see above on **35**:8). The conclusion is added by the Anon. Byz.

8 ἑνὸς … ἐπέμβασιν: The Anon. Byz. adds.

9–10 ἑνὸς … παρέμβασιν: The Anon. Byz. adds.

10 ὡς προείρηται: See **35**:17.

12 ἑπτὰ καὶ μέρους ἕκτου: See above on **35**:8.

13–16 ἐννέα … ἒξ … πέντε καὶ μέρους: Presumably half the diameter of the wheels and the thickness of the decks would be added to get the 60 feet.

Chapter 38. Proportional Relation of the Towers

The Anon. Byz. sets the towers of Diades and Charias and Apollod. in the context of a proportional relationship. Sackur, *Vitruv,* 109, suggested that "der gelehrte Pedant" sought in this comparison of two disparate texts to create "ein Turmproblem." The extensive use of συμμετρία, συμφωνία, ἀναλογία, and λόγος (ratio) here and elsewhere goes far beyond anything found in the classical descriptions. Apollod. makes no mention of such relationships and uses σύμμετρος elsewhere only once (180:10); Ath. Mech. (12:9–10) says of Diades and Charias only Ὁμοίως δὲ καὶ ἐπὶ τοῦ ἐλάττονος πύργου ἡ διαίρεσις τῶν στεγῶν τὸν αὐτὸν λόγον ἐλάμβανεν and does not use σύμμετρος at all. Notably the Anon. Byz. provides (see on **38**:11–12) a definition of συμφωνία that is similar to a definition of συμμετρία found in Aristotle's *De lineis insecabilibus.* For discussion of the possible Pythagorean origin (esp. from Philolaus) of the concept and its applications in art and architecture, see Γ. J. Pollitt, *The Ancient View of Greek Art* (New Haven, Conn., 1974), 12–22 and 256–58, and P. Gros, *Vitruve, De L'architecture, livre II* (Paris, 1990), 56–60. For the Anon. Byz.'s reference to Philolaus see above, **3**:26–27, and to Pythagoreans, below, *Geodesia* **8**:13–14.

6 ὁ πῆχυς . . . : On the measurement system see the Introduction, 23.

11–12 ὅτι . . . μετροῦνται: Cf. Aristotle, *De lineis insecabilibus* 968b6: σύμμετροί εἰσιν αἱ τῷ αὐτῷ μέτρῳ μετρούμεναι; and Heron, *Definitiones* 128: νυνὶ δὲ Εὐκλείδῃ τῷ στοιχειωτῇ (X, def. 1) ἑπόμενοι περὶ τῶν μεγεθῶν φαμεν, ὅτι σύμμετρα μεγέθη λέγεται τὰ ὑπὸ τῶν αὐτῶν μέτρων μετρούμενα. See also below, **51**:28–29, and the Introduction to chap. 38.

18–19 τὸν αὐτὸν . . . λόγον: The phrase is repeated with σώζουσα for ἔχοντες below at **51**:28–29.

19 συμμετρίαν . . . συμφωνίαν: For the combination see below, **51**:18–19 and Heron, *Bel., * 112–13.

20 φορητῶν πύργων: See above on **2**:6.

20–21 οἱ περὶ . . . τοὺς περί: See above on **25**:1.

Chapter 39. Apollodorus' Tower: stability, fire fighting.

The Anon. Byz. draws here on Apollod. 173:9–174:7; for discussion see Lendle, *Texte,* 98–99.

2 ἰσοπέδιος ὁ πρὸς τὴν βάσιν: The Anon. Byz. adds.

3 ἀνωφερὴς τυγχάνῃ: For Apollod.'s κοίλωμα ἔχῃ.

3–5 ποιήσομεν . . . τόπον: The Anon. Byz. here interprets a problematic sentence in Apollodorus, an interpretation Lendle, *Texte,* 98–99, argues is incorrect; Lendle would emend the text of Apollod. (ὑπόθημα τῇ ὁμοίᾳ αὐτοῦ τοῦ πύργου συμπλοκῇ, προσερχομένῃ . . . πλατυνούσῃ) to ὑποθήματ⟨α⟩ ἢ ὁμοίαν αὐτοῦ τοῦ πύργου συμπλοκὴν προσερχομένην . . . καὶ πλατυνούσην. He concludes, "Geländevertiefungen in der Bahn des Wandelturms durch ein 'Gewebe' von sich kreuzenden Balkenlagen, deren Zusammensetzung sich nach dem Grad der zu überwindenden Vertiefung richtete, so auszugleichen, dass am Schluss eine ebene Oberfläche entstand."

3 ὑπόθημα: The term is from Apollod.; cf. above, ὑπόθεμα, **13**:15. For the possible nature of the device see above on **39**:3–5.

4 ἐπὶ τῷ ἀνωμάλῳ: For Apollod.'s ἐπὶ τὸ ἀνάκλιμα.

6–7 ὅπως . . . συντηρῆται: The Anon. Byz. adds.

8–9 ἐκ . . . φλογῶν: The Anon. Byz. adds. See above on **2**:9.

8 πυροφόρων τριβόλων: Philo Mech. 94:9–10 (also 95:8 and 100:20–21) speaks of τριβόλους καιομένους στιππύῳ περιειλι⟨γμένους⟩. Garlan, *Recherches,* 386, compares Philo Mech.'s device to Aeneas Tacticus' (33:2) description of wooden pestles with iron spikes and combustible materials dropped from the walls to stick into siege machines and set them on fire. See also Leo, *Taktika* XIX:58: Καὶ τρίβολοι δὲ μείζονες σιδηραῖ ἢ ἐν σφαιρίοις ξυλίνοις ἧλοι ὀξεῖς ἐμπεπηγμένοι, στυππίοις δὲ καὶ ἑτέρᾳ ὕλῃ ἐνειλημμένη (leg. -μένη) ἐμπυρισθέντα καὶ κατὰ τῶν πολεμίων βαλλόμενα, εἶτα πίπτοντα ἐν τοῖς πλοίοις διὰ πολλῶν μερῶν ἐμπρήσουσιν αὐτά. Kolias, *Waffen,* 175–77, suggests that a fiery τρίβολος may be the prickly plant, attached to a fire arrow or missile, similar to the ἔγκεντρα ματζούκια, to cause it to stick in the wooden equipment. On the pas-

sage see also F. Lammert, *RE* VI.A.2:2414.

9–12 μάλιστα ... εὔθραυστον: The Anon. Byz. adds here to the text of Apollod., apparently from Ath. Mech. 17:14: μάλιστα μὲν φοινικίνοις, εἰ δὲ μή, τῶν ἄλλων ὅσα εὔτονά ἐστι ξύλα πλὴν κεδρίνων, πευκίνων καὶ κληθρίνων· ταῦτα γὰρ ἔκπυρά ἐστι καὶ εὔκλαστα. On the resilience of palm see above on **13**:22; for questions about its resistance to fire, a quality also mentioned by Philo Mech., 91:3, ἐκ τῶν φοινίκων σανίδας ... (ἰσχυραὶ γάρ εἰσι καὶ δυσέμπρηστοι), see Lawrence, *Fortification*, 88.

13–14 ἐπὶ ... περιδρόμοις: See above, **33**:7.

15–17 διά τε ... πληγαί: For Apollod.'s ἵνα ἔχωσι τόπον συνελθεῖν καὶ ἐκλύσαι τὸ βέλος.

21 τῶν ... πεμπόντων: The Anon. Byz. adds.

21–22 εἰργασμένα ὡσὰν τεταριχευμένα: The Anon. Byz. adds. On preservation with salt see *Geoponika* 19:9: Περὶ ταριχείας πάντων κρεῶν; Koukoules, *Bios,* V:64–65; and generally on the method R. J. Forbes, *Studies in Ancient Technology* (Leiden, 1955), I:189.

26 σίφων: The term and its function here is from Apollod. For a description of such a device see Heron, *Pneumatica* I:38 and Landels, *Engineering,* 202. For similar use see *Vita Stephani Iunioris* (PG 100:1069–1186), col. 1176C: τοὺς ἐν αὐτῷ τῷ τόπῳ ἱσταμένους ὑδρυστάτας τῶν ἐμπρησμῶν, οὕσπερ σίφωνας καλοῦσιν. See also D. Oleson, *Greek and Roman Mechanical Water-Lifting Devices* (Toronto, 1984), 28–29.

26–27 κάλαμοι ... ἰξευταί: See above, **19**:27.

30–35 Οὐ μικρὰν ... πληγάς: Cf. Ath. Mech. 18:3–7: ἐπὶ δὲ τούτοις καταλαμβάνονται βύρσαις ῥεραμμέναις ὁμοίως ταῖς τύλαις, καὶ σάττεται εἰς αὐτὰς μάλιστα μὲν ἔλεια ἢ τὸ καλούμενον θαλασσόπρασον ἢ ἄχυρα ὄξει βεβρεγμένα· ταῦτα δέ εἰσι χρήσιμα πρός τε τὰς τῶν λιθοβόλων πληγὰς καὶ πρὸς τοὺς ἐμπυρισμούς, and Philo Mech. 99:26, κωδίοις ὄξει βρέξαντα ἢ ὕδατι. See also Maurice, *Strategikon* X:3:12–13: Καὶ πρὸς τοὺς κριοὺς ἀντίκεινται τύλαι καὶ σακκία, γέμοντα ἄχυρα καὶ ψάμμον; Leo, *Taktika* XV:48: πρὸς τοὺς κριοὺς δὲ ἀντίκεινται τυλάρια καὶ σακκία γέμοντα ἄχυρα καὶ ψάμμον; and *De obsid.* 69:1ff: σοφίζεσθαι δὲ πρὸς τὴν βίαν τοῦ μηχανήματος οὐ μόνον ὅπερ Ἰώσηπος ἐπετήδευσεν, ἀλλὰ καὶ ἕτεροι τῶν παλαιῶν · σάκκους γὰρ ἀχύρου γεμίσαντας, πλὴν βεβρεγμένου διὰ τὸ μὴ ὑπανάπτεσθαι εὐχερῶς (= Josephus, *Bellum Judaicum* III:223). For vinegar as a fire retardant see Theophrastus, *De igne* 25:59–61; Pliny the Elder, *Naturalis Historia* 33:94; and Callebat and Fleury, *Vitruve, 260* n. 3.3. For mats (ὑφάσματα) of hair, wool, or linen used to protect city walls against stone throwers, see ⟨Περὶ Στρατηγίας⟩13:74ff.

31 τύλια: Cf. Ath. Mech. (18:4): τύλαις. For τύλιον = τύλη, see Wescher, 247 n. 16.

32 δίκτυα ἐνύγρων βρύων: The Anon. Byz. is here apparently paraphrasing Ath. Mech.'s θαλασσόπρασον. For βρύον as *alga, muscus marinus,* see Hippocrates, *De mulierum affectibus* 53:3: Ὅταν ὧδε ἔχῃ, καταπλάσσειν βρύῳ τῷ θαλασσίῳ, ὃ ἐπὶ τοὺς ἰχθύας ἐπιβάλλουσι.

34 πυροβόλων: See above 2:9.

36 ἐκ τῶν ... φλογῶν: See above on 2:9.

36–40:1 < ... || 40. ... >: On the lacuna (between folios 28v and 29r) see Dain, *Tradition,* 30–31. Wescher (248:3) noted that the missing material was presumably drawn from Apollod.'s section on ladders, 175:1–185:2.

Chapter 40. Single Ram between Ladders

The Anon. Byz. draws here on Apollod. 185:6–16. For discussion see Lendle, *Texte,* 19–22, with modern drawing, 22. The device is illustrated on folio 29v.

3 ἰσοϋψῆ: The Anon. Byz. adds.

3–6 διὰ σανίδων ... βολάς: For Apollod.'s κανόσι καὶ σανίσι. On βεργῶν see above, 8:3–4, on νεοσφαγῶν 15:18–19, on πηλῷ 15:5, and on πυροβόλα 2:9.

9 πρὸς τὴν ἀνάβασιν: For Apollod.'s τῆς ἀναβάθρας.

12 ἐνεργήσει: For Apollod.'s ἐργάσεται.

13 βαστάγμασιν: For Apollod.'s ἀρτήμασιν; see above on 22:57.

13 παρὰ μικρόν τι: For Apollod.'s μετρίως. The front hanger would be

slightly shorter than the back one so that the ram would be angled upward and thus strike the less unified parts of the wall. See Lendle, *Texte,* 20–21. See also above, chap. **23**.

14–16 ἵνα . . . κριομαχῶσιν: For Apollod.'s ἵνα ἐπὶ τὰς στέγας ἄνω κριομαχῶσιν οἱ ἐπιφέροντες. For discussion of the meaning of Apollod.'s ἐπὶ τὰς στέγας, which the Anon. Byz. here interprets as τὰ ἀνώτερα μέρη τῶν τειχῶν, see Lendle, *Texte,* 21. See also above on chap. **23**.

16 εὐκατάλυτον: The Anon. Byz. adds.

17 ἀνεστηκός: The Anon. Byz. adds.

17–19 ἀσύνδετον . . . ἐπιστηρίζονται: The Anon. Byz. adds.

18 προπύργια: Added by the Anon. Byz; see Demetrakos, *Lexikon,* s.v: προκεχωρημένον ὀχύρωμα . . . προτείχισμα, προμαχών, and below, **55:23** where it refers to a rampart wall on a raft otherwise referred to there as a προτείχισμα.

Chapter 41. Rams on Ladders as Bridges

The Anon. Byz. draws here on Apollod. 185:16–186:3

2 εὐκόλως: The Anon. Byz. adds.

2–3 τοῖς . . . προειρημένοις: For Apollod.'s τοῖς πρότερον. There is no earlier reference in the extant text of the Anon. Byz. to περιφραγαί, but Apollod. 171:7–172:1, in a section on rams on portable towers, has ὅταν δὲ διαβαίνειν δέῃ ἐπ' αὐτοῖς, ἐγείρονται οἱ κάνονες, καὶ ἀεὶ ὀρθοὶ ἑστᾶσι, καλωδίῳ ἐξ ἄκρου ἑλκομένου τοῦ κάμακος δρυφάκτου τρόπῳ. This section of Apollod. was apparently included in the now lost portion preceding chap. 40 of the Byzantine paraphrase.

3 <γενομένων>: Cf. Apollod. 185:17: ὁμοίως τοῖς πρότερον δρυφάκτων ἐφ' ἑκάτερα γενομένων.

3 περιφραγῶν: For Apollod.'s δρυφάκτων ("rails"). For the form cf. *Geoponika* 11:5:4. For an illustration of a ram with guard rails used to mount walls see folio 40r and below on **53:38–39**, ἐπιβατήρια. Cf. also below, **46:34–35**, Περιφραγαὶ . . . ἐκ βυρσῶν, on the sides of a wheeled ladder and attached drawbridge.

4–5 **περιστραφήσονται . . . παρατρεπόμεναι:** For Apollod.'s περινεύουσιν ἐπὶ τὸν κρόταφον.

5–6 **καὶ τὰ . . . διάχωρα:** The Anon. Byz. adds.

6 **καταγραφή:** See above, **1:3**.

Chapter 42. Double Rams on Ladders

The Anon. Byz. draws here on Apollod. 186:4–187:6. See Lendle, *Texte*, 21–24, with modern drawing, 24. The device is illustrated on folio 30v.

1 **τάξιν καί:** The Anon. Byz. adds.

2 **ἐπερχομένην, ἴσην οὖσαν:** The Anon. Byz. adds.

3 **ἤτοι ὀρθήν:** The Anon. Byz. adds.

3–4 **καὶ τὰς μὲν . . . ἔχουσι:** The Anon. Byz. adds.

4–6 **τὰ δὲ ἀπ' ἀλλήλων . . . διάστημα:** For Apollod.'s καὶ διεστᾶσιν οὐχ ὁμοίως, ἀλλὰ καὶ αὐταί εἰσι παράλληλοι.

7–8 **καὶ κατὰ τοῦτο:** For Apollod.'s μόνον ἑνί.

9 **πρὸς . . . πλάγια:** For Apollod.'s τοῖς κροτάφοις ἑκατέρωθεν.

11 **μετακινήσαντες:** For Apollod.'s ἐξώσαντες.

12 **ἐκ τῶν ὄπισθεν:** For Apollod.'s κατὰ νώτου.

12 **ὁμοῦ:** For Apollod.'s ἑκάτεραι.

13 **δύο:** The Anon. Byz. adds.

13–14 **ἀλλ' ἢ . . . τῷ τείχει:** For Apollod.'s ἡ μὲν μία ἐπιτίθεται.

15–16 **καὶ τὸ . . . διάχωρον:** For Apollod.'s ὅσον ἐστὶ καὶ τῆς κλίμακος ἀπὸ τῆς ἑτέρας τὸ διάστημα.

16–18 **καὶ γίνεται . . . ἐπίζευξις:** The Anon. Byz. adds.

Chapter 43. Fighting from the Top Deck of Ladders

The Anon. Byz. draws here on Apollod. 187:7–187:11. See Lendle, *Texte*, 23.

1–3 **ἄνευ . . . τείχει:** The Anon. Byz. adds.

4–5 θορυβοῦσι καὶ καταπλήττουσι: For Apollod.'s περισπῶσι. The Anon. Byz. frequently adds to and elaborates on references to the security of troops and battle psychology found in his sources, both for encouragement of troops, particularly through creating the possibility for more than one man to attack simultaneously and from a superior position, and for creating fear in the enemy. See below, **46**:32–33, 42–44, **47**:12, **49**:19, 22, **50**:14, 24–25, **52**:4, 6–10, **55**:22, **56**:9, etc.

5 προμαχοῦντας: The Anon. Byz. adds.

6 ἐπὶ . . . κινήσει: The Anon. Byz. adds. Cf. below, **44**:9.

7 βύρσαις: For Apollod.'s δέρρεσι.

7 προτείχισμα: The Anon. Byz. adds. Lendle, *Texte,* 23, suggests that while covering the upper two rungs would give no more than 3 feet of protection, it would still be effective if the top deck of the ladder were higher than the wall.

Chapter 44. Torsion Strike-Beam on a Ram

The Anon. Byz. draws here on a brief description in Apollod. 187:11–188:9, elaborating significantly on the nature of the torsion system, in part with material from Heron's *Bel.* For discussion see Lendle, *Texte,* 25–28; idem, *Schildkröten,* 93–95; and Marsden, *Treatises,* 249–65.

4 κατέναντι: The Anon. Byz. adds.

4–5 ἤτοι . . . ἑτέρας: The Anon. Byz. adds.

5–7 ξύλα . . . ἀπαράτρεπτα: For Apollod.'s ἕξουσι περιτομίδας ἐξ ἀμφοτέρων πλευρῶν.

5 ξύλα ἑτεροπλατῆ: For Apollod.'s περιτομίδας, the Anon. Byz.'s paraphrase adding support to Lendle's (*Texte,* 25) rendering of the term as "Schnittbalken," here beams, apparently with cuts in them, fitting over the pins in the ladder legs to secure them in position. See above on **22**:33–34.

7–8 φυλάττοντα . . . διάχωρα: For Apollod.'s ἵνα τὸ πρὸς ἀλλήλας διάστημα διατηρῶσιν ἀλλήλαις.

9 ἐπανοίγεσθαι: For Apollod.'s ἀποχωρεῖν.

9 ἐπὶ ... κινήσει: The Anon. Byz. adds. Cf. above, **43**:6.

10 ἐπικλείεσθαι: For Apollod.'s ἐγκλᾶσθαι.

10–11 ἐκσπῶνται ... ἐκπίπτωσι: For Apollod.'s ἐξάλλωνται.

11 κρατουμένου: For Apollod.'s ἐπιλαμβανομένου.

11 χελωνάρια: For Apollod.'s χελώνια. See above on **22**:33–34.

12 μηρούς: For Apollod.'s κάμαξι.

12–14 ὡς ... γρονθάρια: The Anon. Byz. adds; on the simile see above on **22**:35–37.

15 ξύλα: For Apollod.'s περιτομίδα. See above on **44**:5.

17 ἐπιπήγματα: For Apollod.'s ἐπίπηγας.

18 σιαγόνια: The term is from Apollod. (see also Ath. Mech. 35:5).

18–20 ὀρθὰ ... ἀσφαλιζόμενα: The Anon. Byz. adds, interpreting the σιαγόνια as square boards attached to the sides of the ram and secured below by crossbars. Lendle, *Schildkröten,* 93–94, argues that attachment directly to the ram would not allow the sinews to be long enough to be effective and suggests a boxlike structure that places the side boards further apart.

20–38 Ταῦτα ... κρατούμενον: The Anon. Byz. elaborates significantly here (using in part Heron's *Bel.)* on Apollod.'s brief Ταῦτα τρηθέντα χοινικίδας λήψεται καὶ στροφὰς νεύρων καὶ ἀγκῶνα μέσον μακρόν.

22–23 στεφάναι ... κρίκοι: Apollod. mentions only the washers (χοινικίδες), not these flanges. Heron, *Bel.* 97, uses the term ὑπόθεμα for a ring beneath a washer. See Marsden, *Treatises,* 255 n. 3.

23 χοινικίδας: For discussion of the washer see Marsden, *Treatises,* 53–55, with illustration at 437, and Callebat and Fleury, *Vitruve,* 229–30.

24 ὀστρακίνοις σωληνιδίοις: The simile is added by the Anon. Byz. The illustration (folio 32r) of the washer is compatible with this interpretation.

25 ἀπὸ τόρνου: The Anon. Byz. adds; cf. Heron, *De automatis* XI:2 χοινικίδες ... αὗται ἀπὸ τόρνου τὴν ἐντὸς καὶ τὴν ἐκτὸς ἐπιφάνειαν

εἰργασμέναι. On the lathe see L. R. Palmar, "Mortar and Lathe," *Eranos* 44 (1946), 54–61, and Dar.–Sag., *Dictionnaire,* V:372–375 at "Tornatura." See also above, **17**:14, and below, **46**:4, and E. R. Dodds, *Euripides Bacchae* (Oxford, 1960), 210–11.

25–26 **ἐξ εὐτόνων ... πετάλοις**: For wooden washers coated with metal laminate see Marsden, *Treatises,* 53 n. 30, and more generally for such laminating see Philo Mech., *Belopoeica* 76:18–19: ἦν δὲ κατὰ χεῖρα πάνυ καθαρίως εἰργασμένα τὰ ξύλινα καὶ τῷ σιδήρῳ δεδεμένα σφόδρα.

28–29 **κωλυομένας ... τόπους**: Cf. Heron, *Bel.* 97: καὶ δι᾽ ὅλου ἐντορνία γίνεται, καὶ εἴς τινα σωλῆνα ἐμπίπτει περὶ τὸ περίτρητον γινόμενον ἐν κύκλῳ πρὸς τὸ μὴ παραβαίνειν τὴν χοινικίδα τόπον ἐκ τόπου. γίνεται δὲ ἔσθ᾽ ὅτε ὑπόθεμα τῇ χοινικίδι ἐπικείμενον καὶ συγκεκοινωμένον τῷ περιτρήτῳ, ἐν ᾧ ἐστιν ὁ εἰρημένος σωλήν.

30 **κανόνια τετράγωνα**: Cf. Heron, *Bel.* 97–98: ἐκ τῆς ἄνω πλευρᾶς τῆς κατὰ τὸ ΑΒ εὐθείας ἐκκοπαὶ γίνονται βʹ κατὰ διάμετρον κείμεναι, ἐν αἷς ἐστιν κατερχομένη ἡ καλουμένη ἐπιζυγὶς κατὰ κρόταφον κειμένη. αὕτη δὲ ἔσται σιδηρᾶ, ἐκ καθαροῦ σιδήρου γιγνομένη, καὶ ἐν τῇ χαλκείᾳ καλῶς τετελειωμένη, ὡς πᾶσαν ὑπομενοῦσα τὴν τοῦ ὀργάνου βίαν· περὶ γὰρ ταύτην ὁ τόνος καμπτόμενος γίγνεται, and see Marsden, *Treatises,* 255 n. 5. For an example of washers with rods see D. Baatz, "Teile hellenistischer Geschütze aus Griechenland," *Archäologischer Anzeiger* (1979), 69–72.

30–31 **ὡσανεὶ περιστομίδας**: The Anon. Byz. may here be comparing these rods on the washers to Heron's περιστομίς, *Bel.* 108: ἡ δὲ περιστομίς ἐστι ξύλον μῆκος ἔχον ὡς παλαιστῶν Βʹ ἢ Γʹ, although Heron's term refers to a "clip" rather than the bar across the washer for which Heron uses ἐπιζυγίς. The device is distinct from the περιτομίς mentioned above at **22**:33; for speculation on its nature see Lendle, *Schildkröten,* 119–20.

32 **ὠμιαίοις ... συῶν**: The Anon. Byz. draws here almost verbatim on Heron, *Bel.* 110. For the translation "tendons" (as opposed to "sinews"), see Landels, *Engineering,* 108–9; on animal tendons as less sensitive to moisture than hemp and flax, see A. Neuberger, *The Technical Arts and Sciences of the Ancients,* trans. H. L. Brose (New York-London, 1930; repr. 1969), 221.

34 **διὰ τὸ ἐντόνιον περιειλεῖσθαι:** The reading follows Marsden, *Treatises*, 256 n. 2, who notes that the "stretcher" was used to apply the initial tension.

34–35 **νημάτων σηρικῶν . . . ἐκ λίνου:** Use of animal tendons and women's hair is mentioned by Heron, *Bel.* 110, 112, repeated by the Anon. Byz. below at **45:**11 and 19–20; the Anon. Byz. adds here silk and flax. At *De cer.* 670:1, 12, κόρδαι μεταξοταί are associated with χειροτοξοβαλίστραι and μεγάλαι τοξοβαλίστραι. Whether μεταξοτός in these passages means "of silk" has been contested (see Reiske, *De cer.* II:791, and Kolias, *Waffen*, 251 and n. 62); the Anon. Byz.'s reference here to silk torsion cords would suggest that it does. For other uses of flax see **12:**19 and **49:**3.

35 **μαλάθοις:** Barocius translates "sericis textis," Schneider "Fäden"; Wescher comments: "Vocabulum aliunde non notum." Cf. (?) Demetrakos, *Lexikon*, "μαλάθα (ἡ) δημ. πλεκτὸν κάνιστρον πρὸς οἰκιακὴν χρῆσιν, καλάθα."

36–37 **ἐν σχήματι παλιντόνου ἀγκῶνος:** The comparison is inserted by the Anon. Byz; cf. Heron, *Bel.* 82: εἶτα διὰ μέσων τῶν νεύρων διέβαλλον ἕνα τῶν ἀγκώνων.

37 **κατακλεῖδι:** Heron uses the term at *Bel.* 79 of the pawl on a belly-bow: κόρακα, ὃν δὴ κατακλεῖδα ἐκάλουν ("the pawl, which they named the clicker," trans. Marsden), illustrated by Marsden, *Treatises*, 48. Its use here is apparently due to the Anon. Byz. For a different use of the term see below on **54:**7.

38–39 **οἱ λιθοβόλοι μονάγκωνες . . . καλοῦσιν:** The phrase is from Apollod.; on the one-arm stone thrower ("onager") see Marsden, *Treatises*, 249–65.

39 **Μοχλὸν . . . ῥιζοκρίκιν:** Cf. Heron, *Bel.* 101: δεῖ ἐπιστρέφειν τὰς χοινικίδας μοχλῷ σιδηρῷ κρίκον ἔχοντι, εἰς ὃν ἐμβάλλεται ἡ τῆς ἐπιζυγίδος ὑπεροχή; and 110: ἐπιστρέψεις τὰς χοινικίδας, ὡς προείρηται, τῷ μοχλῷ τῷ σιδηρῷ τῷ ἔχοντι τὸν κρίκον. I do not find the term ῥιζοκρίκι(ο)ν attested elsewhere; *LSJRS*, s.v., gives "app. *ring attached to the base.*" The device is illustrated both alone and in use on folio 32r. On the use of the wrench see Marsden, *Treatises*, 258.

40 περιστομίδας: See above on **44**:30–31.

43–44 ἐπιρρίψει . . . ἀπολυθέντα τὸν μονάγκωνα: For Apollod.'s σχαστηρίαν ("trigger") λαβὼν ἐπαφήσει . . . τὸν μονάγκωνα. Lendle, *Texte,* 28, notes that neither Apollod. nor the Anon. Byz. mentions the possibility of reloading the device.

Chapter 45. Summary on Catapult Torsion Methods

The Anon. Byz. here summarizes portions of Heron's *Bel.,* esp. 109–12 and 115. For discussion of various technical points from Heron, see Marsden, *Treatises,* 55–60; on use of animal tendons and women's hair for torsion springs see, Landels, *Engineering,* 108–10.

1–7 ⟨Α⟩ὕτη . . . ἀπεργάζεται: The opening sentence is the Anon. Byz.'s own summary. This comment and some in the previous chapter, for example, the recommendation for the use of silk, raise uncertainty on whether trebuchets had completely replaced torsion catapults in tenth-century Byzantium. For a discussion of comments in the sources see K. Huuri, *Zur Geschichte des mittelalterlichen Geschützwesens aus orientalischen Quellen,* Studia Orientalia 9 (Helsinki, 1941), 85–87; for recent reviews of the trebuchet/torsion issue, see R. Rogers, *Latin Siege Warfare in the Twelfth Century* (Oxford, 1992), 254–73; P. Chevedden, "Artillery in Late Antiquity: Prelude to the Middle Ages," in I. Corfis and M. Wolfe, *The Medieval City under Siege* (Woodbridge, UK, 1995), 131–73, and my "Tenth Century Byzantine Offensive Siege Warfare: Instructional Prescriptions and Historical Practice," *Byzantium at War (9th–12th c.)* (Athens, 1997), 179–200, specifically 198–99.

3 μακροβολεῖν: For the verb cf. Philo Mech., *Belopoeica,* 49:13–50:3: κατασκευὴν ὀργάνων . . . τὰ μὲν μακροβολοῦντα καὶ εὔτονα ταῖς πληγαῖς ἐποίησαν, τὰ δὲ καθυστεροῦντα, and for the concept Philo Mech., ibid., 51: Τῆς δὲ βελοποιικῆς ὅρος ἐστὶ τὸ μακρὰν ἀποστέλλειν τὸ βέλος.

3–4 εὐθυτόνοις τε καὶ παλιντόνοις: The terms are defined by Heron, *Bel.* 74: τὰ μὲν εὐθύτονα οἰστοὺς μόνους ἀφίησι· τὰ δὲ παλίντονα ἔνιοι καὶ λιθοβόλα καλοῦσι διὰ τὸ λίθους ἐξαποστέλλειν· πέμπει δὲ ἤτοι οἰστοὺς ἢ ⟨λίθους ἢ⟩ καὶ συναμφότερα. For discussion of "straight-spring" (euthytone) and the "V-spring" (palintone), see Marsden, *Treatises,* 44–

45, nn. 5 and 6 with illustrations, 45; idem, *Development,* 22–23, and Drachmann, *Technology,* 187–88.

4 **ἤτοι λιθοβόλοις τε καὶ ὀξυβελέσιν**: The order is perhaps chiastic, as the euthytone was not able to fire stones. On the combination cf. Philo Mech., *Belopoeica* 54:25–27: τὰ μὲν λιθοβολικὰ τῶν ὀργάνων . . . τὰ δ᾽ ὀξυβελῆ, and Constantine Porphyrogenitus, *De legationibus* 551:9: καταπέλτας ὀξυβελεῖς τε καὶ λιθοβόλους. On the latter see Marsden, *Development,* 60, 89, etc.

7–8 **Ὅσῳ . . . πέφυκεν**: Cf. Heron, *Bel.* 115: ἐπεὶ οὖν αἴτιός ἐστιν ὁ τόνος τῆς τοῦ λίθου ἐξαποστολῆς.

9–23 **τῆς τοξίτιδος . . . ἰσχύος**: The section is taken almost verbatim from portions of Heron, *Bel.* 109–12.

12 **ἐν τοῖς σκέλεσι**: The Anon. Byz. adds.

23–24 **βελοποιϊκῇ πραγματείᾳ**: For the text with English translation and commentary of Heron's *Bel.,* see Marsden, *Treatises,* 18–60.

24 **ζητητικωτέροις**: Cf. Proclus, *In primum Euclidis librum commentarius* 227:6–8: καὶ γὰρ ἀπὸ τούτων δυνατὸν καὶ περὶ τὰς ἄλλας γυμνάσασθαι τοῖς ζητητικωτέροις.

25–26 **αἱ . . . διάμετροι**: On the calculation of the diameters see Heron, *Bel.* 114–16, and Marsden, *Treatises,* 58–60.

26–27 **οἵ . . . κύλινδροι**: = Heron, *Bel.* 115:5–6. On the springs as "cylinders" and the calculation, see Marsden, *Treatises,* 58–60, esp. n. 44.

28 **πολυθρύλητος τοῦ κύβου διπλασιασμός**: On this method of calculating catapult dimensions for specific sizes of projectile, see Marsden, *Treatises,* 58–60 nn. 40–44, and W. R. Knorr, *Studies in Ancient and Medieval Geometry* (Boston, 1989), chaps. 1 and 3.

32 **Ἥρωνι**: On Heron of Alexandria see below on **50:2–3**.

Chapter 46. Ladder on Wheels with Drop-Bridge

The device has no clear precedent in the extant classical sources and may be a Byzantine adaptation (cf. Dain, *Tradition,* 16 n. 2). For wheeled ladders in ancient Egypt, however, see Garlan, *Recherches,* 137 n. 2. It is illustrated on folio 34r.

1 ὑπότροχος: For wheeled ladders see *Miracula Demetrii* 186:27: ὑποτρόχους κλίμακας in a list of siege devices, but not otherwise described, and Leo, *Taktika* XV:32: Καὶ σκάλαι σύνθετοι ἢ ἐπιτεθεῖσαι τῷ τείχει, ἢ ἐν ὀρθοῖς ξύλοις ἐπικείμεναι, καὶ διὰ τροχῶν προσφερόμεναι; and Appendix, 54 (PG 1117B): καὶ αἱ κλίμακες προσαγέσθωσαν ξύλοις ὀρθίοις ἐπικείμεναι καὶ διὰ τροχῶν τοῖς τείχεσι προσπελάζουσαι. There is no indication that these had a drop-bridge connected.

3 ἐπιβάθρας: On the terms ἐπιβάθρα and διαβάθρα, which the Anon. Byz. uses interchangeably, particularly in this chapter, see above on **2:11**.

4 ἀπὸ τόρνου: Cf. Heron, *Pneumatica* I:16:28: ἄξων . . . ἀπὸ τόρνου εἰργασμένος. See above on **44:25**.

8 συμμέτρως: See above, chap. **38** introduction.

8 μαγγάνων: Used specifically of a pulley in Heron, *Bel.* 84:10–11: τὸ μὲν ἓν μάγγανον τοῦ πολυσπάστου.

9 πολυσπάστων: On the compound pulley see Drachmann, *Technology,* 52–53 (translating and commenting on Heron, *Mechanics* II:3); Callebat and Fleury, *Vitruve,* 102–3; and Landels, *Engineering,* 85–89. The illustration of the pulleys on folio 34r shows them attached at approximately the middle of the sides of the drop-bridge, with ropes going directly down to men on the ground and thus no fixed point against which to pull.

9 καρείων: Wescher in his note *ad loc.* suggests comparing "κάροια (τὰ), quod inter nomina instrumentorum navalium recensetur a Leone Imp. in Tactic. cap. XIX:5." Sophocles, *Lexicon,* for κάροιον, gives "incorrect for κάρυον," that is, "*nut,* . . . 2. *almond,* . . . 3. *pulley,* particularly, *the block*" (citing the passage in Leo for the last meaning). Leo's text reads κάροια, καὶ τὰ ἄρμενα δὲ αὐτῶν ("blocks and their tackle"). Cf. *Scholia in Lucianum* 73:4:1: ⟨κεροιάκων⟩ τὰ νῦν κάροια λεγόμενα παρὰ τοῖς ναυτικοῖς, ἃ καὶ κρίκους καλοῦσιν οἱ παλαιοί.

11 τροχίλων: Sheaves or wheels in a pulley block; cf. Heron, *Bel.* 85: οἱ μὲν ἐν τῷ ἑνὶ μαγγάνῳ αὐτοῦ τρόχιλοι.

12 **Κωλυμάτια**: "Catch, clutch, stop." The term occurs in 5 instances in Heron's *Pneumatica*, for example, 2:15:9: τρῆμα τοῦ σωλῆνος καὶ ἀνεχόμενον ὑπὸ περονίων κωλυμάτια ἐχόντων πρὸς τὸ μηκέτι ἐκπίπτειν τὸ πλατυσμάτιον. The illustration on folio 34r shows the two side beams of the drop-bridge extended such that they would be stopped by the first rung of the lower ladder.

16 **μονόξυλος**: The term is used in Apollod. (161:7) of battering rams (followed by the Anon. Byz. at **2:6** and **21:3**). The use here of ladder legs appears to be due to the Anon. Byz. himself.

21 **προειρημένων**: Apparently a reference to a section lost in the lacuna following **39:36**.

32–33 **πέντε ... ὁμοψύχως**: For the Anon. Byz.'s interest in the psychological value of more than one soldier working together, see above, **43:4–5**.

34 **Περιφραγαί**: See above on **41:3**.

37–39 **πασσάλοις ... σχοινίοις**: On the use of ropes tied to stakes in the ground to secure ladders and towers, see above, **27:86–91** and **34:13–19** (both taken from Apollod.).

43 **προθυμότεροι ... εὐτολμότεροι**: The Anon. Byz.'s own comment; see on **43:4–5**.

Chapter 47. Drop-Bridge on Filler-Tortoise

The Anon. Byz. draws some material here from Philo Mech. (97:30–34 and 99:27); however, the addition of a drop-bridge to the filler-tortoise does not appear in extant classical sources (so Dain, *Tradition,* 16 n. 2). The device is illustrated on folio 35r.

2 **διαβάθρα**: See above on **2:11**.

2–3 **ἀδυνατῶμεν ... μεστάς**: Cf. Philo Mech. 97:30–34: Ἐὰν δὲ μὴ δύνῃ χῶσαι διὰ τὸ βαθείας καὶ εὐρείας εἶναι, χελώνην δεῖ προθέμενον χωστρίδα σχεδίαν ζευγνύοντα προσαγαγεῖν οὗ βούλεται τοὺς στρατιώτας. The Anon. Byz. here adds the cross-bridge on a filler-tortoise to the first half of Philo Mech.'s sentence, then continues with Philo Mech.'s solution in chap. 48.

4 ὡς ἐμάθομεν: See above, **46**:4–5.

5 χωστρίδος: Cf. above on **2**:2.

5–7 ὑπὸ σχοινίων ... πολυσπάστων: See above on **46**:9.

12 εὐπροθύμως: For the adverb see Sophocles, *Lexicon,* and Demetrakos, *Lexikon;* see also below, **55**:22. For the Anon. Byz.'s interest in battle psychology, see above, **43**:4–5.

13 λαισῶν: See above on **2**:4.

14 τέφρᾳ αἵματι ἀναμεμιγμένῃ: Cf. Philo Mech. 99:27: τῷ αἵματι τέφραν μίξαντα ἀλείφειν τὰ ξύλα (against fire).

15 πυροβόλα: See above on **2**:9.

15–16 τὰ ... ὑγρά: See above, **17**:5–6.

17 προδέδεικται: See above, **13**:32–33.

Chapter 48. Filler-Tortoises on Rafts

The Anon. Byz. here draws on and combines Philo Mech. 97:32–33 and 102:19–27, where Philo Mech. describes the use of iron spikes, pointed and hardened, driven into the crevices in stone or joints in brick walls with hammers by the climbers; iron hooks on knotted ropes thrown to the battlements; and the use of this technique by Egyptians. The device and technique are illustrated on folio 35v. For a Byzantine example of such climbing methods using spikes, see Theo. Sim. II:18:16: τὸν μὲν ἕνα σκόλοπα ἐνείρας τῷ πύργῳ ἀνὰ τὰς ἁρμογὰς τοῦ οἰκοδομήματος ... ἐπιβαίνει ἐπὶ τοῦ σκόλοπος τῷ ποδί, εἶτα τὸν ἕτερον αὖθις ὥσπερ ἐγκεντρίσας σκόλοπα, τὸν λειπόμενον τοῖν ποδοῖν ἐπερείδει.

1 ⟨Ο⟩ἰ δὲ περί: On the usage with personal names see above on **25**:1.

1 Βυζάντιον: On the Anon. Byz.'s designations of Philo Mech. as "Athenian" and "of Byzantium," see above on **12**:2.

2 χωστρίδας: See above on **2**:2.

2 σχεδίας: The accompanying illustration shows a boxlike structure in front of the tortoise. Rochas D'Aiglun, who translates "munies de radeaux," suggests (191 n. 1) that it is a raft "sur lequel on a établi un

fortin en charpente." The term is used of a *raft* by Apollod. (189:4, etc.), followed by the Anon. Byz. (chaps. 55–57). Garlan, *Recherches,* translates the text of Philo Mech. here: "une tortue de terrassiers reliée à une passerelle"; Lawrence, *Fortification,* 101: "to put forward a filling-mantlet and (from its protection) join up a gangway (across which) to move the soldiers forward where desired." The illustration and context suggests that the Anon. Byz. interpreted the passage as referring to a raft on which the tortoise was transported to the wall over the ditch.

5 συμφύσεις: Philo Mech. has διαφύσεις, which may be the preferable reading here (Rochas D'Aiglun adopts it).

7 σφύραις: The term is from Philo Mech. Leo, *Taktika,* VI:27, includes the σφῦρα in a list of equipment for infantry. See also Bryer, "Implements," 66, "a plain wooden two-headed mallet," with illustrations on 61, 62, and 64. It is illustrated here on folio 35v.

8 σχοινίων . . . δικτύοις: For Philo Mech.'s καλωδίων ⟨πρὸς τὰς ἐπάλξεις⟩ ἐπιρριπτοῦνται ἄμματα ἐχόντων. Wescher (260 n. 11) comments, "Haec ex Philone Byzantio confuse excerpta sunt, ita ut sensus non appareat." Earlier in chap. 12, following Philo Mech., the Anon. Byz. described δικτυωταὶ οὖσαι ὡς τὰ λεγόμενα σάρκινα· εἰς δὲ τὰ ἄκρα αὐτῶν ἄγκιστρα προσβάλλονται, ἵνα ἀπὸ τῶν προϋποτεθέντων δερματίνων ἐπιρριπτόμενα ἐπιλαμβάνηται τῶν προμαχώνων καὶ οὕτως τὴν ἐπὶ τὸ τεῖχος ἀνάβασιν τοῖς βουλομένοις διευθετίζωσι. The text here may be corrupt.

10–13 τοιαύτη . . . εἰώθασιν: For Philo Mech.'s καθάπερ Αἰγύπτιοι ποιοῦσιν αὐτό.

Chapter 49. Protection of Ladders and Drop-Bridges, Handheld Swivel Tube Incendiaries

The Anon. Byz. draws here on Philo Mech. (95:39–44) for protection against nets thrown from the wall onto scaling ladders and drop-bridges. The section on the nail-studded triangle on the front of a drop-bridge is not found in extant classical sources, and the handheld swivel tube is clearly a contemporary Byzantine device. The drop-bridge and swivel tube are illustrated on folio 36r.

2 ἐπιβάθραις: See above on **2:11**.

3 ἐκ λίνου: The phrase is from Philo Mech. On use of flax/linen for netting see above, **12**:19, and at **44**:35 for use in catapult windings.

3 ἀμφίβληστρα: The term is Philo Mech.'s.

7–8 ἀγκυρωτῶν δοκίδων: Cf. Philo Mech. 85:37–38: αἱ ἀγκυρωτοὶ δοκίδες καὶ οἱ χηλωτοὶ κοπεῖς πρὸς τὸ κωλύειν καὶ ἐκτραχηλίζειν τὰς προστιθεμένας κλίμακας.

8 ἀνωτέρω: Presumably in the lacuna preceding chap. 40 (so Wescher, 261 n. 10). For stones thrown against rams see above on **2**:8–9.

12 πρὸς ὄνυχα: See above, **13**:13.

19 ἀνεπηρέαστοι: The Anon. Byz.'s own comment. For his interest in security and welfare of troops, see above on **43**:4–5.

20 στρεπτῶν ἐγχειριδίων πυροβόλων: On the handheld device for ejecting Greek fire see J. Haldon and M. Byrne, "A Possible Solution to the Problem of Greek Fire," *BZ* 70 (1977), 91–99, esp. 93 nn. 6–7 for use of τὰ στρεπτά (swivel tubes) in Byzantine sources. On the recent development of the handheld version see Leo, *Taktika* XIX:57: Χρήσασθαι δὲ καὶ τῇ ἄλλῃ μεθόδῳ τῶν διὰ χειρὸς βαλλομένων μικρῶν σιφώνων ὄπισθεν τῶν σιδηρῶν σκουταρίων παρὰ τῶν στρατιωτῶν κρατουμένων , ἅπερ χειροσίφωνα λέγεται, παρὰ τῆς ἡμῶν βασιλείας ἄρτι κατεσκευασμένα. Ῥίψουσι γὰρ καὶ αὐτὰ τοῦ ἐσκευασμένου πυρὸς κατὰ τῶν προσώπων τῶν πολεμίων. Haldon and Byrne note that the σίφων is specifically the pump, the στρεπτόν the swivel tube, but that either is also used of the whole device. The passage and illustration (folio 36r) provide little specific information on how the device worked; on the secrecy surrounding "Greek fire," see A. Roland, "Secrecy, Technology, and War: Greek Fire and the Defense of Byzantium, 678–1204," *Technology and Culture* 33.4 (1992), 655–79. See also on the passage R. J. Forbes, *More Studies in Early Petroleum History* (Leiden, 1959), 87. Dain's comment *(Tradition,* 16 n. 2) on πυροβόλον, "Héron ne dit rien qui ne se trouve dans Apollodore: ce qui est nouveau c'est la vignette," would seem to miss the point of στρεπτῶν ἐγχειριδίων, a phrase not in the Anon. Byz.'s source.

22 πτοήσουσιν: For the Anon. Byz.'s interest in battle psychology see above on **43**:4–5.

Chapter 50. Ctesibius' Land-Based Tube

The Anon. Byz. here draws and greatly elaborates on Ath. Mech. 29:9–31:2. For technical discussion of the device see Lendle, *Texte,* 113–16. It is illustrated on folio 38r. For another Byzantine illustration see Schneider, *Athenaios,* pl. III; for a modern drawing, see Lendle, *Texte,* 116. The Anon. Byz. omits Ath. Mech.'s skeptical concluding comment: Γενναίου δὲ τοῦτο ἄξιον οὐθενός, ἀλλ᾽ ἐκ θαυμάτων τὸ μηχάνημα συγκείμενον καὶ μάλιστα τεχνίτην τὸ θαυμάσαι, on which compare Vitruvius, who omits this device in his discussion of Ctesibius' inventions, X:vii:5: "Reliqua, quae non sunt ad necessitatem sed ad deliciarum voluntatem, qui cupidiores erunt eius subtilitatis, ex ipsius Ctesibii commentariis poterunt invenire." It was apparently the only siege device described by Ctesibius.

2 Ἀσκρηνός: The designation is only found in Ath. Mech. and here, where the Anon. Byz. follows Ath. Mech.; Ctesibius was apparently from Alexandria (see *RE* XI:2074–76).

2 Κτησίβιος: One of the most famous engineers of antiquity, most likely active under Ptolemy II Philadelphus, not long after 270 B.C. See Marsden, *Treatises,* 6–9; idem, *Development,* 62; Lendle, *Texte,* 113 n. 122; and *RE* XI:2:2074–76.

2–3 ὁ . . . καθηγητής: The Anon. Byz. here replaces Ath. Mech.'s designation of Ctesibius as ὁ ἐν Ἀλεξανδρείᾳ μηχανικός. Heron of Alexandria is now dated to approximately the third quarter of the 1st century A.D. (see P. Keyser, *Classical Philology* 83 [1988], 218–20). The Anon. Byz. is either unaware of the correct date or refers to Heron's use of Ctesibius, esp. in his *Bel.,* which is titled Ἥρωνος Κτησιβίου Βελοποιϊκά (on the relation between Heron and Ctesibius, see Marsden, *Treatises,* 1–2, who renders the title of Heron's work "Heron's edition of Ctesibius' *Construction of Artillery*").

3 Ὑπομνήμασι: On the title, which is found in Ath. Mech., of Ctesibius' lost work see Marsden, *Treatises,* 1 and n. 2 with additional bibliography. Cf. also Vitruvius X:vii:5: "ex ipsius Ctesibii commentariis."

4 φησιν Ἀθηναῖος: Ath. Mech. himself quotes Ctesibius with φησι.

5 τετράτροχον For Ath. Mech.'s (Ctesibius') τετράκυκλον.

5–6 περισκεπῆ πάντοθεν οὖσαν: The Anon. Byz. adds.

6 ἢ κριοφόρον χελώνην: The Anon. Byz. adds.

8 ἑτεροπλατές: For Ath. Mech.'s (Ctesibius') τετράγωνον.

9 ἐκκοπάς: For two possible forms of the upright beam-tops and the cut ends of the cross bar on which the tube rests, see Lendle, *Texte*, 114–15 with illustration.

10 αὐλόν: For σύριγγα in Ath. Mech.

10 ἐπικείμενον: Ath. Mech. (Ctesibius) speaks of the tube as κηλωνευομένην, a term that the Anon. Byz. avoids; see also above on Apollod.'s κηλώνια at **27**:30–31.

10–14 σωληνοειδῆ ... περιπεφραγμένον: The Anon. Byz. adds, perhaps influenced by and elaborating on Ath. Mech. (36:5–6): σύριγξι καμαρικαῖς.

14 ἔνοπλον: The Anon. Byz. adds. See on **43**:4–5.

18 τὸ ... ἀναχθήσεται: For Ath. Mech.'s κηλωνεύεσθαι δὲ τὴν σύριγγα. See above on **50**:10 (ἐπικείμενον).

19 σιδηραῖς ἁλύσεσι: The Anon. Byz. adds.

22 τετρατρόχου: For Ath. Mech.'s (Ctesibius') τετρακύκλου.

22 ἀμάξης: The Anon. Byz. adds.

23 κατέμπροσθεν: The Anon. Byz. adds.

24 ἔνοπλον: The Anon. Byz. adds. See on **43**:4–5.

24–25 ὁμοίως ... ἔχοντας: The Anon. Byz. adds. For his interest in the psychological value of soldiers acting together, see above on **43**:4–5.

25–28 Ὑποζώννυται ... φυλάττηται: The Anon. Byz. adds.

27 δέρμασι διαβρόχοις: The Anon. Byz. adds; see above on **15**:18.

28 πυροφόρων: See above on **2**:9.

28–31 Μέτρα ... ἀνατιθέμενον: The Anon. Byz. elaborates on and interprets Ath. Mech.'s Μέτρα δὲ τούτων οὐ συντεταχέναι φαίνεται. See Lendle, *Texte,* 113 n. 123.

31–33 Ἔξεστι ... χρείαν: The Anon. Byz. adds, perhaps influenced by Ath. Mech. 19:1–2, where, however, it is the τεχνίτης rather than the ἀρχιτέκτων who is said to make the adaptation. See above on **1**:9.

32 συμμετρίαν: For the Anon. Byz.'s extensive use of the term, see chap. **38** introduction.

34 τοῖς εἰσαγομένοις: The Anon. Byz. adds; cf. *Geodesia,* 6:42–43 ἡμεῖς δέ, τοὺς εἰσαγομένους πρὸς τὰ μαθήματα ἐρεθίζειν βουλόμενοι.

Chapter 51. The Anon. Byz.'s Numerical Example for the Tube

As he notes at **50**:33–35 the Anon. Byz. here offers his own example of appropriate dimensions. For his other numerical examples see chaps. **27** and **35**.

18–19 σύμμετροι ... καὶ σύμφωνοι: See above on **38**:19.

28–29 ὡς ... λόγον: Similar phrasing is used above at **38**:18–19.

Chapter 52. Larger Land-based Landing Tube

The concept of a tube wide enough for pairs of armed men, the use of realistic representation to terrify the enemy, and the different ways to compensate for the position of the tube vis-à-vis the wall are not found in the extant classical sources and are apparently the Anon. Byz.'s own addition (cf. Dain, *Tradition,* 16 n. 2). The tube is illustrated on folio 38v.

4 ἐνόπλους: The Anon. Byz. adds.

6–10 καταπληκτικαὶ ... πτοηθέντες: The Anon. Byz.'s own comment. For his interest in battle psychology, see above on **43**:4–5.

8 δράκοντος ... λέοντος: For animal figureheads of ships which create fear by appearance and breathe fire, see Anna Comnena, *Alexiad* XI:10:2: ἐν ἑκάστῃ πρώρᾳ τῶν πλοίων διὰ χαλκῶν καὶ σιδήρων λεόντων καὶ ἀλλοίων χερσαίων ζῴων κεφαλὰς μετὰ στομάτων ἀνεῳγμένων

κατασκευάσας, χρυσῷ τε περιστείλας αὐτὰ ὡς ἐκ μόνης θέας φοβερὸν φαίνεσθαι, τὸ διὰ τῶν στρεπτῶν κατὰ τῶν πολεμίων μέλλον ἀφίεσθαι πῦρ διὰ τῶν στομάτων αὐτῶν παρεσκεύασε διιέναι, ὥστε δοκεῖν τοὺς λέοντας καὶ τἆλλα τῶν τοιούτων ζῴων τοῦτο ἐξερεύγεσθαι.

8 πυροφόρον: That is, Greek fire would be emitted through the mouths of the figureheads.

11 ἀπὸ . . . ἐκφύγωσιν: Cf. above 4:14–15.

Chapter 53. Siege Machines on Ships

The Anon. Byz. draws here on Ath. Mech. 27:7–28:6 and 31:3–33:2, but with significant interpretative additions. A slightly different account of the siege of Chios appears at Vitruvius, X:16:9. For discussion see Lendle, *Texte,* 156–60.

1 ἀγομένας: The Anon. Byz. adds.

1 φησιν ὁ ᾿Αθηναῖος: The Anon. Byz. adds.

2 σαμβύκας: For discussion of different devices so named see Marsden, *Treatises,* 90–94; Lendle, *Texte,* 107–13; F. W. Walbank, *A Historical Commentary on Polybius* (Oxford, 1967), II:72 n. 2; and Callebat and Fleury, *Vitruve,* 286 n. 9.2. The *De obsid.* 80:1ff also describes a *sambuca* following Polybius VIII:4.

2 καλοῦσιν: For Ath. Mech.'s προσαγορεύουσιν.

2–3 ἐκ μεταφορᾶς . . . ὀργάνων: The Anon. Byz. adds. The comparison of the device to the triangular harplike musical instrument is not in Ath. Mech.; it is found in Polybius, VIII:4:11, Vegetius, IV:21, Andreas of Panormus (F. Jacoby, *Die Fragmente der griechische Historiker* [Berlin, 1923, repr. Leiden, 1957], no. 571 F1), and in *De obsid.* 81:5–6, following Polybius. For discussion of the analogy see F. W. Walbank, *A Historical Commentary on Polybius* (Oxford, 1967), II:73–74 n. 11, and J. G. Landels, "Ship Shape and Sambuca Fashion," *Journal of Hellenic Studies* 86 (1966), 69ff.

3–4 ἐμφερεῖς . . . αὐλῷ: The Anon. Byz. adds. Cf. above, **50:**11, καμαροειδέσι ξύλοις.

5 καὶ φανεράς: The Anon. Byz. adds.

6 παραλόγως καὶ ἀσυμμέτρως: For Ath. Mech.'s κακῶς. For the Anon. Byz.'s interest in commensurability see chap. **38** introduction.

7 Χίον: The siege, mentioned by Ath. Mech. and Vitruvius (X:16:9), is not otherwise known. For a list of the possibilities see Callebat and Fleury, *Vitruve,* 286 n. 16:9:1.

8 εἰκαστικῶς τοῦ σκοποῦ: The Anon. Byz. adds. See *Geodesia* **1**:8–13, where that treatise is justified by reference to those who have failed to estimate correctly the necessary height of siege engines, etc. and reference is made to this passage: ὡς καὶ ἐν τῷ πρὸ τούτου δεδήλωται συντάγματι.

11 ἐκ τοῦ ὕψους: The Anon. Byz. adds.

12 εἰ δὲ μή : From Ath. Mech. Rochas D'Aiglun, "Athénée," 793 n. 4 considered the passage in Ath. Mech. corrupt. See, however, on the use of εἰ δὲ μή even when the preceding clause is negative and one might expect εἰ δέ, H. W. Smyth, *Greek Grammar* (Cambridge, 1963), 2346(d).

12 ἔξω βάρους: The phrase is from Ath. Mech. For the Anon. Byz.'s interest in the topic see *Geodesia* **8**.

13 ἄνωθεν ἐπικειμένου: The Anon. Byz. adds.

14 τῆς ὀπτικῆς ... πραγματείας: Ath. Mech. has τῶν ὀπτικῶν. Cf. Heron, *Dioptra* II:18–19: παραλογισθέντες τῇ ἀναμετρήσει τῶν τειχῶν διὰ τὸ ἀπείρους εἶναι τῆς διοπτρικῆς πραγματείας, and see below on *Geodesia* **1**:4. Biton (ed. Marsden, sections 52–53) comments: δεῖ δέ σε προειδέναι ὅτι πρὸς τὰς προσβολὰς τῶν τειχῶν καὶ τὰ μεγέθη τῶν ἐλεπόλεων δεῖ κατασκευάζειν, καὶ ὑπεραίρειν τοῖς μεγέθεσι τὰς ἐλεπόλεις. ἔστι δὲ καὶ τοῦτο μεθοδικὴ θεωρία , ἣν διείλεγμαι ἐν τοῖς Ὀπτικοῖς · ἔγκειται γάρ μοι τὸ γένος τοῦ διοπτρικοῦ. Cf. Anna Comnena, *Alexiad* XIII:3:9: Ὀπτικὴν δὲ ἄρα τὴν ἐπιστήμην ἐπλούτουν, ὡς ἔοικεν, οἱ τὸ Δυρράχιον πολιορκοῦντες βάρβαροι. Οὐ γὰρ ἄνευ τοιαύτης δυνάμεως τὰ ὕψη τῶν τειχῶν κατελάμβανον · εἰ δὲ μὴ ὀπτικῆς, ἀλλά γε τῆς ἀπὸ τῶν διοπτρῶν καταλήψεως. See also Leo diac. (82:1–2) on the siege of Antioch: κλίμακάς τε ἀναλόγους τῷ ὕψει τῶν πύργων

τεκτήνασθαι.

15 **καὶ ὅτι** ... : The Anon. Byz. jumps here from Ath. Mech. 28:6 to 32:3.

16 **ἀρχιτεκτόνων**: The term is from Ath. Mech.; see above on **1**:9.

17 **δυσὶ πλοίοις**: For Ath. Mech.'s ὁλκάσι.

17 **πρὸς ὕψος τιθέασι**: The Anon. Byz. adds.

17 **τὸ μηχάνημα**: For Ath. Mech.'s μηχανήματα: the precise nature of the siege devices that Ath. Mech. has in mind here (later called μικρὰς ἐλεπόλεις) is not clear. Lendle, *Texte,* 157–58, reviews the evidence and concludes that they were "leichte Türme mit einer geschützten Plattform ... die dem Angreifer eine überhöhte Position verschaffen sollte." He further suggests that they would be wooden structures with ladders for climbing to upper platforms protected by breastworks, erected with the aid of pulleys just before reaching the walls. For the Anon. Byz.'s interpretation see below at **53**:38–39.

19 **ἐναντίου**: The Anon. Byz. adds.

19 **ἀνέμου**: For examples of yoked ships with siege engines damaged by winds, see Nik. Chon., *Hist.* 38:8–12, and John Kinnamos, *Epitome,* ed. A. Meineke (Bonn, 1836), 22:18–21.

20–22 **ἀναδύνει** ... **μηχάνημα**: For Ath. Mech.'s ἀναπολάζει τὸ ἐπηρεισμένον μηχάνημα.

21 **τὰ πλοῖα**: For Ath. Mech.'s τῶν σκαφῶν.

23–24 **ἀλλὰ** ... **καταδύσει**: The Anon. Byz. adds.

24 **σπαρασσόμενα**: The Anon. Byz. adds.

26 **ἀνθελκόμενα**: The Anon. Byz. adds.

26–27 **εὐτολμίαν μᾶλλον**: The Anon. Byz. adds.

27–30 **Καὶ ἐπείπερ** ... **πεφιλοτιμήμεθα**: The Anon. Byz. draws this sentence with some modification from Ath. Mech. 31:12–32:2. Given the length of the indirect statement, it leaves the impression that the Anon. Byz. himself is the inventor of the πιθήκιον. Schneider, *Athenaios,* 6 and 65 n. 32:1, followed by Lendle, *Texte,* 156, suggested that Ath.

Mech. himself may not be its inventor, but may also be drawing on his own source (Agesistratus).

28 ἀνθρωπίνην: The Anon. Byz. adds.

30 τῶν ... συντεινόντων: The Anon. Byz. adds.

30–31 πρὸς ... ὑποστήριξιν: The Anon. Byz. adds.

31–32 κατὰ μέσον ... πλοίων: For Ath. Mech.'s ἐν τῇ ἐσχάρῃ τῇ ἐπερειδομένῃ ταῖς ὁλκάσιν ... μέσον.

32 πιθήκιον: The term is from Ath. Mech. For a detailed attempt to reconstruct the device, see Lendle, *Texte,* 156–60, who views it (159) as a net with weights, tied at the four corners of the tower base "wie ein Affe, der sich mit Händen und Füssen anklammert und rücklings von oben herabhängen lässt." Rochas D'Aiglun, "Athénée," 795 n. 3, suggests a connection to πίθος.

33–35 βάρος ... θαλασσίου: The Anon. Byz. adds, offering his interpretation of the device. Lendle, *Texte,* 158, comments: "Der Anonymus denkt also offenbar an eine kardanische Aufhängung," that is, a gimbal suspension. Notably the illustration on folio 40r does not appear to follow the verbal description; it has a human bust attached by chains *on top of the deck* joining the ships. The illustrator apparently saw it as a weight that could be moved along the deck to the side that was riding up.

35–36 κλονοῦντος τὰ πλοῖα The Anon. Byz. adds.

36 ἀπαράπτωτον: The Anon. Byz. adds; see above, **2**:12–13.

36 διασώζηται: For Ath. Mech.'s μένῃ.

37 τὰ ἐμπαράσκευα: The term is from Ath. Mech., for which LSJ gives "windscreens." For a discussion of possible meanings see Lendle, *Texte,* 159–60, who concludes: "Eher ist an eine Ableitung von τὰ σκεύη zu denken, womit Schiffsgerät allgemein, insbesondere das Takelwerk, bezeichnet wird. Da Pollux in seiner Zusammenstellung von Begriffen aus dem Schiffswesen das ἐμπαράσκευον nicht erwähnt und sich auch sonst keine Hinweise finden, muss die Bedeutung der Vorrichtung

dunkel bleiben. Von der Sache her möchte man am ehesten an eine Tauverspannung denken."

37 **ἐξ ἑτοίμου**: The Anon. Byz. apparently adds, although Schneider suggests that it may be a gloss on ἐμπαράσκευα.

37 **ἑλεπόλεις**: The term is from Ath. Mech. In classical usage it referred initially to siege towers, usually portable towers on land. Ath. Mech. apparently uses it of towers on ships; see above on **53:17**. At *Geodesia* **1**:5, ἰσοστασίους ἑλεπόλεις τοῖς τείχεσι, the Anon. Byz. uses it specifically of portable towers. Byzantine usage included under the term other siege devices such as battering rams (e.g., Leo diac. 25:13) and stone throwers (cf. Nik. Chon., *Hist.* 38:6–7: ὅθεν ἁλιάδας καὶ ἀκάτια σχεδιάσας καὶ ζεῦγμα διὰ τούτων ἐργασάμενος τὰς ἑλεπόλεις ἐπέστησεν ἄνωθεν). On the term generally see *RE* VII:2:2489; Marsden, *Treatises,* 84ff; and Callebat and Fleury, *Vitruve,* 281 n. 3.6.

38–39 **ὡς θωράκιά . . . ἐπιβατήρια**: The Anon. Byz. adds. Lendle, *Texte,* 158, comments: "Ersichtlich denkt der Anonymus bei der zweiten Kategorie an sambykenähnliche Maschinen, vermutlich zu Unrecht." See above on **53:17** for Lendle's view of Ath. Mech.'s *helepoleis.* The illustrations on folios 39v and the top of 40r show two ships joined by platforms, on which are mounted upright posts with joining crossbeams carrying in one case a drop-bridge, in the other a ram with rails (on which see above, **41:3**), both with a soldier depicted moving across them and both with pulleys and ropes attached; these would appear to be what the Anon. Byz. means here by ἐπιβατήρια. The term is used by Josephus (*Bellum Judaicum* III:252, 254) as an adjective with μηχαναί to refer to gangways. While defensive breastworks are not shown, cf. Polybius' description of preparing each side of the ladders of the *sambuca* (VIII:4:4): δρυφακτώσαντες καὶ σκεπάσαντες ὑπερπετέσι θωρακίοις.

39–40 **κατὰ . . . εὐπρόχειρα**: The Anon. Byz. adds. On the Anon. Byz.'s interest in commensurability see chap. **38** introduction; for εὐπρόχειρος see Koumanoudes, *Synagoge,* 136, citing only this passage.

41 **σχοινίων ἤ**: The Anon. Byz. adds.

41 **προρρηθέντων πολυσπάστων**: The reference to the compound

pulley here is taken from Ath. Mech. (33:3). On its nature see above on **46**:9. The pulleys are illustrated on folio 40r.

43 ὁδοποιοῦντα ἐπίβασιν: The Anon. Byz. adds.

Chapter 54. Mounting the Tubes on Shafts

The Anon. Byz. draws here on Ath. Mech. 35:4–37:2 (for the *carchesion*, the crane and the six movements) and Biton, 57–61 (for the bracket, capstan, and citation of Damis of Colophon). For discussion see Marsden, *Treatises*, 94–97, and Lendle, *Texte*, 107-9. The *carchesion* with mounted tube is illustrated on the lower left, the bracket on the screw shaft on the lower right of folio 40r.

4 ὡς προδέδεικται: See above, **50**:6ff.

5 καρχησίου: The term is from Ath. Mech., whose description reads: Παγήσεται δὲ ἐπὶ τῆς κριοφόρου χελώνης· οὗ τὰ μὲν σιαγόνια ἔσονται μελέϊνα, δεδεμένα λεπίσι ψυχρηλάτοις, ἵνα ἐν ἄξονι ἐμβάλλωνται χαλκῷ σταθμὸν . . . . Καὶ εἰς ταῦτα ἄξων ἐναρμόζεται σιδηροῦς. Two *carchesia* are illustrated on folio 40r. Marsden, *Treatises*, 51 n. 24 (on Heron's use of the term at *Bel.* 88) translates it as "universal joint," describing it as a mechanism that "allow<s> turning to take place simultaneously in both the horizontal and vertical planes." See also Landels, *Engineering*, 97–98, with modern drawing and O. Lendle, "Das Karchesion. Gerät am Masttopp, Trinkgefäss, Drehkipp-Gelenk," *Acta Classica* 32 (1997), 85–118. It allowed the movements described in the next sentence.

5–6 ἕξ . . . κινήσεις: The phrase is from Ath. Mech. For the six movements (forward, backward, up, down, and to each side), see above on **25**:25–26.

6 γέρανοι: The term is found in Ath. Mech. (36:3 and 11), who describes it as mounted on a *carchesion* and carrying vaulted tubes (σύριγξι καμαρικαῖς) covered with ox-hides, apparently similar to the tubes described above in chaps. **50** and **52**. See the lengthy note of Rochas D'Aiglun, "Athénée," 799–800 n. 1, who comments: "Il s'agit ici d'un engin d'escalade analogue à la machine de Ctésibios. La *grue* proprement dite est une longue passerelle recouverte d'arceaux et de cuirs frais.")

7 κατακλεῖδος: The term in this sense is found at Biton (59), εἶτα διὰ

τῆς κατακλεῖδος παρὰ τὸν κοχλίαν διώσθω σαμβύκη, to describe a double "bracket." See Marsden, *Treatises,* 94 n. 43, who comments:"It is a pity that Biton does not describe in more detail this vital part"; see also Marsden's suggested reconstruction (93, diagram 4c). The illustration on the lower left of folio 40r is apparently the Anon. Byz.'s or the illustrator's rendering of the bracket on the shaft.

7 **στύρακος**:The term is not used by Biton (who uses κοχλίας) and is apparently the Anon. Byz.'s substitution.The illustration (folio 40r, lower right) shows a *vertical* screw-shaft, and the Anon. Byz.'s description seems to require so translating. Biton's κοχλίας is interpreted by Marsden as a horizontal roller, by Schramm as a vertical screw (see Marsden, *Treatises,* 94 n. 41); for a different view see Lendle, *Texte,* 107–13. On the Anon. Byz.'s use of στύραξ see also *Geodesia* 7:11.

8 **ἐργάτου**: "Capstan"; see Biton (58–59): καὶ κατὰ τὰς βάσεις τοῦ κοχλίου ... ἔστω ἐργάτης, ὡς ἐπιστρέφειν τὸν κοχλίαν κατὰ τὰς ἐκτάσεις καὶ πάλιν εἰς τὸ ἐναντίον στρέφειν κατὰ τὰς ἐλαττώσεις. Marsden, *Treatises,* 94 n. 42 sees it as working in the vertical plane, while Schramm (cited by Marsden) saw it as horizontal.The device is not shown in the illustration.

9 **Δᾶμις ὁ Κολοφώνιος**:This engineer is not known apart from this reference and its source, Biton (58); see Marsden, *Treatises,* 94 n. 38.

10 **ὁ μηχανικὸς Βίτων**:See above, **1**:13; the citation is from Biton, 57–59. On the μηχανικός see above, **1**:9.

10–11 **ἐν τοῖς αὐτοῦ πολιορκητικοῖς ὑπομνήμασι**: apparently Biton's Κατασκευαὶ πολεμικῶν ὀργάνων καὶ καταπαλτικῶν (see above on **1**:13) which contains the only other reference to Damis of Colophon's *sambuca*.

12 **ἔκκειται**: Dain, *Tradition,* 31, notes that the quire of the manuscript in this section is a ternion rather then the expected quaternion. He raises the possibility that, given the abruptness of the transition between chaps. 54 and 55, a folio may be lost.The illustrations on folio 40r, however, do seem to appropriately reflect the text on folio 39v.

Chapter 55. Rafts as Bridges

The Anon. Byz. here draws on Apollod. 189:4–193:5, betraying no awareness of the criticism of this method of river crossing ("useful only for narrow rivers, and hence subject to enemy fire during construction," etc.), found in the mid-sixth-century ⟨Περὶ Στρατηγίας⟩ 19. For discussion of Apollod.'s text with modern drawings, see Lendle, *Texte*, 176–83; for the impracticality see Blyth, "Apollodorus," 142 and n. 34. The raft is illustrated on folios 41r and 42r.

2 καταστρωθήτω: For Apollod.'s καθηλούσθω.

3 ξυλοπυρίοις ἐμπησσομέναις: For Apollod.'s μὴ πεπηγυίαις ἥλοις συμφυέσιν. The fifteenth-century Latin translation of John Sophianos (on whom see Dain, *Tradition*, 35–40) has for the first term "clavis ligneis" (a phrase Sophianos also uses for ἥλοις ξυλίνοις just below); Schneider renders with "Holzknaggen" and comments "aufgenagelte Holzklammern, die nur lose über die Bretter greifen"; Barocius translates "clavis ligneis." *LSJRS*, taking the word to be an adjective, gives "ξυλοπύριος, ον, perh. *sharpened by fire*, σανίς," citing only this passage and apparently for the meaning following Demetrakos, *Lexikon,* on ξυλοπυρία. It seems preferable, though not certain, to take the word as a noun serving as the alternative to Apollod.'s recommendation not to use ἥλοις συμφυέσιν. Perhaps the term is related to ὁ πυρήν, "pit (of a fruit), eatable nut, knob."

4–5 ἀπελαύνηται . . . ῥηγνύηται: For Apollod.'s ἀπωσθῇ καὶ κατάσσηται.

5 τὰ . . . ξύλα: For τὰ μὲν πλεῖστα in Apollod., who mentions only σανίδες.

6 προσδεδεμένοις: The Anon. Byz. adds.

6 ξυλίνοις: The Anon. Byz. adds.

7–8 τὸ δὲ κατὰ πρόσωπον . . . σχεδίας: For Apollod.'s τὸ πρὸς τῷ ποταμῷ τῆς σχεδίας μέρος.

8–9 σὺν . . . πλαγίοις: The Anon. Byz. adds. The illustration on folio 41r shows the front wall and one side, as well as the top of the rampart on the second side, which is not directly represented due to the angle of view. The Anon. Byz. has apparently considered the possibility of the enemy shooting or attacking from the sides.

10 **κατὰ πῆξιν**: Paris. suppl. gr. 607 of Apollod. has here καταπήγων ὀρθίων ἐνεστώτων (with ὀρθίοις καταπῆξι below at Apollod. 190:1, where the Anon. Byz. uses ὀρθίοις ξύλοις), that is, ὁ καταπήξ = "post," while other mss. of Apollod. have καταπῆξιν. Dain, *Tradition,* 20–21 n. 1, suggests that the reading in Vat. gr. 1605 indicates that the Anon. Byz. was using a manuscript tradition of the poliorcetic corpus followed also by these other manuscripts, rather than that of Paris. suppl. gr. 607, although the reading in the Paris manuscript is the correct one. See also above on **25**:17.

10–12 **ξύλων ... πλαγίαις**: The Anon. Byz. adds. Apollod. states only that the rampart itself is "hinged" (γιγγλυμωτόν), but does not indicate specifically how. He does, however, indicate that the legs of the ladders behind the rampart are drilled and have round pins at either end, one end attached to the uprights and the other bound <by ropes> to the deck (κλίμακες ... τοὺς κάμακας ἑαυτῶν πεπερονημένους ἔχουσαι κατὰ τὰ ἄκρα ἑκάτερα στρογγύλαις περόναις, τὰ μὲν εἰς τὸ προτείχισμα τοῖς ὀρθίοις καταπῆξι τοῖς τοὺς γιγγλύμους ἔχουσι, τὰ δὲ ἐπὶ τὸ ἔδαφος προσδεδεμένα). The Anon. Byz. has apparently extrapolated this description to the idea of hinges at the bottom of the uprights as consisting of round holes with pins inserted into horizontal boards. How such pins could be attached so that the rampart would fold back on them is unclear. Barocius translates: "erectorum stantium lignorum, rotunda foramina inferius suscipientium, politisque clavis connexorum ad laterales tabulas extrinsecus confixas, quibus porro clavis extractis propugnaculum etiam una coincidit." The words "porro clavis extractis" go beyond the Greek text and suggest that Barocius apparently saw the uprights as attached with pins not parallel, but perpendicular. Schneider renders "senkrechten Balken, die unten Löcher haben, in die glatte Durchstecker eingreifen, aussen sind sie mit Querbrettern benagelt," apparently ignoring the preposition ἐπί. The text may be corrupt.

13 **ἔξωθεν**: The Anon. Byz. adds.

13–14 **ἵνα ... προτείχισμα**: The Anon. Byz. adds.

15 **δέρματα ἢ ῥάκη**: For Apollod.'s δέρρεις. On ῥάκη see on **13**:21.

15–16 **μικρὸν ... ἔξωθεν**: The Anon. Byz. adds.

16–17 **τοὺς ἄνωθεν μηρούς**: For Apollod.'s τοὺς κάμακας.

17–19 **πρὸς τοῖς ὀρθίοις … προσδεδεμένους**: For Apollod.'s ἔχουσαι κατὰ τὰ ἄκρα ἑκάτερα στρογγύλαις περόναις, τὰ μὲν εἰς τὸ προτείχισμα τοῖς ὀρθίοις καταπῆξι τοῖς τοὺς γιγγλύμους ἔχουσι, τὰ δὲ ἐπὶ τὸ ἔδαφος προσδεδεμένα.

19–21 **ἵνα … προτείχισμα**: For Apollod.'s ἵνα κρατῆται ὑπὸ διαγωνίων τῶν κλιμάκων ὁ τοῖχος οὗτος καὶ ὀρθὸς μένῃ.

22 **εὐπροθύμως ἀντιμαχήσονται**: For Apollod.'s διαμαχήσονται. For the Anon. Byz.'s interest in military psychology, see **43**:4–5.

23–24 **προπύργια … ἔχοντες**: For Apollod.'s ἐπάλξεις προκειμένας. On προπύργια see above, **40**:18.

25 **ἀνιστάμενον**: The Anon. Byz. adds.

25–26 **ἀλλὰ … ἔστω**: The Anon. Byz. adds.

26 **κατὰ τὴν προσβολήν**: The Anon. Byz. adds.

27 **ἵσταται**: For Apollod.'s μένῃ.

28–30 **πάσας … ἐπιθέντες**: For Apollod.'s πάσαις ἐνδόντες ταῖς κλίμαξιν ἐκ τῆς ἕδρας τοῦτο ποιήσομεν.

31 **τῇ γῇ**: The Anon. Byz. adds.

31 **μακρόθεν διὰ σχοινίων**: For Apollod.'s ἐν ἀπογείῳ. The illustration on folio 41r shows cables going from the raft back to stakes secured on the opposite bank.

32 **ἀποκρατοῦντες ἀσφαλισόμεθα**: For Apollod.'s κατασχόντες ἐκ τοῦ κάτωθεν μέρους τοῦ ποταμοῦ. Apollod.'s note that the raft is secured at the downstream end, which seems quite helpful here, is omitted by the Anon. Byz.

32–34 **καὶ ἐκ … ἄνωθεν**: For Apollod.'s ἐξωθοῦμεν ἀπὸ τῆς ὄχθης ἄνωθεν.

34 **ἀποκρατοῦντος αὐτήν**: The Anon. Byz. adds.

34 **σφηνός**: The term is from Apollod. The precise nature of the mechanism by which the raft is held is not clear, perhaps leading to the Anon.

Byz.'s addition (ἀποκρατοῦντος αὐτήν).

36 καταφορᾶς: For Apollod.'s ῥεύματος.

36 καθάπερ θύρα: The simile is from Apollod.

36 στρατεύματος: For Apollod.'s ὄχλου.

37 χεῖλος: For Apollod.'s ὄχθην.

38 τὸ ... πολεμίους: The Anon. Byz. adds.

40 ἀντιστρέφεσθαι: For Apollod.'s παρελθεῖν.

40–41 Τοῦ ... ἔνδοθεν: For Apollod.'s κατ' ἄκρον.

41 τρυπήματα: For Apollod.'s φρεατίαι.

41–42 πρὸς ... διερχόμενα: The Anon. Byz. adds. The illustration on folio 41r shows three stakes below the front wall of the raft. The Anon. Byz.'s addition here is to clarify that when the raft has reached the opposite shore and comes against it, the stakes are driven through holes just behind the rampart into the bank to secure it.

43 κρυφίως: For Apollod.'s λεληθότως.

Chapter 56. Raft Continued

1–3 ⟨Ἐ⟩πελθόντος ... προτειχίσματος: For Apollod.'s Δεθείσης τῆς σχεδίας ἐν τῇ πολεμίᾳ ἐξ ἄκρου.

3–4 ἐξ ἄκρου καί: The Anon. Byz. adds.

4 ἡ ... καταφορά: For Apollod.'s τὸ ῥεῦμα.

5 πλαγίαν ... ἐπιπέμπει: For Apollod.'s περιφέρει πλαγίαν ἑστῶσαν αὐτήν. For a diagram of the movements see Lendle, *Texte*, 180.

5–6 καὶ παρατίθησι ... ἐφαρμόζουσα: For Apollod.'s καὶ ὅλην παράλληλον τῇ ἑτέρᾳ ἀποδίδωσιν ὄχθῃ.

6–8 τοῦ πλήθους ... ἀντιπαράταξιν: For Apollod.'s ἀθρόως τοῦ πλήθους τεταγμένου ἑτοίμου.

9 ἑστῶτες: The Anon. Byz. adds.

9 τεθαρρηκότες ἀντιμαχήσονται: For Apollod.'s κατὰ κράτος μαχήσονται. For the Anon. Byz.'s interest in battle psychology, see above on **43**:4–5.

10 ἀποστρέψῃ: For Apollod.'s ἀπώσηται.

10–11 ἀπὸ τοῦ προτειχίσματος καταπλήττουσα: The Anon. Byz. adds; for his interest in battle psychology, see above on **43**:4–5.

12 δεσμά: For Apollod.'s ἄμματα.

12 πλαγιάζει: For Apollod.'s ὑπτιοῦται.

12 κατ' ὀλίγον: For Apollod.'s κατὰ μέρος.

13 δηλονότι: The Anon. Byz. adds.

13–14 καὶ ἐπιπιπτόντων τῷ καταστρώματι: The Anon. Byz. adds.

14–15 ὁδὸς ... προτειχίσματος: For Apollod.'s βαθμὸς τὸ μεσόχωρον πληρῶν.

16 διηνεκὴς ... ἔσται: For Apollod.'s εἰς τὸ διηνεκὲς τὸ πόδωμα ἔσται.

16 Τρυπάσθω: For Apollod.'s Διατετρήσθω.

16 κρυφίως: For Apollod.'s λεληθότως.

18 ἀκοντίζειν καὶ τοξεύειν: For Apollod.'s κόντους καὶ βέλη ἐπιφέρειν.

19 καὶ ἐκ ... μέρους: The Anon. Byz. adds.

20 πρόσωπον: For Apollod.'s μέτωπον.

21–22 πρὸς μόνην ... διαμάχεσθαι: For Apollod.'s μίαν ἔχουσι (i.e., "<enemy> having only one <rank>").

Chapter 57. Conclusion of the Raft

1 ὀρθογραφεῖται: The term is from Apollod. (193:1); on its technical nature and nontechnical use by the Anon. Byz. (the latter retained in the translation), see above on **27**:92. The accompanying illustration in Vat. gr. 1605, folio 42 shows an upright view of the front wall of the rampart with three ladders (not attached as described in the text) and

human faces behind it. For a modern elevation see Lendle, *Texte*, 182. The illustration of Apollod.'s text from Paris. suppl. gr. 607 is reproduced by Wescher, 191, and Schneider, *Apollodoros*, pl. xiii, fig. 48.

1 τὸ σχῆμα: The Anon. Byz. adds.

1 φανερά: For Apollod.'s πρόδηλος.

3–4 Τὴν ... θύρας: The Anon. Byz. adds.

4 ἐπὶ τῇ καταφορᾷ: The Anon. Byz. adds.

5 ἐπιπολύ: The Anon. Byz. adds.

6 προσκρούσῃ: The Anon. Byz. adds.

6–7 τὸ ἕτερον χεῖλος ... πολεμίους: For Apollod.'s τῇ πολεμίᾳ ὄχθῃ.

7 καὶ ἀναχαιτίζειν: The Anon. Byz. adds.

8 χείλους: For Apollod.'s ὄχθης.

8 ἀποκρατοῦντας: The Anon. Byz. adds.

8–11 τὴν δὲ τῶν σχοινίων ... ἐπιτεθήσεται: For Apollod.'s καὶ κατὰ μικρὸν ἀνιεμένους ἔχειν, ἵνα ἠρέμα συνέρχηται.

Chapter 58. Conclusion

The summary paragraph is basically the Anon. Byz.'s own conclusion, but for the last line, see Philo Mech.'s final sentence, 104:42–43: Τοῦτον ἄν τις τὸν τρόπον πολιορκῶν τὰς πόλεις ἂν λαμβάνοι μάλιστα μηθὲν αὐτὸς ἀνήκεστον παθών.

1 ἀναγραφήν: Cf. **2**:22, ἀναγράψαντες.

1 σχηματισμόν: On the Anon. Byz.'s use of the term, see above on **1**:39.

3 ἐξάρχοντες: See above on **4**:2.

7 ἀνάκτων Ῥώμης: On the plural see above on αὐτοκρατόρων, **4**:3.

8 Ἄγαρ: For Hagar, mother of Ishmael, regarded as the forefather of the Arabs, see Genesis 16:15. For the common equation Agarenes = Saracens, see Jerome, *In Hiezechielem* 8:25, 1/7. For the tenth century

see, for example *De velitatione* (ed. Dennis, *Treatises*), 198:11 with n.; Dagron, *Traité,* 2 n. 2; and Nikephoros Phokas, *Praecepta militaria* I:74 with McGeer's note.

9 **θεολέστων**: The word occurs three times in the *De cer.* (514:5 and 9, 651:15) in the phrase κατὰ τῆς θεολέστου Κρήτης (on the expedition of 911 under Himerios) and in the Δημηγορία Κωνσταντίνου βασιλέως πρὸς τοὺς τῆς ἀνατολῆς στρατηγούς (ed. R. Vári, "Zum historischen Exzerptenwerke des Konstantinos Porphyrogennetos," *BZ* 17 (1908), 75–85, 5:13: κατὰ τῶν χωρῶν καὶ κάστρων τῆς θεολέστου Ταρσοῦ). Theoph., I:499:21, ὑπὸ τοῦ θεολέστου αὐτῶν ἔθνους, uses the term in connection with Arabs. See R. Jenkins, *Byzantium: The Imperial Centuries* (New York, 1966), 264, regarding the expedition of 949: "And when they referred to Crete, it was the island itself that was 'God-damned,' and not just the Moslem occupants of it." The reference to the use of this compilation on siege warfare against Arabs and this specific rhetorical characterization of them fit well with a mid-tenth-century date for the treatise.

Geodesia

Title: Γεωδαισία: This title, used by Martin, passim, Vincent, 348, and Dain, *Tradition,* passim, is lacking in Vat. gr. 1605, but the term does appear in the introductory paragraph at *Geodesia* **1**:23, on which see below. Lefort, *Géométries,* 30, suggests that the work might better be called *Dioptra.* On the confusion of the Anon. Byz.'s *Geodesia* with the metrological table found in section 4 of Heron, *Geometrica,* see Lefort, *Géométries,* 30 n. 105.

Chapter 1. Introduction

The Anon. Byz. draws, in this introductory chapter, on the first and especially the second chapter of the *Dioptra* of Heron (on its inclusion in the poliorcetic corpus see Dain, "Stratégistes," 379) for both content and wording, for example, the link of dioptrics to construction of siege engines, measuring intervals from distances, the risks of constructing engines of incorrect size, measuring outside enemy range, the other uses of the dioptra. He also uses Afric., *Cest.* VII:15:5–7 (σύμμετρον ἐπαγαγόντας ζεῦγμα . . . εἰς τὸ τὰς ἑλεπόλεις μηχανὰς ἰσοστασίους ἐπενεγκεῖν). He differs, however, in the greater emphasis he puts on siege applications of the dioptra.

3 παραλογίζεσθαι: Vat. gr. 1605 has παραλογίζεθαι, with παρα- abbreviated, but clearly so (Müller, "Handschriftlisches," also read παρα-), while the London ms. 15276 has περιλογίζεσθαι. Barocius, using the Bologna ms., translates "supputare," and Vincent, using Paris. suppl. gr. 817, has λογίζεσθαι. As the phrase παραλογισθέντες τῇ ἀναμετρήσει occurs in the second chapter of Heron's *Dioptra,* and ἐξέσται γὰρ τοῖς βουλομένοις in the first, it seems likely that the same word was used by the Anon. Byz., who has perhaps not adequately adapted it to his context.

4 γνώσει διοπτρικῆς: Cf. Heron, *Dioptra* 2:18–19: παραλογισθέντες τῇ ἀναμετρήσει τῶν τειχῶν διὰ τὸ ἀπείρους εἶναι τῆς διοπτρικῆς πραγματείας. See also above on *Parangelmata* **53**:14, where, following

[249]

Ath. Mech., the Anon. Byz. refers to the importance of optics for correct construction of siege machines.

4 ἰθυφανείας: The term is attested in the *Optica* (12) of Damianus. C. Mugler, *Dictionnaire historique de la terminologie optique des grecs* (Paris, 1974), 205, defines it as "direct sight."

4–5 τὴν ἐπίσκεψιν ποιεῖσθαι: Cf. Aristotle, *Ethica Nicomachea* 1096a5: τρίτος δ' ἐστὶν ὁ θεωρητικός, ὑπὲρ οὗ τὴν ἐπίσκεψιν ἐν τοῖς ἑπομένοις ποιησόμεθα.

11 συντάγματι: That is, the preceding treatise on poliorcetics; see chap. 53 of the *Parangelmata* for this same point on siege devices constructed too large, a section which derives from Ath. Mech.

13 τὴν μετὰ λόγου δύναμιν: Cf. Aristotle, *Metaphysica* 1048a3: καὶ τὰ μὲν κατὰ λόγον δύναται κινεῖν καὶ αἱ δυνάμεις αὐτῶν μετὰ λόγου, τὰ δὲ ἄλογα καὶ αἱ δυνάμεις ἄλογοι.

15 προγενεστέρων καὶ πολυμαθεστάτων: The sources the Anon. Byz. cites by name in the *Geodesia* are Heron of Alexandria, Euclid, and Archimedes. As Martin, 272–73, 317–18, has suggested, the Anon. Byz. apparently also makes use of Ptolemy's star catalog for astronomical values (see commentary on *Geodesia* **11:**74–75). The Anon. Byz. also uses Julius Africanus and may follow Nicomachus of Gerasa, as noted below. For discussions of his sources see Martin, 278 on Heron's *Metrica,* 287 on Afric., *Cest.,* 305 on Heron's *Geometrica;* Vincent, passim; and K. Tittel, *RE* VIII:1077.

16 ἐφόδοις γραμμικαῖς: Cf. Porphyry, Εἰς τὰ ἁρμονικὰ Πτολεμαίου ὑπόμνημα (ed. I. During [Göteborg, 1930]), 24:20: διὰ τῶν ἐν ταῖς γραμμικαῖς ἐφόδοις ἀποδείξεων.

22 λιμένων περιγραφάς: Cf. Heron, *Dioptra* 17:1–2: Λιμένα περιγράψαι πρὸς τὸ δοθὲν κύκλου τμῆμα, τῶν περάτων αὐτοῦ δοθέντων ("to outline a harbor in terms of a given segment of a circle, given the ends," trans. Heath, *History,* II:345).

23 γεωδαισίαν: The Anon. Byz. has altered Heron's τὴν τῶν γεωγραφουμένων πραγματείαν *(Dioptra* 2:9–10) in the list of applications of the dioptra to the term for mensuration; on γεωδαισία (γεωδεσία)

Chapters 1–2   *Geodesia*

see Heath, *History,* I:16 ("not confined to land measuring, but covering generally the practical measurement of surfaces and volumes"), and Proclus, *In primum Euclidis librum commentarius* I:39:22–25: οὐ γὰρ κύλινδρον ἢ κῶνον ἔργον τῆς γεωδεσίας μετρεῖν, ἀλλὰ σωροὺς ὡς κώνους καὶ φρέατα ὡς κυλίνδρους.

24–28 μῆκος ... πλάτος ... ὑψηλόν: The Anon. Byz. comments on the style of his sources in terms of the three mathematical dimensions; cf. below, **8**:3–4.

26 ἰδιωτικώτερον: Cf. *Parangelmata* **3**:3.

29 ταπεινόν: Cf. Aristotle, *Poetica* 1458a31–34: τὸ μὲν γὰρ τὸ μὴ ἰδιωτικὸν ποιήσει μηδὲ ταπεινόν, οἷον ἡ γλῶττα καὶ ἡ μεταφορὰ καὶ ὁ κόσμος καὶ τἆλλα τὰ εἰρημένα εἴδη, τὸ δὲ κύριον τὴν σαφήνειαν.

30 εὐσύνοπτον τὴν πραγματείαν: Cf. Heron, *Definitiones* proem, 1:3–8: τήν τε ἀρχὴν καὶ τὴν ὅλην σύνταξιν ποιήσομαι κατὰ τὴν τοῦ Εὐκλείδου τοῦ στοιχειωτοῦ τῆς ἐν γεωμετρίᾳ θεωρίας διδασκαλίαν· οἶμαι γὰρ οὕτως οὐ μόνον τὰς ἐκείνου πραγματείας εὐσυνόπτους ἔσεσθαί σοι, ἀλλὰ καὶ πλείστας ἄλλας τῶν εἰς γεωμετρίαν ἀνηκόντων.

31 εὐεπιβόλοις: Cf. Afric., *Cest.* VII:15:1: Οἱ τῆς ἐγκυκλίου μετρίως ἐπήβολοι παιδείας, τῶν Εὐκλείδου στοιχείων ἐπὶ ποσόν, ὡς εἰκός, ἐφήψαντο. The Anon. Byz. apparently envisions a similar audience for his work.

Chapter 2. Measuring the Height of a Wall

The Anon. Byz. draws here for method on Heron, *Dioptra* 12, and on Afric., *Cest.* VII:15. This, and the problems presented in chaps. 3–5 involve taking the distance between two points without approaching one or both of the points; the solutions are based on the geometric theorem that the corresponding sides of similar triangles are proportional. In chap. 6 these problems are summarized as applications of εὐθυμετρία.

The lost portion of the problem might be best summarized, as Vincent (354) suggests, from Heron, *Dioptra* 12:1–4: Σημείου ὁρωμένου εὑρεῖν τὴν ἀπ᾽ αὐτοῦ κάθετον ἀγομένην ἐπὶ τὸ δι᾽ ἡμῶν ἐκβαλλόμενον ἐπίπεδον παράλληλον τῷ ὁρίζοντι, μὴ προσεγγίσαντα τῷ ὁρωμένῳ σημείῳ; and Afric., *Cest.* VII:15, 73–74: Τῷ δὲ αὐτῷ λόγῳ καὶ τείχους ὕψος ληφθήσεται ἐπὶ τοῦ αὐτοῦ διαγράμματος ὀρθουμένου.

[251]

1 < . . . >: On the folio loss see Dain, *Tradition,* 31–32. Vincent (350) suggests that the lost material would include a description of the dioptra and two demonstrations: the first, which is referred to in subsequent problems (see on *Geodesia* **2:**12), was to measure with the aid of the dioptra the horizontal distance between two points, only one of which is accessible (= Heron, *Dioptra* 8); the second, to measure the height of a point or building that cannot be approached (= Heron, *Dioptra* 12). The end of this latter problem is preserved (= chap. 2). There would also have been discussion of units of measurement and fractions thereof (περὶ δὲ μοιρῶν καὶ μορίων) as referred to at the end of chap. 2 below.

The term *dioptra,* as used here, refers to a kind of surveyor's theodolite, which is employed primarily for staking out lines to be used in constructing triangles and in chap. 11 for astronomical measurements. Description and discussion of the instrument of Heron of Alexandria are given by Schöne, "Dioptra"; Drachmann, in Singer et al., *Technology,* III:609–12, and O. A. Dilke, *The Roman Land Surveyors* (London, 1971), 75–79. There is also a lacuna in the manuscript of Heron (Paris. suppl. gr. 607) where the Alexandrian describes his dioptra, so that any reconstruction of his device must in part be based on subsequent references in the text. As Martin notes (281), the dioptra of the Anon. Byz. is analogous to, but not identical to, that of Heron. The extant text of the Anon. Byz. also provides much less detail, particularly of the mechanisms which permit the device to tilt and turn. The dioptra of the Anon. Byz. has some parts described with the same terminology as that of Afric., *Cest.* VII:15 (e.g., κάμαξ, λυχνία, ἀγγεῖον). The specific parts mentioned by the Anon. Byz. are τύμπανον (disc), κανών (sight-rod), ἀγγεῖα (housings for the <sight->holes), ὀπή (<sight->hole), τόρμος (stud), χοινικίς (cylinder), στύραξ (<screw->shaft), μοιρογνωμόνιον (degree indicator), κάμαξ (pole), λυχνία (lamp), τύλος (peg).

The descriptions given by the Anon. Byz. of the movements of the various parts of the device are as follows: καθιστάναι τὸ τύμπανον (to set the disc <to a particular position>); παρεγκλίνειν τὸ πρὸς ἡμᾶς μέρος τοῦ τυμπάνου, πρὸς ὕψος τὸ ἕτερον ἀνανεύειν (to incline downward the part of the disc closest to us, to tilt up the other part); περιάγειν τὸ τύμπανον σὺν τῷ κανόνι διὰ τῆς ἐπικειμένης τῷ τόρμῳ χοινικίδος, ἢ στύρακος ἐν τῇ διόπτρᾳ τυχόντος (to turn the disc with the sight-rod around by means of the cylinder resting on the stud, or perhaps by a

<screw->shaft in the dioptra); παρατιθέναι τὸ τύμπανον (to set the disc); διοπτεύειν διὰ κανόνος (to sight with the sight-rod); ἰθύνειν (διιθύνειν) τὸν κανόνα (to direct the sight-rod); μετρεῖν διὰ κανόνος (to measure with the sight-rod); παράγειν τὸν κανόνα (to lead around the sight-rod); περιστρέφειν τὸν ἐπὶ τοῦ τυμπάνου κανόνα (to turn the sight-rod on the disc); ἐπισκέπτεσθαι διὰ τῶν δύο ὀπῶν (to look through the two <sight->holes); διάγειν . . . διὰ τῶν ὀπῶν τοῦ κανόνος (to draw <lines> through the <sight->holes of the sight-rod). The author also indicates that the disc has 360 degrees and intervening minutes (μοῖραι, λεπτά) on it, and hence for astronomical purposes one is able μετρεῖν ἐπὶ τοῦ τυμπάνου τὰς . . . μοίρας (to measure the degrees on the disc). Although not mentioned, the disc would presumably have been divided into four quarters by two diameters to allow staking of lines at right angles for geometrical problems (see Martin, 282). The Anon. Byz., following Afric., *Cest.,* also mentions a separate sighting pole with a target.

'I'hus the Anon. Byz. describes a device that uses a flat disc that can be rotated on a pivot and tilted to various angles. The disc is inscribed with degrees and minutes, presumably divided into four quadrants, topped by a sight-rod with degree indicators and two housings with <sight->holes at either end. There is no specific mention of a water level, although Vincent (350–51) inferred one from the requirements of problems 1 and 9 and the term ἀγγεῖα ("Ces godets, supposés remplis d'eau, remplacent jusqu'à un certain point les lentilles de la lunette que l'on met aujourd'hui sur l'alidade"). Martin (281) describes them simply as housings for the <sight->holes. F. Thee, *Julius Africanus and the Early Christian View of Magic* (Tübingen, 1984), 134, translates ἀγγεῖον as "sight."The dioptra of Heron of Alexandria is illustrated by J. Neumann in Schöne,"Dioptra," 99.

6 διόπτραν . . . λυχνίαν: As Martin (287) notes, this phrase is also found in Afric., *Cest.* VII:15:76–77, the term διόπτρα referring in that passage also not to the sighting instrument itself but to a "target" on which the instrument is sighted (Heron's ἀσπιδίσκη, *Dioptra* 5). On the λυχνία see F. Schmidt, *Geschichte der geodätischen Instrumente und Verfahren im Altertum und Mittelalter,* Arabische Instrumente in orientalistischen Studien 5 (Frankfurt am Main, 1991), 73–74; on the ἀσπιδίσκη see Drachmann in Singer et al., *Technology,* III:611. Martin (287) believed

that the Anon. Byz. has actually used a "target" in his solution to this problem. The reference to the "target" here is, I suggest, parenthetical, and the device is not required in the specific operation the author is describing, only a pole of known height, which is represented by line ΗΘ in the ms. diagram.

12 ὡς ... ἐμάθομεν: A reference to the lost first problem derived from Heron, *Dioptra* 8 (see discussion of the lacuna above and references to the same method below at *Geodesia* **3**:10–11, **4**:12 and **5**:21–22); see also Martin, 253 n. 2, 292 n. 1 and 306. The text of Heron, *Dioptra* 8, reads, "*Given two points, one within our reach, the other distant, to take the interval between them on the horizontal plane without approaching the distant point.* Let the given points be A and B; let A lie within our reach, B at a distance. The dioptra with the semicircular <gear-wheel> is at A and let the sight-rod on the disc be turned until B appears. Then going around to the other side of the sight-rod I tilt the semicircular <gear-wheel> with the other parts remaining unmoved and I take the point Γ in the area within our reach lying on <the extension of> the straight line AB. Then I draw from A with the dioptra AΔ perpendicular to BΓ, and another <perpendicular> ΓE from Γ and I take perhaps a <point> E on it. Having moved the dioptra to E I position the sight-rod so that through it point B appears and another point Δ on AΔ on the straight line BE. The triangle BΓE has AΔ parallel to ΓE. Then as ΓE is to AΔ, so is ΓB to BA. I can now ascertain the ratio of ΓE to AΔ having measured each of them on the horizontal plane, as shown above. Let, perchance, ΓE be found five times AΔ; then BΓ will be five times BA; then ΓA is four times AB. I can measure AΓ on the horizontal; so that the value of AB can be found on the horizontal plane."

14–15 ἐπὶ τὸ τοῦ προμαχῶνος ἄκρον: Martin, 286, Guilland, *Topographie*, I:385, and Dagron, *Naissance*, 322–23, take this as a reference to the tower that carried the quadriga in the Hippodrome. The phrase, however, appears to derive from Afric., *Cest.* VII:15:74–75, which has Ἔστω τὸ μὲν ἄκρον τοῦ προμαχῶνος τὸ A. The specific reference to the Hippodrome begins only in the next phrase. As noted by Guilland (ibid., 385) the presence of a tower carrying the quadriga is, however, confirmed by Nik. Chon., *Hist.* 119:58–61: ἐπὶ τὸν κατὰ τὸ θέατρον πύργον ἀναλάμενος, οὗ κάτωθεν μὲν αἱ τῶν ἐπὶ σταδίου θεόντων ἀφετηρίαι εἰς ἁψῖδας παραλλήλους κεχήνασιν, ἄνωθεν δ᾽ ἵπποι χαλκήλατοι πεπήγασι πίσυρες χρυσῷ ἠληλιμμένοι.

15 **θυρῶν**: Martin (285) understood these θύραι to be the same as the gates from which the chariots started. If, however, the quadriga was above a central arch (see the Appendix), these "doors" may be the gates of that structure. On the starting gates, later referred to as κάγκελλοι, see below on *Geodesia* **3:4**. The measurement of 12 *orgyai* suggests that "some part" of the quadriga would have been approximately 22.44 m above the base of the doors (see Martin, 286; Dagron, *Naissance,* 322–23; Guilland, *Topographie,* I:385).

16 **τεθρίππου**: Presumably the gilded quadriga transported to San Marco after the Fourth Crusade (see Dagron, *Naissance,* 323 and n. 1; Guilland, *Topographie,* I:385). As there was more than one such quadriga in Constantinople, however, see the cautionary note about such identification in L. B. Vlad and A. G. Toniato, "The Origins and Documentary Sources of the Horses of San Marco," in *The Horses of San Marco, Venice,* trans. J. and V. Wilton-Ely (Milan–New York, 1979), 126–36, esp. 128: "In our opinion there is not enough evidence yet to identify with sufficient accuracy which group of horses is the Venetian one."

17 **μοιρῶν καὶ μορίων**: Apparently a reference to material in the lacuna; see Martin, 253.

Chapter 3. Measuring an Interval, Method 1

The Anon. Byz. draws for method here on Heron, *Dioptra* 10:2.

2–3 **πρὸς διαβήτην**: The phrase occurs frequently in Heron's *Dioptra,* where Schöne ("Dioptra") renders "in horizontaler Ebene." Vincent (209–11), based on examination of all the passages in Heron, concludes that the phrase must refer to distance computed horizontally, "distance cultellée." He suggests a possible link to the *chorobates* described by Vitruvius. LSJ gives for διαβήτης both *"compass"* or a *"carpenter's or stonemason's rule,"* citing for the latter *Inscriptiones Graecae* 12(?).11.20: ξύσας ὀρθὸν πρὸς διαβήτην. It is perhaps this latter tool that gives rise to the phrase.

4 **καγκέλλων**: the starting gates, presumably, on comparison to the

Circus Maximus, twelve in number (see Dagron, *Naissance,* 322). Guilland *(Topographie* I:383), however, suggests on the basis of a number of passages in the *De cer.* (e.g., at 360:21 the factions are said to gather before gates one and ten, perhaps indicating that the tenth is the last) the possibility that there were only ten. The Anon. Byz.'s measurement of the distance between gates 3 and 9 would seem to support the latter view (see the Appendix).

6 τῆς ἄνω νύσσης: The turning post *(meta)* closest to the starting gates at the north end of the *spina;* that of the Blue Faction (see Guilland, *Topographie,* I:444).

10 μίαν τούτων: As the *spina* and the north *meta* were not on the main axis of the track, and the starting gates not laid out on a curve centered at point Γ, the triangle cannot be isosceles as the Anon. Byz. assumes. See the Appendix; Vincent, 358; Martin, 302.

11 ὀργυῶν τυχὸν π΄: The distance from the upper turning post to the third gate is then 80 *orgyai* (149.60 m); on the use of the figure to estimate the length of the arena, see the Appendix and Guilland, "Hippodrome," 6–7.

21 μ΄ ὀργυῶν: On the measurement see the Appendix.

Chapter 4. Measuring an Interval, Method 2
The Anon. Byz. draws for method here on Heron, *Dioptra* 10:3

4 σφενδόνης: The "sling" or semicircular end of the Hippodrome; see Guilland, *Topographie,* I:375–76; Janin, *Constantinople,* 183; Müller-Wiener, *Bildlexikon,* 67 fig. 44.

6 ἁπλοῦν: Vat. gr. 1605 has the *spiritus asper* both here and at *Geodesia* 4:17. Martin (291 n. 1), who indicates that his manuscript read ἁπλοῦς (sic), interpreted it as *"simple,"* that is, the part of the arena undivided by the *spina,* while noting that Barocius translated with *inaccessibilis,* as if from ἄπλους. Vincent (360) prints in his text ἄπλουν initially and below ἄπλου, while recording in his apparatus respectively ἁπλοῦν and ἁπλοῦ. He translates the term as "écueil," suggesting (353) that it is a metaphor from navigation, referring to an area where the chariots could not pass, a metaphor perhaps influenced by the use of *euripos* for the *spina.* Guilland,

Topographie, I:446, follows Martin. Given the readings in the archetype, this is surely the correct approach and the area referred to is that between the starting gates and the upper turning post.

12 μίαν τούτων: On the Anon. Byz.'s incorrect assumption or simplification see on *Geodesia* **3:**10 and the Appendix.

13 ὀργυῶν τυχὸν ρκϛ´: On the measurement see the Appendix and Guilland, "Hippodrome," 2–3.

14 ἀγγεῖον: On the term see above on *Geodesia* **2:**1.

27 πέλμα: For the use of the term as "arena" see Martin, 291; Dagron, *Naissance,* 323; and Guilland, *Topographie,* I:442.

29 ὀργυῶν με´: On the measurement see the Appendix and Guilland, "Hippodrome," 2 and 5.

Chapter 5. Measuring an Interval and its Position
The Anon. Byz. draws for method here on Heron, *Dioptra* 10:1

5–6 ἓν τῶν . . . ἑπτὰ τμημάτων: These segments are presumably detached basins of water such as are found on the *spina* at Leptis Magna (see Humphrey, *Circuses,* 38 and 277). On the symbolism, see Dagron, *Naissance,* 334–36. Mango, "L'euripe," 189, cites an illustration on the column of Arcadius that seems to show the seven segments, but for doubts see Dagron, *Naissance,* 324 n. 5. See also Martin, 297 and 301, and Vincent, 362. For a different view see Guilland, *Topographie,* I:447–51, who argues that the segments are not in the *spina* but in the arena.

6 τοῦ εὐρίπου: Here the *spina* or barrier dividing the arena. Humphrey (*Circuses,* 175 and 293) notes that the term was first used of a channel that Julius Caesar had dug around the perimeter of the Circus Maximus to contain animals, but that was filled in by Nero for additional seating. The earliest attested use of the term for the *spina* of the Circus Maximus appears to be in Tertullian, *De spectaculis* 8, when the barrier is also first known on clear evidence to have consisted of basins. For its use specifically for the *spina* of the Hippodrome of Constantinople, see esp. Mango, "L'euripe," passim, critiqued by P. Lemerle, "Bulletin Archéologique II, 1948–50," *REB* 8 (1950), 232–33; and Cameron, *Poryphyrius,* 180 n. 1,

who accepts and further substantiates Mango's view. Guilland's (*Topographie,* I:446–47) assertion that the Anon. Byz. cannot be using εὔριπος here of the *spina* appears untenable.

6 στηθέων: "Balustrades," that is, chest-high railings, and in this instance, around the *spina,* at *Geodesia* **5**:15 on the grandstand wall fronting the arena. Martin, 297, and Mango, "L'euripe," accept the idea of balustrades around the *spina;* Guilland (*Topographie,* I:399–401, 447) argues that the only balustrades were on the grandstand wall. This is in accord with his view of the *euripos* noted above on *Geodesia* **5**:6, but would not allow sufficient space for construction of the figure the Anon. Byz. describes. See the Appendix.

7 βασιλικοῦ καθίσματος: The imperial box of the Hippodrome, situated on the east side; see *ODB* II:934; Guilland, *Topographie,* I:463ff; Mango, "Palace," 46–47. On the Anon. Byz.'s measurement and the location of the *kathisma,* see the Appendix.

8 ἐν τοῖς δρομεῦσι: Barocius (53v) comments: "Cursores in praesentia pro locis, sive intervallis accepit, ubi in ludis publicis cursatur, qui proprio nomine curricula dicuntur"; Vincent (363) translates: "où se tiennent les coureurs qui se préparent." Martin (296) comments: "une construction appelée παρασκευή par les coureurs." It is perhaps best to take ἐν as "among" and with καλουμένων. On foot races in the Hippodrome in the tenth century, see Guilland, "Les courses de l'Hippodrome," *Byzantinoslavica* 26 (1965), 1–39; idem, "Les courses de voeu," ibid., 27 (1966), 26–40; and Vogt, *Livre,* II:168–69.

9 παρασκευῶν: The term is also found in *De cer.* 163:9 and 12 used in the same sense as here. Reiske translates "tabulata," Vogt (*Livre,* II:163) "vestiaires." Mango ("L'euripe," 188) and Vincent (363) translate the term in this passage of the Anon. Byz. "pavillons"; Mango ("Palace," 46) "changing-rooms." Vincent (353) suggests that they may have been mobile tents, Guilland, (*Topographie,* I:457) that they were permanent in nature. See the Appendix.

10 τὴν τῆς κάτω νύσσης ἀντιπεριαγωγήν: That is, the turning post close to the *sphendone,* that of the Green Faction (Guilland, *Topographie,* I:444). For its position see the Appendix.

14–15 τῆς τῶν βαθμίδων ἀναβάθρας: I follow Mango, "Palace," 46, in translating "flight of stairs"; perhaps here steps with lower risers going up through the seats. Guilland (*Topographie* I:402), however, takes the phrase as referring to "l'ensemble des gradins superposés en escaliers."

21–22 ὡς ... ὑπεθέμην: See above on *Geodesia* **2:**12 and Martin, 292 n. 1.

29–30 δώδεκα ... ὀργυῶν: On the measurement see the Appendix.

33–34 κατὰ δύναμιν: That is, 15 squared = 9 squared plus 12 squared; on the use of the term for "squared" value, see Heath, *History,* II:294, and T. L. Heath, *The Works of Archimedes* (Cambridge, 1912), clxi.

Chapter 6. Measuring Rectilinear Surfaces

Martin (304–5) suggests that for the methods of plane geometry, but not the examples, the Anon. Byz. borrows here from Heron's *Geometrica,* especially the method of measuring parallelograms by measuring the triangles created by a diagonal added to the parallelogram. See also Heron, *Dioptra* 23 and 24, and *Metrica* I:1: 12.

1 εὐθυμετρίαν: The term does not appear in the TLG; see Sophocles, *Lexicon,* s.v., "linear measurement"; cf. Heron, *Geometrica* 3:19: Εὐθυμετρικὸν μὲν οὖν ἐστιν πᾶν τὸ κατ᾽ εὐθὺ μετρούμενον, ὃ μόνον μῆκος ἔχει.

2 εὐθυγράμμων ... σχημάτων: Cf. Aristotle, *De caelo* 286b13–14: ἅπαν δὴ σχῆμα ἐπίπεδον ἢ εὐθύγραμμόν ἐστιν ἢ περιφερόγραμμον. καὶ τὸ μὲν εὐθύγραμμον ὑπὸ πλειόνων περιέχεται γραμμῶν, τὸ δὲ περιφερόγραμμον ὑπὸ μιᾶς.

4 ἑτερομηκῶν: Cf. Euclid I:def. 22: ἑτερόμηκες δέ, ὃ ὀρθογώνιον μέν, οὐκ ἰσόπλευρον δέ, and for the method see Heron, *Metrica* I:1.

6 ἐπίπεδον: The term may apply either to the area of a plane figure or to the square number representing the area. See Heath, *Elements,* II:287–88.

8–9 τοῦ ῥηθέντος ... διαγράμματος: The diagram used is the same as for the previous problem with the completion of the lines AB and BZ.

13 ἀναμέτρησιν: A cross above the word links to the marginal scholion,

published in Latin translation by Barocius (57v–58), previously unpublished in Greek, and written in the left margin and bottom of folio 46v and top and right margin of folio 47. Barocius (58) noted that the similarity of terminology (e.g., ἀναμέτρησις, σχηματισμός, στρατηγικὴ ἐπιστήμη, ἐφοδιάζειν) in the opening and closing sentences to terms in the Anon. Byz.'s *Parangelmata* and *Geodesia,* as well as the general content of the scholion, suggest that the Anon. Byz. himself may have been the author.

It is apparently intended to show military uses of geometrical forms and is a pastiche from one of the classical tacticians. The phrase ἀφωρισμένοι λοχαγοί agrees with Asclepiodotus, *Tactica* IV:4, against Aelian, *Tactica* (XI:6) τεταγμένοι λοχαγοί, suggesting that Asclepiodotus is the source. Asclepiodotus discusses square, oblong, and rhomboid formations at VII:4–5, rank-and-file formations at II:6 and IV:2, selecting numbers evenly divisible by two down to unity and the phalanx of 16, 384 at II:7, and open, closed, and intermediate intervals at IV:4. The reading ὑπὲρκεράσεως may be compared favorably to that for Asclepiodotus X:2, υπερασως (sic), found in the archetype for the classical tactician, the mid-tenth-century Laurentianus LV–4; see my paper "A Previously Unrecognized Formula of Archimedes and an Unpublished Pastiche from Asclepiodotus in Vaticanus Graecus 1605," American Philological Association 125th Annual Meeting (Washington, D.C., 1993) *Abstracts,* 154. For the text of Asclepiodotus with English trans., see Illinois Greek Club, *Aeneas Tacticus, Asclepiodotus, Onasander* (London-New York, 1923); for a discussion of the technical terms and numerical recommendations, see also W. A. Oldfather, "Notes on the Text of Asclepiodotos," *American Journal of Philology* 41 (1920), 135–46. The term ἔνταγμα is not found in the classical tacticians or in the TLG; Barocius renders with "ordines." Ἔνταξις, however, is found at Aelian, *Tactica* 31:3, and Arrian, *Tactica* 26:6: ἔνταξιν δὲ ὀνομάζουσιν, ἐπειδὰν τοὺς ψιλοὺς ἐς τὰ διαστήματα τῶν πεζῶν ἐντάξωσιν, ἄνδρα παρ᾽ ἄνδρα. On the use of the tactical writers by Byzantine authors, see Dennis, *Treatises,* 47 n. 1.

20 **διαστροφῆς**: The word rhombus is apparently derived from ῥέμβω, "to turn round and round" (Heath, *Elements,* 13, 189). Proclus, *In primum Euclidis librum commentarius* 171:17–18 comments: ἔοικεν δὲ καὶ ὁ ῥόμβος

σαλευθὲν εἶναι τετράγωνον καὶ τὸ ῥομβοειδὲς κεκινημένον ἑτερόμηκες.

26 For measurement of the pentagon and hexagon, see Heron, *Metrica* I:18–19.

29 and 37 νοήσει τε καὶ αἰσθήσει ... αἰσθήσει τε καὶ φαντασία: On φαντασία as a form of νόησις in Aristotle and especially Proclus, see G. R. Morrow, *Proclus: A Commentary on the First Book of Euclid's Elements* (Princeton, N. J., 1970), 41 n. 5. On the function of the imagination in Neoplatonic mathematical thinking, see ibid., 41 ("the understanding relies upon a special capacity, the imagination or image-making faculty, for exhibiting the variety and complexity of the mathematical forms that it explores"). Such "imagined" objects are thus intermediary between objects perceived by the senses and the universal forms. For an analysis of the evolution of the term, see G. Watson, *Phantasia in Classical Greek Thought* (Galway, 1988), esp. chap. 5, "The Neoplatonists." Cf. also Heron, *Definitiones* 138.

40–41 Ἀρχιμήδης καὶ Ἥρων ἐν τῇ καθολικῇ πραγματείᾳ: Apparently a reference to Heron's *Metrica,* which draws on Archimedes and is in turn being used here by the Anon. Byz.; so K. Tittel, *RE* VIII:1077. On trapezia and trapezoids see Heron, *Metrica* I:10–13.

45–46 ἐν πίθῳ ... κεραμείαν: The proverb is quoted by Plato (*Gorgias* 514e6, *Laches* 187b4) where it signifies to "undertake the most difficult task without learning the elements of the art" (LSJ, at κεραμεία); see also E. R. Dodds, *Plato's "Gorgias"* (Oxford, 1976), 355. Another explanation is attributed by Zenobius to Dicaearchus (see E. von Leutsch and F. Schneidewin, *Corpus paroemiographorum Graecorum,* 2 vols. [Göttingen, 1839; repr. Hildesheim, 1958], I:73): to "learn by relevant experience." Dodds suggests that this interpretation "misses the point." It is likely, however, that the Anon. Byz. so understands the phrase. His ἀφορμαὶ ὑποθέσεων are perhaps a reference to the practical and familiar settings (various sites in the Hippodrome and the cistern of Aspar) that he uses for his geometrical problems, and that may in his pedagogical view constitute "relevant experience."

Chapter 7. Measuring Circles

For the method see Heron, *Metrica* I:25–26.

11 τόρμῳ, etc: For the parts of the dioptra, see the list given above on *Geodesia* 2:1. The potential use of a στύραξ here is an alternative added by the Anon. Byz. to the mechanism described by Heron of Alexandria.

15–16 λίθους . . . σκοπούς: The reference in Afric., *Cest.* VII:15:40–41, is to a single point viewed across a river; the adaptation to various points on the perimeter of a circle is apparently due to the Anon. Byz. as is the accompanying illustration.

16–17 τὰ Β . . . Π: The letters of the ms. diagram, which has Β Γ Δ Ε Ζ Η Θ Ι Κ λ μ Ν, are at variance with those in the text. The depiction of the circle is notable for its attempt at realistic presentation of the natural physical characteristics described in the text.

19–20 ὡς . . . ἐμάθομεν: See above on *Geodesia* 2:12.

21–22 τῆς ἐκ τοῦ κέντρου: On the absence for a term for "radius" in Greek (= ἡ ἐκ τοῦ κέντρου εὐθεία), see Heath, *Elements,* II:2.

22 τριπλασιεφέβδομός ἐστιν: The formulas are found at *Metrica* I:26, where Heron indicates that he follows Archimedes' *Dimensio circuli* and Περὶ πλινθίδων καὶ κυλίνδρων. In the same passage Heron notes that Archimedes' approximation of pi (diameter x 310/71 < circumference < diameter x 31/7) is not well suited to practical measurement and so has been reduced to the smallest integers as 22 to 7 (εἰς ἐλαχίστους ἀριθμούς, ὡς τὸν κβ′ πρὸς τὰ ζ′.)

31 πολλαπλασιαζόμεναι: On this method of multiplication, that is, multiplying each figure of one number by each figure of the other and then adding the partial products, and its rate of error in Byzantine land surveying texts, see Lefort, *Géométries,* 243–44.

47–48 ἀρχῇ . . . ἀρχῆς . . . ἀρχήν: Barocius (61v) saw here an allusion to the Trinity, a view followed by Vincent (375), doubted by Dain (*Tradition,* 17); Barocius also notes Platonic and Neoplatonic uses. In this mathematical context and in view of the Anon. Byz.'s other Neoplatonic allusions, this latter usage is more likely. The concept seems quite similar to the various Neoplatonic views of the circle found in Plotinus and Proclus. Cf. esp. Proclus, *In primum Euclidis librum commentarius* 155:5–9: κέντρον, ἀφ᾽ οὗ πᾶσαι μέχρις ἄντυγος ἴσαι ἔασιν. Ἀλλ᾽ ὡς μὲν τῆς διαστάσεως ἀρχὴ τῶν γραμμῶν τῷ "ἀφ᾽ οὗ" σημαίνεται, ὡς δὲ μέσον τῆς περιφερείας τῷ "πρὸς ὅ." πρὸς γὰρ τὸ κέντρον αὕτη συνάγεται κατὰ πᾶσαν ἑαυτήν. See also M. Atkinson, *Plotinus: Ennead V.1* (Oxford, 1989) 215: "Plotinus sometimes uses the image of a circle and its center as an illustration of the relationship between the One and the Intellect, or the Intellect and the soul. The center is in a sense a part of each radius, yet because each radius has its point of reference at the center, in that the center is the source of each radius, the center is at the same time different from each." See also J. Bussanich, *The One and Its Relationship to the Intellect in Plotinus* (Leiden, 1988), 84–85. On the Anon. Byz.'s "Neoplatonism" see above on *Parangelmata* chap. 3.

52 **τὰ Β ... Θ**: The ms. illustration shows an α on the periphery of the circle just below the human figure and the rope, but the letter is not found in the text; the previous ms. illustration of the circle had the α at the center of the circle, and this was specifically mentioned in the text.

Chapter 8. Measuring Solids

3–4 **πᾶν σῶμα ... ὕψος**: Cf. Diogenes Laertius, VII:133–35: Σῶμα δ᾽ἐστίν, ὥς φησιν Ἀπολλόδωρος ἐν τῇ Φυσικῇ, τὸ τριχῇ διαστατόν, εἰς μῆκος, εἰς πλάτος, εἰς βάθος and Heron, *Geometrica,* Introduction: φυσικὸν σῶμα, ὅ ἐστι τριχῇ διαστατόν.

13–14 **Πυθαγόρειοι ... ἁρμονίαν**: Cf. Proclus, *In Platonis Timaeum commentaria* II:224:29–32: τὸν γὰρ κύβον ἁρμονίαν εἰώθεσαν καλεῖν οἱ ⟨Πυθαγόρειοι⟩, διότι μόνον τῶν σχημάτων τὰς γωνίας ἔχει μέσας ἀνὰ λόγον τῶν τε πλευρῶν καὶ τῶν ἐπιπέδων and Nicomachus of Gerasa ("the Neo-Pythagorean"), *Arithmetica Introductio* II:26:2: Τινὲς δὲ αὐτὴν ἁρμονικὴν καλεῖσθαι νομίζουσιν ἀκολούθως Φιλολάῳ ἀπὸ τοῦ παρέπεσθαι πάσῃ γεωμετρικῇ ἁρμονίᾳ, γεωμετρικὴν δὲ ἁρμονίαν φασὶ τὸν κύβον ἀπὸ τοῦ κατὰ τὰ τρία διαστήματα ἡρμόσθαι ἰσάκις ἴσα ἰσάκις. Heath, *History,* I:85–86, comments: "Nicomachus too says that the name 'harmonic mean' was adopted in accordance with the view of Philolaus about the 'geometrical harmony,' a name applied to the cube because it has 12 edges, 8 angles, and 6 faces, and 8 is the mean between 12 and 6 according to the theory of harmonics."

26–27 ἐλαχίστοις καὶ πρώτοις: Cf. Euclid VII:21: Οἱ πρῶτοι πρὸς ἀλλήλους ἀριθμοὶ ἐλάχιστοί εἰσι τῶν τὸν αὐτὸν λόγον ἐχόντων αὐτοῖς, and the comments of Heath, *History,* II:285–86.

36 ὡς ἀνωτέρω προείρηται: See *Geodesia* 7:22.

41–42 ψπδ′ . . . ιδ′: Vincent (379 n. 3) explains: "784 = 616 (1 + 1/4 + 1/44) = 616 + 154 + 14 = 616 x 14/11." One might add 1/4 = 11/44; 11/44 +1/44 = 12/44 = 6/22 = 3/11; 1 + 3/11 = 14/11. The formulation presumably reflects the preference for expression of a fraction as a submultiple, as "an 'aliquot part,' that is, a fraction with a numerator unity," on which see Heath, *History,* I:41–42. Barocius (65 n. f) comments: "Adnotandum quod melius est dicere, quod 784 ad 616 habet rationem supertripartientem undecimas, sive supertriundecimas sicut 14 ad 11: quam dicere quod continet eum, ac eius partem quartam, et quadragesimam quartam. nam quemadmodum 14 continet 11 et eius 3/11, sic et 784 continet 616 et eius 3/11: quae sunt 168, excessus videlicet, quo ipse 784 ipsum 616 superat. ter enim 56, 168: et undecies 56, 616 faciunt."

55 β̈: On the expression of myriads by the symbol representing the number of myriads with two dots over it and generally on large number notation with the word μυριάδες see Heath, *History,* I:39.

76–84 ["Εστι . . . τέταρσιν.]: Vincent (380–1) bracketed these lines as an interpolation on the grounds that: (1) they presuppose the definition of a cone, not given until the next paragraph; (2) they contain erroneous propositions. He notes that the surface of the double cone inscribed in a sphere is equal to the circumference of its base multiplied by the apothem, that is, 88 x 20 = 1760, taking as approximately equal to 20 the radius 14 multiplied by the square root of 2. As to the volume of the same solid it has the area of the great circle multiplied by a third of the diameter, that is, 616 x 91/3 = 57491/3. Thus the surface of the double cone equals approximately 5/7 that of the sphere, and its volume is half that of the same sphere. Barocius (65–65v), noting only the difficulty regarding the calculation of the surface, concluded, "aut ergo textus corrupte legitur, aut bonus dormitavit Homerus." While the errors are perhaps not beyond the Anon. Byz. himself, their extent and the assumption of the definition of the cone would seem to favor Vincent's approach.

98–99 ἡ δὲ τοῦ κώνου ἐπιφάνεια: Vincent (383) notes that as above the calculation of the surface of the cone is incorrect; the formula for the mantle of the cone here should be πrs where r is the radius, s the slant height (and thus $s^2 = r^2 + h^2$); the result would be 13771/5. The Anon. Byz. has apparently failed, perhaps in an attempt to maintain proportional relationships for all the solid figures, to realize that the 1:3 ratio of the cone to the cylinder holds only for the volume, not for the surface area. The statements in Archimedes are also not explicit on this limitation. See, for example, *De sphaera et cylindro* 4:8–9: πᾶς κῶνος τρίτον μέρος ἐστὶν τοῦ κυλίνδρου τοῦ βάσιν ἔχοντος τὴν αὐτὴν τῷ κώνῳ καὶ ὕψος ἴσον.

108–13 Καὶ . . . γινέσθω: The formulas for centers of gravity of the cylinder, prism and cone are found in Archimedes' *Ad Eratosthenem methodus,* Introduction, lemmas 8, 9, and 10, a work preserved only in a single palimpsest manuscript. That of the pyramid is not found elsewhere in extant texts. As the first and second, then third and fourth formulas are linked to one another in the Anon. Byz., it seems likely that he had access to a manuscript or handbook summary of Archimedes on centers of gravity no longer extant; see the abstract of my paper "A Previously Unrecognized Formula of Archimedes" (as above on *Geodesia* **6**:13). For Archimedes on centers of gravity, see Heath, *History,* II:350–51. The text of the Anon. Byz. here also provides confirmation of the conjectures on the text of Archimedes' *Ad Eratosthenem methodus.* For the topic see *Parangelmata,* chap. 53, and cf. Anna Comnena, *Alexiad* XII:4:1, on men flocking to the emperor: καθάπερ τὰ βαρέα τῶν σωμάτων ἐπὶ κέντρα φέρεται.

Chapter 9. Volume of the Cistern of Aspar

2–3 ἐπὶ τῆς Ἀετίου κινστέρνης: The Aetius in question was probably the prefect of the city in 419 (see Janin, *Constantinople,* 203, but R. Janin, "Les citernes d'Aetius, d'Aspar et de Bonus," *REB* 1 [1943], 89–101, for alternatives, and *ODB* I:518). The cistern, built in 421, was the largest open one of the city; Müller-Wiener, *Bildlexikon,* 278, gives the dimensions as 244 x 85 m with a height of 13–15 m.

4 Ἄσπαρος: Flavius Ardaburius Aspar, an Alan, consul (434), *patrikios,* and *magister militum.* The cistern was constructed in 459 and was 152 m square; see Janin, *Constantinople,* 205–6, and Müller-Wiener, *Bildlexikon,* 279. C. Mango, "The Water Supply of Constantinople," in *Constantinople and Its Hinterland,* ed. C. Mango and G. Dagron (Cambridge, 1995), 9–18, specifically 17 with n. 41, observes that the Anon. Byz.'s text proves that the square open cistern in Constantinople was that of Aspar and tentatively suggests that the accompanying illustration in Vaticanus gr. 1605 (fig. 41), which shows the cistern filled with blue water, may indicate that the open-air cisterns continued in use in this period.

5 Πλινθίς: The "brick" is defined as a solid in the form mn² (m<n); see Nicomachus of Gerasa, *Arithmetica Introductio* II:17:6, and D'Ooge, *Nicomachus,* 256 n. 4.

9 δοκίς: The "beam" is defined as a solid in the form mn² (m>n); see Nicomachus of Gerasa, *Arithmetica Introductio* II:17:6, and D'Ooge, *Nicomachus,* 256 n. 4.

11 ὀργυῶν οʹ: On the capacity see the Appendix and Müller-Wiener, *Bildlexikon,* 279.

14 κεραμίων: See Heron, *Geometrica* 22:2:8: χωρεῖ δὲ ὁ στερεὸς πούς κεράμιον αʹ; and F. Hultsch, *Griechische und römische Metrologie* (Berlin, 1882), 115, who cites this passage of the Anon. Byz., suggesting, "Die gesetzliche Bestimmung des Hohlmasses blieb unverändert bis in die späteste byzantinische Zeit. Noch Heron von Konstantinopel, der im zehnten Jahrhunderte lebte, setzt die Amphora (κεράμιον) gleich 1 römischen Kubikfuss und das Wassergewicht derselben gleich 80 λίτραι Ἰταλικαί." The κεράμιον does not appear in Schilbach, *Metrologie,* however, and the Anon. Byz. may be using archaic terminology.

18 μήκει ... στερεῷ: Cf. <Iambilici> Θεολογούμενα τῆς ἀριθμητικῆς (ed. V. de Falco, rev. U. Klein (Stuttgart, 1975), 2:10–13: οὕτω κἂν τῇ τῶν μερῶν τὰ μὲν μήκει ἡμίση δυνάμει ⟨μὲν⟩ τεταρτημόρια, στερεῷ δὲ ὀγδοημόρια, τὰ δὲ μήκει τρίτα δυνάμει μὲν ἔννατα, στερεῷ δὲ ἑπτακαιεικοσιμόρια.

38 πεντήκοντα . . . μετὰ ἑνὸς καὶ πέμπτου: The Anon. Byz.'s attempt to relate the cubic *pous* based on 16 *daktyloi* to a λίτρα of 12 *oungiai* apparently has led to a rough approximation, the first system with the power sequence 16, 256, etc. influencing the attempted equivalent in the second (i.e., 256 divided by 5 = 51 1/5 *daktyloi* equated to 12 *oungiai); see Barocius (67) and Vincent (387), the latter who translates "16 doigts (*lisez* 17?)." Seventeen and one-fifteenths would be needed.

41–42 κεραμίου λιτρῶν Ἰταλικῶν π': The Roman cubic foot, "quadrantal," was officially equated to 80 pounds of wine by the lex Silia, ca. 200 B.C. It was equated with the amphora or κεράμιον (see P. Chantraine, *RE* XXIV:667–72, and Hultsch, cited above on *Geodesia* 9:14). On the λίτρα see Heron, *De mensuris* 60:20: Λίτρα παρὰ Ῥωμαίοις ἑρμηνεύεται λίβρα . . . ἔχει δὲ ὀγκίας ιβ'.

51 ἀετώσεως: The term is attested at Ath. Mech. 13:3 for the upper part of a tortoise (τὸ δὲ ὕψος χωρὶς τῆς ἀετώσεως τῆς ἐφισταμένης ὕστερον), and cf. ἀέτωμα above at *Parangelmata* 22:41 and 36:7. For measurement of the capacities of various structures, see Heron, *Stereometrica* I:41–54.

51 σῖτον, κριθήν τε καὶ ὄσπρια: On the measurement of σῖτος and κριθή in ὄρρια (horrea), see Heron, *Stereometrica* II:53–54, where a conversion table for various measurements of the cubic foot is provided. *De cer.* 701:4 describes the imperial inspection of granaries; the emperor is to bring an ἀρχιτέκτων with him to measure the cubic capacity for audit purposes (see A. Toynbee, *Constantine Porphyrogenitus and His World* [Oxford, 1973], 579–80). For the combination of the three crops, see *De obsid.* 46:9–10, 48:17, and *Geoponika* II:12.

52–53 μεδίμνους, μοδίους τε καὶ χοίνικας: On the dry measures, see Schilbach, *Metrologie,* 94ff. For a tenth-century use of the *medimnos,* cf. Leo diac. 156:9–10: καὶ σῖτον ἐδίδου, ἑκάστῳ ἀνδρὶ μετρῶν ἀνὰ μεδίμνων δύο.

55 στερεοῦ ποδός: See Heron, *De mensuris* 23, and above on *Geodesia* 9:51 for a conversion table.

Chapter 10. Measuring the Discharge of a Spring

The chapter draws heavily on Heron, *Dioptra* 31. For paraphrase and discussion of the passage in Heron see K. D. White, *Greek and Roman Technology* (London, 1984), 214.

6 γεννητικαί: For Heron's γενναῖαι.

23–24 ἐξ ἡλιακοῦ ὡροσκοπίου: The phrase is taken verbatim from Heron.

26, 27–28 [κατὰ τὸν ὄγκον] … [ἀλλὰ καὶ τὸ τάχος]: The phrases are also lacking in the source, Heron, *Dioptra* 31.

29–36 Εἰ γὰρ πᾶν νυχθήμερον … ἀποφανούμεθα: This numerical example is added by the Anon. Byz. For "equatorial times" (i.e., "360 degrees of the equator cross the meridian in about one day, one 'time-degree' equals 1/15 of an equinoctial hour or about 4 minutes"), the seasonal hour (the hour as 1/12 of the actual length of daylight or night-time at a given place and time of year and hence variable by time and place), and the νυχθήμερον (the "solar day" of 24 hours), see Toomer, *Almagest,* 23, and V. Grumel, *La chronologie* (Paris, 1958), 163–65.

34 κάδων: Apparently here the classical technical measure of liquid volume, on which see P. Chaintraine, *Der Kleine Pauly Lexikon der Antike,* III (Munich, 1969), 42–43. The term is not found in the source text (Heron, *Dioptra*) and is added by the Anon. Byz. Whether this is a con-temporary or antiquarian use is not clear; it is not in Schilbach, *Metrologie.* Cf. Heron, *Geometrica* 23:63:1–2: Ὁ ἀμφορεὺς παρ' ἐνίοις λέγεται μετρητής· ἔχει οὖν ἡμιαμφόρια δύο, ἃ καλοῦσί τινες κάδους, Ῥωμαῖοι δὲ οὔρνας; but *De cer.* 671:17: κάδους ρ', in a list of equipment for the expedition against Crete.

Chapter 11. Astronomical Observations

The first paragraph of this chapter draws heavily on Heron, *Dioptra* 32; the remainder is added by the Anon. Byz. Martin (315-19), followed by Vincent (400-7), provides a detailed discussion of the Anon. Byz.'s er-rors in astronomical methodology. Primarily they note that in addition to the use of "zodiac" for ecliptic and the confusion (unless scribal error) of meridian with equator (*Geodesia* **11**:34, 36) for placement of the dioptra, the Anon. Byz. "paraît avoir confondu, de même que les anciens astrologues, les *ascensions droites* avec les *ascensions obliques,* et avoir confondu aussi les *déclinaisons* avec les *latitudes*" (Martin, 316).

4 ἡλίου τε μέγεθος ... διακρίνοντες: The Anon. Byz. adds; cf. Heron, *Geometrica,* Introduction: ἐπεὶ γὰρ ἡ ἀστρονομία περὶ μεγεθῶν τε καὶ ἀριθμῶν καὶ ἀναλογιῶν διαλαμβάνει, τό τε γὰρ μέγεθος ἡλίου καὶ σελήνης πολυπραγμονεῖ καὶ τὴν τῶν ἄστρων ποσότητα καὶ τὴν πρὸς ἄλληλα τούτων ἀναλογίαν. Ptolemy, *Almagest* V:16, is titled Περὶ μεγεθῶν ἡλίου καὶ σελήνης καὶ γῆς. Toomer (*Almagest,* 257 n. 66) comments "there is no point in estimating the relative volume of the bodies, but it was apparently traditional in Greek astronomy." See also N. M. Swerdlow, "Ptolemy's Theory of the Distances and Sizes of the Planets" (Ph.D. diss., Yale University, 1968).

5 ἀπλανῶν: For the term "fixed" see Ptolemy, *Almagest* VII:1: "Concerning the terminology we use, in as much as the stars themselves patently maintain the formations [of their constellations] unchanged and their distances from each other the same, we are quite right to call them 'fixed'" (trans. Toomer, *Almagest,* 321).

7–9 Ἐκ ... λεπτῶν: Cf. Heron, *Dioptra* 32:7–10: ἐν γὰρ τῷ ὑπὸ γαστέρα τοῦ τυμπάνου τοῦ ἐν τῇ διόπτρᾳ κύκλον γράψομεν περὶ τὸ αὐτὸ κέντρον τῷ τυμπάνῳ, ὃν γράψει τὸ τοῦ μοιρογνωμονίου ἄκρον τοῦ ἐν τῷ κανόνι· καὶ τοῦτον διελοῦμεν εἰς μοίρας τξ΄. The Anon. Byz. has added the λεπτά.

24, 27 τὰ προηγούμενα ... τὰ ἑπόμενα: For another view of the translation of the terms, see Toomer, *Almagest,* 20.

34, 36 ἰσημερινῆς ... μεσημβρινῆς: Martin (316) comments: "la dioptre, mise dans le plan de l'équateur, ne peut évidemment servir à mesurer les différences de latitude des étoiles. Nous croyons donc que l'auteur lui-même, ou quelque copiste, a mis ici méridien pour équateur, et réciproquement."

37 παρακυπτηρίῳ: I have not found this form attested elsewhere, but παρακυπτικόν, "an imperial loge, a place from which the emperor could observe the area beneath him" (*ODB* III:1585), is found in *De cer.,* specifically at 144:12 and 164:15, of rooms above the *kathisma* in the

Hippodrome for viewing the games (see Cameron, *Porphyrius,* 200–1). On this latter term employed in another text see Downey, "Mesarites," 869, XIV n. 2. Mango, "Palace," 41, observes that the word Boukoleon is applied in texts of the ninth and most of the tenth century to a stretch of shore, a harbor, a terrace, and a staircase, but not to the Imperial Palace. He cites (ibid., 49 n. 3) for the terrace various texts (e.g., Leo Grammaticus, *Chronographia,* ed. I. Bekker [Bonn, 1842], 298: ἐν τῷ τοῦ Βουκολέοντος ἡλιακῷ) and connects them with this passage in the Anon. Byz. A terrace with balustrade overlooking the Sea of Marmara would allow for placement of the dioptra with a 360 degree field of view and placement of the meridian and equator lines described; it appears to be the best approach to a term that remains uncertain. Martin's (309) rendering as "donjon" (? presumably referring to a tower) and Vincent's (395) "observatoire" are perhaps too specific, and Vincent himself suggests in a note (401–2) the alternatives "donjon, balcon" and comments that it may be better to avoid a translation that creates the impression of a specific astronomical observatory. Guilland, *Topographie,* I:265, renders as "balcon (?)" and (363) suggests tentatively that it may refer to the "rond-point" or balcony of the terrace of the Pharos.

37–38 ⟨ἐν⟩ τοῖς Βουκολέοντος: Mango's suggestion ("Palace," 49 n. 3) "[ἐν?] τοῖς Βουκολέοντος," which takes Boukoleon as (perhaps in origin) a personal name, has the distinct advantage of retaining the τοῖς of the archetype. It might be noted that the initial ἐν of this sentence comes at the end of a line in the archetype, and the *nu* is written unusually large; the following line ends with παρακυπτηρίῳ, the next begins with the τοῖς. Perhaps the presence of the quite visible ἐν directly above παρακυπτηρίῳ has led to its omission immediately following it.

On the use of τά with the genitive of a personal name to designate a monument, building, etc. with which the person was associated and hence a surrounding locality within Constantinople and ἐν in this context as "in der Nähe von," see A. Berger, *Untersuchungen zu den Patria Konstantinupoleos* (Bonn, 1988), 166–68. On the Boukoleon as a stretch of shore, a harbour, a terrace overlooking the harbour, and eventually a palace see Mango, "Palace," passim.

38–39 ἐπὶ τῶν πρασίνων ... κοσμηταρίων: I have not found the substantive attested elsewhere (although Pausanias (VII:5) has ἐκ τοῦ καλουμένου κοσμητηρίου κομίζουσι, of a storage area for ἀγάλματα). Barocius translates the phrase "super viridibus," explaining in a note "super quadam viridi superficie," ignoring κοσμηταρίων. Martin (309 and n. 3) translates "sur les architraves vertes," taking the word as a diminutive of κοσμητής or as commonly accented κοσμήτης (cf. *De admin.* 29:251: κίονες πυκνοί, ἔχοντες ἐπάνω κοσμήτας; Downey, "Mesarites," XXXVII:2: "string courses"; Sophocles, *Lexicon,* s.v., 3, and G. W. H. Lampe, *A Patristic Greek Lexikon* [Oxford, 1961–68], s.v., II: "entablature"). Vincent, however, renders with "salle," commenting (402 n. b) that an architrave seems inappropriate for the placement of such lines, suggesting as alternatives "plafond,'"parquet." Guilland, *Topographie,* I:265, translates "sur l'architrave en marbre vert."

38 **τῶν πρασίνων**: A possible connection with the Green Faction is considered but rejected by Martin (309 n. 3), but entertained by Vincent (402), who suggests that it may have been a place where they assembled. Martin's view is preferable. Cf., for example, *De admin.* 29:280: μετὰ κιόνων πρασίνων καὶ λευκῶν.

39–40 **Θέσει τῶν ἡλιακῶν . . . ὡροσκοπίων**: For the interpretation of the phrase as a reference to another treatise by the Anon. Byz., see Martin, 308; Vincent, 394–95 (by his use of upper-case Θέσει and translation "dans notre Méthode pour tracer les cadrans solaires"); Dain, *Tradition,* 23, and Dain, "Stratégistes," 358. As the Anon. Byz. uses ἀναγράφειν (*Parangelmata* **2:**22) of his poliorcetic treatise, this seems the correct approach, although the work is not otherwise known.

47–48 **ἐπὶ τὴν πρώτην τοῦ Κριοῦ ἢ τοῦ Ζυγοῦ . . . μοῖραν**: On the use of first degree of Aries to specify the spring equinox (necessary because other norms existed in antiquity), see Ptolemy, *Almagest* II:7, and Toomer, *Almagest,* 90 n. 70. Similarly the first degree of Cancer is used below (*Geodesia* **11:**53–54) to mark the summer solstice.

52 **μοίρας λβ′ β′′**: Martin's and Vincent's manuscript apparently read simply λβ′. Martin (310–13), noting that the ortive amplitude of the solstice increases with latitude, concluded that the Anon. Byz. did not draw his value from Ptolemy, but that the observation was, in this instance, made by the Anon. Byz. himself or by a contemporary. Martin calculated that 32 degrees would correspond to a latitude of 41°1′11′′,

while that of Constantinople is 41°1′27″. He concluded that the small difference was due to rounding. The additional 2/3 of a degree in the archetype, while it indicates that the Anon. Byz. did not round the value, does not contradict Martin's basic conclusion. The walled portion of Constantinople extends from approximately 40°59′ to 41°2′30″. At the summer solstice the angle of the sun's rising relative to due east at Constantinople is between 32 and 33 degrees. While theoretical measurement would be closer to 32 degrees, actual measurement due to such factors as refraction, elevation of the observer, and parallax would be closer to 32 1/2 to 33 degrees.

55–56 δεκαὲξ καὶ κη′: That is, the Anon. Byz. gives the ortive amplitude at one month and two months before and after the two equinoxes as 16 and 28 degrees. Martin (313–14) notes that at Constantinople ca. A.D. 938 the values would be 15°21′57″ (for 16) and 27°19′10″ (for 28). The correct round numbers would thus be 15 and 27 degrees, the Anon. Byz.'s rounding error most likely being due to calculation mistakes of 9′ and 11′ respectively, errors that Martin suggests would not be unexpected in a tenth-century author. For the method of calculation see Martin, 313 n. 3, and Vincent 403–4.

64 Λαμπαύρας: That is, Aldabaran, used as a sighting star by Ptolemy, *Almagest* IX:8, etc. Ptolemy, *Almagest* VII:5 (Toomer, *Almagest*, 362), gives a value of 12 2/3, the Anon. Byz. 20 2/3, that is, exactly 8 degrees more. See below on *Geodesia* **11:74–75**.

65 Βασιλίσκου: That is, Regulus. Ptolemy (*Almagest* VII:2) uses his observation of Regulus compared to that of Hipparchus to formulate his precession rate. Ptolemy, *Almagest* VII:5 (Toomer, *Almagest*, 367), gives a value of 2 1/2, the Anon. Byz. gives 10 1/2, that is, exactly 8 degrees more. See below on *Geodesia* **11:74–75**.

74–75 ἐπικινήματι τῶν ἀπὸ τοῦ Πτολεμαίου χρόνων: For Ptolemy's attribution of the discovery of precession to Hipparchus, see Toomer, *Almagest*, 138 and 321 n. 2. Martin (317) has shown that the Anon. Byz. has not actually observed these stars himself (the dioptra alone would be insufficient; an armillary astrolabe would be needed), but has added to the values in the catalog of Ptolemy one degree per century, the value Ptolemy, in A.D. 138, attributes to the precession rate (Ptolemy,

Almagest VII:2; Toomer, *Almagest,* 328), thus providing a date of ca. 938 (i.e., eight centuries after Ptolemy) for the Anon. Byz. (see the Introduction, 3–4). For ἐπικίνημα cf. Proclus, *Hypotyposis astronomicarum positionum* 3:53.

78 ἀνὰ λ′: That is, 30 degrees for each sign of the zodiac.

78 ἐπὶ τοῦ Ταύρου θ′ γ′′ : That is, 30 minus 202/3.

84 μοίρας λ′ καὶ μίαν: Martin (318–19) calculates the correct declination for Arcturus in A.D. 938 as 24°31′15′′ and suggests that the Anon. Byz. has derived his value of 31 degrees from Ptolemy's citation of Hipparchus' value of 31 (*Almagest* VII:3; Toomer, *Almagest,* 333), while ignoring or forgetting that precession also changes declinations. The sentence in Ptolemy reads: "Also, Arkturus, which was found to be 31 degrees north of the equator in Hipparchus' time, but 295/6 degrees in our time, has [thus] moved southward 11/6 degrees" (trans. Toomer). If this is the Anon. Byz.'s source, he would seem to have ignored information explicitly provided by Ptolemy.

85 νδ′ ἔγγιστα: That is, 191/2 in Leo, 30 in Virgo, and 5 in Libra.

86 ε′ μοῖραν: Ptolemy, *Almagest* VII:5 (Toomer, *Almagest,* 347), gives for Arcturus 27 degrees, the Anon. Byz. 5, that is, exactly 8 degrees more. See above on *Geodesia* **11**:74–75.

90–91 πρώτου καὶ δευτέρου μεγέθους: On the system for the magnitudes of the stars, see Ptolemy, *Almagest* VII.4, and Toomer, *Almagest,* 16, who notes that it certainly preceded Ptolemy and was conjecturally attributed to Hipparchus.

91 ε′ πλανήτων: That is, Saturn, Jupiter, Mars (the inner planets), and Venus and Mercury (the outer planets). See Ptolemy, *Almagest* IX:1.

94 κρᾶσιν: "Mixture," "temperature," used astrologically "to designate the resultant qualities derived from the mingling of various influences" (F. E. Robbins, *Ptolemy, Tetrabiblos* [Cambridge, Mass., 1940], 64) and used widely in the *Tetrabiblos*. Martin (314) and Vincent (399) translate as *"influence"* and note the astrological significance. The Anon. Byz.'s concern here is specifically weather prediction; see below on *Geodesia* **11**:107. G. J. Toomer, "Ptolemy," *Dictionary of Scientific Biography*, XI:197

(New York, 1975) notes, "Predicting the weather from the 'phases' of the well-known stars long preceded scientific astronomy in Greece." For tenth-century Byzantine examples see S. Lampros, Κείμενα περὶ τοῦ ναυτικοῦ . . . , *Neos Hellenomnemon* 9 (1912), 162–72, and R. H. Dalley, "Meteorology in the Byzantine Navy," *Mariner's Mirror* 37 (1951), 5–16.

95 **τὰ νεφελοειδῆ λεγόμενα συστήματα**: The standard term for a nebula is νεφελοειδὴς συστροφή (Ptolemy, *Tetrabiblos* I:9:23, etc.; Geminus, *Elementa astronomica* III:4). See also Ptolemy, *Tetrabiblos* II:13: οὐ μὴν ἀλλὰ καὶ τῶν ἰδίως νεφελοειδῶν συστροφῶν, οἷον τῆς Φάτνης καὶ τῶν ὁμοίων, ἐπὰν αἰθρίας οὔσης αἱ συστάσεις ἀμαυραί.

100 **φάσεις ζ'**: Vincent (406) cites the seven figurative forms of the moon listed in <Iambilici> Θεολογούμενα τῆς ἀριθμητικῆς (ed. V. de Falco, rev. U. Klein [Stuttgart, 1975], 60:26): μηνοειδής, διχότομος, ἀμφίκυρτος, πανσέληνος, ἀμφίκυρτος, διχότομος, μηνοειδής.

101 **σχηματίζονται**: Cf. Ptolemy, *Tetrabiblos* I:2:5: ὡς τοῖς ναυτιλλομένοις τὰς κατὰ μέρος τῶν χειμώνων καὶ τῶν πνευμάτων ἐπισημασίας, ὅσαι γίνονται κατὰ τὸ περιοδικώτερον ὑπὸ τῶν τῆς σελήνης ἢ καὶ τῶν ἀπλανῶν ἀστέρων πρὸς τὸν ἥλιον συσχηματισμῶν.

103–4 **ἐκ τοῦ προχείρου . . . κανόνος**: An anonymous reader suggests that this is a reference to Ptolemy's *Handy Tables*. As that work is generally referred to in the plural (Πρόχειροι κανόνες) and the Anon. Byz. uses κανών for the sight-rod on his dioptra, I have retained the latter usage in the translation. The suggestion may, however, be correct.

107 **ἐπισημασιῶν**: On the stars and planets as signifiers of weather see Ptolemy, *Tetrabiblos* I:2: αἵ τε τῶν ἀστέρων τῶν τε ἀπλανῶν καὶ τῶν πλανωμένων πάροδοι πλείστας ποιοῦσι ἐπισημασίας τοῦ περιέχοντος καυματώδεις καὶ πνευματώδεις καὶ νιφετώδεις . . . ; Toomer, *Almagest*, 283 n. 18 (ἐπισημασία = "prognostication [concerning weather]"), and above on *Geodesia* **11**:101.

Appendix

The Measurements in the Hippodrome[1]

In the *Geodesia* the Anon. Byz. provides a number of measurements in the Hippodrome, as well as of the cistern of Aspar. It should be noted that the author says of his measurements at three points "perhaps (τυχόν) 80 *orgyai*" (**3**:11), "perhaps 126 *orgyai*," "perhaps two and one half *orgyai*," (**4**:14, 25). Also as noted below his reference points are not always specific and sometimes involve alternatives. Thus he apparently does not intend the values to be taken as precise. In some cases his results are at variance with archaeological evidence and what may be suggested through comparison with other hippodromes. Following Schilbach,[2] I use 1 *orgya* = 1.87 m. The measurements are as follows:

Geodesia 2

1. 12 *orgyai* (22.44 m) from the base of the doors (θύραι) to some point on the quadriga above the starting gates or central arch.

Geodesia 3

2. 80 *orgyai* (149.60 m, ΙΆ on Diagram 1) from the upper (ἄνω) turning post to the third starting gate (κάγκελλος). The Anon. Byz. assumes the same distance to the ninth starting gate and the accompanying manuscript diagram indicates an isosceles triangle. As the *spina* was angled and not on the main axis, and the gates were laid out on a curve, this supposition is incorrect.

3. 40 *orgyai* (74.80 m, AB on Diagram 1) between the third and ninth starting gates; whether measured from the outer edges or centers of the gates is not stated.

---

[1] I am much indebted to Jonathan Bardill for his assistance in preparing this appendix. The suggested position of the angling in of the west flank of the Hippodrome is the result of his comparison of the plans of Mamboury and Wiegand and Müller–Wiener, as are the resulting scale drawings. The text has also benefited at a number of points from his insightful comments.

[2] *Metrologie*, 22–26.

Appendix

Geodesia 4

4. 126 *orgyai* (235.62 m, γα on Diagram 1) from a point in the "undivided area" (ὁ ἁπλοῦς) sufficiently back from the upper turning post to allow sighting to the points where the curve of the *sphendone* begins, initially that to the left. The Anon. Byz. assumes the same distance to the beginning of the curve of the *sphendone* on the right and the accompanying manuscript diagram indicates an isosceles triangle. He might have found a position in the "undivided area" where this was possible.

5. 45 *orgyai* (84.15 m, αβ on Diagram 1) as the width of the *sphendone* at its opening.

Geodesia 5

8. 90 *orgyai* (168.30 m, ΓΑ on Diagram 2) from the lower (κάτω) turning post to a point A on the *spina*.

9. 12 *orgyai* (22.44 m, ΓΕ on Diagram 2) from the lower turning post to a point E towards the flight of stairs along a line perpendicular to ΓΑ.

10. 81 *orgyai* (151.47 m, EB on Diagram 2) from point E as in the previous item to the point B on the ground by the *kathisma* or one of the flanking pavilions along a line parallel to ΓΑ.

11. 15 orgyai (28.05 m, AB on Diagram 2) from point B to point A on the *spina*.

Geodesia 9

12. 70 x 70 x 12 *orgyai* (130.90 X 130.90 x 22.44 m) as the dimensions of the cistern of Aspar.

The Diagrams show the outline of the Hippodrome based on archaeological plans and on comparison with other hippodromes, and are to scale. The imposed lines indicate the distances that the Anon. Byz. is attempting to ascertain, but their lengths do not in all cases correspond to the measurements he gives.

Appendix

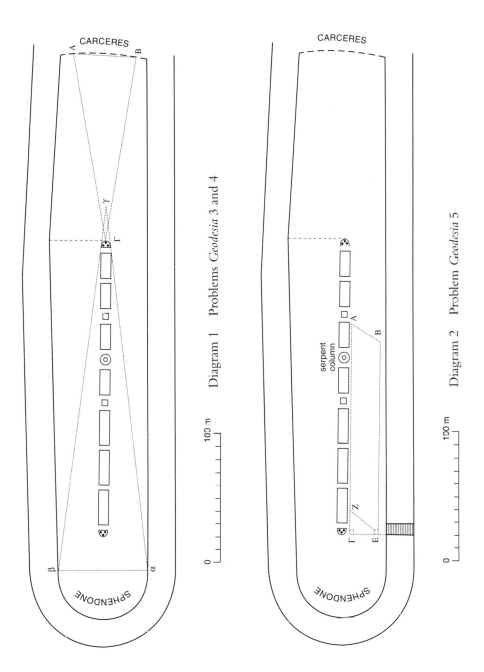

Diagram 1   Problems *Geodesia* 3 and 4

Diagram 2   Problem *Geodesia* 5

Appendix

The following conclusions may be suggested:

1. The value 40 between starting gates 3 and 9 (which is the correct solution to the problem posed, and appears twice in the text and once in the accompanying manuscript diagram) presents two difficulties. Addition of the remaining gates (in total at least ten and in the currently prevailing view twelve[3]) would make the starting gate complex wider than the *sphendone* (i.e., 45 *orgyai* = 84.15 m). Martin (299–300), assuming a total of twelve gates in concave arrangement with a central arch between gates 6 and 7, suggests that the arena must have widened (abruptly) as it approached the north facade. Guilland, ("Hippodrome," 5) notes Martin's solution and suggests the alternative that the arena may have narrowed gradually as it went from the *carceres* to the *sphendone*. Neither solution is in accord with the plans of E. Mamboury and T. Wiegand[4] and Müller-Wiener[5] which taken together indicate that the west side of the Hippodrome widened gradually from the *sphendone*, but then moved in again toward the starting gates. Similar narrowing is also found in other hippodromes, for example, the Circus Maximus and the Circus of Maxentius.[6]
A second problem concerns the width of the individual gates. Even assuming, on the comparison with the Circus Maximus and that of Maxentius, a central arch between gates 6 and 7 and that the whole width of gates 3 and 9 was included in the measurement (*pace* Guilland, *Topographie,* I:384, idem, "Hippodrome," 5), the individual gates with one pier would have to measure ca. 8-9 m, depending on the width of the central arch. The concave arrangement of the gates would lessen this figure only slightly. As Humphrey[7] notes, the gates at Leptis Magna were ca. 2.7 m wide with piers of 1.04 m, those of the Circus Maximus ca. 5 m wide with piers of 1.25 m. Thus a width of 8-9 m at Constantinople seems implausible and the Anon. Byz.'s value of 40 *orgyai* suspect. If given any credence, however, the measurement would seem to favor a central arch and only ten gates. It is worth noting in this regard that Guilland (*Topographie,* I:383) suggests on the basis of passages in the *De cer.* that there may have been only ten. If the Circus Maximus was the model, however, twelve would seem more likely. I have assumed following Guilland (*Topographie* I:393 and 399) that the gates were numbered beginning from the left as one

---

[3] On the number see Dagron, *Naissance,* 322.
[4] *Kaiserpaläste,* fig. cii.
[5] *Bildlexikon,* 69 and 124.
[6] See Humphrey, *Circuses,* 120 and 587.
[7] *Circuses,* 49 and 152.

Appendix

faced them from the upper turning post, although this is not certain.

2. The Anon. Byz. saw his two main triangles (see Diagram 1 above) as isosceles (he indicates in both problems that only one side need be measured and the two manuscript diagrams show the same measurement for both sides). The distance in his terms then from approximately the center of the *carceres* to the upper turning post would be ca. 77.5 *orgyai* and from his position somewhat north of the same turning post to the center of the opening of the *sphendone* 123.9 *orgyai*. The depth of the *sphendone* would be half the diameter, or 22.5 *orgyai*. Estimating 8-13 *orgyai* for the uncertain distance he moved back north from the upper turning post to obtain a clear view, and allowing for the fact that the measurement from the *carceres* is not on the center line, the total length of the interior track in the Anon. Byz.'s terms would be approximately 213.4 *orgyai* or 399.05 m. Mamboury, on the unproven assumption that the Serpent Column was at the center of the Hippodrome, suggests 400 m.[8] One measurement of the Anon. Byz. here, however, may be significantly in error. The line γα in *Geodesia* 4 from the "undivided area" to the opening of the *sphendone* on the left side is given as 126 *orgyai* or 235.62 m. In the Circus Maximus and that of Maxentius the upper turning post is beside the break line and the angling in of the grandstand. In Constantinople the position of this angling in can be approximately established by viewing the plans of Mamboury and Wiegand[9] and Müller-Wiener[10] in combination. From a turning post at this point in the track to the opening of the *sphendone* on the left side would be about 260 m. To take his measurement γα the Anon. Byz. would have been measuring from a point (γ) some distance north of the turning post to obtain a clear line of sight. In reality this position may well have been about 15–25 m from the turning post, and the distance γα as much as 288 m. Clearly the Anon. Byz.'s measurement (126 *orgyai* = 235.62 m) appears too short. Better archaeological indication of the position of the upper turning post would help clarify this question.

3. The value of 81 *orgyai* (151.47 m) from point E opposite the lower turning post to the point B on the ground by the *kathisma* or a flanking pavilion may give some indication of the position of the imperial box on the east side of the Hippodrome. That is, the depth of the *sphendone* (22.5 *orgyai*) plus

---

[8] "Les fouilles," 272.

[9] *Kaiserpaläste*, fig. cii.

[10] *Bildlexikon*, 69 and 124.

81 *orgyai* would give 103.5 *orgyai* plus the unknown distance between the lower turning post and the opening of the *sphendone*. The plans of Leptis Magna and of the Circus of Maxentius given by Humphrey[11] suggest that the lower turning post might be 20–25 meters[12] (about 10.6–13.3 *orgyai*) from the opening of the *sphendone*. If that were so in Constantinople, then point B would be situated approximately 115.5 *orgyai* north of the beginning of the *sphendone*. A difficulty is created by the uncertainty of whether the Anon. Byz. is sighting on the *kathisma* and if so on what part of it, or on one of the flanking pavilions, and by the unknown scale of the *kathisma*.

Imposition of the Anon. Byz.'s measurements on a scaled drawing (see Diagram 2 above) suggests that point B is north of the Serpent Column. This is at variance with the *kathisma*'s proximity to the Boukoleon palace posited by Mango ("Palace," 46–47) and may be yet another instance in which the Anon. Byz.'s measurements are not to be taken as precise.

Also the line to the *kathisma* reference point begins at E only 12 *orgyai* from the lower turning post toward the grandstand wall fronting the arena, while the full distance would be approximately 22.5 *orgyai*. Similarly the diagonal from the *kathisma* reference point to the *spina* (BA) of 15 *orgyai* also seems too small, even allowing for the fact that the *spina* was angled toward the grandstand wall on that side. Thus both points E and B were apparently somewhere in the track. If the pavilions were temporary tents erected in the track during footraces only, one of these might be the reference for point B.

See also on the problem Mango's ("Palace," 46–47) solution and diagram. In his diagram he places the point Γ not at the lower turning post, but 9 *orgyai* south of it, although in his text he defines Γ as "namely the lower or south turning post"; he positioned it at the turning post in the diagram in Mango, "L'euripe," 185. The effect in his later diagram is to bring the *kathisma* 9 *orgyai* further south. The Anon. Byz. says that Γ is πρὸς τὴν τῆς κάτω νύσσης ἀντιπεριαγωγήν and after taking line ΓΑ he says μετελθὼν πρὸς τὸ πλάγιον τῆς διόπτρας τὸ ἐπὶ τῇ νύσσῃ. While the localizing effect of ἀντιπεριαγωγή is not completely clear, point Γ would seem to be in the immediate vicinity of the turning post, not 9 *orgyai* behind it, while the second statement suggests that the dioptra, and hence point Γ, was indeed at the turning post itself. A. Berger, "Bemerkungen zum Hippodrom von Konstantinopel," *Boreas* 20 (1997), 5–15, especially 5–6, makes the measurement of the 81 *orgyai* to the *kathisma* reference

---

[11] *Circuses,* 23, 587.
[12] See also Mango, "Palace," 50 n. 36.

point **B** from the upper (north) turning post rather than from the lower one. This appears to be at variance with the Anon. Byz.'s statements.

4. The value 45 *orgyai* (84.15 m) for the width of the *sphendone* at its opening is at variance with the archaeological result given by Mamboury ("Les fouilles," 272), 79.6 m.

5. The cistern of Aspar is ca. 152 m square.[13] The Anon. Byz.'s values would give 130.9 m square, again at significant variance with the archaeological evidence.

Thus the Anon. Byz.'s measurements are perhaps best viewed as mathematical examples that cannot be used to obtain precise information on the interior dimensions of the Hippodrome and the placement of the *kathisma*, but can at best provide only approximations.

[13] See Müller–Wiener, *Bildlexikon*, 279.

Ἥρων᾽
βελο..

A   Vaticanus graecus 1605, folio 1 (photo: Biblioteca Apostolica Vaticana)

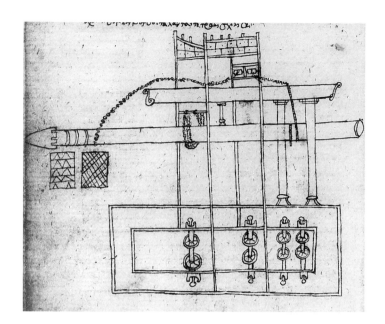

(a)

(b)

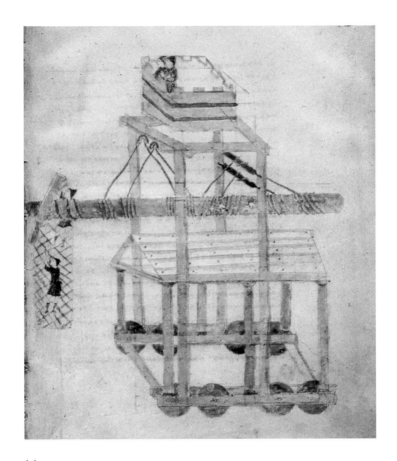

(c)

B Ram of Hegetor
    (a) Vindobonensis phil. gr. 120, folio 32
         (photo: Österreichische National Bibliotek)
    (b) Parisinus supplementus graecus 607, folio 23
         (photo: Bibliothèque nationale de France)
    (c) Vaticanus graecus 1605, folio 20
         (photo: Biblioteca Apostolica Vaticana)

1 Tortoises and defenses against objects rolled down from cities on hills, Vat. gr. 1605, folio 7v (photo: Biblioteca Apostolica Vaticana)

2   Tortoises and more defenses against rolling objects, Vat. gr. 1605, folio 8
      (photo: Biblioteca Apostolica Vaticana)

3   Inflatable leather ladder, Vat. gr. 1605, folio 9v (photo: Biblioteca Apostolica Vaticana)

4   Excavating tortoise, Vat. gr. 1605, folio 11 (photo: Biblioteca
     Apostolica Vaticana)

5   Excavating through a wall, Vat. gr. 1605, folio 11v (photo: Biblioteca
    Apostolica Vaticana)

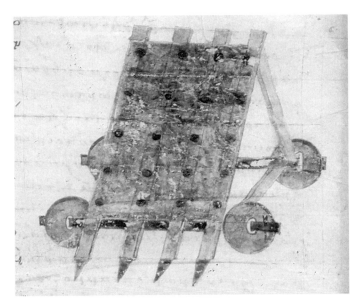

6   Excavating tortoise coated with clay, Vat. gr. 1605, folio 12v (photo: Biblioteca Apostolica Vaticana)

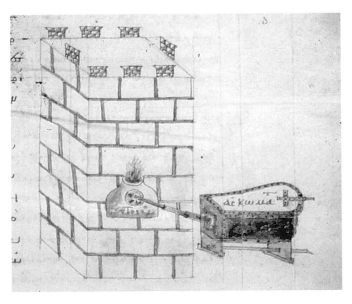

7   Bellows and firepot, Vat. gr. 1605, folio 13 (photo: Biblioteca Apostolica Vaticana)

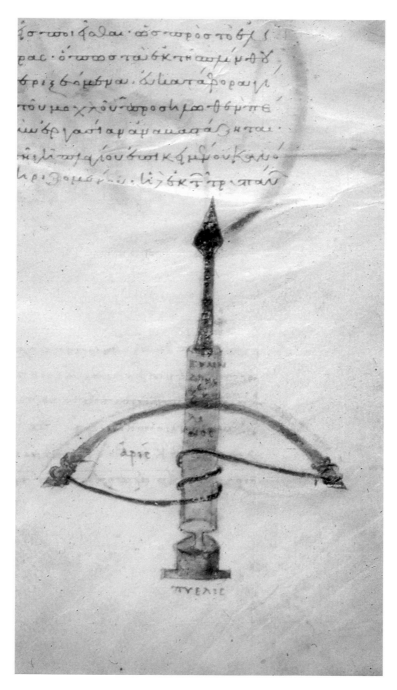

8   Borer, Vat. gr. 1605, folio 14 (photo: Biblioteca Apostolica
     Vaticana)

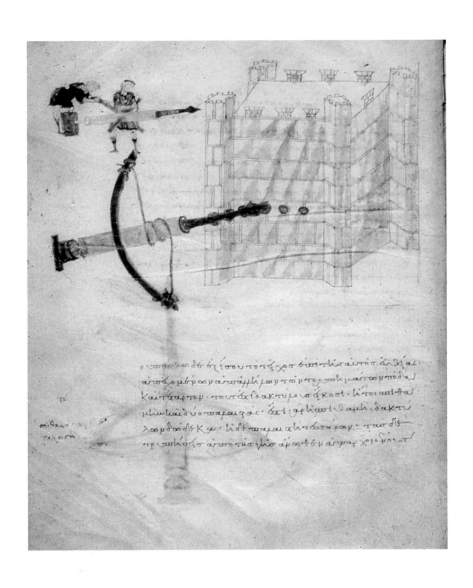

9 Borer in operation, Vat. gr. 1605, folio 14v (photo: Biblioteca
   Apostolica Vaticana)

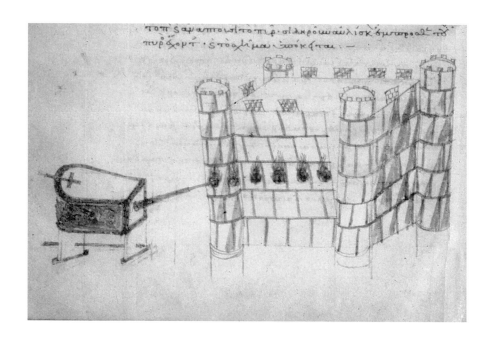

10 Bellows fanning bore holes, Vat. gr. 1605, folio 15v (photo:
Biblioteca Apostolica Vaticana)

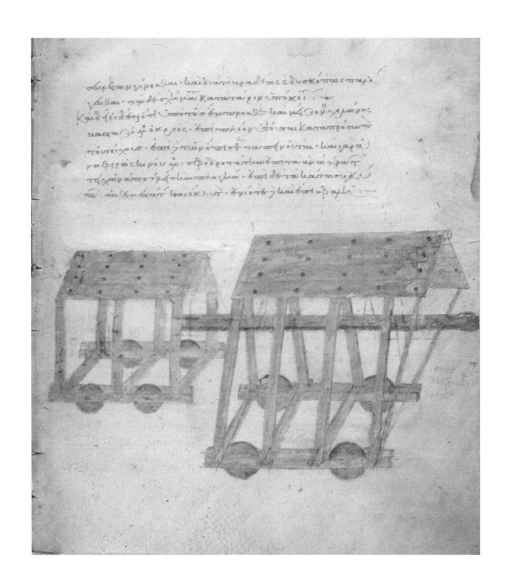

11 Multiple tortoises to protect a ram, Vat. gr. 1605, folio 18 (photo: Biblioteca Apostolica Vaticana)

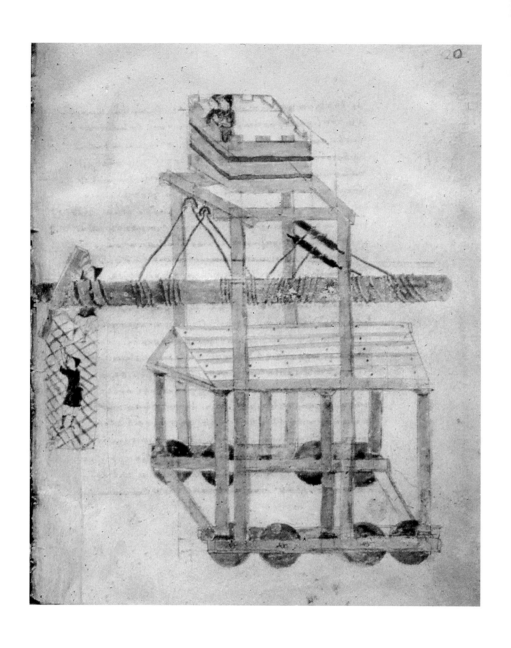

12   Ram of Hegetor, Vat. gr. 1605, folio 20 (photo: Biblioteca
      Apostolica Vaticana)

13 Scout–ladders, Vat. gr. 1605, folio 22v (photo: Biblioteca Apostolica
    Vaticana)

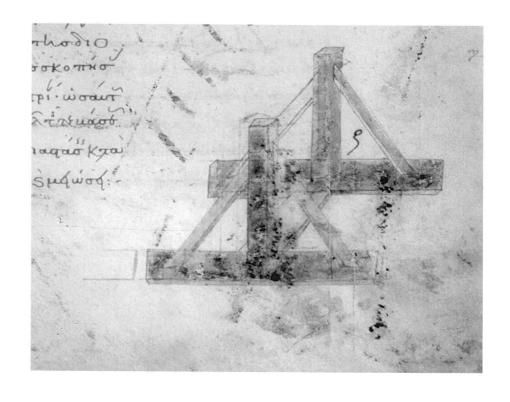

14 Additional base for a scout ladder, Vat. gr. 1605, folio 23 (photo:
   Biblioteca Apostolica Vaticana)

15 Portable siege tower, Vat. gr. 1605, folio 26 (photo: Biblioteca
    Apostolica Vaticana)

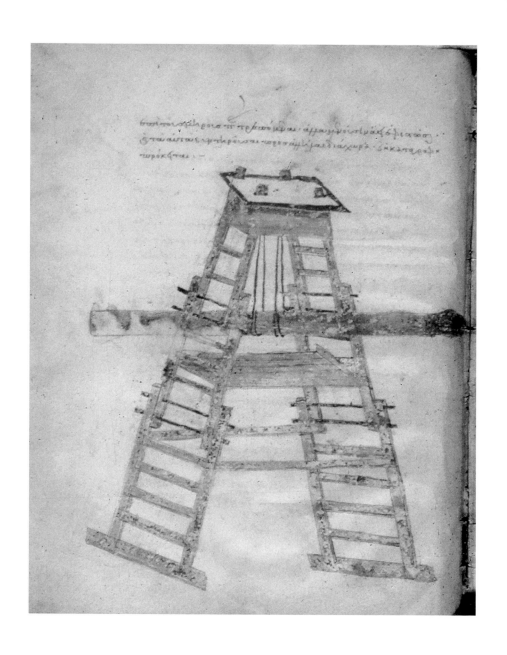

16 Ram between ladders, Vat. gr. 1605, folio 29v (photo: Biblioteca
    Apostolica Vaticana)

17   Dual rams on ladders, Vat. gr. 1605, folio 30v (photo: Biblioteca
    Apostolica Vaticana)

18 Torsion flail on a ram, Vat. gr. 1605, folio 32 (photo: Biblioteca
Apostolica Vaticana)

19 Wheeled ladder with drop-bridge, Vat. gr. 1605, folio 34 (photo: Biblioteca Apostolica Vaticana)

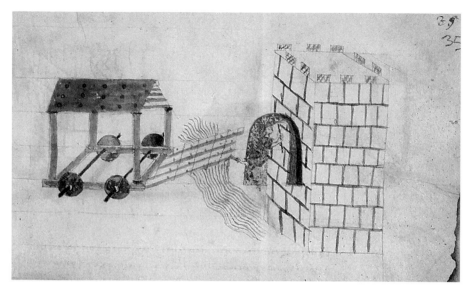

20 Cross-bridge on a tortoise, Vat. gr. 1605, folio 35 (photo: Biblioteca
    Apostolica Vaticana)

21 Using iron spikes and rope ladders to scale a wall, Vat. gr. 1605, folio 35v
    (photo: Biblioteca Apostolica Vaticana)

22   Using flame throwers on drop bridges, Vat. gr. 1605, folio 36 (photo:
     Biblioteca Apostolica Vaticana)

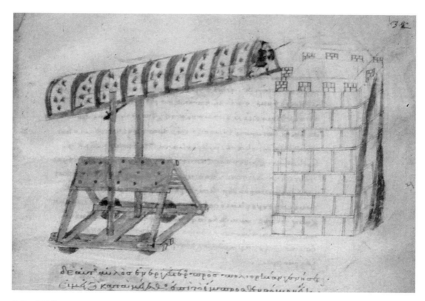

23 Tube on a wagon for landing troops on a wall, Vat. gr. 1605, folio 38 (photo: Biblioteca Apostolica Vaticana)

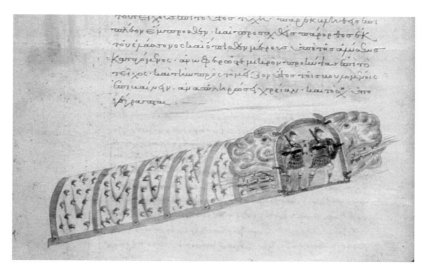

24 Tube with animal figureheads on the doors, Vat. gr. 1605, folio 38v (photo: Biblioteca Apostolica Vaticana)

25 Tower on a ship, Vat. gr. 1605, folio 39v (photo: Biblioteca Apostolica Vaticana)

28 Raft, front view, Vat. gr. 1605, folio 42 (photo: Biblioteca
    Apostolica Vaticana)

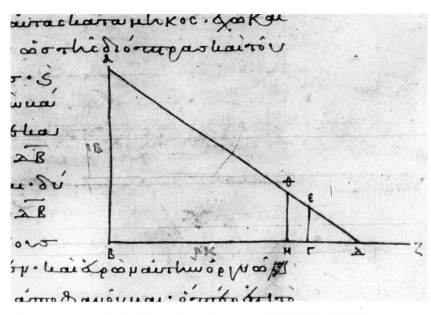

29 Measuring the height of a wall, Vat. gr. 1605, folio 43 (photo: Biblioteca Apostolica Vaticana)

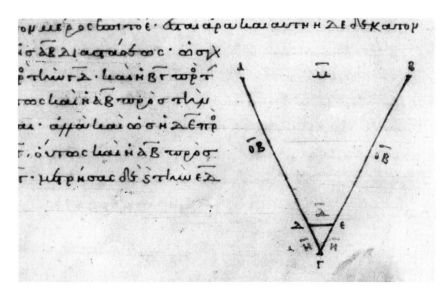

30 Measuring an interval from a distance, method 1, Vat. gr. 1605, folio 43v (photo: Biblioteca Apostolica Vaticana)

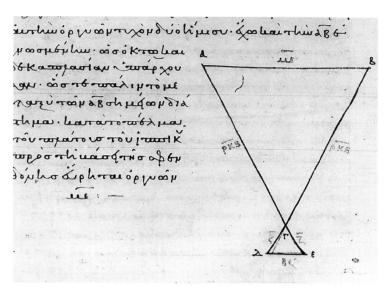

31   Measuring an interval from a distance, method 2,
     Vat. gr. 1605, folio 44v (photo: Biblioteca Apostolica
     Vaticana)

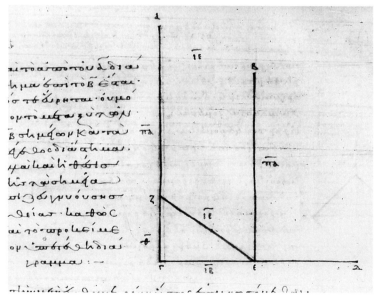

32   Finding the position of a line, Vat. gr. 1605, folio 46
     (photo: Biblioteca Apostolica Vaticana)

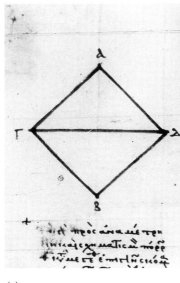

(a)

(b)

33 (a) The rhombus as two isosceles triangles, Vat. gr. 1605, folio 46v

(b) The quadrilateral divided into two triangles, Vat. gr. 1605, folio 47

(photos: Biblioteca Apostolica Vaticana)

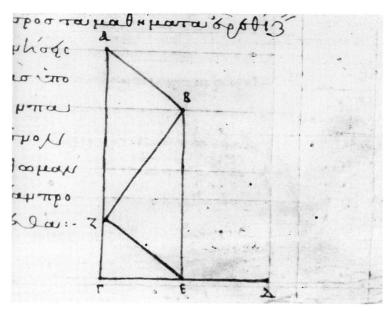

34 Measurement of areas, Vat. gr. 1605, folio 47 (photo: Biblioteca Apostolica Vaticana)

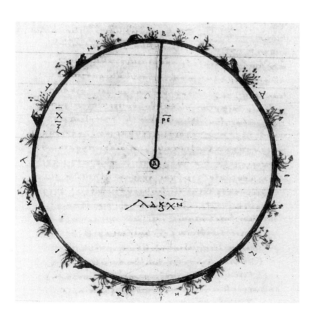

35 Measurement of a circle, method 1, Vat. gr. 1605, folio 48v (photo: Biblioteca Apostolica Vaticana)

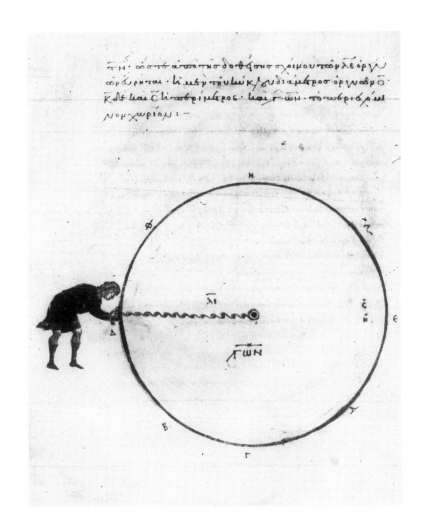

36 Measurement of a circle, method 2, Vat. gr. 1605, folio 49v
    (photo: Biblioteca Apostolica Vaticana)

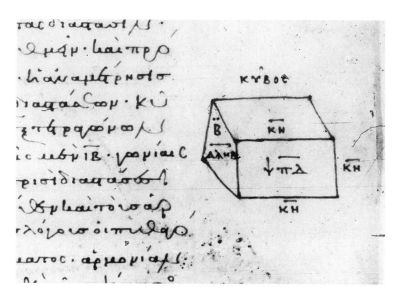

37 Measurement of a cube, Vat. gr. 1605, folio 50 (photo:
Biblioteca Apostolica Vaticana)

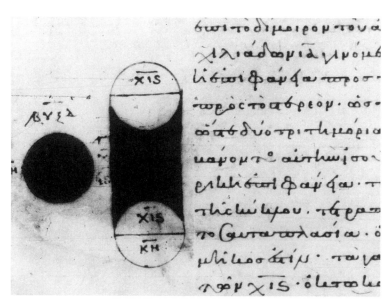

38 Measurement of a sphere and a cylinder, Vat. gr. 1605,
folio 51v (photo: Biblioteca Apostolica Vaticana)

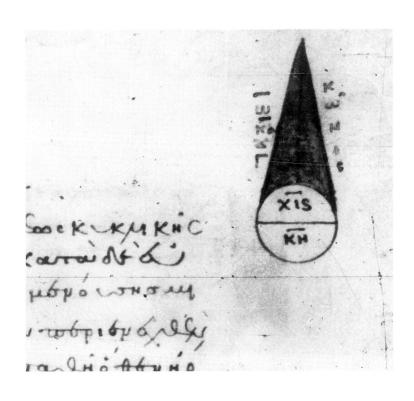

39   Measurement of a cone, Vat. gr. 1605, folio 52
     (photo: Biblioteca Apostolica Vaticana)

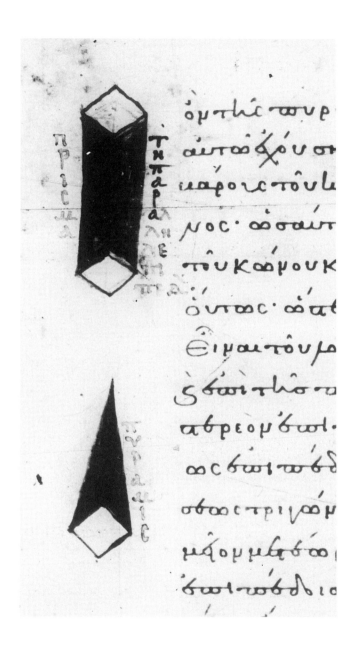

40   The pyramid and prism, Vat. gr. 1605, folio 52v (photo:
     Biblioteca Apostolica Vaticana)

41 Measurement of the capacity of a cistern, Vat. gr. 1605, folio 53
    (photo: Biblioteca Apostolica Vaticana)

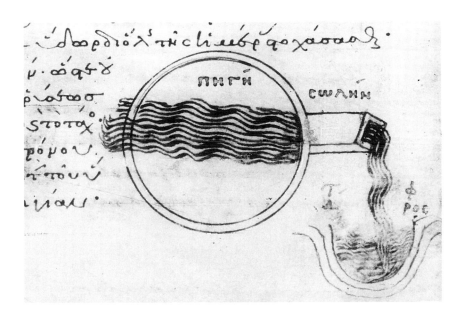

42 Measuring the discharge from a spring, Vat. gr. 1605, folio 54v
    (photo: Biblioteca Apostolica Vaticana)

Greek Indices

General

References are to chapter and line number of the texts; G— *Geodesia*; a star indicates that the term is discussed in the commentary at that point. The index is selective, and frequently occurring terms may be listed only at the initial reference or in instances where they are discussed in the commentary.

ἀγγεῖον **5**:5; **G4**:14

ἄγκιστρον **12**:22; **48**:7

ἀγκύλη **45**:16

ἀγκυρωτός **49**:7

ἀγκών **44**:37; **45**:16, 19

ἄγνοια (διπλῆ) **3**:20★

ἀγνωσία **1**:4★; *Intro.* 9–10

ἀέτωμα **22**:41; **36**:7

ἀέτωσις **G9**:51★

αἷμα **47**:14

αἴσθησις **G1**:12; **G6**:29★,37

ἀκοντίζω **49**:21; **56**:18

ἀκόντιον **11**:16★

ἀκρωτήριον **39**:24

ἀλοιφή **12**:14

ἅλυσις **22**:3; **25**:11; **50**:19; **52**:19

ἅλωσις **1**:17; **44**:45

ἅμαξα **5**:4; **7**:28; **50**:5, 22; **51**:2

ἄμμος **15**:10★

ἀμπέλινος **9**:2

ἀμπελοχελώνη **10**:3; **13**:2

ἀμυντήριος **53**:38

ἀμφίβληστρον **49**:3, 15

ἀναβάθρα **G5**:15★

ἀναγεμίζω **11**:7; **12**:15; **15**:6; **19**:2; **39**:19

ἀναγραφή **58**:1

ἀναγράφω **2**:22; **G6**:24; **G11**:40★

ἀναδενδράς **10**:11★

ἀναλογία **29**:15; **30**:9, 16; **38**:5, 10, 18; **51**:28

ἄναξ **58**:7

ἀναπτόμενα, τά **2**:9★; **15**:16; **39**:9, 36

ἄνεμος **19**:24; **53**:19, 37

ἀνεπηρέαστος **49**:19

ἄνεσις **46**:10

ἀνθηρυλεκτέω **3**:54★

ἀνθολογέω **G6**:43

ἄνθραξ **16**:10, 14

ἀντιζυγίς **31**:22★

ἀντικόρυφος **G4**:22

ἀντιμηχάνημα **1**:16

ἀντιπεριαγωγή **G5**:10

ἀντίσπαστος **26**:3

ἀνωμαλία **G11**:105

ἀξιάγαστος **G11**:37

ἀξίωμα **1**:30★

ἀξόνιον **46**:4

ἄξων **13**:14; **24**:10; **33**:12, 16

ἀπαγκαλίζω **7**:13★

ἀπαράπτωτος **2**:13★; **53**:36

ἀπαρεμποδίστως 13:32; 14:4;
  33:20
ἀπλανής G11:5*
ἀπλόγραμμος 28:4
ἀπλότης 1:34*
ἀπλοῦς, ὁ G4:6*,17
ἀποστάτης 4:4*
ἀρίς 17:14
ἀριστερός 7:6, 10; G4:4,11
ἁρμονία 22:47; G8:14*
ἁρμονικός G8:13
ἁρμός 34:9
ἄρτησις 21:3*
ἀρχή G7:47*, 48², 49, 50, 51
ἀρχιτέκτων 2:15*; 38:23; 50:31;
  53:16
ἄρχων 4:2*
ἀσκός 12:14; 39:23, 28
ἄσκωμα 16:14; 19:27
ἀσπίς 7:7; 27:78*
ἀστερίσκος 17:23
ἀσυμμέτρως 53:6
ἄτακτος G6:40
ἀταραξία 3:36, 52
ἀττικίζω 3:1*
αὐλίσκος 16:13; 19:29
αὐλός 50:10, 25, 26; 51:6;
  52:1, 8, 12; 53:4; 54:2
αὐτεπιβούλευτος 53:25
αὐτοκράτωρ 1:11; 4:3*
ἀφορμή G6:44
ἄχυρον 39:31

βαθμίς 27:37; 42:3; 46:17, 27;
  G5:14*
βαθμός 40:2, 6, 7; 42:14; 43:6;
  44:4

βασιλικός G5:7; G11:37
βασταγή 22:57*
βάσταγμα 25:9*; 40:13
βελοποιΐα 3:40
βελοποιϊκός 1:15; 3:46; 45:23
βέλος 10:20; 13:23; 45:8, 29;
  46:36; G1:18
βέργα 8:3; 9:2; 13:22; 40:3
βίβλος 1:22*
βιωφελέστατος 3:60; G1:14
βόθρευμα 11:23
βόρειος G11:52, 83
βορρᾶς G11:35
βοῦς 15:18; 17:4; 39:21; 40:5;
  47:14
βρύον 39:32*
βύρσα 27:77; 40:4; 43:7; 46:35;
  47:14; 50:13

γαλήνη 53:18
γεννητικός G10:6
γέρανος 54:6*
γερροχελώνη 2:5*; 8:1; 15:17
γέφυρα 47:1; G1:7
γεφυρόω 55:2
γεωδαισία G1:23*
γεωμετρία G1:33
γεωργικός 11:21
γιγγλυμωτός 55:9
γλυφή 52:6
γλωσσίς 28:5*
γραμμή G1:4; G11:34, 36, 44
γραμμικός G1:16
γραφή 53:4
γριφάνη 11:22*
γρονθάριον 22:35*; 31:17; 44:14
γυμνασία 50:34

γυρόθεν **10**:6; **17**:9; **25**:7

δᾴς **14**:14★; **19**:8
δεινότης **3**:2★
δεκάστεγος **30**:7; **37**:9, 12
δέλτος **2**:21★
δεξαμενή, ἡ **G9**:2, 42, 49
δέρμα **10**:15★, 17; **13**:21; **15**:9, 18;
    17:4; **39**:12; **50**:27; **55**:15
δερμάτινος **12**:13, 23
δεσμός **27**:37; **56**:12
διαβάθρα **2**:11★; **21**:5; **30**:3;
    46:24, 33, 36; **47**:2, 8; **49**:20;
    G1:7
διαβήτης **G3**:3★
διάβροχος **15**:18★; **50**:27
διάγραμμα **G1**:17; **G4**:2; **G5**:39;
    G6:9,19
διαδοχή **4**:10★
διάθεσις **3**:20★
δίαιτα **3**:51
διαιτητικός **1**:17★
διάλειμμα **19**:11★; **25**:9★
διαλεκτικός **3**:8★
διαλόξως **29**:3,9
διάμετρος **51**:4, 18, 20; **G7**:1
διάστασις **13**:37
διάστημα **10**:8
διαστροφή **G6**:14,20
διατύπωσις **G9**:35
διάχωρον, τό **14**:2, 4; **19**:16; **41**:6;
    42:5, 16; **44**:8
διδασκαλία **1**:33; **3**:38
διδάσκω **3**:39
δίκελλα **11**:24★
δίκτυον **25**:13; **39**:32; **48**:8
δικτυωτός **12**:21

διοπτεύω **G5**: 11; **G11**:23, 27, 33,
    46, 66, 70, 81
διόπτρα **G2**:6★; **G3**:6, 14; **G4**:5,
    14; **G5**:10, 13, 17, 18; **G7**:2, 6,
    11, 39; **G10**:14; **G11**:2, 14, 34,
    44
διοπτρεία **G1**:14; **G7**:7; **G11**:102
διοπτρικός **G1**:4; **G11**:1
διορίζω **1**:38, 39★; **29**:12; **49**:9;
    G1:16; **G9**:52; **G11**:41; Intro.
    11–12
διορυγή **2**:10★
διπλασιασμός (τοῦ κύβου)
    45:28★
δίρρυτος **13**:5★
διχοτόμημα **G11**:96
διχοτομία **G8**:109
δοκίς **49**:8; **G9**:9★
δράκων **52**:8★
δρομεύς **G5**:8★
δύναμις **G5**:34★
δυσεύρετος **32**:1
δυσκρασία **G11**:106
δύσφραστος **1**:40; **G1**:25

ἐαρινός **G11**:49
ἐγγλύφω **22**:36; **31**:17; **44**:13
ἐγχειρίδιος **49**:20★
εἰκασία **G1**:12
εἰκαστικῶς **53**:8★
εἰκοσάστεγος **30**:14
εἰσαγόμενοι, οἱ **50**:34; **G6**:42
ἐκκοπή **50**:9★,19
ἐκφράζω **3**:55
ἔλαιον **5**:8; **14**:17; **15**:10; **19**:10;
    45:21
ἔλαφος **45**:12

[323]

κατάστημα (ἀέρων) **G11**:105
κατάστρωμα **36**:6; **40**:14;
  55:19, 30, 41; **56**:14
κέδρινος **39**:10
κέντρον **13**:19; **G7**:3, 5, 19, 22, 27
κέντρον, τό (τοῦ βάρους)
  G8:108*
κένωμα **22**:30
κεραμεία **G6**:46*
κεράμιον **11**:12*, 15;
  G9:14*, 41, 43
κεράτισις **20**:10*
κηπουρικός **17**:13
κινστέρνη **G9**:3, 11, 13
κλήθρινος **39**:11
κλῆμα **9**:2
κλῖμαξ **2**:7*
κλίσις **17**:33*
κλόνος **39**:6
κλύδων **53**:35
κορύφωσις **53**:23
κοσμητάριον **G11**:39*
κρᾶσις **G11**:94*
κριθή **G9**:51*
κρίκος **27**:37; **34**:17; **44**:23, 28;
  G7:43, 50
κριοδόχη **25**:10, 22
κριοκοπέω **13**:4
κριομαχέω **20**:4; **22**:48; **40**:16
κριός **2**:6*
κριοφόρος **2**:3*; **21**:4; **22**:2; **50**:6
κρόταφος **27**:8
κτείς **11**:21
κυβίζω **G9**:36
κύβος (= ἁρμονία) **G8**:14
κύβος (διπλασιασμός τοῦ κύβου)
  45:28

κύθρινος **16**:8
κύκλος **G7**:1, 3, 5, 8, 15, 17, 21,
  26², 30, 32, 35
κύλινδρος **26**:3; **45**:27*
κῦμα **53**:20, 23
κωλυμάτιον **46**:12

λαβδαραία **6**:2*
λαίσα **2**:4*; **9**:1; **11**:5; **47**:13, 17
λακκίζω **20**:6; **24**:20
λάκκισμα **11**:7*
λεπτά, τά **35**:9*, 10, 11; **G11**:9, 17
λέων **52**:8*
λίθινα τείχη **16**:1; **18**:6–7; **24**:17;
  48:6
λιθοβόλος **15**:20; **27**:84; **39**:16, 35;
  44:38; **45**:4
λίθος **5**:3; **6**:9; **16**:3, 15; **20**:7;
  22:53; **24**:21; **40**:6; **45**:17;
  G7:15
λιμήν **G1**:22
λίνον **10**:15; **44**:35; **49**:3
λιτός **27**:15*; **28**:4
λίτρα **G9**:39², 40, 41
λόγχη **11**:16*
λυχνία **G2**:6*

μάγγανον **46**:8*
μάθημα **G6**:42
μαθηματικός **3**:32*; **50**:30
μαθηματικῶς **45**:31; **G1**:27
μαθητής **30**:2
μακροβολέω **45**:3*
μάλαθον **44**:35*
μέδιμνος **G9**:52*
μέθη **12**:12
μέθοδος **48**:11; **G2**:18

μεσημβρινός **G11**:36★
μεσονύκτιον **G11**:81
μεσοστάτης **22**:39; **31**:8★, 12, 20,
    24, 28, 30; **32**:2; **33**:10;
    34:2, 4, 7
μεσουράνημα **G11**:28
μεσόχωρον, τό **56**:15
μεταπύργιον **4**:14★; **52**:11
μετάρσιος **27**:41
μετασχηματίζω **G6**:21
μεταφορά **53**:2
μετοπωρινός **G11**:49
μέτρον **2**:16; **3**:34; **38**:12; **44**:5;
    46:28; **50**:28
μηνιαῖος **G11**:43, 55, 59
μηχανή **2**:12; **53**:1, 15, 26
μηχάνημα **1**:1; **2**:1; **4**:9; **11**:9;
    38:24; **50**:4; **53**:17, 22, 25, 31,
    36, 42; **58**:2; **G1**:9
μηχανικός, ὁ **1**:9★; **26**:2; **30**:3;
    38:22; **54**:10; **G9**:35
μόδιος **G9**:53★
μοῖρα **G2**:17; **G11**:8
μοιρικῶς **G11**:101
μοιρογνωμόνιον **G11**:18, 20, 51,
    69
μολιβδουργός **16**:18★
μολιβοῦς **G10**:9
μονάγκων **44**:38★,44; **45**:1
μονόξυλος **2**:6; **21**:3; **22**:49; **46**:16
μονόπτερος **13**:7★
μόριον **G2**:17
μουσικός **53**:2★
μοχλός **17**:7,27; **44**:39
μυρίκη **8**:4★

νεάκιον **7**:9★

νεοσφαγής **15**:19★; **17**:4; **40**:5;
    47:14
νευρά **45**:9,14
νεῦρον **44**:32★; **45**:11, 22
νεφελοειδής **G11**:95
νῆμα **44**:34
νηματικός **44**:35
νηνεμία **19**:25
νόησις **G6**:29
νότιος **G11**:57
νότος **G11**:35, 37
νύσσα (ἡ ἄνω) **G3**:6★, 13; **G4**:7
νύσσα (ἡ κάτω) **G5**:10★, 13
νυχθήμερον, τό **G10**:29★, 36

ξύλον **7**:9
ξυλοπύργιον **2**:6★
ξυλοπύριον **55**:3★
ξύσμα **14**:16★; **19**:19

ὄγκος **G9**:45, 49; **G10**:20, 27
ὀδοντωτός **11**:22
οἰακίζω **26**:2
οἴκημα **G9**:2, 50
οἰκοδομή **20**:3
ὀϊστός **45**:15
ὀκτάτροχος **25**:17; **30**:20
ὀλιγαρκής **3**:44, 50
ὁλοσίδηρος **11**:17
ὁμοταγής **44**:4
ὁμοψύχως **46**:33
ὀνίσκος **25**:10★; **26**:4
ὄντα, τά **3**:14★; *Intro.* 12
ὄνυξ **13**:13, 19; **49**:12
ὄξος **16**:16★; **39**:31
ὀξυβελής **45**:4
ὀξύρρυτος **22**:11, 38

ὀπή **G11**:45
ὁπλίτης **10**:5, 13; **G6**:13 scholion
ὀπτικός **53**:14★
ὀργανικῶς **45**:31
ὄργανον **1**:14; **3**:47; **11**:14; **15**:20;
    17:7; **39**:25; **45**:4, 6, 25, 29;
    50:32; **53**:3
ὀρθογραφέω **57**:1★
ὀρθοστάτης **22**:24, 27; **27**:35, 88,
    31:31
ὀρθόω **27**:92★
ὀρυκτρίς **2**:2★; **13**:5★; **47**:16
ὄσπριον **G9**:51★
ὀστράκινος **16**:9; **44**:24
οὐγκία **G9**:37, 38
οὐράνια, τά **G1**:23; **G11**:3
οὖρον **16**:16

παίγνιον **12**:12
παλιλλογέω **G1**:24★
παλίντονος **44**:37; **45**:4★, 15
παράγγελμα (**Tit.**); **1**:18; **3**:8
παράθεσις **45**:5; **46**:11
παραίτιος **G11**:99
παρακυπτήριον **G11**:37★
παραλογίζομαι **G1**:3★
παραλόγως **53**:6
παρασκευή **G5**:9★
παραστάτης **22**:25★; **31**:32; **32**:2;
    34:3, 5, 7; **37**:2, 13
παρέμβασις **37**:4, 10
παρεξοχή **17**:16★; **27**:48; **31**:6, 8;
    46:13
παροιμία **G6**:45★
πάσσαλος **19**:5, 8, 11, 22; **27**:90;
    34:16; **46**:37; **48**:4; **55**:31, 42

πελέκημα **19**:19★
πέλμα **G4**:27★
πεντεκαιδεκάστεγος **30**:12★
περιγραφή **G1**:22
περίδρομος **33**:7★; **39**:14
περίπτερος **33**:7★; **39**:13
περιστόμιον, τό **G10**:15
περιστομίς **44**:31★,40
περιτομίς **22**:33★; **31**:16
περιφραγή **41**:3★; **46**:34
περίφραγμα **25**:23
περόνη **24**:9; **27**:25, 26, 32, 35, 45,
    60, 70, 83; **34**:16; **40**:10;
    44:3, 6, 15; **55**:12
πέταλον **16**:9, 11; **17**:10, 27; **33**:13;
    44:26
πεύκινος **39**:11
πηγή **G10**:1, 7, 8, 11, 12, 18, 20
πηλός **15**:5★; **24**:4; **39**:18; **47**:13
πῆξις **55**:10
πιθήκιον **53**:32★
πίθος **G6**:45★
πίσσα **14**:17★; **15**:10★; **19**:10
πισσόω **19**:9
πλατυκέφαλος **15**:2; **24**:1
πλατυλίσγιον **17**:13★
πλήσμιος **3**:46
πλίνθινα τείχη **17**:1; **24**:18; **48**:6
πλινθίνη οἰκοδομή **20**:3
πλινθίς **G9**:5★
πλοῖον **7**:21; **53**:1, 12, 17, 19, 21,
    22, 32, 36, 40; **54**:3
πολιορκέω **4**:4; **48**:12; **G1**:1
πολιορκητήριος **2**:12; **58**:2
πολιορκητικός **1**:1, 11; **54**:11
πολιορκία **1**:13, 16; **2**:1, 20;

ὑπόθεσις 27:57; **G4**:3; **G6**:44
ὑπόμνημα **1**:13; **50**:3, 30; **54**:11
ὑπότροχος **11**:2; **13**:13; **15**:21;
    46:1★
ὑπόφορος **12**:4
ὕπτιον **3**:3★

φαινόμενα, τά **G11**:103
φαντασία **G6**:37★; *Intro.* 13
φάσις **G11**:100★
φιλομαθέω **3**:8; **G1**:20
φιλόχριστος **58**:7
φιλύρα **8**:4★
φλόξ **15**:16; **16**:7, 15; **39**:9, 36
φόβος **52**:9
φοινίκινος **39**:10
φοῖνιξ **13**:22★
φορητός **2**:6★; **38**:20
φορτίον **53**:13
φρεατία **17**:22
φρύγανον **14**:13; **19**:20

χεῖλος **56**:2, 5; **57**:3, 6, 8, 10
χειμερινός **G11**:58
χελωνάριον **44**:11
χελώνη **2**:1★
χελώνιον **22**:34★; **31**:16
χηλή **45**:15
χοινικίς **44**:23★, 29, 33, 41; **45**:5;
    G7:11
χοῖνιξ **G9**:53★
χοίρειος **15**:5
χωστρίς **2**:2★; **11**:2; **47**:5; **48**:2

ψευδογράφος **3**:19
ψυχρήλατος **33**:13

ὡριαῖος (χρόνος) **G10**:28
ὡροσκόπιον **G10**:24; **G11**:40
ὡροσκόπος, ὁ **G11**:28

Proper Names

Ἅγαρ **58**:8
Ἀγησίστρατος **1**:12
Ἀδριανός **1**:10
Ἀέτιος **G9**:2
Ἀθηναῖος (μηχανικός) **1**:11;
    50:4; **53**:1
Ἀλέξανδρος **30**:2
Ἀνθέμιος **1**:31
Ἀπολλόδωρος **1**:10, 26, 36; **31**:1;
    33:1; **37**:1; **38**:20
Ἀπολλώνιος **3**:27
Ἀριστοτέλης **3**:26
Ἀριστοφάνης **3**:27
Ἀρχιμήδης **G6**:40; **G7**:26
Ἅσπαρ **G9**:4, 11
Ἄτταλος **1**:13

Βίτων **1**:13; **54**:10
Βουκολέων **G11**:38; *Intro.* 2

Δᾶμις **54**:9
Διάδης **30**:1; **32**:2; **36**:2; **38**:21

Εὐκλείδης **G8**:86

Ἡγήτωρ **25**:1
Ἥρων **3**:31; **45**:32; **50**:3; **G6**:41

Ἰσοκράτης **3**:26

Proper Adjectives and Places

Rare Terms

The following are terms not found on the *Thesaurus Linguae Graecae* CD-ROM (Version D) or in the Anon. Byz.'s main poliorcetic and mathematical sources (that are not yet included on the *TLG*), Apollodorus of Damascus, Archimedes, Athenaeus Mechanicus, Onasander, or Philo of Byzantium. A star (*) indicates an apparent *hapax legomenon* or term used more than once in the Anon. Byz. but not recorded as used elsewhere by Demetrakos, *Lexikon,* Du Cange, *Glossarium,* LSJ, *LSJRS,* Lampe, *Lexicon,* Sophocles, *Lexicon,* or Trapp, *Lexikon* (fascs. 1–2).

*ἀδιάκλαστος **46**:20
ἀνθηρολεκτέω **3**:54
*ἀντιζυγίς **31**:22
ἀντικόρυφος **G4**:22
ἀπαγκαλίζω **7**:13
*ἀπαράπτωτος **2**:13; **53**:36
*ἁπλόγραμμος **28**:4

Βόθρευμα **11**:23

*γριφάνη **11**:22
γρονθάριον **22**:35; **31**:17; **44**:14

διαλόξως **29**:3, 9
*διπλόγραμμος **27**:16

*ἐνθραύω **53**:25
ἔνταγμα **G6**:13 scholion
ἐξάστεγος **37**:4, 7
ἐξονυχιστής **3**:1
*ἐπικεφαλίς **17**:17
εὐθυμετρία **G6**:1
*εὐπρόχειρος **53**:40

ἰθυφάνεια **G1**:4
*ἰσοβαρῶς **22**:53

*ἰσοζύγως **22**:53
ἰσοτετράγωνος **30**:8; **31**:22; **32**:3

*κάρειον, τό (? κάρυον, τό) **46**:9
κεράτισις **20**:10
*κοσμητάριον **G11**:39

λαβδαραία **6**:2
*λάκκισμα **11**:7

*μάλαθον, τό (? μάλαθος, ὁ) **44**:35

νεάκιον **7**:9

*ξυλοπύργιον **2**:6
*ξυλοπύριον, τό (? ξυλοπύριος -ον) **55**:3

*ὀξύρρυτος **22**:11, 38

*παρακυπτήριον **G11**:37
*παρεξέχω **22**:22; **44**:6; **46**:18; **55**:16
*παρεξοχή **17**:16; **27**:48; **31**:6, 8; **46**:13
*πεντεκαιδεκάστεγος **30**:12

περιφραγή **41**:3; **46**:34
*πλατυλίσγιον **17**:13
   (cf. πλατυλίσκιον)

*ῥιζόκρικι(ο)ν **44**:39
*ῥυκάνισμα **19**:20

συγκάθεσις **17**:31
σχάριον **25**:17, 19; **31**:23;
   51:1, 9, 11

*τεκτόνευσις **1**:8
*τοξίκιον **7**:22
τύλιον **39**:3

Terms found in one instance on
the *TLG*.
ἀναγεμίζω **11**:7; **12**:15; **15**:6; **19**:2;
   39:19
ἔξογκον, τό **30**:21; **33**:17; **47**:7
ἐπικρημνίζω **22**:45
εὐπροθύμως **47**:12; **55**:22
λακκίζω **20**:6; **24**:20
μονόπτερος **13**:7
παρέμβασις **37**:4,10
σύμπαχον **20**:3; **27**:1; **36**:6
ὑπεμβαίνω **16**:15; **17**:16; **19**:12;
   24:8; **27**:38

English Index

Achmetis, 196
Aetius, 265–66
Agar, 4, 16, 20, 247–48
Agesistratus, 156
Aldabaran, 272
Alexios I Komnenos, 169
Almagest, 3, 272–73
Anaxarchus of Abdera, 167
animal figureheads, 234
Anthemios, 5, 158
Apollodorus of Damascus, 1, 4, 5, 7, 14, 20, 21, 155
Apollonios (Dyskolos), 166
Arabs, 5, 15, 16, 17, 18, 247, 248
arch, 175
archetype, 1, 8, 9, 21, 22, 257
Archimedes, 15, 161, 261, 262, 265
architects, 154-55, 163, 267
architrave, 271
Archytas, 10, 166
Arcturus, 273
Aristophanes (of Byzantium), 166
Aristotle, 10, 11, 166, 168, 190, 267
arrows, 190
Asclepiodotus, 260
Aspar, 23, 266, 281
Athenaeus Mechanicus, 2, 4, 18, 20, 155
Attalus of Pergamum, 156
Atticism, 164
axiom, 5, 158

balustrades, 258
barrels, 171
barriers (tripod), 160, 172
battle psychology, 221
beaks, 171–72, 176

bellows, 190, 191, 195
Biton, 2, 4, 156, 241
blowpipe, 191, 195
Bononiensis ms. 1467, 1
boots, 180, 182
borer, 209
Boukoleon, 2, 270
bow-drill, 191
brick, 196

caltrops, 160, 179
capstan, 241
carchesion, 240
casks, 171
Categories (of Aristotle), 12, 165
center of gravity, 265
centones, 177, 185
Chandax, 18, 169, 180
"changing-rooms," 258
Charias, 208, 210, 214
Chios, 235, 236
Cilicia, 15
cistern, 265–66, 275, 281
column drum, 171
commensurability, 23, 239
Constantine VII, 3 n. 4, 4 and n. 4
Constantinople, 3, 266, 270, 271, 272
contraction of area, 209–10, 213
craftsmen, 154, 213
crane, 240
Crete, 15, 16, 18, 176, 187, 248
Ctesibius, 232
curtain walls, 171

Damis of Colophon, 240, 241
defectors, 169